National interest and solidarity: Particular and universal ethics in international life

Edited by Jean-Marc Coicaud and Nicholas J. Wheeler

United Nations University Press

TOKYO · NEW YORK · PARIS

The views expressed in this publication are those of the authors and do not necessarily reflect the views of the United Nations University.

United Nations University Press
United Nations University, 53-70, Jingumae 5-chome,
Shibuya-ku, Tokyo 150-8925, Japan
Tel: +81-3-3499-2811 Fax: +81-3-3406-7345
E-mail: sales@hq.unu.edu general enquiries: press@hq.unu.edu
http://www.unu.edu

United Nations University Office at the United Nations, New York
2 United Nations Plaza, Room DC2-2062, New York, NY 10017, USA
Tel: +1-212-963-6387 Fax: +1-212-371-9454
E-mail: unuona@ony.unu.edu

United Nations University Press is the publishing division of the United Nations University.

Cover design by Mea Rhee

Printed in Hong Kong

ISBN 978-92-808-1147-6

Library of Congress Cataloging-in-Publication Data

National interest and international solidarity : particular and universal ethics in international life / edited by Jean-Marc Coicaud and Nicholas J. Wheeler.
    p. cm.
  Includes bibliographical references and index.
  ISBN 978-9280811476 (pbk.)
  1. National interest. 2. International relations. 3. International cooperation—Case studies. I. Coicaud, Jean-Marc. II. Wheeler, Nicholas J.
JZ1320.3.N38 2008
172'.4—dc22   2007037007

To Jeffrey Gross

Contents

Contributors

Alex J. Bellamy is Professor of International Relations at the University of Queensland, Australia. His research interests include humanitarian intervention, peace operations, the responsibility to protect and the ethics and laws of war. His most recent book is *Just Wars: From Cicero to Iraq*. He is currently writing a book on the ethics of terrorism.

Jean-Marc Coicaud heads the UNU office at the United Nations in New York. He has served as Senior Academic Officer in the Peace and Governance Programme at UNU in Tokyo and in the Executive Office of the United Nations Secretary-General as a speechwriter for Dr. Boutros Boutros-Ghali. Coicaud is the author, co-author and co-editor of a number of books focusing on authoritarian democracy, political legitimacy and international ethics. He has recently published *Beyond the National Interest*.

Alan Collins is Senior Lecturer in the Department of Politics and International Relations at Swansea University, United Kingdom. He is the author of *Security and Southeast Asia: Domestic, Regional and Global Issues* and the editor of *Contemporary Security Studies*. He has published articles on international security with a particular interest in Southeast Asia in *Pacific Review*, *Asian Survey* and *International Relations of the Asia-Pacific*.

Timothy W. Docking is Senior Advisor to the CEO of Millennium Challenge Corporation (MCC). Since joining MCC in 2004 he has managed the front office and helped to lead the US$2 billion per year international development agency during its start-up phase. He also served as a White House Fellow (2003–2004) and, prior to that (2000–2003), he directed research on African affairs at the US Institute of Peace.

Geoffrey C. Gunn is currently Professor of International Relations in the Faculty of Economics, Nagasaki University. He has previously held academic positions in Garyounis University (Libya), the University of New South Wales, the National University of Singapore and Universiti Brunei Darrusalam. In 2000 he served as consultant to the UNTAET mission in East Timor. Gunn's most recent book is *First Globalization: The Eurasian Exchange 1500–1800*.

Parviz Mullojanov is Executive Director of the Public Committee for Democratic Processes, a Tajik non-governmental organization that is an outgrowth of the Inter-Tajik Dialogue, an American–Russian peace initiative. He has been a member of Inter-Tajik Dialogue since 1997. In the mid-1990s he worked for Human Rights Watch Helsinki, UNCHR and the African Development Bank offices in Dushanbe.

Ekaterina Stepanova is Project Leader on Armed Conflicts and Conflict Management at the Stockholm International Peace Research Institute, where she is head of the research group on unconventional threats, on leave of absence from the Center for International Security, Institute of World Economy and International Relations, Moscow. She is a guest lecturer at the Geneva Centre for Security Policy. She is the author of *The Role of Illicit Drug Business in the Political Economy of Conflicts and Terrorism, Anti-terrorism and Peace-building during and after Conflict* and *Civil-Military*

Relations in Operations Other Than War, and co-editor/co-author of *Kosovo: International Aspects of the Crisis*.

Doug Stokes is Senior Lecturer in International Relations at the University of Kent, Canterbury, and has published extensively on US foreign policy, US intervention and international relations theory. He is currently working on two new books, one provisionally titled *US Hegemony and Transnational Conflict*, and an edited volume with Michael Cox titled *US Foreign Policy: From Republic to Hyperpower*.

Mira Sucharov is Associate Professor of Political Science at Carleton University in Ottawa, Canada. She is the author of *The International Self: Psychoanalysis and the Search for Israeli–Palestinian Peace*, and has published articles on global politics, foreign policy and the Arab–Israeli peace process. Her upcoming project investigates the roots of loyalty in international relations.

Nicholas J. Wheeler is Professor of International Politics at Aberystwyth University, UK. He has authored a number of publications, most prominently *Saving Strangers: Humanitarian Intervention in International Society*. His new book (with Ken Booth) is *The Security Dilemma: Fear, Cooperation and Trust in World Politics* (Palgrave Macmillan, forthcoming).

Samina Yasmeen, Associate Professor, is director of the Centre for Muslim

States and Societies and lectures in political science and international relations in the School of Social and Cultural Studies, University of Western Australia, Perth. She is a specialist in political and strategic developments in South Asia, the role of Islam in world politics and citizenship among immigrant women.

Acknowledgements

This book is the product of a research project conducted under the auspices of the Peace and Governance Programme of the United Nations University, based in Tokyo. Over the course of the project, the editors and authors benefited from the hospitality offered by the University of Western Australia at the occasion of a workshop organized in 2002 by Professor Samina Yasmeen (one of the contributors to the volume). Another workshop was organized in Tokyo in 2003 by Ms. Yoshie Sawada, Programme Administrative Assistant at UNU's Peace and Governance Programme. The editors and authors wish to thank the commentators of the chapters and the participants to these workshops. Their comments were instrumental in helping to give a better focus to the chapters brought together in the book. The authors would also like to thank the anonymous reviewers of the manuscript for their helpful suggestions. In Tokyo, Ms. Sawada's administrative support to this project has been valuable. From UNU Press, we wish to thank former Publications Officer Mr. Scott McQuade, Editor Mr. Robert Davis and Senior Publications Coordinator Ms. Yoko Kojima for their help in bringing this book to life. We would also like to acknowledge Ms. Jibecke Jönsson, Ms. Lamis Abdel-Aty and Ms. Charlotte Månsson at the UNU Office at the United Nations, New York, for their assistance with the final stages of this book.

Introduction: The changing ethics of power beyond borders

Jean-Marc Coicaud and Nicholas J. Wheeler

This book has its origin in the intellectual and political climate of the 1990s, in the geopolitical and normative changes that followed the end of the Cold War.[1] During this period, humanitarian interventions in particular became one of the key features of international and multilateral life, and the analysis of their motivation and implementation the topic of heated debates.

Few were left indifferent to the suffering of millions of people, which international interventions were meant to alleviate. Yet, since helping meant challenging the mainstream conception of international order – a conception associated with the traditional and somewhat narrow understanding of the principle of national sovereignty (entailing non-interference in the internal affairs of other states) and of national interest – the issue of humanitarian intervention came to divide policymakers, academia and public opinion. Taking a clear and well-thought-out stand on humanitarian intervention, weighing the positive against the negative aspects, proved to be a demanding exercise.

What this book is about

Although this book originated from the issue of humanitarian intervention, it was never meant to be limited to that. Rather, from the outset the idea was to examine the relevance of the debates (arguments and

National interest and international solidarity: Particular and universal ethics in international life, Coicaud and Wheeler (eds),
United Nations University Press, 2008, ISBN 978-92-808-1147-6

counter-arguments) generated by the question of humanitarian intervention at a more general level. Extrapolating the discussions around humanitarian intervention to a broader international environment, the aim was to gain a better understanding of the motivations of actors who intervene in areas of crisis, and their evolution. Being understood, also, that intervening actors are usually from the top echelons of the international hierarchy of power, and that the areas where the interventions take place tend to be at the weaker end of the international distribution of power.

It is in this perspective that the extent to which national interest and internationalist, or solidarity, considerations enter actors' rationale to get involved in international crises became a primary concern of the editors of and contributors to this book. Focusing on crises in the context of which it is not obvious from a traditional national-interest point of view why international actors would choose to intervene, or how committed they are to solving the crises, the goal was to evaluate the respective weights of national interest (including security) on the one hand and internationalist (solidarity) considerations on the other.

Since they are part of the framework of analysis, it may be helpful to first clarify what is, by and large, meant in this book by the notions of national interest, solidarity in general and solidarity at the international level, especially in relation to democratic values.

The question of national interest

The use and understanding of the term "national interest" is relatively straightforward. It refers to the self-interest of nations, how states envision their defence and projection of power beyond their borders. In this regard, traditionally, national interest has been divided into those interests that states consider core or vital, such as security, and those that relate to the promotion of more secondary interests. Moreover, the notion of national interest has historically been associated with a geopolitical understanding of international relations. Indeed, it has been felt that the pursuit of the national interest is closely linked to geography – the locations where acts unfold (for economic, energy, military or other reasons) and which constitute potential fault lines that have to be carefully watched.[2] While this geographic anchoring remains significant,[3] it has been balanced in recent times by the changes brought about by the deterritorialization of politics at the national and international level[4] – a deterritorialization that includes normative factors such as identification with human-rights imperatives, the influence that it has on individual and collective interests and values and their interaction, as well as on policies at home and abroad.

Solidarity, generally and at the international level

Considering that the initial impetus for this book was to look into the meaning of the emergence of the norm of humanitarian intervention for the greater context of the evolution of international life, the idea of solidarity was destined to be a significant signpost. Here, this idea is conceived and used first and foremost in connection with the protection of human rights. Put simply, it is a notion that invokes the need to help people who are beyond one's own borders. In this perspective, based on the internationalization of the democratic idea of human rights,[5] solidarity has a universalist character. The idea being that, whilst human beings live in a plurality of cultures, which exhibit a range of particular moral practices, all have basic needs and rights that have to be respected. These basic needs and rights, constituting the core commonality of individuals across the world, are also what bring them together and impel them to identify with, and care about, each other's suffering. Violation of these needs and rights calls for a sense of international solidarity. Failing to respond to the plight of the other, failing to show solidarity, diminishes the humanity of all. As such, international solidarity points to the international community's responsibility and obligation toward victims of conflict regardless of their personal circumstances and geographical location. This is how the idea and practice of international humanitarian intervention can be viewed as one expressing an ethics of international solidarity.

This being said, the notion of solidarity is problematic in the field of international relations. Some elaboration is therefore necessary to unpack it a bit more, in order to stress its importance in the context of this book and reveal how it lies at the core of the current dilemmas of international action.

In traditional forms of social organization, solidarity connotes a tight bonding among people (kinship) that renders it imperative for the group to look after its members. This sense of solidarity runs deep and permeates the group's internal relations. Another dimension of this "thick" solidarity is its sharply exclusive character. The translation of the "us versus them" divide into the deep "in versus out" divide, to which traditional societies are prone, has a heavy bearing on who benefits from solidarity and who does not.[6]

Compared to traditional solidarity, the modern form of solidarity that springs from democratic values and rights is wider and more diffuse.[7] Rather than being locked into forms of membership that tend to be narrow and exclusive, modern solidarity seeks the broadest inclusion possible. The values and rights of universality and equality, at the core of democratic culture, introduce and call for a certain connectedness among people, which initiates an experience of community that goes far beyond the boundaries of immediate society. This modern solidarity-driven process entails three facets.

First, democratic values of universality and equality, and the rights associated with these, celebrate the basic process of identification between people. From this derives, second, a sense of obligation. Because "the other" (whoever and wherever he/she is) is not foreign, his/her fate triggers responsibility. People – the members of one's human community – are the repository of everyone's rights. Responsibility makes them accountable to help ensure that the rights of others are respected. Third, the spread and embrace of the values and rights of universality and equality, by recognizing individuals in their variety as members of one world, provide tools to build a case for the rights of all and, consequently, to fight for improved inclusion.

Historically, these three facets have worked in favor of a widening and deepening of solidarity at the national level and, subsequently, at the international level.[8] To some extent, international law is a product of this state of affairs. The spectacular development, after World War II, of the universalization of human rights is a real articulation of international solidarity as exercised in favor of individuals.

Yet, the values and rights of universality and equality, which trigger international solidarity, are also part and parcel of what accounts for its limitations.

From a general standpoint, to begin with, solidarity is based on key democratic values and rights that are constrained at three levels. Modern democratic solidarity, although wider than traditional solidarity, tends to be thinner. This is the first problem. Arguably, universality and equality introduce a distance among people that lessens the level of social solidarity among them. In other words, as solidarity widens, it becomes attenuated. What brings people together is also what keeps them apart.[9] A second problem is that values and rights of universality and equality do not get rid of the ideas of priority and hierarchy, and they do not dispense with the need for these ideas. How could they, considering that prioritizing and establishing hierarchies is essential to human life, partly because without them there is no particular direction, and partly because the limited resources at hand ask for choices in their allocation? The result is that the values and rights of universality and equality cannot impede the hierarchy of priorities from playing a selective, and therefore restricting, role in the projection of solidarity. Third, as the circle of human community expands under the influence of the values and rights of universality and equality, the ability to relate to people becomes more and more abstract and fragile. As such, the extension of democratic solidarity tends to give a renewed importance to traditional bonds of proximity, including kinship ties.[10]

The cumulative effects of these constraints on solidarity have the largest role at the international level. Because it is the widest circle of humanity, the international realm does not benefit from the level of identification and participation that is characteristic of the national realm, at least in unified and developed countries. The "pull" power of international solidarity is weakened further when considerations of self-interest enter into the calculus, as they often do. The inconsistency that comes with self-interest prevents international solidarity from being a universal imperative. Under these conditions, compared to national solidarity, and despite the rhetoric of universality and equality, it is hard to see how international solidarity could be considered other than secondary.

National interest, solidarity and the dilemmas of international action

Indeed, solidarity beyond borders is not a primary concern for the projection of power at the international level. The national bent of international life, that is, the fact that international politics centres around the national perspective, explains this state of affairs. This focus on the particular as opposed to the univeral tends to give solidarist projects such as the protection of human rights a relatively marginal status.

To be sure, in the aftermath of the Cold War, at least until 11 September 2001, the pressure of globalization and progress in international governance, along with the lessening of global security competition, boosted the internationalization of social reality.[11] But these forces did not fundamentally alter the structure of international life, which is still based on the primacy of the nation-state. As a result, the national political community remains the principal context of socialization. People continue to identify and participate, to form expectations and obligations – four key elements of socialization, at first and foremost the national level, in spite of the parallel local and international affiliations that they may have.

Ultimately, this translates into tensions between the national interest and solidarity in the context of the international projection of power, from which dilemmas also spring. In this perspective, the notion of dilemmas of international action is another one that readers should keep in mind while going through the chapters. As a whole, the concept has to be understood in relation to the multilayered character of international life and to its impact on international decision-making and action. It refers to the trade-offs (costs and benefits) entailed in choosing one course of action over another. Despite the continued primacy of the national realm, the increasing intertwining of rational interest and international solidarity that characterize the post–Cold War era gives much relevance to dilemmas. But it also makes them a source of difficulty: deliberating and acting in the midst of the dilemmas that ensue becomes a constant juggling act. To address the dilemmas successfully calls for keeping several balls of political reality in the air at the same time. Surely, when hard choices have to be made, what is owed to the national realm tends to prevail over what is owed to the international realm. Nevertheless, since the demands of international solidarity affect the ways in which national interest is fulfilled and how it evolves, what defines national interest and the best way to serve it is not a clear cut proposition – and certainly not one that simply requires a focus on a particularist vision of ethics in the international realm.

As an examination of the extent to which the balance between national interest and solidarity shapes the projection of power at the international level, and of how such a balance is evolving, this book amounts to being an analysis of how the "us versus them" divide structures international life. It ends up being a study of how this divide influences the conception and projection of national interest at the international level, and how they interact with internationalist considerations.

The book is of course not the first to reflect on the nature and role of the "us versus them" divide at the international level. In fact, this divide has preoccupied international relations from the outset. It is a tradition that this book continues, but with the difference of trying to conduct an analysis that avoids the "either/or" approach (with, in particular, the inclination to endorse the divide as an absolute – realism – or to call for its elimination – radicalism) around which the main schools of International Relations have a tendency to rally.

International relations and the "us versus them" divide

The "us versus them" divide is not specific to international relations. It begins at the most basic human level, that of the self. While the self and the other are ontologically linked (it takes the other to experience the self, as there is no self without the other), the inseparability between the self and the other creates a distance that cannot be eliminated. The instinctive primacy of self-preservation is a by-product of this reality. Beyond the level of the self, this basic reality shapes the relations of the collective. This happens at the national level, where gaps between, for instance, social, economic and ethnic groups have historically kept people apart, along "us versus them" divides; and it does even more so at the international level. With international life being largely structured around a national bias, the "us versus them" divide constitutes a defining element.

Against this background, it does not come as a surprise that the various schools of International Relations,[12] to a large extent, address and position themselves in relation to this divide. The ways in which these schools have come to interpret and handle this divides reflect their respective intellectual and political agendas.

Realism and the confrontation between "we" and "they"

Realism has evolved over a long period of time and exhibits many different strands. Perhaps the most significant divergence between its various strands is how realist thinkers treat the origins of international instability, and how states should act to avoid that instability. For example, Hans Morgenthau argues that international instability and power politics are rooted in human nature and, as human nature will not change, international politics will always remain characterized by a struggle for power.[13] Kenneth Waltz takes a different approach to explain conflicts.[14] He points to the anarchical nature of the international system, rather than to human nature. As for what has been at times called the liberal realism of Hedley Bull, as exhibited by *The Anarchical Society*,[15] here it is also claimed that interstate relations are characterized by a state of anarchy. But, in contrast to Waltz, Bull sees it possible for states to mitigate anarchy through the development of an international society built on common rules and norms.[16]

Beyond the differences that exist between the various strands of realism, there is, however, a common feature regarding how they relate to the "us versus them" problem. Indeed, whatever their cause, struggles for power and conflicts rest upon, and stage, a confrontation between "we" and "they" that constitutes the "horizon indépassable" of the realist philosophy of power and relations among states.[17] It is based on this philosophy that realists articulate three central beliefs: statism, survival and self-help. Statism refers to the idea that states are, if not the only, then at least the main actors of the international system. Any other actor, such as the United Nations, is of secondary importance, to be evaluated on the basis of whether or not it is useful for the national interest, and on the extent to which it is so. As the central actor of the international system, the principal goal of the state is to ensure its survival and that of the citizens over which it purportedly stands guard. It does so by elevating the defence of the national interest to a primary purpose a defence of the national interest that takes precedence over the national interest of other countries. And since all states aim for the same objective, international politics tends to be characterized by distrust and competition, which makes self-help a key tool for survival.

As we can see, the realist depiction of international affairs as a struggle between "we" and "they" leads to rather pessimistic prospects for eliminating international tension. This also explains the realist thinking that states call upon international cooperation and international law only when it advances their interest. Moreover, considering that political realities constrain the commitments that states accept, and that the interests of more powerful states set the terms of cooperation, international rules and institutions have little, if any, independent effect on state behaviour. All this means that, for realists, reaching out to others is no more than a self-interested act, conditioned and limited by the primacy of the national interest. This applies to the ways in which realism envisions solidarity vis-à-vis other states, as well as to solidarity geared toward international human rights.

Liberalism and the mitigation of the divide

Liberalism, which also has a long history and various strands, is distinct from realism namely in the sense that it developed as a response to the realist view that conflicts are natural and can be contained only by balance-of-power strategies. In addition, it is different in its conception and handling of the "us versus them" divide. Unlike realism, liberalism tries to tame this divide. Its taming approach unfolds in three related ways.

First, most liberal theories of international life, while acknowledging the duality of "us versus them", attempt to limit it by giving much importance to international cooperation. This is in line with the value that liberal theories of society see in cooperation among individuals in general. Second, liberalism is open to recognizing a plurality of actors in the international realm (especially since the 1980s). In this regard, although states are still by and large considered central players in international affairs, non-state actors are viewed as occupying a significant role. This makes interstate politics in the liberal perspective more complex and fluid than realists assume. For instance, the liberal approach takes into account both domestic (including the preferences of individuals and private groups) and transnational politics (including global entities or networks). In the process, the divide between "us" and "them" tends to be blurred. Although the existence of competition is acknowledged, it is also recognized that actors are connected by relations of interdependence – that create some sort of continuum of fate and interest among them. In other words, the ways in which they interact is not conceived as a zero-sum game. Third, the most progressive liberals see the individual as a subject of international law. This echoes the fact that, as the inclusive character of democratic values is part and parcel of liberalism, equality and the universality of rights of individuals constitute crucial aspects of the liberal creed. As such, liberalism cannot easily overlook the commitment to human rights of the solidarist message. Projecting a sense of international solidarity in the name of human rights becomes one of the constitutive elements of liberal legitimacy at the international level.[18]

Liberal theories, nevertheless, are limited to, and by, the "us versus them" divide. The commitment of liberalism to human rights does not structure it enough to allow in practice a harmonious dovetailing of its particularist ethics with its universalist orientation. It does not allow the primary value given to the pursuit of the national interest to be reconciled with defending seriously the fate of individuals beyond borders.[19] When all is said and done, liberalism tends to condition the latter to the former. It tends to fail to conceive the former within the latter, to integrate the former into the latter. Hence the difficulty that it faces in envisioning and implementing a socially inclusive view of the world that is based on full international reciprocity of rights and duties.

Re-engineering and widening the sense of community

It is largely as an attempt to go beyond this state of affairs that the various strands of the radical (left) tradition of International Relations developed. They made it one of their key goals to describe how international life might, and should, be transformed to improve the sense of justice, within and among states. In this regard, Kant's ideas did not contribute only to the development of liberalism in international politics. His views that international politics is about relations among the human beings who make up states, that the ultimate reality of international affairs is the community of humankind and that, on this basis, all individuals should work for human brotherhood, were picked up, built upon, and radicalized by successive waves of revolutionist conceptions of international politics, especially Marxists.[20]

Where realism and liberalism take the state system for granted, Marxism offers a different explanation for international conflict and a blueprint for how to fundamentally transform the existing international order. As Michael Doyle puts it: "From Marx and Engels's work we can follow a distinct dialogue through the democratic Socialists to Lenin, Stalin, Mao, and current-day interpreters of the canon. For them world politics is intraclass solidarities combined with interclass war waged both across and within state borders.... Despite an analytic tradition that (as do the Realists) explicitly describes normative questions as ideological, Marxists also rely upon an idealist commitment to human welfare that makes the determination of international progress an essential feature of both their scientific explanation and their plan for revolutionary liberation."[21] Although developments within international politics in the 1970s contributed to enhancing some of the Marxist ideas, not least Immanuel Wallerstein and his world-system's theory,[22] in the end, the ways in which communism unfolded in reality, domestically and internationally, weakened its intellectual standing beyond repair.

This does not mean that the critical stance toward reality, including international reality, that is put forward by Marxism totally vanished from international studies. As a matter of fact, some of its key characteristics, among which is the idea that reality is an historical and social construct that consequently can be changed and improved,[23] came to be the pillars of critical approaches to international affairs.

Critical social theory, which emerged in International Relations in the 1980s,[24] casts itself mainly as an alternative to positivist and empiricist epistemology. Instead of being purely observational or explanatory, this type of theorizing seeks to be emancipatory. In the process, it aims at unveiling and overcoming the exclusionary effects of the "us versus them" divide.

Postmodernism,[25] another critical approach, pursues this agenda by emphasizing the power relationships and dominations that underlie what is seen as natural. In doing so, its goal is to reveal the marginalized and the excluded other, and put an end to marginalization and exclusion.

Another perspective, feminism, stressing that gender is socially and culturally constructed, argues that it is important to recognize gender bias, not just in social relations at large, but specifically within the study of International Relations.[26]

Constructivism is perhaps most successful when it comes to encapsulating theoretical and liberating aims. Springing from a variety of approaches[27] and offering a plurality of strands,[28] it gives an explanation, or a set of explanations, of international life meant to close the analytical gaps of realism, liberalism and Marxism, without rejecting their contribution altogether. Constructivists are most concerned with understanding the behaviours and institutions of international life as social constructs, and how these human constructs have come to be taken for granted.[29] The exercise of denaturalization that the conception of international life as a social construct brings leads constructivism to have history, and historicity, built in as part of its approach. This means that much attention is given to contingency, and change.[30] It also means that the understanding of international life as a social reality implies not only that history is to a large extent a human-made reality subject to contingency and change, but also that it will continue to evolve in the future. Combined with peo-

ple's ability to learn (part of what Emanuel Adler calls "cognitive evolution"[31]), this approach opens the gate to the idea of the plasticity of
international life.[32] It is here that the explanatory programme of constructivism becomes part of an emancipatory agenda, promoting, at least implicitly, a progressive and inclusive vision of the "us versus them" divide.

Take, for instance, what constructivism has to say on identity and national and transnational interests, and what it signifies for the rearrange-
ment and mitigation of the sense of "we" and "they" in the context of
security communities and human rights discourse. Constructivists argue
that states' identities and interests evolve from the dissemination and
convergence of normative understandings across national boundaries, a
high level of communication, economic interdependence and cooperative
practices.[33] This shows that the "we-feeling", or identities of national
groups, may expand across national borders. For example, building on
Karl Deutsch's concept of security communities, Emanuel Adler argued
that the importance of security communities is that they provide their
members with compatible core values, deriving from common institutions, mutual responsiveness and a sense of mutual loyalty – a sense of
"we-ness", or a "we-feeling" among states.[34] Crucially, they make possible a situation where interstate relations are not shaped by the threat or
use of force.

In a complementary manner, Kathryn Sikkink has shown how collective beliefs about human rights contribute to the construction of Western
identities, with a significant role played by non-governmental actors. In
this perspective, human rights norms become not only regulative injunc-
tions designed to overcome the collective-action problems associated with
interdependent choice, but also constitutive elements of the identity and
self-understanding of actors. In the process, changing interests and values,
as part of an evolving identity, transform the notion of national interest.
As human rights become part and parcel of national identities, they end
up shaping national interests and how they are conceived and (best) pursued in the international realm in the handling of issues and interactions
with other nations.[35] The transformation of identity and national interest
associated with the rise of human rights is of particular importance to
leading democratic powers, such as the United States. In principle, these
states more than others are meant to identify with human rights values.
Their ability to take human rights seriously internationally determines
not only the legitimacy of their foreign policy but also, to the extent that
they contribute to underwrite international order, the overall legitimacy
of the international system.[36] As Kathryn Sikkink points out, to overlook
this aspect is to misunderstand current political realities and, essentially,
not to serve well the national interest.[37]

Situating this book in the traditions of international relations

Obviously some of the concerns of this book are not foreign to international relations studies which favour a critical approach. For example, evaluating how in the post–Cold War era national interest and solidarity considerations motivate states to get involved in international crises is a way to address the three following questions that are of major interest to constructivist scholars. First, to what extent do the political realities of international life now have a hybrid character, made up of traditional national interest and internationalist considerations? Second, to what extent does the alleged hybrid character of the political realities of international life blur the line between national and international (internationalist) demands? And, third, where and how does the blurring of that line invite national interest (especially that of key states) to be less particularist and exclusionary, and more inclusive and universalist?

At the same time, however, the contributors to this book do not intend to put forward an emancipatory agenda per se. They probably all hold "progressive" views regarding the directions in which international life should go (favouring, for example, human rights and the minimization of the "us versus them" divide). But emancipation is not at the centre of the chapters. As mentioned earlier, the book has a rather straightforward purpose, that is, mainly to analyse case studies to acquire some sense of the respective weights of national interest and internationalist considerations in current international life.

The book shares two other ideas with constructivist approaches to International Relations. First, the idea that the national interest is not fixed and that the progressivist evolution of international politics calls for moving away from a traditional conception of the national interest. In this perspective, although the analysis provided by the chapters tends to show that realist self-interested motivations continue to be a decisive factor in states' rationales for international action, they also indicate that such motivations can not afford to be "raw". It is more and more difficult, especially for the big powers, to present as legitimate international interventions that are initiated only for self-centred reasons, ignoring or even undertaken at the expense of other countries and people.

This is all the more the case, considering that the findings of the chapters go against another realist idea, the idea that the foreign policy of a country can to a large extent be conducted in an asocial manner, as if the interests and rights of other states and their citizens did not have to be taken into account.[38] The chapters show that the pursuit of national interest is likely to be self-defeating when it ignores altogether the security and rights of other countries and their citizens. In other words, while solidarity is about doing the right thing, through the recognition and implementation of rights and duties, it can also bring the international realm closer to enjoying security. Conversely, to overlook solidarity is to invite resentment, if not violence. Hence, recognizing the mutual interdependence between the ideas of solidarity and security helps to "secure security", both materially and psychologically.

These findings help understanding of how the book situates itself vis-à-vis liberalism and its values. On the one hand, the chapters illustrate that in the contemporary political context democratic values have acquired much importance in defining the normative guidelines of legitimacy and good governance, at home and abroad.[39] As such, liberal values are one of the winners of the time. On the other hand, the analyses of the contributors caution against an international instrumentalization of liberalism and its values. The "unilateral" use of them, which disregards the need to recognize the rights of others (countries and people), undermines the possibility of justifying involvement beyond borders and of establishing security at home and abroad.

Organization of the volume

As a whole, the book is organized into three main parts. These parts correspond to three versions of interstate and intrastate relations, in the context of national interest and international solidarity, and their interplay.

Solidarity versus security

Part I, "Solidarity versus security", focuses on the balance between security and solidarity considerations in relation to states locked into tense relationships with a real risk of conflict. In this perspective, transborder solidarity is quite minimal, although not necessarily completely non-existent. The security tensions at work among actors do not exclude the development of cross-border solidarity with potential benefits at the intrastate or even at the interstate level, or the emergence of security communities between countries. This is linked with the need to seriously manage tensions to avoid them degenerating into open conflict. This is a role that partly accrues to powerful external actors, particularly when they have a strong presence in the region and have relations, in one way or another, with the antagonists. To examine these themes, this section focuses on two case studies: the India–Pakistan dispute over Kashmir and the quest for mitigating tensions; and US–China relations, especially in connection with the Taiwan dispute.

In Chapter 1, on India and Pakistan, Samina Yasmeen explains why Pakistan and India have maintained such a negative relationship. Are they guided by a single-minded adherence to a logic of relations according to national interest, or do alternative views that favour solidarity exist within these countries? If present, what role do these alternative views play in determining the nature of Indo-Pakistani relations? How can these voices be strengthened and what is the likelihood of India and Pakistan moving into an era of mutual cooperation and solidarity in the future? Finally, what is the role played by external actors or, rather, what is the interplay between the dynamics of the India–Pakistan relations and the input from external actors? In other words, the chapter seeks to highlight the tense interaction between national interest and solidarity beyond borders in the relations between India and Pakistan, as well as the changing regional and international context, including the evolving attitude of external actors (especially the United States, as "facilitator") who are particularly interested in the India–Pakistan dispute. Samina Yasmeen argues that developments in Indo-Pakistani relations after 11 September indicate that the relationship is unlikely to move in the direction of shared goals and common understandings in the foreseeable future.

Alan Collins's chapter on Sino–US relations examines what underpins the relationship between the United States and China. In particular, Collins tries to determine if the relations between the United States and China are shaped by a pursuit of national interest where the core assumption about the other is constant and unlikely to change, or if there are changes that indicate a growing sense of communality. For Collins, these questions are essential, not only for the actors directly involved, but also because Sino–US relations are fundamental to the likelihood of peace or conflict in East Asia. Ultimately, his prognosis is mixed. On the one hand, though remote, war between China and the United States is still a possibility. On the other hand, the relationship is not on the verge of conflict; the two countries have, particularly since 11 September, engaged in dialogue to manage a series of crises, most notably North Korea and Taiwan. Sino–US relations lie therefore somewhere between enmity and amity. Yet, and more positively, Collins sees promising signs for the emergence of a security regime between the United States and China – a regime that suggests a level of cooperation in which members are not concerned solely about their individual short-term interest.

Solidarity, national interest and great power interventionism

Part II, "Assessing the logic of solidarity and national interest in great power interventionism", concentrates on cases in which powerful external actors are deeply involved in conflict management. Here, the case studies demonstrate that external actors' motivation displays a combination of national interest and international solidarity considerations. As a matter of fact, in some cases, it is not easy to distinguish and rank which considerations are behind great powers. This is partly due to the complexity of the crises and their political and normative ramifications, particularly when it comes to the Israeli–Palestinian conflict. The case studies examined in the section are the following: Russia's foreign policy and its attitude toward the idea of international solidarity championed by Western powers since the end of the Cold War; the reconfiguration of interests vis-à-vis Central Asia in the post–Cold War and post–11 September contexts; the role of the United States and the European Union in the search for a solution to the Israeli–Palestinian conflict; and American policy toward the Colombian conflict.

Ekaterina Stepanova's chapter on how Russia relates to the issues of national interest and international solidarity unfolds in the context of what separates the developed countries from the rest of the world. She notes that for the developed world (composed mostly, but not exclusively, of the Western world, as the interesting positioning and role of Japan's development aid policies exemplifies), the increasing prevalence of behavioural patterns motivated by a combination of moral considerations and self-interest brings the issue of complementarity and competitiveness between the national interest and solidarity paradigms to the forefront. She goes on to say that, "while there is no question that the world's most-developed democratic states are frequently guided by solidarity culture in shaping their behaviour toward one another, and demonstrate elements of international solidarity in addressing selected issues of global concern, in their relations with states that do not share some or most Western values, national interests and geostrategic considerations ... often prevail". According to Stepanova, this to a large extent explains the West's relations with Russia. But the dual use of national interest and international solidarity that Stepanova detects in (powerful) Western nations' foreign policies is also a trait that applies to Russian foreign policy itself. According to her, the case of Russia is perhaps most exemplary in demonstrating that the two main theoretical approaches described above present a spectrum/continuum rather than being mutually exclusive. For Stepanova, the continuum between national interest and international solidarity in Russian foreign policy is largely shaped by Russia's own national and cultural identity, as well as its subsequent relations with the rest of the world, in particular the West.[40] She argues that from this identity a synthesis of both cooperative (extroverted, internationally oriented) and geostrategic (geopolitical, self-centered) paradigms has emerged. Stepanova stresses the fact that in the post–Cold War era, Russian foreign policy has undergone several shifts. It went from the relative infatuation with the democratic solidarity discourse of the early 1990s (which, according to Stepanova, occurred at the expense of Russia's strategic interest) to disillusionment with Western policies (fuelled by the NATO enlargement process and the resurgence of geostrategic thinking by the mid- and late 1990s) and, finally, to the more balanced approach of the early 2000s (with international cooperation embedded in a formulation of Russian national interest). Stepanova's chapter tests, as well as illustrates, these ideas, first in the context of Russia's recent involvement in conflicts within the Commonwealth of Independent States (CIS); second, in the context of its involvement in conflict management outside the CIS; and, third, in the context of the post-11 September "war against terror", including the war against the Taliban regime in Afghanistan and the war against Iraq.

In Chapter 4, Parviz Mullojanov analyses the renewal of interest in Central Asia. He lists the variety of interests that Russia has had over time in Central Asia, and examines competing views inside the Russian bureaucracy throughout the 1990s on how Moscow should relate to Central Asia. His analysis confirms and completes Stepanova's chapter. Mullojanov shows how the model of evolution put forward by Stepanova concerning the various shifts of Russian foreign policy in the past 15 years applies to Central Asia. But Mullojanov also analyses the challenge that Russia now faces as a multiplicity of new actors arrives in the region. Indeed, it is not only the United States that is trying to be more present in the various countries of Central Asia. It is also China, Iran and Turkey. Most of these external state-actors that are taking a renewed interest in Central Asia are animated less by solidarist motivations than by national-interest considerations. In this perspective, the multilateral efforts deployed to address the humanitarian needs of the region, as well as to aid in its development, are likely to be overshadowed by the games of power politics. This is all the more the case, argues Mullojanov, considering the fact that multilateral initiatives are themselves not free of national-interest calculations. Mullojanov recognizes that the West's growing involvement in Central Asia has positive aspects, such as helping to undermine persistent authoritarianism. But he concludes that Central Asia is likely to continue to also be one of the key fault lines of international politics.

In Chapter 5, Mira Sucharov analyses the attempts by the European Union and the United States to resolve the Israeli–Palestinian conflict. Sucharov begins by saying that the attempt to uncover the determinants of external involvement in the Israeli–Palestinian conflict (specifically, whether actors are motivated by geopolitics or a sense of international solidarity) is particularly salient in the context of this crisis, as well as in the broader context of the Middle East. Sucharov's overall assessment is that a sense of solidarity generally shapes the outlook of the European

Union and the United States, but that it is intimately tied to the national interest in connection with polity identities. Sucharov argues that this is in line with the thesis "that the degree to which a state understands its fate to be intertwined with that of others (a stance that represents a culture of solidarity) emerges from the overall identity of the state.... That identity in turn leads to particular conceptions of the national interest". Regarding the United States, Sucharov indicates, for example, that President George W. Bush's decision to call for a Palestinian state in October 2001 largely derived from an ethics of solidarity toward people's desires for self-determination as much as from intrinsic geopolitical imperatives. As for the European Union's motivations for involvement in the Israeli–Palestinian conflict, Sucharov tells us that it involves some elements of geopolitics (particularly the consolidation of the organization's foreign-policy machinery and checking the global power of the United States), but also includes a sense of international solidarity, in assisting Palestinian self-determination (an evening out of the international playing field in favour of those who appear to have been neglected). Ultimately, Sucharov indicates that this "suggests not only that the national interest can derive from identity, but that the moral question posed by the Babylonian Jewish sage Hillel may indeed hold resonance for global politics in the new millennium: 'If I am not for myself then who is for me, but if I am only for myself, then what am I?'"

Doug Stokes's chapter looks into US foreign policy toward Colombia in relation to drug trafficking, insurgency, terrorism and other elements endangering the viability of the Colombian state and contributing to the region's instability. This chapter represents a critique of the logic of solidarity at the international level. It illustrates the limits of the concept by adopting a critical/radical, and somewhat Marxist, interpretation. Although Stokes indicates that there are some solidarist considerations animating the ways in which the United States relates to Colombia, he stresses the fact that the United States, dating back to the Cold War, views the Colombian crisis first and foremost in terms of national interest and geopolitics. Stokes's thesis is that American involvement in Colombian affairs is a form of "transnational class solidarity designed to insulate the Colombian state and ruling class from a wide range of both armed and unarmed social forces" that threaten the mutual interests of US and Colombian capital. On this basis, he argues that the purpose of involvement is the preservation of Colombia as a pro-US state and "the effective incorporation of Colombia as a stable circuit within the global circulation of capital". As such, Stokes's chapter is an analysis of a great power actor's rationale for intervention combined with a sociological analysis of Colombia's economic dynamics and the positioning of elites within. This focus allows him to show that the discourse and practice of solidarity at the international level can be very selective (geared toward the few rather than the many), self-serving (for the benefit of the national interest of the United States, regardless of the interests of the Colombian people as a whole) and, consequently, oblivious to the inclusive and distributive justice demands meant to be at its very core.

Ethics of human solidarity

Part III, "Toward an ethics of human solidarity" focuses on cases in which the projection of power is principally geared toward helping people caught in the midst of intrastate (humanitarian) crises. Three examples are investigated: US foreign policy toward Africa and its variety of crises; the involvement of the international community in the attempts to resolve the Yugoslav wars of succession; and the international community's handling of the East Timor crisis.

US foreign policy toward Africa and the extent to which it is shaped by national interest and international solidarity considerations is the focus of Timothy Docking's discussion in chapter 7. According to Docking, the end of the Cold War led to a re-evaluation of the realism that had guided American policies toward Africa for forty years. Initially, the prospect of a changed US foreign policy calculus toward Africa was greeted with enthusiasm by American activists, scholars and policymakers alike, many of whom were hoping that the end of the Cold War would usher in an era of enlightened US foreign policy toward the African continent – an enlightened policy based on new, creative thinking and principles, including international solidarity. But, in practice, post–Cold War American policy vis-à-vis the region has had a mixed impact. The withdrawal of support for former US clients often contributed to the unleashing of the destructive forces of civil war in which the US was unwilling to engage. According to Docking, the US proclivity to "cut and run" from Africa's problems came to characterize most US policy decisions toward the continent throughout the 1990s. This led a number of analysts to label America's Africa policy as one of "cynical disengagement". The glimpses of international solidarity that could be seen in Somalia at the beginning of the 1990s and in Bush's pronouncements on AIDS in Africa in the early 2000s are not enough to change this impression. Docking notes that the Bush administration has over time strengthened its policy of international solidarity toward Africa (he mentions in particular the 2002 announcement of the Millennium Challenge Account). But he concludes that the fact that Washington continues to see Africa as a foreign-policy backwater does not help make the case for international solidarity toward the continent.

In Chapter 8, Alex Bellamy focuses on the wars of succession in the Balkans. In this chapter, Bellamy charts the shift in the relationship between interest and solidarity from 1991 onwards. He charts how perceived geopolitical considerations overrode concerns over the emerging humanitarian disaster in Yugoslavia until the post-Kosovo era, when interest and solidarity appeared more closely aligned. He argues that, by the end of the 1990s, the international community and European states had come to recognize that in the Balkans both humanitarian concerns and national interests would be satisfied by policy responses aiming to end humanitarian emergencies and create more democratic societies. Bellamy makes the point that this significant shift began to take place in the immediate aftermath of Srebrenica in 1995 and was based on a growing acceptance, as the war unfolded, that there was an intimate link between respect for basic human rights and long-term geopolitical stability. At the same time, he stresses the fact that the display of solidarity at work in the Balkans by the end of the 1990s did not bring about a triumph of solidarism. Solidarism remained very constrained, in particular by domestic politics, including the reluctance of intervening powers to place their citizens in harm's way.

Geoffrey Gunn, writing on East Timor, begins Chapter 9 by showing how a culture of national interest (demanded by Indonesia and blessed by Australia and the United States) derailed East Timor's quest for decolonization for decades. He underlines the point that not even the end of the Cold War brought immediate redress to the sovereignty question. The weight of Indonesian national interest might have continued to deny East Timor's access to independence had it not been for the political juncture produced by Indonesia's economic collapse, the resignation of President Suharto and the domestic instability that followed in the late 1990s. A push from the United Nations and Portugal, manifested in the tripartite talks held between the UN, Indonesia and Portugal on the future of East Timor, led Jakarta to accept (though reluctantly) the idea of independence for East Timor. Gunn goes on to show that the analysis of the successive UN involvements in East Timor, starting in May 1999, starkly demonstrates that, provided that a number of procedural steps have been met, a full-blown ethics of solidarity at the service of humanitarian concerns can emerge, notwithstanding the most severe geopolitical limitations. As such, the case of East Timor stands in sharp contrast to the refusal of the international community to get involved in Rwanda's even more horrific situation just a few years earlier. Gunn's conclusion is somewhat positive. He argues that the willingness of ASEAN members and China to overcome a prevailing logic of non-interference by accepting the idea of humanitarianism dressed up as universalism (even if some reservations remained), goes a long way toward illustrating how the ethics of international solidarity progressed in the 1990s.

The lessons drawn in the concluding chapter lead to a call for an enlargement and deepening (to use European integration vocabulary) of the international rule of law. Nevertheless, this is not to say that universalist considerations may turn into a sense of global public policy, or a form of thick international solidarity similar to the one existing in the best-functioning democratic polities or at the regional level as in the case of Europe. The enduring particularist tendencies of international life are one of the reasons that will probably prevent this from happening. Yet, as legitimacy constraints increasingly weigh on foreign policies, as it becomes less and less manageable for the unilateral or exclusively self-interested international projection of power to make might right, it is essential that the international rule of law be significantly strengthened. The enhancement of international solidarity is indeed one of the best ways to respond to demands of national and international security.

Notes

1. This chapter has benefited from the comments and suggestions of Louise Bergström, Jibecke Jönsson and Lamis Abdel-Aty.
2. Lucien Poirier (1994) *La crise des fondements*, Paris: Economica. For more on the link between national interest and geography, and therefore on geopolitics, refer to John Agnew (1998) *Geopolitics: Re-visioning World Politics*, New York: Routledge.
3. Yves Lacoste (2006) *Géopolitique: La longue histoire d'aujourd'hui*, Paris: Larousse.
4. John Gerard Ruggie (1998) *Constructing the World Polity: Essays on International Institutionalization*, London: Routledge, pp. 172–197; David Held, Anthony McGrew, David Goldblattt and Jonathan Perraton (1999) *Global Transformations: Politics, Economics and Culture*, Stanford, Calif.: Stanford University Press, pp. 27–28. For a more philosophical, as well as speculative and radical, understanding of deterritorialization, see Gilles Deleuze and Félix Guattari (1987) *A Thousand Plateaus: Capitalism and Schizophrenia*, Brian Massumi, trans., Minneapolis, Minn.: University of Minnesota Press.
5. Any society that is not exclusively based on force, and that is mindful of its own people's well being, embodies a sense of human rights, which can be different from a sense of individual rights. (On this later issue, refer for example to Daryush Shayegan (1992) *Cultural Schizophrenia: Islamic Societies Confronting the West*, John Howe, trans., London: Saqi Books, pp. 27–28.) But what is quite specific to Western democratic culture, and therefore links international solidarity to the idea of international democratic culture, is the idea that human rights are universal, that is, that all human beings ought to have access to the same basic rights, whoever and wherever they are. For more on this, see Philip Allott (2001) *Eunomia: New Order for a New World*, Oxford: Oxford University Press.
6. On these questions, see, for instance, Georg Simmel (1964) *Conflict and the Web of Group-Affiliations*, Kurt H. Wolff and Reinhard Bendix, trans., New York: The Free Press.

7. See Emile Durkheim (1997) *The Division of Labor in Society*, W. D. Halls, trans., New York: Free Press; and Ferdinand Tönnies (2002) *Community and Society*, Charles P. Loomis, trans. and ed., Mineola, N.Y.: Dover. For more on the notion of solidarity, its history and application at the national and international levels, refer to Serge Paugam, ed. (2007) *Repenser la solidarité*, Paris: Presses Universitaires de France.

8. The movement toward a wide and profound sense of the realization of justice, fueled by democratic values and rights, is one of the defining vectors of modernity at the national and international levels. But this is not one that is free from struggle. Despite the declarations of principles, the beneficiaries of democratic universalism and equality initially formed and, to some extent, continue to form an exclusive club. And it is around the boundaries of inclusion and exclusion that the battles for political, economic and social justice have focused throughout the evolution of modern democratic culture. On this question, see Andrew Linklater (1998) *The Transformations of Political Community: Ethical Foundations of the Post-Westphalian Era*, Columbia, S.C.: University of South Carolina Press, pp. 117–118.

9. The seriousness of this issue has been a constant concern in the study of modernity. In this regard, Anglo-American scholars have been particularly apt at identifying mechanisms of rational choice that ensure the cohabitation of self-interest and social cooperation. See Jane J. Mansbridge (1990) "The Rise and Fall of Self-Interest in the Explanation of Political Life", in Jane J. Mansbridge, ed., *Beyond Self-Interest*, Chicago: University of Chicago Press, pp. 3–22. On the other hand, continental European analysts tend to explore a sense of community that is able to reconcile the autonomous agent and the social being by insisting on the role of shared culture and history, in which the reciprocity of rights and duties is embedded.

10. Although much of the scholarly literature on modern democratic culture focuses on its atomization, modern democratic culture remains inhabited by elements of kinship. This culture's decisive contribution to the organization of collective life in connection with the distribution of goods (be they political, economic, social or intellectual) based on talent and merit (hence the importance of access to education for a fair competition for goods) does not eliminate the remnants of kinship's influence. For instance, familial social relations can prove to be, in one way or another, a crucial determinant.

11. See, for example, Thomas M. Franck (2000) "Legitimacy and the Democratic Entitlement", in Gregory H. Fox and Brad R. Roth, eds, *Democratic Governance and International Law*, New York: Cambridge University Press, pp. 25–41.

12. These traditions and their various versions have deep historical and political roots beyond the contemporary era, and the differences among them can be rather blurred at times. For a more general analysis of these traditions, refer, for example, to Martin Wight, Gabriele Wight and Brian Porter, eds (1992) *International Theory: The Three Traditions*, New York: Holmes & Meier; and Michael W. Doyle (1997) *Ways of War and Peace: Realism, Liberalism and Socialism*, New York: W. W. Norton. See also Stephen M. Walt (1998) "International Relations: One World, Many Theories", *Foreign Policy*, No. 110, Spring: 29–46; and Kenneth W. Abbott (1999) "International Relations Theory, International Law, and the Regime Governing Atrocities in Internal Conflicts", *American Journal of International Law* 93(2), April: 361–379.

13. Hans J. Morgenthau (1978) *Politics among Nations: The Struggle for Power and Peace*, New York: Knopf.

14. Kenneth Waltz (1979) *Theory of International Politics*, Reading, Mass.: Addison-Wesley.

15. Hedley Bull (1995) *The Anarchical Society: A Study of Order in World Politics*, New York: Columbia University Press.

16. James C. Hsiung, writing in the neorealist tradition, takes an interesting view on the anarchical state of international society. He argues that in direct connection to human nature, it is in fact the anarchical nature of international society that is the primary motivation for multilateral cooperation and global governance. It is therefore in the interest of multilateral cooperation to keep the anarchical nature of international society, as without it there would be neither a need nor a desire for states to cooperate. James C. Hsiung (1997) *Anarchy and Order: The Interplay of Politics and Law in International Relations*, Boulder, Colo.: Lynne Rienner Publishers.

17. Jean-Paul Sartre used to say that Marxism is the "horizon indépassable" of humanity.

18. Allen Buchanan (2004) *Justice, Legitimacy, and Self-determination: Moral Foundations for International Law*, Oxford: Oxford University Press.

19. Value and interest tend to be seen as at odds. Yet they are not by definition antithetic notions. After all, one has to value something (or someone) to take an interest in it (or him/her). Also, the existence and pursuit of an interest (survival, for example) is what gives value to the object (or action or person) that is seen as needed to satisfy this interest. Furthermore, ethics, which can be described as the organization of relations among actors based on an exchange of mutually recognized rights and duties, is not only on the side of value. It is also on the side of interest. If the value of ethics lies in not ignoring the other (and the other interest), it also requires not ignoring oneself (and one's own interest). For, although ethics brings upon the self the burden of looking after and feeling responsible for the other, it is as much in need of the self as it is in need of the other: unless one does well for himself/herself, it is difficult to do good for others.

   It is worth adding that the tension that can exist between interest and value is echoed by the difficult relationship between power and principle (specific neither to liberalism nor to political action). More often than not, the gap separating the concrete exercise of power and principles is on display. In this perspective, power is apt to be seen on the side of interest and of its self-serving temptations, while principles are prone to be placed in the camp of values and of their socializing aims and effects. But, as with interest and value, power and principle are not opposed by definition. In a win-win situation, they work together. For instance, the implementation of principles of conduct in a social setting requires a sense of agency, that is, power.

20. Hedley Bull (1992) "Martin Wight and the Theory of International Relations", in Martin Wight, Gabriele Wight and Brian Porter, eds, *International Theory: The Three Traditions*, New York: Holmes & Meier, p. xii.

21. Doyle, *Ways of War and Peace*, p. 20.

22. Immanuel Wallerstein (1989) *The Modern World-System*, San Diego, Calif.: Academic Press.

23. See, for instance, Roberto Mangabeira Unger and Zhiyuan Cui (1997) *Politics: The Central Texts, Theory against Fate*, London: Verso.

24. For example, Yosef Lapid (1989) "The Third Debate: On the Prospects of International Theory in a Post-Positivist Era", *International Studies Quarterly* 33(3): 235–254.

25. The heading "postmodernism" comprises a great number of scholars with diverging views (who may not all agree to one definition of postmodernism). This approach is described here in only the broadest of terms. For an indicative debate on what postmodernism is and is not, see the exchange between Øyvid Østerud, Steve Smith and Heikki Patomäki in *Journal of Peace Research* 33(4), 1996, and 34(3), 1997.

26. See J. Ann Tickner (1997) "You Just Don't Understand: Troubled Engagements between Feminists and IR Theorists", *International Studies Quarterly* 41(4): 611–632. Lamis Abdel-Aty makes the point that while radical approaches call into question and can help surmount the "us versus them" divide through their faith in change and aspiration for liberation, they also solidify this divide by emphasizing and espousing

difference, particularism and plurality. The interplay between these two tendencies is especially interesting in the case of feminism. On the one hand, feminism tends to encourage empathy and empathetic involvement to learn from subjects, signaling a form of inclusiveness. On the other hand, feminism emphasizes the relational and oppositional categories of masculine and feminine.

27. Emanuel Adler indicates that four currents of thoughts have strongly influenced constructivism in international relations: neo-Kantian "objective hermeneutics", linguistic "subjective hermeneutics", critical theory and pragmatist philosophy of science. See Emanuel Adler (2002) "Constructivism and International Relations", in Walter Carlsnaes, Thomas Risse and Beth A. Simmons, eds, *Handbook of International Relations*, London: Sage Publications, pp. 96–97. As a whole, international relations constructivism lends much to continental European critical sociology and its unpacking of the social character of reality at the national level. Considering how relatively weak the study of International Relations is in continental Europe, particularly when it comes to theoretical questions, it is ironic that one of the currently most vibrant approaches to International Relations has some of its main roots in a modern European continental intellectual tradition.

28. Emanuel Adler lists four strands of international relations constructivism: a modernist type of constructivism, modernist linguistic constructivism, radical constructivism and critical constructivism. See "Constructivism and International Relations", pp. 97–98.

29. Emanuel Adler (1997) "Seizing the Middle Ground: Constructivism in World Politics", *European Journal of International Relations* 3(3): 322: "Constructivism shows that even our most enduring institutions are based on collective understandings; that they are reified structures that were once upon a time conceived *ex nihilo* by human consciousness; and that these understandings were subsequently diffused and consolidated until they were taken for granted."

30. Martha Finnemore and Kathryn Sikkink (2001) "Taking Stock: The Constructivist Research Program in International Relations and Comparative Politics", *Annual Review of Political Science* 4: 393: "Understanding how social facts change and the ways these influence politics is the major concern of constructivist analysis".

31. Adler, "Seizing the Middle Ground", pp. 342–343.

32. On the notion of plasticity applied to social reality, refer to Unger and Cui, *Politics: The Central Texts, Theory against Fate.*

33. Emanuel Adler (1997) "Imagined (Security) Communities: Cognitive Regions in International Relations", *Millennium: Journal of International Studies* 26(2): 252.

34. Ibid. See also Emanuel Adler and Michael N. Barnett, eds (1998) *Security Communities*, Cambridge: Cambridge University Press; and Emanuel Adler and Michael N. Barnett (1996) "Governing Anarchy: A Research Agenda for the Study of Security Communities", *Ethics & International Affairs* 10(1): 63–98.

35. "The emergence of human rights policy is not a simple victory for ideas over interest. Instead, it demonstrates the power of ideas to reshape understandings of national interest. The recent adoption of human rights policies did not represent the neglect of national interests but rather a fundamental shift in the perception of long-term national interests. Human rights policies emerged because policy makers began to question the principled idea that the internal human rights practices of a country are not a legitimate topic of foreign policy and the causal assumption that national interests are furthered by supporting regimes that violate the human rights of their citizens." Kathryn Sikkink (1998) "Transnational Politics, International Relations Theory, and Human Rights", *PSOnline*, Washington, D.C.: The American Political Science Association, p. 519, September, available from www.apsanet.org. Refer also to Martha Finnemore (1996) *National Interests in International Society*, Ithaca, N.Y.: Cornell University Press, and

(2004) *The Purpose of Intervention: Changing Beliefs about the Use of Force*, Ithaca, N.Y.: Cornell University Press.

36. For more on this, see Jean-Marc Coicaud (2007) *Beyond the National Interest: The Future of UN Peacekeeping and Multilateralism in an Era of U.S. Primacy*, Washington, D.C.: United States Institute of Peace Press.

37. Kathryn Sikkink (2005) "Mixed Signals: U.S. Human Rights Policy and Practice", paper presented at the Center for Democracy and the Third Sector, Washington, D.C.: Georgetown University, 18 April, unpublished.

38. See, for instance, Jack L. Goldsmith and Eric A. Posner (2005) *The Limits of International Law*, Oxford: Oxford University Press.

39. At the most general level, legitimacy is the recognition of the right to govern. It tries to offer a solution to the fundamental problem of simultaneously justifying power and obedience. Translated to the international level, this understanding of legitimacy amounts to justifying the way in which international order is organized, including why and how power is projected beyond borders. On the question of legitimacy in general, see Jean-Marc Coicaud (2002) *Legitimacy and Politics: A Contribution to the Study of Political Right and Political Responsibility*, David A. Curtis, trans., Cambridge: Cambridge University Press. For legitimacy in the international context, refer to Ian Clark (2005) *Legitimacy in International Society*, Oxford: Oxford University Press.

40. On the question of Russia's identity and its relations with the (modern) West, see Martin Malia (1999) *Russia under Western Eyes: From the Bronze Horseman to the Lenin Mausoleum*, Cambridge, Mass.: The Belknap Press of Harvard University Press; and Orlando Figes (2002) *Natasha's Dance: A Cultural History of Russia*, New York: Picador.

Part I
Solidarity versus security

1

India and Pakistan: From zero-sum to shared security

Samina Yasmeen[1]

After remaining mired in a mutually conflicting relationship in the post–Cold War era, South Asia is experiencing a spring of optimism not known in the last six decades. Mutual suspicions and conflicts, which had become the hallmark of Indo-Pakistani relations, are giving way to cooperative experiments: Kashmir is being discussed by the two states as an issue, and people are moving with relatively less unease than before. This is in marked contrast to the tensions the two states experienced only very recently. The Kargil crisis (1999) remained confined to Kashmir but it did create fears of a conflict between the two erstwhile enemies. Only three years later, the yearlong mobilization of Indian and Pakistani forces along the international boundary in 2002 raised the spectre of an all-out war between the two nuclear neighbours. The eventual de-escalation by 2004 reduced the immediacy of a major conflict but the fear of one being sparked at a later stage remains one of the major concerns of the international community. The question arises as to why the two South Asian neighbours maintained a negative relationship for more than five decades instead of focusing on the developmental needs of their citizenry. Have they been guided by a single-minded adherence to a geo-strategic logic of relationships, or do alternative views favouring a culture of solidarity exist within these countries? What role have these alternative views, if present, played in determining the nature of Indo-Pakistani relations? How can these alternative voices be strengthened and how durable/permanent is a new spring of understanding between the two historical adversaries India and Pakistan? What role has the United States

National interest and international solidarity: Particular and universal ethics in international life, Coicaud and Wheeler (eds),
United Nations University Press, 2008, ISBN 978-92-808-1147-6

played in this process? Also, in the new geostrategic environment, does the United States role hold a promise of improving Indo-Pakistani relations?

This chapter attempts to answer these questions by developing a framework for analysing the movement of states along the spectrum that has one end occupied by the logic of "us versus them" (identified as the geostrategic approach) and the other end representing a culture of solidarity. It argues that the nature of Indo-Pakistani relations can best by understood in terms of a multiplicity of views in both states on the appropriate ways of dealing with the "other" across the border. The dominant view remains one of mutually negative perceptions of each other. Created and encouraged by the state and reinforced by societal forces, the images of the "other" as unreliable, hostile and irrational provide the context in which India and Pakistan deal with each other. They also create the conditions in which the geostrategic logic remains prevalent and enables both the state and society to translate all developments in their relationship into a zero-sum game. Alternative moderate views, however, do exist on the nature of the self and the other, and the appropriate ways of dealing with the neighbouring state. While relatively less pronounced, these views focus on the need for a more cooperative relationship between the two major South Asian states. Taking place against a changing regional and international context, the interplay between these different views creates conditions in which Indo-Pakistani relations essentially move between extreme hostility and notions of shared security. A view of solidarity as human-rights empathy remains absent in this context. At best, the approach of shared security can be identified with solidarity as cooperation and security community. Those subscribing to different sets of ideas are influenced by the regional and international environment but these remain the primary determining factors of Indo-Pakistani relations. External actors can and do play a role but have to date been unable to reduce the significance of views held by people within India and Pakistan. The developments in Indo-Pakistani relations after 11 September 2001 provide a recent example of the manner in which opposing views and ideas shape the nature of their interaction. They also highlight the role the United States has played in managing the tensions between the two South Asian neighbours. However, given the role played by domestic debates and views, despite the US role, the relationship is unlikely to move in the direction of a culture of solidarity emanating from a shared belief in the value of human rights as the primary determinant of their interrelationship. At best, the two states are going to explore some areas of shared security – occupying the space of solidarity representing security considerations.

Geopolitics versus solidarity: A framework for analysis

The starting point for this chapter remains a view of international relations where states move along the spectrum of conflicting and cooperative relationships. The conflicting end of the spectrum is identified as the geostrategic or realist view of world politics, which accepts the permanence of conflict in relations between states and, by extension, other actors in the international system. Their respective notions of national interest and a need to maximize this interest at the expense of others guide relations between states inhabiting this end of the spectrum. This induces a tendency to view international relations as a zero-sum game in which gain for one side means a loss for the other. The geostrategic approach, with its emphasis on the ideas of balance of power, is often elevated to the status of a value that needs to be cherished and sought. The other end of the spectrum is occupied by an understanding of world politics that conceptualizes the world in terms other than national interest. This end of the spectrum elevates cooperation to the status of a value that draws inspiration from universally held notions of human rights. The threat or use of force is considered unthinkable with a declared and actual commitment to cooperative mechanisms, as in the case of European Union.[2]

The space between the two extreme ends of the spectrum is occupied by gradating acceptance of the logic of competition or cooperation. The extent to which competition is favoured over cooperation determines the nature of a relationship between a set of parties. It also establishes the space they occupy on the spectrum. They may, for instance, occupy the space closer to the solidarity end of the spectrum. This would approximate at the interstate level a grouping like ASEAN, which is not a full-blown security community but is a very strong security regime in which cooperation reflects more than simple cost-benefit analysis. Alternatively, states may be willing to cooperate with others as an instrument of protecting their perceived national interest. But this conception of cooperation does not exclude the notion of competition. This selective acceptance of the logic of cooperation and competition may place them in a space where notions of solidarity either are not entertained, or, at best, encompass the idea of solidarity as cooperation. Parties cooperate because they realize the value of cooperation and not because they hold it as a value in itself. Assigning specific titles to each of these sets of relationships may be difficult. But developing a space of shared security (which could also be identified as a space of solidarity as cooperation) along the spectrum can circumvent the problem. Parties in a relationship could be placed in this space if their ideas or actions reflect an understanding that absolute security needs to be sacrificed for the sake of relative security. This could take the form of agreements and/or understandings that acknowledge limits to their competition or establish areas of cooperation in identified areas.

The apparent simplicity of the spectrum to understand and explain relationships between states or other parties, however, hides an inherent complexity. This complexity is directly linked to the multiplicity of ideas and views held in any given political unit about the appropriate ways of dealing with the other. This diversity is not restricted to decision-making circles but extends to members of the civil society as well.[3] Closely related to the notion of identity, it emanates from differing views in every state or society about the self, the other and the extent to which cooperation with the other is possible and/or feasible. It is also closely related to a reading and re-reading of history with an inherent need to find data to validate the already held views about the self and the other. While operating broadly within a common perceptual context, therefore, groups in a state or society can and do differ on which end of the spectrum or space is most relevant to their interaction with another state or society. The interplay between these different views determines the policies a state may pursue vis-à-vis the other. A predominance of geostrategic concepts, for example, could cause state A to opt for competitive policies toward state B. A shift in this balance may cause the same state to start preferring shared security instead of a geostrategic approach. At the same time, however, the multiplicity also creates conditions in which the debates are not resolved and the state pursues policies that reflect the difference of opinion and power balance among various groups. Effectively, therefore, a state may pursue policies that occupy different spaces along the spectrum of geostrategy and solidarity. They may sign agreements in some areas that reflect a commitment to shared security while simultaneously pursuing competitive policies in other areas.

The shifts along the spectrum and the multiplicity of policies, it is important to point out, are not totally driven by domestic factors in states party to a relationship. These shifts can be shaped by and interact with regional and global environments. External actors and their agendas may, for instance, support and empower one set of views, thus increasing its chances of being reflected in the state's policies. At the same time, the same efforts could paradoxically empower totally opposing groups who might interpret the actions of external actors as validation of their own worldview. In other cases, external actors may simply empower certain groups by their inaction and thus alter the domestic balance of views and resulting policies. American policy toward Iran after the Islamic revolution of 1979 provides an example of such a complex interplay of factors. By withdrawing from the situation, the United States inadvertently strengthened the ability of the clergy to shape events in Iran. Moderate voices felt powerless and had no option but to accept the revolutionary foreign policy agenda of the Islamic regime. More recently, the awarding of the Nobel Peace Prize to Shirin Ebadi in 2003 indicates the mixed impact of external actors: while moderate factions in Iran treat it as a vindication of their ideas, the orthodox clergy perceives and portrays it as evidence of western intervention in their Islamic country.[4]

Given this complexity, one could argue that analysing relations between states or parties along the geostrategic and solidarity spectrum requires an understanding of the multiplicity of views within the states and parties concerned, as well as their interaction with the international environment. Appreciating these linkages could also assist us in predicting the likely nature of relations between states engaged in cooperative or competitive policies.

Indo-Pakistani relations: Multiplicity of views

Since their independence in August 1947, Indo-Pakistani relations have been characterized by negativity and mutual hostility. The two states have fought three major wars, in 1948, 1965 and 1971. They have come close to armed conflict on numerous other occasions, including the crises in 1986, 1990, 1999 and 2002. These historical experiences have engendered a sense of mistrust of the other. They have also created a perceptual blockage that impedes a real understanding of the neighbouring state. Encouraged by the state structures and reinforced by the media and educational institutions, views have emerged that form part of the folk and scholarly myths about each other. Both Indian and Pakistani societies generally view the other as manipulative, aggressive, unreliable and incapable of rational thinking. Instead of being questioned, the extremely low levels of cooperative interaction between the two countries perpetuates these myths and forms the milieu in which opinions and views develop about the appropriate approaches to deal with the other. These views, which exist both in the decision-making circles and the civil society, can broadly be categorized as orthodox and moderate.[5]

Essentially, the differences between the orthodox and moderate views stem from differing notions of the identity of the self and the other. In Pakistan a debate has existed on the nature of the state created in August 1947.[6] For some, it is an Islamic state destined to provide optimal conditions for Muslims of the subcontinent to realize their true potential as Muslims. For others, it is a state for Muslims that reflects the aspirations of its citizenry without being overly prescriptive in religious terms. These differences notwithstanding, a sense exists among some groups at the elite and societal levels (which could be identified as the orthodox) in Pa-kistan about the distinctive Islamic character of their state. This stands in marked contrast to the perceived Hindu character of India. Drawing upon the conflicting stands taken by the All India Congress and the Muslim League, this characterization ignores the fact that India has the second largest number of Muslims in the world. Pakistan is seen and por-trayed as the logical home for Muslims in the subcontinent. At the same time, continuation of the logic of the freedom struggle in a post-colonial state gives rise to a claim to equality not matched by reality. The ortho-dox groups expect Pakistan to be treated as an equal to India despite the apparent power imbalance between the two states. Indian refusal to ac-quiesce to such religiously derived claims to equality is interpreted by these groups as evidence of Indian unconditional hostility. They argue that India has not accepted the reality of Pakistan and is determined to undo the partition of 1947. Its refusal to hold a plebiscite in Kashmir, the decisive role played by India in the dismemberment of Pakistan in 1971 and India's build-up of conventional and nuclear arms are some of the examples presented by these groups to prove their claims of Indian hostility. These acts, in their opinion, stem from irrationality and or im-morality inherent in the Indian psyche. Negotiations with India to con-tain threats from the east are, therefore, viewed as futile, as the Indian leaders are seen as being motivated by the need to "undo Pakistan" and not by any kind of cost-benefit analysis. Their prescriptions for dealing with the situation, therefore, range from being selectively offensive to de-veloping strong defensive capabilities that would dissuade India from threatening Pakistan.[7] For some, this translates into forming alliances or partnerships that would secure continued supply of conventional weapons for Pakistan and establish a balance of power vis-à-vis India. Such pre-scriptions relate to a perception that India is consistently acquiring de-fence capabilities that would tilt the balance against Pakistan and open more avenues for New Delhi to threaten its neighbour. While alliances with external patrons is not seen as a guarantee of obtaining a perfect balance, these groups still consider infusion of additional military capa-bility as a means of deterring Indian threat. For others, the idea of a bal-ance also involves developing nuclear capability that matches the Indian nuclear programme in proportionate, if not absolute, terms; they do not suggest that Pakistan needs to acquire exactly the same number of nu-clear weapons and missiles as India but favour developing a capability that would clearly communicate to New Delhi that Pakistan retains the ability and will to inflict damage on India if it chooses to do so. Still others favour exploiting the Indian government's inability to deal with domestic situations. By relying on non-conventional means and supporting insurgencies within India, they aim to bleed India, with the ultimate objective of keeping New Delhi's aggressive ambitions under control.

Islamists in Pakistan share the prescriptions suggested by the orthodox groups. The logic for this support, however, is embedded in their strong belief in Pakistan's identity as an Islamic state.[8] Having gained strength during the Zia-ul-Haq regime and the Afghan jihad supported by the United States, these groups have proliferated with differing views on the exact nature of the Islamic state. Nevertheless, they agree on certain common themes, including the categorization of the world in terms of Ummah, anti-Muslim western states and friendly non-Muslim states. Pakistan, as an Islamic state, is placed in a central position in this schema with the responsibility of countering the threats posed by alliances among the Christian, Jewish and Hindu adversaries. Translated into actual terms, it involves taking a stand against US, Israeli and Indian policies either regionally or globally. Within the regional context, it requires Pakistan to maintain a military balance of power vis-à-vis India in the arenas of both conventional and nuclear arms. More specifically, the Islamist view accords the Kashmir issue a central place in Indo-Pakistani relations.[9] The resolution of the dispute is presumed to lead to Kashmir's accession to Pakistan as an Islamic state. To this end, they favour supporting and actively engaging in insurgency in the Indian part of Kashmir so as to force New Delhi into submission and negotiations.

The moderates in Pakistan approach the Indo-Pakistani relationship through a different prism. Instead of placing religious identities of the two states at centre stage, these groups emphasize the need to develop policies on the basis of a dispassionate analysis of the existing balance of power in various spheres. In other words, the state is partly divested of its religious identity and credited with realist notions of national interest and balance of power. The state is also credited with rationality and the ability to engage in mutually beneficial interactions. Interestingly, the moderates do not restrict these notions of rationality to Pakistan. These attributes are extended to India as well, which leads them to question the idea of unconditional Indian hostility. They argue that Indian behaviour indicates its acceptance of Pakistan as a reality but that its leadership has not always understood Pakistan's security needs. Such lack of understanding is seen as having complicated the context in which the two neighbours have related to each other. These groups also implicitly acknowledge the inequality between India and Pakistan and that Indian defence and foreign policies pose a threat to Pakistan. However, they maintain that carefully designed policies could enable Pakistan to neutralize this threat and establish a correct if not cordial relationship with its neighbour. Hence, while these moderates favour forming alliances with external patrons, including both China and the United States, they do not see these linkages as replacing the need to engage India in a cooperative relationship with Pakistan. Instead, they favour exploring areas in which India and Pakistan can arrive at some understandings that are mutually beneficial to both parties. In other words, moderates argue in favour of striving for shared security in areas where a clear need exists and is appreciated by both neighbours. Although the focus remains predominantly in the military arena, the moderates also emphasize the need to establish understanding in areas of "low" politics, as well.

A similar division of opinion exists across the border in India. As in Pakistan, the variations are related to differing notions of identity and their meaning for relations with the "other".[10] Traditionally, for a vast majority of Indians, secularism has been the defining feature of their polity. The demands made by the Indian National Congress prior to 1947 and the policies pursued by New Delhi since independence are believed to vindicate this sense of identity. Added to the notion of secularism is the concept of Indian destiny as a great nation. Its size, diversity, history and secularist tradition are seen as the indicators of this destiny. By virtue of these attributes, India is viewed as a state capable and deserving of playing a major role at regional and international levels. For the orthodox groups in India, Pakistan is perceived to be the antithesis of this identity. Drawing upon the experiences of the independence struggle and the statements made by some sections in Pakistan, the orthodox groups consider Pakistan's essence to be determined and perpetuated by an unswerving adherence to the notions of "Two Nation Theory". Pakistan's claim that it was created for Muslims in the subcontinent is seen as an expression of its identity as a theocratic state, which is unlikely to adjust to a secular state next door. Irrationality and unconditional hostility are seen as the natural consequences of Pakistan's Islamic identity. Pakistan is seen not as a normal state that knows and accepts its limits but as a theocratic one that fails to appreciate that India is the larger power in the region. Islam, quite interestingly, is seen as having induced this irrational insistence upon equality among Pakistani leadership. Islamabad's search for allies, including the US and China, is viewed as corroborating evidence of Pakistan's commitment to threatening India. The prescriptions for dealing with this threat focus primarily on taking a strong military stand so as to convince Pakistan of the futility of threatening India. Intimidation with the option of using military means at its disposal is considered to be the best strategy for containing Pakistani aggression and irrationality.

In a mirror image of Pakistan, Hindu fundamentalist groups in India share the prescriptions suggested for dealing with the neighbouring state.[11] However, they have a different conception of the Indian identity.

For them, India is a Hindu state. The idea is not purely religious but civil in nature. Hinduism is seen as the true reality of the subcontinent with its relevance to all aspects of the lives of its inhabitants. Islam, in contrast, is portrayed as the religion of the invaders who succeeded in imposing their traditions for some time.[12] The creation of Pakistan is seen as a continuation of this process. Its Islamic identity and claims of representing Muslims of the subcontinent is seen as directly threatening India's Hindu identity. Any statements in favour of Indian Muslims are seen in this light and perceived as evidence of a Muslim threat to India.

The moderates in India question the validity of prescriptions by orthodox and Hindu fundamentalists. To some extent this reflects a tendency to de-link Pakistan's present identity from the experiences of the freedom struggle. While conceiving of Indian identity in secular terms, they discount the predetermined role of Islam in Pakistan's domestic and foreign policy merely because of the independence experience. Pakistan is seen as a weaker neighbour, which has been unable to follow the path of democratization. This is seen as having introduced structural weaknesses in the society, giving rise to negative tendencies and insecurities in Pakistan. However, Pakistan is not viewed as unconditionally hostile. Instead, while unable to accept its subordinate status, Pakistan is seen as a neighbour that can be engaged in a cooperative relationship. Given the history of animosity between the two states, the moderates shy away from identifying a culture of solidarity as a realizable goal in the foreseeable future. But they do acknowledge and stress the need to explore areas in which shared security concerns can lead to some agreements between the two states. India's status as a great regional and global power is seen by them as conferring additional responsibility upon New Delhi to demonstrate benevolence toward the lesser equals. Shared security and not intimidation is seen as the best way of dealing with a relatively weaker Pakistan.

The multiplicity of prescriptions on dealing with the "other" in India and Pakistan has created a situation where the nature of their relationship across time is determined by the relative ascendancy of views. Given that orthodox elements have been relatively predominant in both states for a major part of their post-colonial existence, their relationship has essentially remained tense, negative and conflict-ridden. Apart from being reflected in the armed and near-armed conflicts, this negativity has found expression in the arena of economic, social, cultural and diplomatic interaction. Groups convinced of the Indian threat to Pakistan's economic viability, for instance, opposed the proposal of according India Most Favoured Nation status. Similarly, any suggestions of similarity between Indian and Pakistani cultures have been questioned by those afraid of Indian cultural domination. This has been the case despite the fact that the two states do share some common cultural traits. On occasion, Indo-Pakistani sport links have also been hostage to the ascendancy of ortho-dox groups in the two states who have refused to allow even cricket matches to be played on each other's soil. The same is true of the treat-ment accorded to the diplomatic staff of the two neighbours. The nega-tivity in their relationship is expressed through harassing, targeting and expelling diplomats from the "other side" without genuine grievances.

The moderate views, however, have also been relevant in shaping the relationship. While not always in a position to dictate the logic of the re-lationship, they have at least succeeded in limiting the extent of hostility between the two countries. This has been evident both during times of war and peace. The Indus Water Treaty signed between India and Paki-stan in 1960, for instance, was one of the earliest examples of moderates determining the nature of their relationship in the arena of sharing water resources. Similarly, the agreement to accept Soviet mediation during the 1965 Indo-Pakistani war would not have come about without some mod-erate elements arguing in favour of limiting the costs of war. The same logic prevailed in the post-1971-war days when the necessity of limiting the costs to Pakistan led the two sides to sign the Simla Agreement (1972) and play down the need to resolve the Kashmir issue in line with UN resolutions. More importantly, moderates in India and Pakistan have caused the two states to sign a number of agreements to limit the possi-bility of future conflict. In 1988 they formally agreed not to attack each other's nuclear installations and, as part of the agreement, have consis-tently exchanged the lists of their nuclear facilities. The process has not stopped even during the periods of high tension between the two neigh-bours. Following the heightened tensions between the two sides in 1990, they have also signed agreements in 1991 to respect each other's air-space, provide advance notifications of air exercises and follow agreed procedure for military flights within 5 to 10 kilometres. They have also agreed to provide advance notification of certain military exercises as a means of avoiding conflict.

The Lahore Declaration signed in February 1999 was one of the best examples of the role played by moderates in promoting the agenda of shared security. Signed in the immediate aftermath of the nuclear tests of the two sides in May 1998 and the concern expressed both domesti-cally and internationally about the possibility of a nuclear exchange, India and Pakistan agreed to "take immediate steps for reducing the risk of accidental or unauthorized use of nuclear weapons and discuss concepts and doctrines with a view to elaborating measures for confi-dence building in the nuclear and conventional fields, aimed at preven-tion of conflict". They undertook to provide each other with advance notification in respect to ballistic missile flight tests, expressed their com-

mitment to undertaking national measures to reduce the risks of accidental or unauthorized use of nuclear weapons under their respective control
and decided "to identify/establish the appropriate communication mechanism".[13] The declaration was significant not simply for the areas it cov-
ered but also for the fact that the initiative was taken by the two parties
without direct pressure from external actors, particularly the US. This is
not to suggest that the concerns expressed by the international community and the fears of an inadvertent nuclear war between the two new nuclear states may not have played a role in the willingness of the two states
to sign the declaration. But significantly, the two sides did not wait for an
incident like the Cuban missile crisis to appreciate the need for negotiations on nuclear issues. Also, the invitation for the visit and the willingness of Indian Prime Minister Atal Bihari Vajpayee to visit Pakistan was
initiated and secured through the moderate factions in the two countries,
without external involvement. Equally importantly, recognizing the concern among some sections in Pakistan that India had not accepted Pakistan's reality, the Indian Prime Minister visited Minar-e-Pakistan, the site
where the Pakistan Muslim League passed the resolution for the country's creation in March 1940. One could see here the signs of an emerging
appreciation of the need for new policies of shared security.

Given the unequal coexistence of orthodox and moderate approaches,
one could argue that some scope for cooperation and/or shared security
has always existed in Indo-Pakistani relations. This has been the case despite the predominance of orthodox views and their impact upon how the
two neighbours have related to each other. The manner in which these
views have been presented and the language used, however, has evolved
over a period of time. As the conception of what is of value has changed,
the issue areas in which orthodoxy and moderation have interacted has
also undergone a change. Such shifts have been apparent in areas of nuclear policy and Kashmir.

During the first two decades of their existence, hawks and moderates
had mainly focused on a conventional balance of power: the issues being
dealt with included the advisability of acquiring or not acquiring new
and/or more capable weapons. In the early 1970s, however, as India
conducted its first nuclear test, the debates expanded to encompass the
role and relevance of nuclear weapons in determining the nature of
Indo-Pakistani relations. On the Indian side, moderates and hawks
argued over the advantages and disadvantages of going openly nuclear:
while hawks remained mostly in favour of acquiring nuclear capability,
moderates cautioned against it. Across the border in Pakistan, initially
the debate on the need to acquire or not to acquire nuclear weapons to
balance Indian capability remained rather limited. Taking place against
the background of the Pakistani defeat in the 1971 Indo-Pakistan war

and the separation of East Pakistan, moderates were reticent to question Pakistan's right to go nuclear. From the 1980s onwards, however, the debate on nuclear policy in Pakistan began taking shape with a small group arguing against the need to acquire nuclear weapons. At the same time, orthodox and moderate groups in both India and Pakistan began to discuss the pros and cons of a recessed or ambiguous versus a declared nuclear capability. By the 1990s, therefore, moderates in Pakistan and India were cautioning against conducting nuclear tests but orthodox groups were supporting a policy of moving away from an ambiguous to a declared nuclear capability through tests. After India and Pakistan tested their nuclear weapons in May 1998, the nature of debates in the nuclear arena once again changed. Orthodox and moderate groups in the two states began to discuss questions such as the relevance of maintaining a credible minimum deterrence, the need to acquire a more sophisticated counterforce capability and the command structures needed to avoid inadvertent nuclear war in South Asia. As moderates in India favoured the idea of a minimum nuclear deterrence, those across the border began to suggest ideas of nuclear sufficiency. Instead of trying to keep pace with Indian nuclear and missile capability, they argued, Pakistan's interests would be better served by acquiring sufficient number of nuclear weapons and missiles so as to make its policy of First Use credible. Meanwhile they also favoured negotiating with India to avoid accidental nuclear conflict in the region. That India and Pakistan signed the Lahore Declaration in 1999 was evidence that, despite the presence of orthodox ideas, moderate views prevailed in the region, at least on the nuclear and missile issues.

The influence of moderate elements emphasizing shared security was also apparent, though to a very limited degree, on the Kashmir issue in the 1990s. The historical positions of the two sides remained dominant during this decade: Islamabad argued for resolving the Kashmir issue in line with UN resolutions on the assumption that a plebiscite would deliver the whole princely state to Pakistan. Meanwhile, an alliance between Islamists and the orthodoxy also enabled intelligence agencies to promote and support jihadi elements that infiltrated into the Indian part of Kashmir with a view to its "liberation". India retorted by identifying Kashmir as an integral part of the Union and even laid claims to the rest of Kashmir under direct or indirect Pakistani control. Despite the evidence that the insurgency in the Indian part of Kashmir stemmed from the failure of the Centre to deal with problems in the state, the orthodox groups viewed it as purely a function of Pakistani infiltration.

By the mid-1990s, the entrenched positions were mildly criticized by moderate elements in both countries: those in Pakistan began to question the value of disproportionate emphasis on the Kashmir issue to the exclusion of more pressing issues like poverty and economic fragility of the state. The logic of strengthening Pakistan internally guided them into arguing for more creative solutions to the Kashmir problem. Across the border, Indian moderates also began acknowledging the domestic sources of insurgency in Kashmir, including the disillusionment among the Kashmiri youth with the Centre's policies. While these views did not attract a lot of attention in the two states, they did partially influence the manner in which they dealt with the Kashmir issue. This influence was most apparent during the Agra Summit between President Pervez Musharraf and Prime Minister Vajpayee in July 2001. The draft agreement suggested by Pakistan indicated that it was prepared to shelve references to UN resolutions. Although the summit did not succeed, due to the reluctance of orthodox elements from both sides to make substantive concessions, the episode did reflect the limited success of moderate elements in shifting the debate on Kashmir toward the area of shared security.

Continued relevance of multiplicity

The multiplicity of views about the "other" and the attendant policy prescriptions have continued in the new millennium. The manifestation of this multiplicity, however, differs from the past. The language used by different groups in India and Pakistan to describe each other's identity and the issue areas considered significant have altered to reflect the time-specificity of these ideas and images.

This change is often most noticeable among the hawkish elements in both societies. They have developed a set of ideas that are remarkably reminiscent of the views held by the orthodox historians of the Cold War. They draw upon a series of social, structural, institutional and personality factors to refine the archetype of the "other" that has formed the basis of their prescriptions in the past. For the orthodox in India, Pakistan remains a theocracy with a strong commitment to the Two Nation Theory. The rise of Islamic fundamentalism since the early 1980s is presented as a vindication of this characterization.[14] The military is placed in a central place in this conception of Pakistani polity. Given the historical imbalance in favour of the armed forces, it is credited with shaping and implementing Pakistan's domestic and foreign policy. However, while in the past the Pakistani military was portrayed as a secular institution, the Islamization of the society is seen as having altered the nature of the armed forces as well. The Pakistani military is considered and portrayed as an "Islamized" force that has acquired an additional religious justification for its anti-Indian policies. The Inter-Services Intelligence (ISI) is accorded a special place in this scenario. It is seen as supporting and actively aiding Islamists in the military and the larger society. Just as orthodox historians of the Cold War have identified Stalin as the main culprit, the Indian orthodoxy extends this place to Pervez Musharraf. As the architect of the Kargil incursions, he is presented as a dangerous enemy who would undermine any understanding aimed at securing shared security for the two states. His handling of the Agra summit and particularly the fact that his meeting with Indian editors was telecast without prior notice or agreement has earned him the attribute of being cunning, unreliable and shifty. Effectively, therefore, Pakistan is viewed as a state and society that continues to be hostile and negative toward India.

The Pakistani orthodox view mirrors the ideas held by their Indian counterparts. India is divested of a secular identity and instead is portrayed as an essentially Hindu society.[15] The social reality is perceived as determining the nature of the polity. India, in other words, is seen as continuing the trends set by the Hindu Ashoka Empire with a strong emphasis on expansionism. Since 1998, the Bharata Janata Party (BJP) has been accorded a special place in this understanding of Indian society and state. As a party committed to promoting Hindu interests due to its strong connection to the Rashtriya Swayamsevak Sangh, the BJP is seen as the vehicle for promoting Indian/Hindu hegemony in the region. It is also considered a natural expression of an aggressive and expansionist religion.[16] The credit of promoting the agenda of a Hindu society is given to vocal anti-Pakistani groups. During the BJP rule, for instance, former Indian Deputy Prime Minister (and future party president) L. K. Advani was often presented as the main hawk who was determined to undermine Pakistan as part of his larger agenda. He was portrayed as an opportunist and an arch manipulator who could successfully exploit domestic situations to promote the agenda of his party. The imagery drew its vindication from the experience of the Agra Summit (2001). It was consistently argued that Pakistan made a number of concessions with the aim of improving relations with India. In marked departure to the past, the Pakistani draft did not mention the relevance of UN resolutions to resolving the Kashmir issue.[17] But the chances of the Summit leading to some concrete results were undermined by Advani at the last minute, due to his refusal to endorse the nearly agreed-upon draft document. The communal massacre in Gujarat (2002) and the re-election of Narendra Modi in December 2002 were also presented as evidence of the cross-regional lines of control established by the hawks in India.[18] That Pakistani President Musharraf was targeted in this election campaign was presented as a further evidence of Indian Hindus mobilizing domestic support by presenting Pakistan in a bad light. Essentially, irrespective of the time period, for orthodox groups in Pakistan the fault continues to lie with India and not with Pakistan.

As in the past, the mutually negative perceptions of each other have been reinforced in the new millennium by the state and media. But another element has been added to the list, with the active use of films and satellite technology to present the other in a negative light. On the Indian side, a number of films have been produced that portray Pakistan as an aggressive, irrational and cunning enemy.[19] In some cases, the production has been assisted by active participation by the Indian armed forces. On Pakistan's side, the absence of a vibrant film industry has made it difficult to produce similar movies targeted against India. Instead, they have relied on a strong television industry that produces plays highlighting Indian complicity and connivance. As a result, the myth of the enemy across the border continues to exist among the masses of the two neighbouring states. As before, however, this mythology coexists with moderate views on both sides of the border.

Moderate voices in India at the turn of the new millennium have generally argued for the need to come to terms with Pakistan and engage it in a mutually cooperative relationship. This prescription is partly related to the perception of Pakistan as a failing state, or a state with structural weakness.[20] The enormity of economic, political and law and order problems in Pakistan is seen as raising the chances of its implosion from within. Such a possibility is considered dangerous for an India that is emerging as a global power. A policy of encouraging Pakistan's viable existence is seen as increasing the chances of controlling a possible instability in India's neighbourhood. Given that the idea of India as a global power is closely tied to its economic development, the prescriptions of a moderate policy also emanate from a neo-liberal understanding of world politics.[21] At one level, cooperative relationship with Pakistan is viewed as providing additional markets for Indian goods and services. At another level, it is seen as contributing to the image of South Asia as a safe environment for foreign investment, which is, in turn, considered essential for maintaining the pace of India's economic growth.

In Pakistan, moderates have shifted the emphasis from the "other" to the "self". Pakistan's identification as a failing state since the mid-1990s has provided the context in which they have refined their arguments for cooperation and shared security with India. As the country has suffered economically due to a set of political, social and institutional factors, they have highlighted the need to create a favourable regional environment to assist with domestic reconstruction. To this end, they argue the need to accept the reality of power balance in South Asia. Unlike in the past when they made only implied references to relative equality, they are becoming more vocal in accepting that India is a regional power.[22] Such an acceptance, they argue, would not undermine Pakistan's status as a significant actor at the international level. Rather, it would create conditions that would enable Pakistan to realize its true destiny as a state for Muslims. Such renegotiated emphasis on the self has resulted in suggestions of a different approach to resolving the Kashmir issue. Instead of adhering to the demand that the issue be resolved in line with the UN resolutions, moderates have argued for more flexible and creative strategies that take into account the interests of India, Pakistan and the Kashmiri people.[23] Moderates are also reassessing the place of nuclear weapons in Pakistan's security policy. The idea of sufficiency that emerged soon after the nuclear tests of May 1998 is still being floated by the moderates: instead of matching Indian nuclear and missile capability in quantitative terms, they prefer to acquire weapons that would credibly deter an Indian attack on Pakistan.[24] Equally important, moderates in Pakistan are also increasingly stressing the need to cooperate with India on issues including AIDS, drug trafficking, poverty, environmental problems and human trafficking.[25] To this end, they have consistently stressed the need for greater people-to-people interaction. Such interaction, they argue, would break the traditionally held mythology of "enemy across the border". Effectively, therefore, Pakistani moderate voices have been drawing attention to the enlarged space where the two states could explore ideas about shared security. While these ideas draw inspiration from universal conceptions of human rights as the basis of solidarity, they nonetheless remain focused on the value of such cooperation from the perspective of long-term security.

Interplay of multiplicity post–11 September 2001

The developments in Indo-Pakistani relations after 11 September 2001 have been shaped by these differing views on cooperation and competition. But these debates and views have also been influenced by changes in the regional environment, particularly the US presence in the region after the terrorist attacks on American soil. This interplay can best be understood in terms of changes in American policy toward South Asia since the end of the Cold War. After relying on Pakistan to oust the Soviets from Afghanistan in the 1980s, Washington ended its special relationship with Islamabad in October 1990. Not only was Pakistan denied American military assistance but Washington also came close to identifying it as a state supporting terrorism. Meanwhile, against the background of economic liberalization in a changed global environment, the US began to establish a close military and economic relationship with India. This

Indo-centric policy suffered from a major flaw: it generally treated India in isolation from the regional context in which New Delhi was formulating and implementing its policies. The nuclear issue was the only exception: concerns about the possibility of Pakistan and India acquiring nuclear capability often attracted attention from American policymakers and analysts. The level and nature of this interest increased after India and Pakistan tested nuclear weapons in May 1998. Concerned that the two South Asian states could engage in an unplanned, inadvertent nuclear war, Washington adopted a two-pronged policy toward India and Pakistan: it imposed sanctions on the two states but at the same time attempted to "educate" them about dealing with their nuclear capability. Meanwhile, however, the US persisted with its policy of engaging India while ignoring Pakistan.

The Kargil crisis (1999) forced Washington to reassess its South Asia policy. Fearful that incursions by the Pakistani military could trigger a conventional conflict with the possibility of escalation into a nuclear war, the US government became actively involved in the region. President Bill Clinton acted as a facilitator between the two states and put pressure on Pakistan's Prime Minister Nawaz Sharif to withdraw troops from Kargil. That India implicitly accepted such an American role set the scene for future American policy towards the region. President Clinton's visit to South Asia in March 2000 provided an outline of this new policy: America was to establish and sustain a close relationship with India, the emerging global actor. Pakistan, on the other hand, was to be managed as a failing state with little or no support from Washington.

The terrorist attacks on the US in September 2001 altered this outlook. After ignoring Pakistan for more than a decade, Washington declared a "war on terrorism". In South-west Asia, it needed Pakistan due to the close nexus between Islamabad and the Taliban regime. Given the links between the ISI and the Islamic regime, Pakistan was in the best position to provide the necessary information for American reprisal attacks on Afghanistan. President Musharraf, who took power in October 1999, was aware of the costs involved in not cooperating with the Bush administration. In a 180-degree shift in Islamabad's foreign policy, Pakistan joined hands with Washington and emerged as the "front-line state" in the American war on terrorism.

Orthodox groups on both sides perceived a shift in US policy in geostrategic terms in the wake of the terrorist attacks. In India, the attacks were perceived as vindicating the stand taken by New Delhi against Pakistan's support for insurgency in the Indian part of Kashmir. At one level, therefore, parallels were drawn between America and India as state victims of terrorism. At the same time, however, the notion of India as a global power guided the orthodox groups to suggest that the attacks had created opportunities for New Delhi and Washington to cooperate in combating terrorism. Specifically, it was seen as opening up space for Indo–US cooperation against Pakistan as a state that had supported terrorism. The influence of such a reading of the situation and associated prescriptions was apparent in the Indian government's decision to hand over incriminating evidence to American authorities against both Osama bin Laden and the details of training camps in the Pakistani part of Kashmir. New Delhi also offered the US government the use of its defence bases and refuelling facilities for mounting air attacks against the Taliban and Al Qaeda. Effectively, the Indian orthodoxy viewed the situation in zero-sum terms.

Across the border, orthodox groups adopted a similar approach. Aware of the pressure Pakistan had come under as a result of its support for the Taliban with an attendant need to revise its Afghan policy, orthodox groups saw the terrorist attacks as containing the possibility of strengthening Pakistan vis-à-vis India. Instead of simply joining the US war on terrorism, they wanted to extract maximum benefit from the situation by asking for US support against India.[26] However, given that President Pervez Musharraf had already acquiesced in providing logistical support to American forces, the orthodoxy shifted their emphasis to limiting any possible gain that may accrue to India through US counter-terrorism activity. Having already alienated the Islamists, President Musharraf could hardly ignore such suggestions. While emphasizing moderation, therefore, he demanded that India and Israel be kept out of any operation in Afghanistan.[27] He also asked that the Northern Alliance not be engaged in the operations due to its traditional links to New Delhi. The language used in the process catered to the orthodox sensibilities: India was asked to "lay off".

The orthodox groups gained more ascendancy in India after the terrorist attacks on the Indian Parliament on 13 December 2001. The attack was seen as targeting the symbol of Indian democracy as well as an evidence of Pakistan's persistent role in undermining Indian unity and security. The language of counter-terrorism provided the context in which orthodox groups promoted their agenda in India. It was argued that the US retaliatory attacks against the Taliban across a long distance provided the blueprint for Indian response to Pakistani terrorism. Instead of accepting the situation, it was argued, India could also launch attacks across the border on terrorist training camps in Pakistani-controlled Kashmir. The Indian government communicated this intention within days of the attack on the Indian Parliament in the form of a number of retaliatory actions. It blamed Pakistan for creating the conditions in which the attacks on the symbol of Indian democracy could take place. As a state supporting terrorism, Pakistan was threatened with retribution unless it ceased the infiltration of terrorists across the Line of Control (LOC). It was also asked to hand over 20 criminals wanted by New Delhi.[28] Before the year was over, the Indian government recalled its High Commissioner in Pakistan and stopped land surface contacts between the two countries. The train links between Indian and Pakistan – Samjhota Express, which had remained in operation even during the Kargil crisis – were stopped.[29] Indian airspace was closed to Pakistan International Airlines, which was asked to close its offices in India.[30] More importantly, Indian troops were mobilized along the international border, indicating an Indian resolve to translate its threats into actions.

Pakistan's response to the Indian moves was shaped by the balance of power within the decision-making circles. Having made the break with its pro-Taliban policy, moderates, led by President Musharraf, were keen to retain the support of the orthodox groups. At the same time, they were cautious not to undermine the emerging relationship with Washington by being branded a "terrorist state". Therefore, Islamabad sought evidence from New Delhi to substantiate its claims that groups supported by Pakistan had perpetrated the attacks. Meanwhile, Pakistani troops also moved along the international border. Soon, however, faced with pressure from the United States, which wanted to continue its operations against Al Qaeda in South-west Asia, the Pakistani government initiated steps to control terrorist groups operating from Pakistan. In a major speech on 12 January 2002, President Musharraf banned terrorist organizations, including Lashkar-e-Taiba and Jaish-e-Mohammad.[31] He also declared that the Pakistani government would not permit its territory to be used for terrorist activities against any state. The moves, which were ostensibly made as part of a "national security agenda" but were in reality the outcome of strong behind-the-scenes pressure from Washington, failed to elicit a positive response from New Delhi.

The ascendancy of orthodox views combined with anger against the attacks led the Indian government to brand the steps taken by President Musharraf as merely cosmetic in nature and for "domestic consumption".[32] New Delhi argued that any judgement on the sincerity of Musharraf's moves depended upon the handing over of the named criminals and the cessation of infiltration across the LOC. Given that Pakistan's performance on the second criteria could not take place until the onset of spring, such a precondition justified maintaining troops along the international border. Meanwhile, New Delhi maintained pressure against Pakistan. The Indian Foreign Minister, Jaswant Singh, identified Pakistan as a state pursuing "a path of compulsive and perpetual hostility as part of its national identity".[33] His counterpart in the Ministry of Defence, George

Fernandes, stated that India would give Pakistan time but would not wait indefinitely.[34] At the same time, leaders of Shiv Sena issued statements endorsing the idea of attacks across the LOC and extending full support to the Indian Prime Minister "in all his efforts against Pakistan".[35]

The emphasis on retribution through pre-emption was questioned by moderate voices in India. They argued that cessation of cross-border terrorism was a qualitative change that required longer periods for accurate measurement.[36] Instead of maintaining troops along the border, therefore, they suggested extending the time period in which the sincerity of President Musharraf's commitment could be judged. Some analysts also portrayed Musharraf as a reformed moderate who had realized the need to change Pakistan's policy toward India. Instead of branding him as unreliable, therefore, suggestions were made to give him some credit for his changed priorities and outlook.[37] These voices, however, were unable to tilt the balance in favour of a moderate response from India. The Indian orthodoxy was convinced that in the new age of counter-terrorism and acceptance of retribution for terrorism, New Delhi could count on American support against Pakistan's policy on Kashmir. Importantly, they viewed the new situation as opening up the space for them to "deal with the Pakistani problem" on a permanent basis. Hence, Indian forces remained poised along the international border. Pakistan was consistently reminded of Indian resolve to retaliate if Islamabad did not cease cross-border terrorism. Such communications did not make a distinction between Islamabad's willingness and ability to control militants (jihadi elements) as part of their Kashmir strategy for years. The relevance of this distinction became apparent with the terrorist attack on a military camp in Kaluchak on 14 May 2002. Instead of entertaining the possibility that the Pakistani government had not actively supported the attack, New Delhi blamed Islamabad for the massacre of mostly children and women at Kaluchak. On 17 May, the Indian Parliament authorized the federal government to take action against Pakistan's support for terrorism.[38] Pakistan's High Commissioner, Jehangir Qazi, was expelled from India. Soon Indian Prime Minister Vajpayee was talking of a "decisive battle" with Pakistan. A number of analysts began making statements that appeared to justify a possible "significant" Indian punitive attack across the LOC to demonstrate the limits of Indian patience.[39] These references, it needs to be pointed out, drew inspiration from the still-emerging Bush Doctrine with its emphasis on pre-emption and unilateralism by powerful (and primary) actors. They reflected a view in New Delhi that in a changed geostrategic environment, India retained the right to use force against Pakistan either pre-emptively or in retaliation against Islamabad's support for Islamic militant organizations like Lashkar-e-Taiba and Jaish-e-Mohammed.

That the Indian government was seriously considering such an attack became apparent through a series of steps taken by New Delhi in the next few days. The paramilitary forces in Kashmir and the coast guard were placed under the command of the army and the navy respectively. At the same time, five Indian warships were moved from the Eastern Fleet in the Bay of Bengal to the Arabian Sea. These moves, coupled with the continued presence of Indian troops along the Indo-Pakistani boundary indicated an Indian willingness to accept the broadening of the conflict beyond the Kashmiri theatre.[40]

These messages were interpreted by the orthodox groups in Pakistan as evidence of Indian unconditional hostility. They argued that Pakistan had compromised its Afghan policy and clamped down on the Kashmiri freedom fighters without evoking a positive response from India. The build-up of tension, for them, was evidence that New Delhi was using the post–11 September emphasis on counter-terrorism to subjugate Pakistan. Faced with such a situation, they reiterated their prescription of taking a tough stand against Indian "bullying". Moderates led by President Musharraf were forced to address these concerns due to the emerging reality on the ground after the snow began to melt in Kashmir. The number of terrorist attacks across the LOC had begun to increase. So had the observations by outside actors that the training camps dismantled after 12 January 2002 were beginning to reappear. It was becoming increasingly apparent that a "soft" approach by President Musharraf would increase the likelihood of the orthodoxy supporting the Islamists in Pakistan. Fearing the implications of such an alliance for Pakistan's domestic and foreign policy, Islamabad opted for taking a tough stand. Taking into account these views, the Pakistani government announced on 24 May that it would be conducting a series of missile tests during the next four days.[41] It also came to use language that reflected an orthodox reading of the Indian identity. In his nationally televised speech on 27 May 2002, President Musharraf identified the Indian government as tyrannical and repressive in nature. Indian Christians and Muslims were urged to shake off this "tyranny" and "repression". He also referred to the struggle in Kashmir as a fight for freedom.[42] However, the Pakistani government's action also indicated a reluctance to let the situation escalate into an inadvertent conflict. Prior to testing the missiles, for instance, the Indian government was notified of the tests in line with the understanding contained in the Lahore Declaration. President Musharraf's 27 May speech also identified the Kashmiri situation as a "freedom struggle" but was coupled with the denial of any role in insurgency. The subtext was one of asking the Indian government not to blame the Pakistani government for actions of Islamic groups that were not necessarily under Islamabad's control.

The US role: A facilitator

These implied preferences for moderation notwithstanding, India and Pakistan might not have come back from the brink of an armed conflict if it were not for active US facilitation. The United States was motivated by a number of interests in South-west and South Asia. In addition to its traditional interest in preventing a nuclear conflict between India and Pakistan, Washington was also committed to establishing a strategic partnership with New Delhi in a new international environment. At the same time, the logic of counter-terrorism dictated that it maintain and deepen the relationship with Pakistan for a variety of reasons. Having replaced the Taliban with an Afghan regime led by Hamid Karzai, the United States still needed Pakistan's support for providing the most efficient transit routes to proceed with Afghan reconstruction. At the same time, Washington needed Pakistan's help in targeting members of Al Qaeda who had fled into the tribal areas bordering Pakistan as well as into Pakistani cities. Without Pakistan's active help, locating and/or arresting Islamic militants would have been difficult. Equally significant, America wanted to contain Islamic militancy in Pakistan by supporting a series of programmes aimed at improving the educational institutions. These multiple interests are not necessarily overlapping or complementary. For instance, while the logic of retaining Pakistan's role in the war on terrorism required that Washington support Islamabad in its emerging conflict with India, the need to build upon the emerging strong strategic relations pointed towards supporting Indian criticism of Pakistan's role in the Kashmir insurgency. At the same time, preventing a nuclear war in the region required cooperative relationships with both India and Pakistan. Faced with such a situation, Washington devised a policy of urging both parties to reduce the level of tension. Initially it put pressure on Pakistan to respond to Indian concerns that Islamabad was supporting the insurgency in the Indian part of Kashmir. Through a series of high-level missions, Washington successfully convinced Musharraf to announce his government's opposition to supporting terrorism in January 2002.

Once the tensions mounted in mid-2002, the US government modified its strategy. Aware of the limits of President Musharraf's government's ability to completely eradicate cross-border infiltration, it started counselling both sides into moderation. A number of senior American officials visited India and Pakistan during these months of heightened tensions. The list included, among others, the Secretary of State, Colin Powell, the Secretary of Defence, Donald Rumsfeld and the Deputy Secretary of State, Richard Armitage. They continued to insist that Pakistan take all necessary measures to prevent Islamic militants from crossing into the Indian part of Kashmir as well as ensure that training camps on the Pakistani side of the border were dismantled. At the same time, they urged India to respond favourably to the steps taken by President Musharraf in order to reduce tension. It is important to point out that crisis management rather than promoting notions of shared security was America's main concern during mid-2002.

Interestingly also, Washington was not always the dominant facilitator suggesting ideas. The complex interplay between local and external influences created a situation where groups within India and Pakistan exploited American concerns to gain some advantage. Indian hawks, for instance, used a language of counter-terrorism similar to that used by Washington. The references to pre-emption also followed the American lead in a subtle attempt to draw parallels between the American experience of 11 September 2001 and the Indian experience of 13 December 2001. The ultimate aim appeared to secure Washington's support for a hawkish Indian stand on Pakistan's Kashmir policy. Across the border, Pakistani groups also identified elements considered important by Washington as a means of securing American support for Islamabad's peaceful overtures. As Indian suggestions of a pre-emptive strike against "training camps in Kashmir" increased in May and June 2002, moderates in Islamabad communicated to the American government that an Indian attack would attract an equal and similar response. Such messages played on American fears of a nuclear war in South Asia. At the same time, the Pakistani government shifted its forces from the western to the eastern border with an implied inability to prevent Taliban and Al-Qaeda from infiltrating into Pakistan. It was basically an indirect way of increasing American pressure on the Indian government for reconciliation. The success of such ideas was apparent at the height of tensions in 2002 when the United States issued a travel advisory cautioning its citizens against visiting India and Pakistan. Given the impact of such an advisory on US–Indian economic links,[43] Indian businessmen put pressure on their own government to cool the situation on the Pakistan border. These steps appear to have strengthened the hands of moderates in both states. They also induced some willingness among the orthodox elements to reassess the value of playing a zero-sum game in a nuclearized region.

The first indication of the moderate agenda re-gaining some ground appeared with New Delhi's admission in June 2002 that the level of infiltration by jihadis in the Indian part of Kashmir had partly subsided. A few months later, on 16 October 2002, the Indian government announced its decision to withdraw troops along its international border with Pakistan while maintaining the military presence along the LOC in Kashmir. Pakistan reciprocated by taking a similar decision the next day.[44] The process of de-escalation, however, did not gain momentum in the next six months. As the Bush administration shifted its attention toward planning and then executing an attack on Iraq, the space was left open for the orthodoxy on both sides of the border. Probably emboldened by the absence of American pressure, they reverted to using the language of animosity and negativity. The trend, however, was more obvious in India, where a number of senior cabinet ministers castigated Pakistan as a terrorist state. The allegation that the Pakistani government was masterminding terrorist activities in the Indian part of Kashmir was repeated frequently,[45] as was the demand that it must cease completely prior to any improvement in Indo-Pakistani relations. President Musharraf and the newly elected Jamali regime responded to such characterizations by suggesting negotiations between the two sides. But these offers were made against the perpetuation of the view in some Pakistani decision-making and civil-society sectors that India was committed to exploiting the new environment to its goal of weakening Pakistan. Such views and the tendency to engage in competitive behaviour resulted in India and Pakistan expelling diplomats from across the border in a tit-for-tat manner in February 2003.

The situation changed with the American invasion of Iraq in March 2003. As the invasion proceeded, the US government indicated a resolve to address the South Asian situation as well. There appear to be two explanations for this renewed interest. First, the United States had developed an appreciation of cross-regional linkages among Islamic militants and the possibility of them impacting upon the American presence as an occupying force. But Washington was also motivated by a desire to create a peaceful environment in South Asia that would enable it to focus on restructuring the Middle Eastern scenario. These interests guided the US government to intensify its pressure on both sides to improve their mutual relations. The emphasis shifted from simple crisis management to one of also creating space for shared security concepts. Signs of such a shift were already apparent in July 2002, when the US-funded Seeds for Peace programme arranged for Pakistani and Indian youth to spend time together in America. But, as the invasion in Iraq progressed, American pressure for a change in the South Asian situation increased.

American pressure was reflected in a gradual shift from an orthodox to a moderate approach in India. Prime Minister Vajpayee took the initiative on 18 April by issuing conciliatory statements on the Kashmir issue. The Pakistani government reciprocated and soon diplomatic relations were upgraded with the exchange of High Commissioners. The road links severed in December were re-established, with the revival of buses linking Delhi and Lahore. More importantly, the Pakistani government extended a public assurance to Washington that there were no training camps operating on the Pakistani side of the LOC.[46] President Musharraf also guaranteed that if there any camps were discovered, they would not be there the next day. In other words, Islamabad expressed a willingness to translate its claims of non-interference into an actual policy. Coupled with the relatively consistent and secret contact between senior Pakistani and Indian decision-makers in London, the moves once again expanded the space for positive interaction.

As before, the orthodox on both sides were reluctant to concede the space to moderates. They continued to influence the course of events in areas where it was possible. The negotiations surrounding the access to airspace provided a useful indicator of such a struggle.[47] While the people-to-people interaction was revived at numerous levels, India and Pakistan were unable to reach an agreement on opening up their respective airspace to each other. This was partly linked to the Pakistani side realizing that the ban on overflights had hurt India more than it had hurt Pakistan. It had affected around 90 flights per month from Pakistan to South-east Asia and the Far East. In contrast, around 120 Indian flights per month to the Middle East and Europe had been affected. The cost of additional hours required to re-route Indian flights, therefore, was higher for India than for Pakistan. Aware of this advantage, Pakistan demanded a categorical assurance from India that it would desist in future from unilaterally closing off its airspace. New Delhi was reluctant to extend such assurance and the process of negotiations faltered. The impasse was broken only when, under US pressure, President Musharraf announced his decision to open Pakistani airspace to Indian carriers in November 2003, taking some of the Pakistani negotiators by surprise.

Thereafter, India and Pakistan moved quickly along the path of normalization. The Indian Prime Minister, Vajpayee, agreed to participate in the SAARC summit held in Islamabad from 4 to 6 January 2004. The occasion was used to engage in bilateral negotiations despite the previous reluctance toward using SAARC for such purposes. India and Pakistan agreed to revive bilateral talks in February 2004. The most significant part of the understanding was the concession made by Pakistan to the idea of a "composite dialogue". The position markedly differed from the past, when Islamabad insisted on the centrality of the Kashmir issue and its resolution along the lines of the UN resolutions. These concessions were parallelled by a change of language used by both governments. They stressed the need to start a new chapter in the history of Indo-Pakistani relations and referred to the needs of the people. Pakistani officials mentioned the irrelevance of weapons in the new millennium, while Indian counterparts expressed a willingness not to blame Pakistan for acts of terrorism. The number of staff in the High Commissions was also increased. On the economic front, Pakistan expressed a desire to purchase diesel from India – a shift from the previous tendency to bypass Indian providers as a sign of independence! At least for the time being, the moderates appear to be in ascendancy. The emphasis appears to be shifting away from geostrategic to accepting the logic of a shared security spectrum.

A triumph for the shared security approach?

The conclusion of a series of agreements between India and Pakistan and the success of the moderates needs to be viewed in perspective. In May 2004, the BJP government lost elections and the Indian National Congress once again returned to power as part of a coalition. Under the leadership of Prime Minister Manmohan Singh in India and President Musharraf in Pakistan, the two South Asian neighbours continued a process of rapprochement. Despite the emerging positivity in 2004 and the language of shared security, orthodox views persist on both sides of the border. So do groups that perceive the "other" through the prism of religious identity. These groups are unlikely to concede the space to moderates on a permanent basis. The signs of such reluctance are already apparent in some Islamists and orthodox groups in Pakistan questioning the altered approach to resolving the Kashmir issue.[48] Referring to the UN resolutions and their sanctity, they oppose an agreement that would validate Indian claims to the princely state. They also claim that the increased people-to-people contacts since 2004 have not contributed to resolving the Kashmir issue: the issue has merely been sidelined with suggestions that "Kashmir might as well be sacrificed to wolves".[49] The signs of dissatisfaction with a moderate approach increased with the failure of talks in January 2005 between two governments on the proposed Baghliar Dam on River Chenab. As the Pakistani government decided to refer the case to the World Bank for arbitration under the terms of the Indus Water Treaty, critical voices in Pakistan were claiming that the dialogue was designed only to serve Indian interests and that New Delhi did not show any flexibility.[50] Similar misperceptions about the "other" were apparent during the earthquake in Pakistan (October 2005). The response to Indian offers of assistance at the time of need was muted due to the possible strategic advantage India might have acquired by virtue of their presence in the disputed territory of Azad Kashmir.

The ability of the US to drastically alter this relationship will also remain limited. While it can suggest ideas and put pressure on both sides, different American interests and the need to keep both India and Pakistan on its side limit Washington's ability to push for a change beyond a certain limit. At best, Washington could suggest greater cooperation in the area of shared security. However, the internal dynamics between different groups in India and Pakistan will ultimately determine the shape of their relationship with the country across the border. They might conclude some more agreements (for example, in the area of nuclear weapons and missiles) but a culture of solidarity as human-rights empathy would remain a distant future for the two South Asian neighbours.

Notes

1. During the course of researching and writing this paper, I lost my beloved mother, Begum Sarfraz Iqbal. She taught me all I knew in life and accepted my absence when she needed me the most. I hope that her optimism and passion for a peaceful South Asia eclipses my less than optimistic analysis.
2. I am grateful to Nicholas Wheeler and Jean-Marc Coicaud for their comments, which have been incorporated in revising this part of the chapter.
3. Graham T. Allison talked of bureaucratic politics but in a globalized world, the number of actors has proliferated with multiplicity emerging as a feature of civil society as well.
4. See, for example, Scott Peterson (2003) "Iran's Nobel Winner Does Not Make the News at Home", *Peace Women*, 12 December, available at http://www.peacewomen.org/news/Iran/Dec03/home.html, accessed 4 February 2005.
5. Samina Yasmeen (1995) "The Kashmir Dispute in the 1990s: A Possible UN Role?", paper presented at the international conference The United Nations: Between Sovereignty and Global Governance?, La Trobe University, Melbourne, July 2–6, unpublished. See also Samina Yasmeen (2003) "Pakistan's Kashmir Policy: Voices of Moderation?", *Contemporary South Asia* 12(2), June: 187–202.
6. This section draws heavily upon personal interviews conducted during 2002 and 2003 by the author.
7. See, for example, MAH (2002) "Fifty-Five Years of Indian Itch", *Dawn*, 17 December, p. 7.
8. These views are expressed with differing intensity by a number of organized Islamic parties and groups.
9. Based upon personal interviews conducted in Islamabad and Lahore in April and May 2003.
10. The discussion of Indian views is based upon a series of personal interviews conducted in January 2003 in New Delhi.
11. Personal interviews conducted in January 2003, New Delhi.
12. Salil Tripathi (2002) "Civilisation Split: Fighting over Identity", *Asian Wall Street Journal*, 9 January.
13. Pamela Philipose (1999) "Two Prime Ministers Give Friendship a Chance", *Indian Express*, 22 February, pp. 1, 9. For the text of the agreements and of the Lahore Declaration, see *Dawn: The Internet Edition*, 22 February 1999.
14. This is despite the fact that a sizeable majority in Pakistan continues to subscribe to liberal Islamic values.
15. MAH, "Fifty-Five Years of Indian Itch".
16. This identification of a political party to the nature of the society resembles the view taken by orthodox historians of the Cold War who considered the Communist Party to be the natural expression of an exploitative society. Such a view is sometimes substantiated by referring to the research conducted by Indian scholars; one such example is A. G. Noorani (2001) *The RSS and the BJP*, New Delhi: Leftword Press.
17. Personal interview with a senior Pakistani official, January 2003.

18. See, for example, Abdul Hamid Tabassum (2002) "Gujrat mein Muslim kash Fasadat karaney wala Nirender Moodi" (The Organizer of Muslim Massacre through Communal Violence – Nirender Moodi), *Ausaf* (special edition), 18 December, p. 1.
19. Hamid Mir (2003) "Media War", *Ausaf*, 24 November.
20. See, for example, the ideas presented in *South Asia Foundation: Regional Cooperation through Education and Sustainable Development*, Beaulieu-sur-Mer, France: Imprimerie, 2002. A former Indian diplomat, Madanjeet Singh, floated the idea of a Foundation.
21. Personal interviews in New Delhi, January 2003.
22. See, for example, reference to the statements made by former Pakistani Chief of Army Staff Jehangir Karamat on Indo-Pakistani relations, in Sushant Sareen (2001) "Pakistan Clamors for Resuming Negotiations", 31 January, article on file with author.
23. These voices have become more pronounced since mid-2004 but their existence was apparent even earlier. See, for example, Ayaz Amir (2001) "There Is No Kashmir Solution", reprinted from *Dawn* in *Sentinel*, 7 January; Ayaz Amir (2001) "Kashmir & Power of Illusion", *Dawn*, 19 January; and Ikram Sehgal (2001) "Untangling the Kashmir Knot", *The Nation*, 20 January.
24. Interview with a senior Pakistani official, January 2000.
25. See, for example, Toufiq A. Siddiqi (2003) *A Natural Gas Pipeline for India and Pakistan: Global Environment and Energy in the 21st Century*, Honolulu, Hawaii: Balusa.
26. Interview with a senior journalist, Islamabad, December 2001.
27. Kamran Khan (2001) "Parameters for Cooperation Fixed", *The News*, Islamabad, 15 September.
28. Sumanta Bose (2002) "Indo-Pak Brinkmanship: At the End, What Are We Left With?", *Economic and Political Weekly*, 29 June, p. 2550.
29. "Last Bus to Lahore Leaves New Delhi", *Dawn*, 29 December 2001.
30. Faraz Hashmi (2001) "Islamabad Hits Back", *Dawn Weekly Service*, 27 December.
31. Ihtasham ul Haque (2002) "Lashkar, Jaish, TJP, TNSM & SSP Banned; ST under Watch: Political, Diplomatic Support to Kashmiris Will Continue, Says Musharraf", *Dawn*, 13 January.
32. See, for example, text of an interview with Indian Foreign Minister Jaswant Singh, *Press Trust of India*, 28 January 2002.
33. Ibid.
34. Dinesh C. Sharma (2002) "India–Pakistan Relations: New Delhi Adopts Cautious Tone to Musharraf Speech", *Bangkok Post*, 16 January.
35. "Sena–BJP Talks on Seat Sharing Still On", *Times of India*, 20 January 2002.
36. See, for example, "Cold-Shouldering Peace", *The Hindu*, 9 March 2002.
37. Rajindar Sachar (2002) "Disperse the War Clouds", *The Hindu*, 19 January.
38. Sujan Dutta and Mukhtar Ahmad (2002) "Parliament Authorises Action", *Telegraph*, Calcutta, 18 May.
39. See interview with Indian academic P. T. Singam, "Fingers on Triggers as Crunch Nears", *West Australian*, 1 June 2002.
40. Sadanand Dhume (2002) "India Threatens Pakistan with 'Decisive Fight'", *Wall Street Journal Europe*, 23 May, p. A1; "Naval Ships Head West", *The Hindu*, Delhi, 22 May 2002.
41. "Hataf-V Marks 3rd Test of Ghori", *Dawn* (Islamabad), 26 May 2002.
42. "Musharraf Denies Exporting Terrorism", *Business Standard*, 28 May 2002.
43. See, for example, "US Travel Advisory under Review", Rediff.com, 2002, available from http://www.rediff.com/news/2002/jul/20war.htm, accessed 7 February 2005.
44. "India to Withdraw Troops from Border", *Dawn*, Karachi, 17 October 2002; and "Pakistan to Withdraw Troops Shortly", *Dawn*, Karachi, 18 October 2002.

45. George Fernandes talked of Pakistan in terms of a terrorist organization. Vajpayee talked of Pakistan developing into a terrorist nation.

46. The assurance was extended during Richard Armitage's visit to Pakistan in May 2003.

47. Based on information provided by a Pakistani official.

48. Qazi Hussein Ahmed, for instance, has declared that Jamaat-e-Islami would continue Jihad in Kashmir. "Qazi Vows to Continue Kashmir Jehad", *The Nation*, 6 February 2005, available from http://www.nation.com.pk, accessed 6 February 2005.

49. See, for example, M. A. Niazi (2004) "Not So Composite", *The Nation*, 31 December, p. 1.

50. See, for example, Kaleem Omar (2005) "Dilly Dallying over Baghliar Dam", *The News*, 10 January.

2

Sino–US relations: A nascent security regime?

Alan Collins

What underpins the relationship between the US and the Peoples' Republic of China (PRC) and does it have the potential to develop into our notion of solidarity? To determine this we have to know whether the relationship is underpinned by a pursuit of national interest where the core assumptions about the other have not changed, and appear unlikely to do so, or if changes to those core assumptions that indicate a growing sense of shared identity or communality are detectable. This is a critical question, not merely for the actors involved but because the Sino–US relationship determines, more than any other, the likelihood of peace or conflict in East Asia.

Drawing on the theoretical framework in the introduction, this chapter will use security complex theory to determine whether the Sino–US relationship resembles a conflict formation, a nascent security regime or a security community. A conflict formation indicates that little meaningful cooperation is evident; a security regime suggests a level of cooperation that indicates the members of the regime are following more than just their short-term self-interest; and a security community indicates they have developed such a sufficient closeness in outlook that there exists a mutual expectation that they can achieve a peaceful resolution to any dispute that occurs between them. A security community is underpinned by our notion of solidarity but since Sino–US relations are quite obviously not operating in a security community, solidarity does not underpin their relationship. Nevertheless if their relationship resembles that of a nascent security regime then it is pertinent to ask whether the seeds of solidarity

National interest and international solidarity: Particular and universal ethics in international life, Coicaud and Wheeler (eds),
United Nations University Press, 2008, ISBN 978-92-808-1147-6

can be discerned. Before examining security complex theory the chapter begins by giving a brief account of Sino–US relations during the Bush administration.

In the aftermath of 11 September the relationship between Beijing and Washington has improved quite considerably. When George W. Bush took office in 2001 his administration sought to distance the United States from the engagement policies pursued by the outgoing Clinton administration. Whereas Clinton had sought to establish a "constructive strategic partnership" with China, Bush spoke of China as a "strategic competitor".[1] In his 1998 visit to Beijing, Clinton had praised China for not devaluing its currency during the Asian financial crisis, while being critical of America's regional ally, Japan, for not doing more. He went further than any previous US president by publicly stating in China that the United States opposed Taiwanese membership of organizations where sovereignty was a requirement for membership. He therefore appeared to tacitly support the third of Beijing's "three nos"; the first two the United States already acknowledged. The "three nos" are: no support for Taiwanese independence, no support for two Chinas, or one-China, one-Taiwan, and no support for Taiwanese admission to international organizations.

In contrast, Bush's Asia-Pacific policy was focused on improving relations with key allies. Japan was encouraged to play a more cooperative security role with the United States, while Taiwan was offered a wider range of military equipment than had been on offer previously. This included submarines, which would have a considerable impact on China's ability to either invade Taiwan or impose a blockade of the island. Bush also appeared to break with the American preference for strategic ambiguity over the defence of Taiwan, when he declared in April 2001 the United States would do "whatever it takes" to defend the island and that the use of military force was "certainly an option".[2] Not only was Bush focusing US attention on its allies, he was also distancing the United States from Beijing. In the administration's strategic overview before 11 September – the Quadrennial Defense Review – it was noted that the United States would restructure its armed forces by shifting from "threat-based" assessments of potential enemies to "capabilities-based" assessments. In the North-east Asian region, the main security challenge was identified as the possible rise of "a military competitor with a formidable resource base".[3] This could be only China. The deterioration in relations was captured in April 2001 when an American reconnaissance plane was involved in a mid-air collision with a Chinese fighter plane. The Chinese pilot was killed while the American crew made a forced landing on Hainan Island. After two weeks of diplomacy the United States made a muted apology and the crew was released.

The Hainan incident proved to be a turning point. The then-US Secretary of State, Colin Powell, credits it with propelling US–China relations to a new level.[4] Then, in September, Al Qaeda's attack on the World Trade Center and the Pentagon brought a sudden change to US foreign policy with the American declaration that the world's only superpower was now at war against international terrorism. International terrorism gave these two states the opportunity to unite against a common foe, since China too has its fears about Islamic terrorism; a separatist movement is active in Xinjiang, a Chinese province in Central Asia. The tentative understandings reached over the Hainan incident were now seized upon by both Beijing and Washington to improve their relations. The then-Chinese Premier, Jiang Zemin, set aside the prepared agenda at the APEC meeting held in Shanghai in October 2001 so that Bush could use the occasion to put terrorism at the top of the international agenda. Bush now referred to their relationship as "cooperative and constructive" while Jiang delivered what Bush was seeking when he told the APEC conference "terrorism is an international public hazard".[5] With international terrorism providing a common ground, cooperative ventures were achieved. The United States, although wary of treating all Chinese internal adversaries as terrorists (such as the Tibetans and the quasi religious Falun Gong movement), nevertheless did add the East Turkistan Islamic Movement to its terrorist list. China reciprocated by enacting legislation to control the export of those materials that had raised US concern about missile and weapon of mass destruction proliferation. The improvement in relations also enabled the United States to deploy troops to Central Asia without raising fears in China that these forces could support Muslim groups demanding more freedom from Beijing.

What, though, are we to make of these fluctuating relations? Is it simply a case of these two states pragmatically reacting to their immediate concerns or does their cooperation have deeper roots than merely short-term self-interest? In order to address this question, the next section applies the concept of regional security complex theory to determine, first, whether the relationship is an example of an emerging security regime or a conflict formation and, second, if it is the former, does it have the potential to become a security community?

Regional security complex theory

The theory of regional security complexes (hereafter security complex theory) developed by Barry Buzan postulates that because threats are more acutely felt from neighbouring powers it is possible to divide the globe into regional clusters. The criterion for determining how a cluster, or security complex, is formed is that it is a region where the states' "primary security concerns link together sufficiently closely that their national securities cannot realistically be considered apart from one another".[6] Within a security complex the relations between its members can be plotted along a spectrum depending upon the levels of amity and enmity exhibited. For Buzan, amity refers to the "expectation of protection or support", while enmity refers to relationships beset "by suspicion and fear".[7] Where the states' security interdependence is marked by enmity, Buzan refers to the security complex at this extreme end as an example of what Raimo Väyrynen called a "conflict formation". Toward amity lies a security regime while at the amity-extreme end of the spectrum is Karl Deutsch's security community.[8]

In order to make judgements as to the type of security complex in operation, the theory uses a blend of realist and constructivist explanations of state behaviour. Thus, while the focus is on regional dynamics, as opposed to the neorealist preference for structural explanations, it is nevertheless concerned with the material resources available to the states and consequently the region's balance of power. It does, though, complement this by examining the less tangible ideational factors that influence state behaviour and treating these as an independent variable from the distribution of power. Specifically, though not exclusively, the constructivist approach pursued in security complex theory is the Copenhagen School's notion of securitization, where the focus is on when and under what conditions an elite interprets others' actions as threatening and thus engages in securitization discourse.[9]

In view of this chapter's concern with Sino–US relations it might seem odd to refer to a regional security complex, since the United States is not geographically located in East Asia. Two points need to be made in this respect. First, it is possible for a state to belong to more than one security complex. China, for example, is a member of both the North-east Asian and South-east Asian security complexes because the states in these regions take Chinese actions into account when analysing their security environment. The United States is also a member of a number of regional security complexes, including those in East Asia, because its global reach makes it a player that states take into account when they analyse their security environment. The second point is that while the United States is an outside power, its presence in East Asia is so considerable, both in ideational (notions of democracy, free market economics) and material terms (troop deployments in Japan and South Korea), that US security policy is uppermost in the minds of Beijing's decision-makers when they analyse their security environment. Hence Buzan's claim that what determines if East Asia's security complexes resemble a conflict formation or security regime "lies in what happens with China and the US".[10]

Conflict formation, security regime and security community

A conflict formation describes a region where fear and suspicion characterize the interaction between states. In East Asia, where the Korean Peninsula remains divided, historical animosity exists between China and Japan and Chinese attempts to reunify with Taiwan give rise to the possibility of clashes with the United States, a conflict formation would appear an apt description.[11] While it is true that the actors remain wary of one another, in the post–Cold War period they have sought to reduce the likelihood of conflict by engaging in dialogue. They are members of the ASEAN Regional Forum (ARF) and the Korean Six-Party talks and since 2002 the foreign ministers of South Korea, Japan and China have held annual three-way meetings under the auspices of the ASEAN Plus Three (APT) process. Thus, while suspicion is evident in these relationships, this does not equate to the likelihood of conflict being high.

At the other end of Buzan's spectrum is a security community. A security community exists where states share common values, mutual sympathies and loyalties; where a state has at least a partial identification with another's image that creates a "we-feeling". The similarity in their outlooks leads to enhanced cooperation that deepens those common values and is manifest in various transnational linkages and membership in international institutions. Finally, a community exhibits a degree of reciprocity where members manifest a sense of obligation and responsibility toward one another. States in a security community become integrated to such an extent that – and this is the defining feature of a security community – the members do not consider the use of force, or threat to use force, as an appropriate means of resolving their disputes. The members of the European Union thus exist in a security community since it is inconceivable that, for example, the United Kingdom and France would go to war against one another to resolve a dispute.

Although rationalist explanations for state behaviour, such as neo-realism and neo-liberalism, can explain a non-war relationship, their explanation derives from the actors' determining that cooperation advances their interests through a cost-benefit calculation. Once it no longer pays to cooperate, the states will renege or defect. A non-war relationship in a security community arises because the actors' identities have transformed to such an extent that it becomes a shared identity that generates a sense of obligation toward one another. Cooperation arises therefore because it is mutually beneficial to do so; the benefit accrued benefits the community as a whole and therefore defection need not be feared. A security community is thus understood through a constructivist explanation of state behaviour.

In an anarchical environment, defection exists because there is no guarantor of state sovereignty; states must be egoists. A security community overcomes this because it is a type of mature anarchy where a level of governance is in operation. This does not mean that there has to be legally and formally prescribed responsibilities, although in the case of the European Union there are, but rather defection is overcome because the collective norms that govern state behaviour are established from the shared values, mutual loyalties, the "we-feeling"; that is, their shared identity and self-understanding.

This sense of commonality is likely to be replicated in the domestic environment as state identities adjust. Hence Emanuel Adler and Michael Barnett's view that "states govern their domestic behavior in ways that are consistent with the community".[12] There would therefore be an expectation that members of a security community would have similar domestic political systems. It is perhaps not surprising given these conditions that East Asia, with its variety of political systems and cultures and where force is quite clearly an option, cannot be described as a security community. This does not, though, mean that parts of the region do not exhibit elements of a nascent security community, such as South-east Asia.[13]

Between a conflict formation and security community lay various cooperative arrangements to enhance security that differ in terms of motivation and scale. These are variously referred to as cooperative security, comprehensive security, security regime and common or mutual security. Unlike a security community, the cooperation prevalent in these arrangements is underpinned by self-interest. The states are egoist actors that engage in cooperation because they perceive it as enhancing their own security. Since the actors are egoists it will matter how much the other state(s) gain from the cooperation and if one state is gaining more from the cooperative venture then others, then one or more of the others are likely to defect. On the security complex spectrum a security regime lies closer to a security community than a conflict formation. The reason is not because the members of the regime are motivated by a solidarity rationale; they remain egoists, but because the regime reduces the likelihood of defection and thus encourages a greater degree of cooperation. How does it do this?

The existence of a security regime, while indicating a greater degree of amity than in a conflict formation, does not presuppose a lack of conflict. However, unlike a conflict formation, the members of a security regime have agreed to cooperate to manage conflicts that occur. This level of co-operation indicates an acceptance of the status quo, a desire to avoid war and an expectation that the members will act with restraint when disputes occur.[14] This understanding is manifest in the establishment of norms of behaviour with which the members operate in accordance. These norms can be tangible, such as in a signed declaration or treaty, or they can be intangible where states operate according to commonly held conventions. The "ASEAN Way" is arguably an example of the latter, where ASEAN members' interactions take place within commonly accepted norms of be-haviour. The defining feature of a security regime is that this form of co-operation is "more than the following of short-run self-interest".[15]

The regime's norms of behaviour help to dampen fears of defection since they create a degree of certainty in the members' interactions. With the fear of defection lessened, regime members can afford to suffer short-term losses in the knowledge that other members will not take ad-vantage of their temporary weakness; they will act with restraint. States can therefore pursue long-term national interests, even those that require them to compromise their interests in the short-term. We can thus distin-guish normal state cooperation from regime cooperation because in the latter it is more than the following of short-run self-interest.

What best describes the Sino–US relationship? It is evidently not a se-curity community. Not only do both states consider war between them as possible but shared values that necessarily underpin the sense of commu-nity do not exist either. Cooperation does though occur between China and the United States, and our interest is in determining whether in their pursuit of their national interests a nascent security regime is forming.

Sino–US engagement

The US policy toward China has been one of containment and engage-ment. Both are designed to prevent China's growing influence displacing American power in East Asia. They seek to do this by adjusting Chinese objectives so they are conducive to US interests. Containment policies are coercive in nature and seek to achieve this through deterring China. They are based on a zero-sum interpretation of Sino–US relations and such policies include strengthening alliances, such as the April 1996 Japan–US Joint Declaration on Security and the release in September 1997 of new guidelines for US–Japan defence cooperation, maintaining US forces in the region and providing Taiwan with military equipment. Engagement policies are cooperative in nature and are characterized by seeking a peaceful resolution of conflicts of interest as they arise. While engagement policies vary in their type they share the requirement of participation by both states; hence the importance of dialogue, and indeed the form of dialogue, when assessing engagement policies.

Advocates of containment argue that the problem with engagement is that it assumes Chinese objectives are reactive to US policies. They claim this is false and instead argue China seeks to accumulate enough economic, military and diplomatic power to oust the United States from East Asia and achieve its ultimate goal of regional hegemony. US efforts to enter into dialogue and seek a peaceful resolution of conflicts therefore only encourage China to encroach on more US interests because it indicates American unwillingness to penalize China and resist its hegemonic ambitions. Advocates of engagement respond by arguing that Chinese long-term objectives are not immutable and therefore they are open to influence. Entering into cooperative enterprises with China can influence the perception that Beijing decision-makers have of the US. Thus, advocates of engagement claim that if the United States treats China as an enemy then it will become an enemy, but if it treats it as a partner then this can be avoided.[16]

The US pursuit of both containment and engagement has been referred to by Gerald Segal as "constrainment" and essentially it means pursuing engagement but maintaining containment policies just in case Beijing proves unwilling to adjust its objectives.[17] Our interest is in engagement and whether this cooperative approach indicates a nascent security regime is forming.

Engaging China can simply mean gaining Chinese willingness to enter into bilateral discussions with the United States, and/or Chinese admission to international institutions. In this instance it is hoped that dialogue between the two states would affect perceptions that the elite hold of each other, correct misperceptions and create opportunities for cooperation, thus developing a stable regional order. For a security regime to form, though, engagement is more than just entering into dialogue. Engagement must have a purpose, and in this instance it means restricting China's policy options by changing Chinese objectives so they are conducive to US interests, or more commonly referred to as socializing China so it operates within agreed norms of behaviour. That is, ensuring China is willing to act within restraints when conflicts of interests arise, a key feature of a security regime. That engagement means adjusting China's strategic ambitions to fit US interests immediately raises the question of what motivates Beijing to engage with the US. After all, as Alastair Iain Johnston and Paul Evans forcefully argue, "adjusting one's behavior to the anticipated preferences of others says nothing about whether this cooperation is in some sense coerced, bought, or carried out for normative reasons".[18] Thus, our interest is not simply in whether China acts within acceptable norms, but also why.

While a definitive answer is not possible to this question we can never-theless make some judgements about the type of Chinese participation and what this reveals. If Chinese participants simply attend, add little to the discussion and/or obstruct agreement, then very little socializing is oc-curring and no norms of behaviour are established. However, if Chinese participants are proactive and recommend proposals to guide state inter-action this could indicate a willingness to establish norms of behaviour. It would certainly suggest that the Chinese elite saw the benefits of estab-lishing restraints on a particular issue. While this is an improvement on being a silent or obstructive participant since it indicates recognition that norms of behaviour can be useful, a clearer indication of Chinese willing-ness to operate in a security regime would be if China adjusted its poli-cies because of the rules or norms that were in operation.

In the field of arms control, Johnston and Evans note there is evidence not only that China has become a proactive participant but also that it has adjusted its policies to fit norms of behaviour that are already in exis-tence. For example, they note that in both the negotiations leading to the 1997 Chemical Weapons Convention and the verification issues in the Comprehensive Test Ban Treaty (CTBT), Chinese specialists made orig-inal contributions to the discussions. This reflected a change because previously the Chinese had just been reiterating rather vague proposals announced elsewhere. The Chinese were now active participants collabo-rating with other members in producing, amongst other things, detailed working papers on the language that would govern activities prohibited by the treaties and the definition of terms adopted. This certainly indi-cates that Beijing recognizes the value of establishing rules or norms that restrain state behaviour. Are the Chinese, though, willing to do this if these norms of behaviour require China to adjust its policies?

On this issue, Johnston and Evans note that most of the arms control agreements China has adopted have entailed little cost to Beijing. That is, agreeing to the outer space, Antarctic or the South Pacific nuclear-weapon-free zone treaties has not required the Chinese to adjust their policies. However, in the 1990s China became a signatory to the CTBT and, although it is not a member of the 1997 landmine treaty (Mine Ban Treaty/Ottawa Convention), it did agree to the landmine protocol. Both the CTBT and landmine protocol required a sacrifice from China. This sacrifice was that developments of certain weapons, specifically nuclear, and the export of anti-personnel landmines would no longer be per-mitted. The Chinese were thus prepared to adjust their procurement plans to operate within these regulations. While this again indicates that for the Chinese norms matter, what is particularly revealing is that Chinese ac-cession to these treaties took place in the face of opposition from the Peoples' Liberation Army and the Chinese weapons-manufacturing community. This indicated something important had changed in Beijing's decision-making calculations. That change, Johnston and Evans argue, was China's self-image.

They argue that during the 1990s China's self-identification began to change. China's self-image of a sovereign-centric, autonomous major power was now tied to a new image of China as a responsible major power, "whose status is measured in part by participation in institutions that increasingly regulate state behavior".[19] While the source of this change is unclear, they do note that China has abandoned the image of a radical Third World state leading the global have-nots and espousing an ideology of revolutionary Marxism. This change of image has led Chinese decision-makers to become sensitive to accusations of China being an obstructionist actor in international institutions. Johnston and Evans back up this assertion by claiming,

> In interview after interview of arms control specialists, a common response was that China had to join such and such treaty or process because it was part of a world historical trend, because it was part of China's role as a responsible major power, because it would help improve China's image, and, more concretely, help China to break out of the post [Tiananmen Square] attempts by some Western states to isolate China diplomatically.[20]

Critically, then, Johnston and Evans argue that determining whether to sign a particular treaty or not is not based solely on the specifics of the treaty but more generally on the negative image others will have of China if it does not sign. Beijing is therefore sensitive to the image others have of China and this helps to explain its increasingly active participation in international institutions and operating within their norms of behaviour, because this is seen as a means of enhancing China's image as a responsible power. Chinese self-identification as a responsible actor is thus an important explanatory tool as to why China has agreed to act within certain norms of behaviour. Johnston and Evans thus argue, "China has undergone a socialisation process to the extent that it is sensitive to the normative (as opposed to concrete material) image effects generated by participation in institutions".[21]

In terms of what is motivating Chinese cooperation, this claim from Johnston and Evans is extremely important. The importance of operating within norms and participating in their creation certainly indicates that China is prepared to establish constraints on its actions, at least in the arms control arena. While this can be explained by material considerations – that is, an egoist China is calculating that these constraints enhance its security – Johnston and Evans are also arguing that China's motivation is ideational because cooperating is what responsible major powers do; China is sensitive to the image others have of it. This indicates that China's identity is malleable and therefore, through a continuing process of socialization, China's identity might change sufficiently for there to be at least a partial identification with America's identity. If this were to occur, then it is possible that future cooperation could be based on solidarity; here lies the path to a security community. This prospect is explored later in the chapter.

While Johnston and Evans's claim is revealing, China's current interest in institutions and multilateralism, especially in the context of Sino–US relations, is better explained as a pursuit of national interest by an egoist. China's willingness to participate in international institutions and multilateral processes has been borne out at the turn of the century. Historically wary of institutions constraining China, the PRC is now a member of APEC, ARF, APT, and the World Trade Organization; has sought a multilateral solution to the South China Sea dispute by signing in 2003 the Declaration on the Conduct of Parties in the South China Sea; acceded to ASEAN's Treaty of Amity and Cooperation in the same year; established in 2001 with Russia, Kazakhstan, Kyrgyzstan and Tajikistan the Shanghai Cooperation Organisation (SCO); and is an original member of the Six-Party Talks seeking a peaceful resolution in the Korean Peninsula. In the late 1990s China signed the two main UN conventions on human rights and sent personnel to participate in UN peacekeeping operations. "In short", Michael Yahuda states, "China was becoming a participant in many of the international institutions and practices [that] befitted a country that sought recognition as a responsible great power".[22] The explanation for this, while partly ideational, reflects a change in attitude toward the US.

For much of the 1990s China viewed the post–Cold War world as multipolar and one in which the United States was a declining power, or at least a declining one in East Asia. The Chinese attitude toward the United States was a mixture of admiration, for the United States was the yardstick by which the Chinese could measure their own progress and power, but also distrust and suspicion, for the United States was perceived to be blocking China's rise and imposing on China its own political values. China thus sought to balance US power in the region and this helps to explain its initial interest in joining and establishing the institutions noted above. By 1999, however, the Chinese had accepted that, far from sinking into relative decline, the gap between America and the rest of the world was widening. Multipolarity was not the likely outcome but, rather, unipolarity had emerged, and since regional allies had shown they were not going to help balance against the United States, the Chinese have sought to use this regional multilateralism to strengthen their presence, not in competition with the United States, but as a growing influence alongside that of America.

This change was made explicit by China's fourth generation of leaders, who ascended to leadership in 2002 and were confirmed by the National People's Congress in March 2003. In his visit to Washington in December 2003, China's Prime Minister, Wen Jiabao, articulated the view that the "overriding trend of the present-day world is towards peace and development. China's development is blessed with a rare period of strategic opportunity".[23] This "rarity" distinguished modern day circumstances from the usual historical trend of a major war occurring between the rising power and the hegemon. For Yahuda, China's leader was revealing that the Beijing elite had accommodated themselves to American pre-eminence as the sole superpower because this system facilitated China's economic growth and rising power while also ensuring there would be no major wars between the great powers of the region. Yahuda writes,

> In short, China has what has been called a period of strategic opportunity in which it can focus on the domestic tasks of economic growth and transformation, while being assured of a peaceful international environment that is conducive to its growing economic significance in the world.[24]

The explanation is therefore self-interest. China cooperates with the United States because it is in its economic interests to do so. Does this self-interest, though, extend to suffering short-term losses to gain long-term benefits? Is there evidence that China can operate within a security regime?

David Shambaugh, a leading US expert on China, notes, when examining the improving relationship between China and the states of Southeast Asia, that

> China's efforts to improve its ties with ASEAN are not merely part of a larger "charm offensive." They represent, in some cases, fundamental compromises that China has chosen to make in limiting its own sovereign interests for the sake of engagement in multilateral frameworks and pursuit of greater regional interdependence.[25]

This willingness to pursue its national interest by placing limits on its own sovereign interest is strong evidence that China's use of multilateralism is more than just the following of short-run self-interest. It indicates that Beijing is willing to operate within norms of behaviour that restrain its actions. Shambaugh writes, "China's expanded engagement with ASEAN and the SCO ... reflects an increased appreciation by the Chinese government of the importance of norms",[26] and, as a consequence, "most nations in the region see China as a good neighbor, a constructive partner, a careful listener, and a nonthreatening regional power".[27] It does therefore appear that a security regime is forming because China is willing to accept the current status quo in East Asia, operate with restraint and do so for more than just their immediate self-interest. While this is true for China's relationship with some of the other East Asian states, our interest is in the cooperative relationship between China and the United States, and specifically, whether this cooperation indicates more than just the following of short-run self-interest. To determine this we now turn to the two regional security issues that dominate the Sino–US relationship in East Asia: Korea and Taiwan.

North Korea

The Korean crisis erupted in October 2002 when the North Korean leadership announced that it was pursuing a nuclear arms programme; it declared itself a nuclear power in February 2005 and detonated an atomic device on 9 October 2006. In response to the 2002 announcement, the United States demanded that North Korea return to its non-proliferation agreements before any talks could be resumed, and in December 2002 the United States boarded and inspected a North Korean ship in the Arabian Sea that was carrying missiles to Yemen. The North Koreans responded by removing the presence of the International Atomic Energy Agency (IAEA) from their country and in January 2003 withdrew from the Non-Proliferation Treaty. In 2003 Beijing stepped in to act as a mediator between the United States and North Korea. The reason for China's involvement is that Beijing does not want the Korean peninsula to become nuclearized; the United States and China thus share the same objective of denuclearizing North Korea and this explains Chinese support for UN Security Council Resolution 1718 condemning Pyongyang for its nuclear test in 2006. The importance of this crisis for China is manifest in President Hu Jintao taking a direct role in China's management of the crisis. In April 2003 China convened a three-way meeting between North Korea, the United States and China and has since expanded the talks to include South Korea, Japan and Russia. The first six-party talks were held in August 2003 and since then they have met on five further occasions.[28] The six-party talks have become the means through which a resolution to this crisis has been sought by all the interested parties. At present the Bush administration has agreed to a deal, drawn up by the Chinese, that is very similar to the 1994 Agreed Framework that the US administration initially criticized. In return for the United States releasing financial assets frozen since September 2005 and providing emergency supplies of fuel, North Korea will shut down and seal the Yongbyon nuclear facility, including the reprocessing facility, and invite back IAEA personnel to conduct all necessary monitoring and verifications.

China's newfound enthusiasm for multilateral solutions has led some commentators to speculate that the six-party talks might be the forerunner of an institutionalized arrangement for managing North-east Asian affairs.[29] Whether this occurs will depend upon whether the United States remains committed to multilateralism. The United States has been largely indifferent to the creation of Asian multilateral institutions, but with Washington's attention focused on the other two members of Bush's "Axis of Evil" the six-party talks, and especially China's involvement, has been welcomed as the best means of resolving the Korean crisis. The reason why America wants China's involvement is because the United States does not have sufficient leverage to force North Korea to denuclearize; China, as North Korea's only ally and supplier of fuel and food does have this leverage. In order to encourage China to use this leverage not only does the United States directly seek to persuade Beijing to pressure North Korea, as US Secretary of State Condoleezza Rice did in her March 2005 visit to China,[30] but the United States also shows restraint in its dealings with China. By limiting its criticism of China, Washington seeks to maintain cordial relations. This US restraint was manifest after North Korea announced it had nuclear weapons and withdrew from the six-party talks in February 2005. Pyongyang's announcement coincided with a US–Japanese summit in which these two allies were going to express their growing concern about China's military modernization programme. However, in light of North Korea's dramatic announcement, America and Japan moderated their language and instead emphasized their "cooperative relationship with China, welcoming the country to play a responsible and constructive role regionally and globally".[31] The influence China is able to wield over North Korea was given evidence when, soon after Wang Jiarui, a high-level Chinese envoy, had been dispatched to Pyongyang, North Korea announced it would reverse its decision to withdraw from the six-party talks.[32] The US State Department's willingness to delay the Patriot missile defence arms sale to Taiwan because they did not want to anger China when the United States wanted Beijing's help over North Korea is also evidence of US restraint.[33]

This willingness to show restraint could indicate the emergence of a security regime; a prospect that could be enhanced if the six-party talks are institutionalized. However, there are reasons to believe that Sino–US cooperation currently falls short of that needed for regime formation. While China and the United States share the objective of a denuclearized Korean peninsula, they differ over the virtue of seeing the Pyongyang regime remain in power. Therefore, while Beijing will encourage the North Korean leadership to resume dialogue, it is less willing to do this by using its leverage to force Pyongyang back to the negotiating table.[34] China is not therefore prepared to compromise on its own immediate interests of maintaining cordial relations with Pyongyang for the attainment of a denuclearized North Korea. Beijing is engaging in the cost/benefit calculations of an egoist actor that epitomizes the use of cooperation for its own self-interest. Likewise, although the United States appreciates the virtue of cooperating with China to resolve the crisis, Condoleezza Rice made it clear in her discussions with the Chinese elite that if progress was not forthcoming the United States would impose its own sanctions on Pyongyang.[35] In other words, the United States would defect on the six-party talks if these were not fulfilling US national interest in favour of a unilateral solution. This form of cooperation is not evidence of a security regime since they are not looking beyond their immediate self-interest. In other words, the signs of restraint on America's behalf and China's dispatching of envoys to encourage continued North Korean participation in the six-party talks are too directly linked to their own immediate self-interest to invoke the concept.

Taiwan

The tension in the Chinese–Taiwanese relationship dates back to the Chinese civil war when in 1949 Mao Zedong's communist forces routed Chiang Kai-Shek's Kuomintang (KMT) and forced the latter to flee to Taiwan (then known as Formosa). Since then China has been represented by two regimes; one in Beijing (the People's Republic of China, PRC) and one in Taipei (the Republic of China, ROC). The KMT held China's seat in the United Nations Security Council until 1971 and it was only in the late 1980s that Taipei moderated its claim to being the representative of mainland China. The existence of two regimes representing one state underpins the "One China" policy that both have pursued.

For the PRC the "One China" policy means that Beijing is the legitimate representative of all China, and Taiwan is a province of China with the regime in Taipei a subordinate authority. The ultimate goal for Beijing is reunification between Taiwan and the mainland, with Beijing the central authority. This is known as the "one country, two systems" formula in which Taiwan enjoys autonomy within the PRC. Beijing has sought to do this through a carrot-and-stick approach. The carrot is called peaceful inducement and is designed to encourage Taiwanese investment in China, increase contact between the two and ultimately ameliorate historical animosity. This is Beijing's preferred approach to achieving reunification because, although it is long-term, it offers the prospect of increasing economic prosperity for both the PRC and ROC and enhancing societal cohesion; in colloquial terms this is a "soft" landing. The fact that it is long-term is not a hindrance to this approach since China's territorial size has fluctuated throughout its history and it matters little if reunification is achieved sooner or later. Reunification must though happen at some point and, to ensure this, China has a stick, which is to warn Taiwan that moves to declare itself an independent sovereign state would be regarded as an act of secession. The Chinese elite have consistently reaffirmed that such an action would result in war. This is not Beijing's preferred approach to reunification but if Taiwan alters the current status quo then it will force China's hand and Beijing will seek to bring about a "hard" landing. Since Beijing views Taiwan as a part of China, actions in support of Taiwan by outside powers is considered interference in China's internal affairs. This helps to explain why Beijing expects outside powers to accept the "One China" principle since to not do so is tantamount to recognizing Taiwan as a sovereign state.

The Taiwanese have not refuted the "One China" policy but now they interpret it as a reflection of the shared history and culture the island has with the mainland. Since the mid-1990s the Taiwanese elite have not seen it as preventing them from referring to the ROC as an "equal" and "independent" state. The relationship between the PRC and ROC is referred to as "state-to-state", with the caveat that it is a relationship between two states within one nation. This formulation was created by Lee Teng-hui, the Taiwanese president until 2000, and his successor Chen Shui-bian has continued with this description; in 2002 Chen said that there is one state on each side of the Strait. The differences in the interpretation of "One China" is deliberately left ambiguous so that both the PRC and ROC can affirm their support for the principle, which until 2002 was a PRC precondition for entering into dialogue with ROC officials.[36]

Taiwan is seen as a touchstone of Sino–US relations because the United States has committed itself, via the 1979 Taiwan Relations Act, to view any military action, boycott or embargo against Taiwan as a matter of grave concern to the United States. The Act requires the United States to provide Taiwan with enough military capability to maintain a self-defence force and, although in 1982 President Reagan agreed to limit and reduce US arms sales to Taiwan, the United States has continued to sell sizable quantities of military equipment. In 1992 the United States sold 150 F-16 fighter planes to Taiwan and currently has an arms package, which includes submarines and the Patriot anti-missile defence system, worth US$18.2 billion waiting to be completed. US support for Taiwan has not only been shown in the sophisticated military equipment sold to Taipei, but the US has also deployed its own forces to the region during periods of increased tension. This was the case during the 1996 Taiwanese presidential election. This was the first election in which the president would be directly elected and the PRC decided to conduct a military exercise opposite Taiwan in order to intimidate the Taiwanese electorate – it spectacularly failed with Lee Teng-hui re-elected with 54 per cent of the vote and the United States deploying two of its aircraft carrier fleets to the area.[37] This 1996 incident is worth noting in detail not only because it reveals the potential for war between China and the United States, but also because it reveals that both wish to avoid this outcome.[38] Indeed, since 1996 and even more so after the 2000 Taiwanese presidential election, both have sought to maintain the status quo.

The origins of the 1996 incident can be traced back to June 1995 when Lee Teng-hui visited his alma mater, Cornell University. Lee was already perceived by Beijing as distancing Taiwan from the mainland and on his visit to the United States he appeared to be acting in a manner not dissimilar to that of a visiting state leader. It confirmed Beijing's opinion that far from leading Taiwan down the path of reunification, Lee was taking the province in the opposite direction. The visit also undermined those in China preferring to bring about reunification via peaceful means because Qian Qichen, the then-Chinese Foreign Minister, had been given assurances by the then-US Secretary of State, Warren Christopher, that Lee would not be granted a visa. Qian Qichen had passed these assurances onto the Politburo. Lee's subsequent visit thus undercut the carrot approach favoured by the Foreign Ministry and was replaced by the stick approach advocated by the People's Liberation Army.

In July 1995 the Chinese conducted military exercises opposite Taiwan that simulated an invasion, and they fired missiles into the sea 85 miles north of Taiwan. One week before parliamentary elections in November the Chinese launched another military exercise and then in the lead up to the March 1996 presidential election they launched three missiles within 30 miles of the island's main ports in the north and south, effectively closing them during this period. The deployment by the United States of two aircraft carrier fleets in response to these military exercises constituted the largest deployment of US naval forces in the Pacific since the Viet Nam War.

China's "stick" approach reveals the willingness to threaten the use of force to achieve national goals, and likewise America's military reaction shows the continuing value for Washington of force as an instrument of policy vis-à-vis China. This would appear to support the view that Sino–US relations can be best described as a conflict formation. However, the threat of force in 1995/96 was not designed to initiate war; it was designed to avoid war. The logic runs like this: (1) China would have to wage war against Taiwan if the latter declared independence, so (2) military threats are designed to deter such moves by making it patently clear the costs Taiwan would incur, and therefore (3) military threats would make war less likely by reducing the likelihood of a declaration of independence.[39] The US force deployments were likewise a visible attempt to deter China from resorting to force. The US action, along with the Taiwan Relations Act, is part of a US twin-track approach to maintaining the status quo. In addition to deterring China by threatening war, the United States also seeks to deter Taiwan's moves to sovereign independence. It does this by pressuring Taipei to tone down its rhetoric and leaving its commitment to Taiwan's defence ambiguous so that the Taiwanese elite cannot be certain of US support in the event of hostilities with the mainland. The US objective is to maintain the current status quo while waiting for China to liberalize enough for reunification to be acceptable to the Taiwanese.

The deliberate rising of tension in 1995/96 was thus an attempt by the PRC and the United States to avoid war and maintain the status quo. While this indicates a preference in Beijing and Washington to maintain the status quo, such actions can hardly be said to show restraint and thus do not support the notion of their relations operating in a security regime. Nevertheless, the reaction of both after 1996 was to improve their relationship so that they could avoid a repeat of this episode. This improvement was marked by Clinton referring to China as a "strategic partner" in 1998 and his support for Beijing's "three nos" while visiting China in the same year.

In the period since, China and the United States have steadily established a tacit understanding of how to maintain the status quo. This does not equate to reaching an agreement on a peaceful resolution to the Taiwan issue, rather an understanding of how to dampen those dynamics that could lead to war. This is not to suggest that tensions haven't risen since 1996; the Bush administration's initial approach to East Asia was a cause of concern in Beijing and during Taiwan's presidential election in 2000 China engaged in more sabre rattling.[40] It has, though, become appreciated that these approaches reduce, not enhance, security. China's bellicose approach in 2000 help end KMT rule in Taiwan and brought to power Chen Shui-bian, the leader of the pro-independence Democratic Progressive Party (DPP). Importantly, China has learnt that its actions have been self-defeating and at the March 2004 election there was no repeat performance from Beijing. Although Chen was re-elected, he won by only 0.2 per cent of the vote and this after a controversial gunshot incident just hours before polling began. The 2004 election was fought between a pan-green camp (led by the DPP) and a pan-blue camp (led by the KMT); the pan-blue camp has, after the leadership of Lee, returned to its pro-reunification stance while the pan-green camp favours Taiwan independence over Chinese reunification. While the result of the presidential election was not what Beijing wanted, Chen's marginal victory and the KMT's success at the parliamentary election in December 2004, which gave the pan-blue alliance a parliamentary majority, should rein in Chen's pro-independence moves.

This tacit understanding between Beijing and Washington is therefore that Beijing refrain from pressuring Taiwan because this only confirms the view in Taipei that the PRC is a bully, and in return for this restraint the United States applies pressure on Chen to curb his pro-independence aspirations. This has been evident since November 2003 when Taiwan passed a referendum bill that could be used on sovereignty issues such as the flag or changing the name of the ROC to Taiwan. In December, Chen, trailing in the opinion polls, sought to present himself as a crusader of national dignity by announcing his intention to hold a referendum at the same time as the presidential election. The referendum would call upon China to dismantle its missiles aimed at Taiwan. The response from the United States was a strongly worded rebuke. Bush announced that the United States was opposed to either China or Taiwan unilaterally changing the status quo and that Chen's referendum proposal indicated Taiwan was willing to do this. This certainly seemed the case when during the 2004 campaign rally Chen announced his intention to hold a referendum in 2006 on a new constitution for implementation from May 2008. Chen was put under pressure by Washington to tone down the rhetoric.[41] This resulted in a watering down of the referendum question to be put to the electorate in 2004. The deliberately confrontational demand for Beijing to dismantle its missiles was replaced by asking whether, if China refused to withdraw the missiles, the government should acquire the Patriot anti-missile defence system. The result of Washington's pressure could also be seen in Chen's inaugural address when he promised that his constitutional reform plan would not touch on the sensitive issues of sovereignty, territory, national title or the country's flag. US pressure could also be seen in late 2004 during Taiwan's parliamentary elections. Once again, Chen had used the campaign to promote Taiwanese identity. He said Taiwan should seek UN membership under the name of Taiwan rather than ROC, and embassies should use Taiwan instead of the less attention-grabbing name Taipei. This time, US Deputy Secretary of State Richard Armitage stated that Washington was not obliged to defend Taiwan and that Taiwan was probably the biggest "landmine" in Sino–US relations.[42]

Does this improving Sino–US relationship mean an intangible security regime based upon an emerging tacit understanding is forming with regard to Taiwan? While we can witness restraint and reciprocity in their relationship, the degree of cooperation shown falls short of that required for a security regime. In the first instance, the reason is the same as the

North Korean case; they share the same objective, in this case avoiding war, but this does not take priority over more immediate interests. The United States will continue to supply Taiwan with sophisticated military equipment and China will attack Taiwan if it declares itself an independent sovereign state. This latter statement is an absolute; a matter on which there can be no compromise. It reveals the second reason why a security regime is problematic; the Taiwan issue is really about regime legitimacy for the communist party in Beijing. The Chinese Communist Party's (CCP's) legitimacy is partly based upon restoring China's great power status and a key element in this is returning territories lost during the "century of shame". Taiwan is the principle territory; the leader of Beijing that presided over the loss of Taiwan would be labelled a *qianguzuiren*, an eternally guilty man. It is therefore impossible for the Chinese elite to ignore Taiwanese statements that favour pro-independence. Taiwan is therefore an independent variable; domestic considerations take precedence over the state of Sino–US relations in determining China's actions. While this limits the extent that the norms of behaviour necessary for a security regime can develop, the tacit understanding based on restraint and reciprocity helped the two states diffuse a potential crisis in early 2005.

Chen's various pro-independence statements in 2004 forced China's relatively new elite, which was still establishing its credentials, to respond. They responded by passing an anti-secession law at the National People's Congress in March 2005; the law provides a legal pretext for the use of force in the event of Taiwan declaring itself a sovereign independent state. Despite Taiwanese fury at this action, which culminated in a rally of over 275,000 people in Taipei on 26 March, the anti-secession law simply codifies China's position, and can be regarded as a restrained response to Chen's provocative rhetoric during Taiwan's 2004 election year. The anti-secession law is as much directed at a hard-line domestic audience in the PRC, as Hu Jintao solidifies his position in power, as it is at Chen.[43] Indeed, in reference to the parliamentary victory for the pan-blue camp in December, Hu spoke of "signs of relaxation" in relations, with "new and positive factors" dampening support for Taiwanese independence.[44] The pan-blue camp's victory has certainly ensured that Chen's objective of a new Taiwanese Constitution for 2008 will not be realized. On her return from Asia in early 2005, Condoleezza Rice revealed that the PRC leadership "talked a good deal about what they were going to try to do to reduce tensions in the Taiwan Strait".[45] A soft landing remains the ultimate goal. While they may differ over the ultimate solution, they both wish to retain the current status quo. Thus, Rice's comments about the anti-secession law were muted; they merely reaffirmed the US position that neither the PRC nor the ROC should take unilateral steps to change the status quo. Rice simply noted the law as an unwelcome development because it increased tensions and the United States "are not pleased when either side does anything unilaterally to either try to change the status quo or that increases tensions".[46] The US response does indicate that a tacit understanding based on restraint is emerging in Sino–US relations over Taiwan.

Future prospects

It is evident that cooperation in the Sino–US relationship conforms to our understanding of rational egoist actors pursuing their national interest by calculating whether it pays to cooperate or defect. Although there is evidence that since 11 September 2001 a greater degree of restraint in their relationship can be discerned, this has not yet established the norms of behaviour that would make defection seem costly and therefore unlikely; a security regime is not in operation. Is a security regime possible? While the degree of restraint shown over North Korea is not in itself evidence of a security regime, the possibility would be enhanced if the six-party talks became institutionalized. In the case of Taiwan, however, China's domestic imperative complicates regime formation. The preference for the status quo and willingness to show restraint are positive factors, but whether a security regime can develop, where Sino–US relations indicate more than the following of short-run self-interest, is unlikely when a powerful domestic imperative (regime legitimacy) ensures that reunification, even the hard way, takes precedence over anything else. What the anti-secessionist law, and America's response, indicates is that currently both calculate that cooperation is their best means of constraining Chen and avoiding war.

Although current Sino–US relations exemplify cooperation between two rational egoists, is a deeper level of cooperation possible based on our understanding of solidarity? Does the Sino–US relationship have the potential to form a security community? It is important to recall that a security community is a non-war community based upon a shared sense of identity. It is that "we-feeling", the recognition that one's security is bound to the other, which means war is simply not an option for resolving disputes that arise. There is a general assumption amongst scholars working on security communities that this shared sense of identity is based upon a common commitment to liberalism and democracy. Adler and Barnett note two reasons for this. They argue that, first, with an emphasis on the rule of law, tolerance, duty of citizens and the role of government, liberal ideas can create a shared transnational civic culture, and thereby engender a sense of common identity. Second, they note that liberal ideas can promote the existence of strong civil societies between the member states because they encourage the exchange of people, goods and ideas. While this is true, Adler and Barnett note that other ideologies could also promote transnational exchanges, policy coordination and establishment of institutions, which ultimately promote a collective purpose from which a sense of shared identity is formed. They note the developmentalist ideology of South-east Asia as an alternative to liberalism, which has underpinned a number of ASEAN projects initiated since Burma, Cambodia, Laos and Vietnam joined.[47] The key point though is that the members share this common ideology, whether it be liberalism or not, and this is evidently not the case in the Sino–US relationship.

The implication is that if a security community is to form, domestic change in China will be a necessary precondition. China's political system enables the elite to deny their workers trade union rights; to ruthlessly suppress organizations that the elite regard as a threat, whether they are political or religious; to suffocate ethnic minorities; and with corruption rampant, to place themselves above the law. The differences between China and America that make a sense of "we-feeling" difficult to establish can be easily appreciated in terms of human rights. It is a topic that produces frequent condemnation from Washington; indeed the United States has filed a UN resolution condemning China's human rights record almost every year since the suppression of the Tiananmen Square protests in 1989. The difficulty arises because the emphasis placed on individualism in the West stands in contrast to the traditional Asian emphasis on society. Steeped in Confucian philosophy that prizes social harmony, the Chinese have traditionally seen protection for their social and economic welfare grounded in members of the society fulfilling their obligations and a strong government ruling righteously; not the expansion of their individual liberties. Confucianism is a system of obligations in which the members of society show deference to their rulers and the rulers reign in a benevolent manner for the best interests of society. The CCP's approach to human rights "bears the heavy imprint of traditional Confucianism", which was also seized upon in the 1990s by Malaysia and Singapore to explain why Asian values underpinned the economic success of the Asian "Tiger" economies.[48]

It is from a Confucian perspective that the CCP defends its human rights record. The CCP therefore highlights the improving living standards, education provision, medical care and welfare services that have seen dramatic improvements in raising average incomes, literacy and life expectancy since 1949 as evidence that it is meeting its obligations to provide for Chinese society.[49] The importance of being seen to be "righteous" rulers also underpins the drive against corruption in government. Corruption amongst government officials has increasingly been singled out by the CCP as undermining their rule and is routinely referred to as determining the "life and death of the party".[50]

The problem for the West, and the difficulty of establishing a sense of shared identity, for the most part arises in the political realm. In keeping with the traditional notion of deference, the CCP has not tolerated challenges to its authority; indeed, criticism of the government is illegal according to one of the Party's "Four Cardinal Principles". Portraying itself as defenders of Chinese society, the CCP has crushed internal criticism by arguing that internal disorder invites foreign intervention and exploitation. This was captured in the brutal suppression of students peacefully protesting in Tiananmen Square in June 1989, on the grounds they were dangerous subversives acting on behalf of foreign enemies of China. Since the late 1990s the CCP has targeted the quasi religious Falun Gong movement. Fearing that this movement could act as an alternative for people's loyalty, the CCP has banned the Falun Gong and arrested its leaders. It is this unwillingness to countenance criticism, maintaining a one-party authoritarian political system, that makes cooperation between Beijing and Washington based on solidarity principles a non-starter.

There is then little prospect of a "we-feeling" developing with America and, despite China's sensitivity to its international image, there is little prospect of imminent change. Evidence of this was provided in April 2004 when Beijing used its "right of re-interpretation" of the Basic Law (the mini-constitution for Hong Kong) to change the process of broadening democracy in the Special Administrative Region. The Basic Law allowed the Region to propose changes, debate them and pass them through the Region's institutions, only then could Beijing have a say. Beijing's re-interpretation allows it to now determine in advance whether change is needed. Yahuda writes, "its fear of democratization is so great that Beijing has been willing to weaken the 'high autonomy' promised to Hong Kong, despite its clear understanding that its actions could damage its standing with Western countries and weaken still further the already low appeal that its proposed formula of 'one country, two systems' enjoys in Taiwan".[51] Clinton put it succinctly when in 1998 he told Jiang Zemin China was on the "wrong side of history" as long as its rulers did not accept democracy as the organizing principle of modern governance; only a post-communist China would deserve the world's respect.[52]

Conclusion

Sino–US relations are clearly not at the security community end of Buzan's security complex spectrum. Not only is war between them a possibility but the type of shared identity that underpins solidarity is also not evident. The relationship is not though at the conflict formation end of the spectrum either, as they have, especially since 11 September 2001, engaged with one another to manage a series of crises, most notably Korea and tacitly Taiwan. Sino–US cooperation therefore lies somewhere between the enmity and amity end of Buzan's spectrum.

Since solidarity does not underpin Sino–US cooperation, this reveals that the two are egoist actors that are calculating whether cooperation is beneficial; they are self-interested, not other-regarding. The implication is that if they calculate that it no longer pays to cooperate they will defect. Defection would, for example, be manifest by the United States or China withdrawing from the six-party talks and in broader US terms it would mean placing more emphasis on containing rather than engaging China. The closer the Sino–US relationship is to the amity end of the spectrum the less likely it is that defection will occur. Toward the amity end of the spectrum is a security regime, hence the question of whether a nascent security regime is forming in Sino–US relations because, if it is, this will lessen the fear of defection.

There are some promising signs that a security regime could emerge. It has been shown that China's self-image as a responsible power has made it increasingly sensitive to the image others have of it and this has encouraged Beijing to operate within norms of behaviour; more often referred to as socializing China into acceptable international norms of behaviour. This helps to explain its continuing membership of various institutions and its willingness to adopt multilateral solutions to resolve points of contention. It indicates that the state elite increasingly no longer see multilateralism as a sacrifice of national interests but rather as a means of achieving national interests. This helps to explain why, when Sino–US relations improved after 11 September, a multilateral approach was pursued by Beijing to manage the Korean crisis. The appreciation that national interests can be accomplished via cooperation has engendered a degree of restraint in the way China and the United States have pursued their objectives. This restraint can be witnessed in both their management of the Korean crisis and Taiwan. It does not, however, indicate a security regime is forming.

A security regime lessens fears of defection because there is an expectation that by acting within norms of behaviour the members will restrain their behaviour. Such restraint has been witnessed in the Sino–US relationship. However, the form of cooperation that arises has to denote more than the following of short-term self-interest for it to form a security regime. It is not evident that this is happening. Therefore, the Sino–US relationship can be plotted on the security complex spectrum near, but not at the same point as, a security regime. Although the form of cooperation is too closely associated with the pursuit of short-term self-interest for the relationship to be a security regime, the building blocks for what is required for a security regime are forming – preference for the status quo, desire to avoid war, establishing norms to guide state actions (six-party talks; tacit understanding over Taiwan), restraining their behaviour – and given time these could create confidence in Beijing and Washington that the other will not gain from defection. If this occurs then a security regime can form because they will be able to sacrifice their short-term self-interest in the knowledge the other will not take advantage. However, since this has not yet happened it is too soon to claim a nascent security regime has formed.

In terms of policy prescription, this would entail Washington continuing to engage with China and, given China's newfound preference for multilateralism, such an approach is likely to find a receptive audience in Beijing. While a multilateral approach is largely unproblematic for the Korean crisis, in the case of Taiwan, which Beijing regards as a domestic issue, it is not feasible. Instead, the United States should continue to maintain its strategic ambiguity and dissuade either Taipei or Beijing from changing the status quo. This is the best means of managing the issue of Taiwan because the decision-makers in Washington and Beijing see time as on their side; they both calculate that with China's integration into the world economy, and increasing economic and social contacts between the mainland and Taiwan, the more problematic resort to a "hard landing" will become to achieve reunification. It is also pertinent to note that, despite the current Taiwanese administration's stance on independence, the Taiwanese people also favour the current status quo.

A word of caution, though, needs to be noted. Sino–US cooperation is managing crises, it is not resolving them. Beijing would prefer a divided Korea with Kim Jung-Il's communist state in place, rather than border a united Korea under the rule of America's ally, Seoul. Likewise, the future of Taiwan is bound to the CCP's legitimacy and this takes precedence over tacit understandings with Washington. While Beijing has no desire to force reunification the "hard" way this is preferable, even if it means war with the United States, to allowing Taiwan to secede. Not only would Taiwanese independence encourage other secessionist demands from, for example, Tibet or Xinjiang, but more importantly it could also undermine CCP rule. A resolution to the crises in North-east Asia therefore requires Beijing to de-link Taiwan from the regime's legitimacy and recognize the greater long-term stability a united, rather than artificially divided, Korea will create. Whether such a change in policy can be accomplished while China remains communist is a moot point.

Notes

1. Clinton used the term "strategic partner" during his 1998 visit to China. It was during the presidential election in 2000 that Bush referred to China as a competitor.
2. Martin Kettle and John Hooper (2001) "Bush Says U.S. Force Is an Option to Defend Taiwan", *Guardian*, 26 April.
3. Michael Yahuda (2006) *The International Politics of the Asia-Pacific*, 2nd ed., London: RoutledgeCurzon, p. 266.
4. Susan V. Lawrence (2004) "How China Relations Improved: An Insider's View", *Far Eastern Economic Review*, 28 October.
5. John Gittings (2001) "U.S. Claims China and Russia as Allies", *Guardian*, 22 October.
6. Barry Buzan (1991) *People, States and Fear: An Agenda for International Security Studies in the Post–Cold War Era*, 2nd ed., Hemel Hempstead, England: Harvester Wheatsheaf, p. 190.
7. Barry Buzan (1992) "Third World Regional Security in Structural and Historical Perspective", in Brain L. Job, ed., *The Insecurity Dilemma: National Security of Third World States*, Boulder, Colo.: Lynne Rienner, p. 168.
8. For conflict formation, see Raimo Väyrynen (1984) "Regional Conflict Formations: An Intractable Problem of International Relations", *Journal of Peace Research* 21(4): 357–359. For security community, see Karl Deutsch (1957) *Political Community and the North Atlantic Area: International Organization in the Light of Historic Experience*, Princeton, N.J.: Princeton University Press.
9. Barry Buzan and Ole Wæver (2003) *Regions and Powers: The Structure of International Security*, Cambridge: Cambridge University Press, p. 71.
10. Barry Buzan (2003) "Security Architecture in Asia: The Interplay of Regional and Global Levels", *Pacific Review* 16(2): 164.
11. For a recent reference to continuing Chinese–Japanese animosity see Jonathan Watts (2005) "Tokyo Makes Protest after Anti-Japanese Violence in China", *Guardian*, 11 April.
12. Emanuel Adler and Michael Barnett (1998) "A Framework for the Study of Security Communities" in Emanuel Adler and Michael Barnett, eds, *Security Communities*, Cambridge: Cambridge University Press, p. 36.
13. Amitav Acharya (2001) *Constructing a Security Community in Southeast Asia: ASEAN and the Problem of Regional Order*, London: Routledge.
14. Robert Jervis (1982) "Security Regimes", *International Organization* 36(2), Spring: 360–362.
15. Ibid., p. 357.
16. For details of the containment/engagement debate see David Shambaugh (1996) "Containment or Engagement of China? Calculating Beijing's Responses", *International Security* 21(2), Fall: 180–209. Also see Denny Roy (1994) "Hegemon On the Horizon? China's Threat to East Asian Security", *International Security* 19(1), Summer: 149–168; Avery Goldstein (1997) "Great Expectations: Interpreting China's Arrival", *International Security* 22(3), Winter: 36–73.
17. Gerald Segal (1996) "East Asia and the 'Constrainment' of China", *International Security* 20(4), Spring: 107–135.
18. Alastair Iain Johnston and Paul Evans (1999) "China's Engagement with Multilateral Security Institutions", in Alastair Iain Johnston and Robert S. Ross, eds, *Engaging China: The Management of an Emerging Power*, London: Routledge, p. 245.
19. Ibid., p. 252.
20. Ibid., p. 253.

21. Ibid.
22. Yahuda, *The International Politics of the Asia-Pacific*, p. 299.
23. Wen Jiabao (2003) "Turning Your Eyes to China", *People's Daily*, 10 December, available from http://english.peopledaily.com.cn/200312/12/eng20031212_130267.shtml, accessed 30 May 2006. Also see Farah Stockman (2003) "Visit Takes Political Flavor: Chinese Premier Says Democracy Is Goal; Chinese Premier Touts Democracy", *Boston Globe*, 11 December.
24. Yahuda, *The International Politics of the Asia-Pacific*, p. 306.
25. David Shambaugh (2004) "China Engages Asia: Reshaping the Regional Order", *International Security* 29(3), Winter: 76.
26. Ibid., p. 77.
27. Ibid., p. 64.
28. The second round was held in February 2004 and the third in June 2004; the fourth, held in 2005, was divided into two phases (26 July–7 August, 13–19 September); the fifth round extended from November 2005 until February 2007 and was divided into three phases (9–11 November 2005, 18–22 December 2006, 8–13 February 2007) and the sixth round, at the time writing, has completed its first phase (19–22 March 2007).
29. Francis Fukuyama (2005) "Re-Envisioning Asia", *Foreign Affairs* 84(1), January/February: 83–86. Also see Shambaugh, "China Engages Asia", p. 88.
30. Chris Buckley (2005) "Rice Warns N. Korea Standoff Can't Last", *International Herald Tribune*, 22 March.
31. Quoted from Satoshi Ogawa and Aya Igarashi (2005) "Bilateral Talks Revive Old Issues", *Daily Yomiuri*, Japan, 22 February.
32. Anna Fifield and Richard McGregor (2005) "Hopes Rise for Resumption of Nuclear Talks After U-Turn by North Korea", *Financial Times*, 23 February. Also see Joe McDonald (2005) "Chinese Leader Steps Up Pressure On North Korea to Resume Nuclear Talks, Calling Them 'Only Correct Choice'", *Associated Press*, 23 March.
33. Walter Pincus (2005) "End to Arms Sale Delay Sought", *Washington Post*, 2 February.
34. Joel Brinkley (2005) "China Balks at Pressing the North Koreans", *New York Times*, 22 March.
35. Nicholas Kralev (2005) "Rice Warns N. Korea of 'Other Options'", *Washington Times*, 22 March.
36. In 2002 one of China's vice-premiers, Qian Qichen, said the One China principle could be set aside when discussing the issue of direct cross-strait transport links.
37. Most experts state that China's actions gave Lee an additional 5 to 10 per cent of the popular vote. See Michael A. Glosny (2004) "Strangulation from the Sea? A PRC Submarine Blockade of Taiwan", *International Security* 28(4), Spring: 152.
38. For greater coverage of this incident see Mel Gurtov and Byong-Moo Hwang (1998) *China's Security: The New Roles of the Military*, Boulder, Colo.: Lynne Rienner, pp. 266–279.
39. For details on how, by applying pressure on Taiwan, China could achieve unification without resorting to a military invasion see Bruce Gilley (1998) "Operation Mind Games", *Far Eastern Economic Review*, 28 May, pp. 31–32. For China preferring reunification via economic exchanges rather than forcibly via military action, see Robert S. Ross (2002) "Navigating the Taiwan Strait: Deterrence, Escalation Dominance, and U.S.–China Relations", *International Security* 27(2), Fall: 71.
40. See Danny Gittings (2000) "China Threatens to Attack Taiwan", *Guardian*, 22 February.
41. "Not So Fast, Mr Chen", *Economist*, US Edition, 18 December 2004.
42. Lawrence Chung (2004) "U.S. Not Obliged to Defend Taiwan", *Straits Times*, Singapore, 23 December.

43. Edward Cody (2005) "China's Law On Taiwan Backfires: Anti-Secession Measure Hurts Efforts Abroad", *Washington Post*, 24 March.
44. "Hu Warns Against Independence Moves", *Taipei Times*, 5 March 2005.
45. "Mainland Interpreting Subtle Messages from Taipei's Protest March", *South China Morning Post*, 28 March 2005.
46. Flor Wang (2005) "Taiwan Welcomes Rice's Comments on Anti-Secession Law", *BBC Monitoring Asia Pacific – Political*, 22 March.
47. Adler and Barnett, *Security Communities*, pp. 40–41.
48. Robert Weatherley (1999) *The Discourse of Human Rights in China: Historical and Ideological Perspectives*, Basingstoke, England: Macmillan, p. 102. For the Asian Values debate and human rights, see Michael K. Connors (2004) "Culture and Politics in the Asia-Pacific: Asian Values and Human Rights", in Michael K. Connors, Rémy Davison and Jörn Dosch, eds, *The New Global Politics of the Asia-Pacific*, London: Routledge-Curzon, pp. 199–213.
49. Kenneth Christie and Denny Roy (2001) *The Politics of Human Rights in East Asia*, London: Pluto Press, pp. 219–233.
50. For example, see Joe McDonald (2004) "China's Communist Party Calls for Better Government, Warning That Its Rule Could Hang in the Balance", *Associated Press*, 26 September.
51. Yahuda, *The International Politics of the Asia-Pacific*, p. 308.
52. Gerald Segal (1998) "It's Not Such a Big Dragon, After All", *Sunday Times*, 28 June.

Part II

Assessing the logic of solidarity and national interest in great power interventionism

3

Cultures of solidarity and national interest: Russia's conflict management policies

Ekaterina Stepanova

Russia's involvement in post–Cold War regional conflicts in neighbouring states and, occasionally, in other regions, has been most commonly explained as a result of Russia's geostrategic thinking and policy driven by Russia's national interests as they are understood, interpreted and formulated by its leadership. As geostrategy is commonly defined as designing foreign policy around the idea of the national interest, nation-states are by definition more inclined to stick to geostrategic approaches than are international organizations whose very existence is a result of international cooperation and where geostrategic interests of the leading member-states have to be mutually reconciled, are present in a more moderate form and may be reinforced and supplemented by shared values, cultures and so on.

In the early years following the end of the Cold War, the geostrategic paradigm seemed to give way to more idealistic, normative and value-based approaches. International organizations and multilateral policy-making gained increased prominence at the expense of certain traditional prerogatives of nation-states. At the same time, international affairs remained primarily driven by state interests that may, although do not necessarily have to, reflect the imprint of unilateralism that may lead to more tension, instability and confrontation. One of the most vivid and high-profile examples of this approach at the global level was and remains the US unilateralism further reinforced at the outset of a new century by the new focus on the fight against terrorism. In a post–11 September environment, the United States, driven primarily by its own strategic

National interest and international solidarity: Particular and universal ethics in international life, Coicaud and Wheeler (eds),
United Nations University Press, 2008, ISBN 978-92-808-1147-6

concerns, went to extremes in its unilateralist approach, as it undertook its unconstrained 2003 intervention in Iraq that served as a peak of the US "unipolar moment".

In contrast to the national interest paradigm, the international solidarity approach is based on a strong belief that norms and values can reconstitute state behaviour. According to this theory, a genuine solidarity culture stems, first and foremost, from values (norms, beliefs etc.) that are shared and that create a moral commitment to the welfare of others. International solidarity manifests itself at both regional and global levels and, as viewed in this chapter, at both state and broader public level. As far as regional models of security cooperation are concerned, the clearest expression of international solidarity has been a security community where war between members is unthinkable (such as NATO in the Euro-Atlantic region or the EU in Europe). It is, however, solidarity at the global level on issues, largely overlooked, if not completely ignored during the Cold War, due to preoccupation with security and strategic considerations, that was most vividly stimulated by the economic, social, technological and political developments of the late twentieth century, such as the end of the East–West confrontation, in particular. The ever-growing prominence of human rights, the moral dimension of humanitarian interventions in the 1990s, the increasingly widespread view of state sovereignty as a responsibility and the world-wide humanitarian response to such catastrophic natural disasters as the December 2004 tsunami that badly hurt countries of South and South-east Asia are all clear expressions of an emerging global solidarity culture.

Even within this briefly defined, morally based international solidarity framework, a number of questions remain about the nature of the "shared values" that are supposed to form the basis for the post–Cold War solidarity culture. This leads us to distinguish between at least two general types of solidarity culture. The so-called "traditional human solidarity" is based on a limited, but more or less universally accepted set of values, reflecting the most basic human principles – that is, those embedded in the human rights provisions of the UN Charter – and stressing commonality and conformity rather than the ideological nature of the values. In contrast, the Western[1] "liberal democratic solidarity" concept implies that a genuine culture of international solidarity can emerge only as an intrinsic part of cooperation between fully developed democracies. While, in this case, a set of values to be shared is more extensive, the claim about their more inclusive nature, made by proponents of the concept, is hardly acceptable for many in the non-Western world. This is especially evident when the so-called "modern democratic values", emphasizing Western-type democratic development and interpretation of human rights, are compromised by attempts to impose them by violent means, as demonstrated by NATO's 1999 war against Yugoslavia. The world is too complex and too culturally diverse to be dominated by only one type of solidarity – a uniform Western "liberal democratic solidarity". The proponents of this concept emphasize, among other things, seeing the "other" as part of "we", as well as a sense of "international responsibility", as characteristics unique and specific to this concept. But similar characteristics bearing a different cultural and value substance can arguably be applied to non-Western parts of the world as well (for instance, to the Muslim solidarity and "sense of responsibility").[2]

Another important distinction (that is not always easily made) is between moral solidarity, which may be based on either "modern democratic" or more traditionally understood shared values but is still driven by the solidarity logic, and various strategic, economic, political and other incentives to cooperate that may lead to the so-called functional cooperation that stems from national interest logic and does not imply value-based solidarity logic. In other words, the national interest logic does not have to be confrontational or unilateralist and may lead to cooperative behaviour ("functional cooperation"), when it is realized that the long-term national interest is in cooperation with the other.[3]

With "pure" moral incentive remaining a fragile motivation indeed, most real-world cooperative behavioural patterns and scenarios in fact fall short of the morally defined solidarity pattern described above, normally presenting a common denominator of partners' self-interests. While the approach does not imply "solidarity" as such, it is not amoral by definition. It might even be argued that the strong advantage of this approach, in contrast to the morally defined solidarity paradigm, is sensitivity to, understanding of and ability to consider and even partly reconcile cultural and normative differences between actors belonging to radically or significantly different cultural and value systems (or culturally defined "civilizations"), such as the West and various parts of the Muslim world.

For the "developed" world, the increasing prevalence of behavioural patterns motivated by a combination of moral considerations and self-interest of some kind brings the issue of complementarity and/or competitiveness between the geostrategic and solidarity paradigms to the forefront. For instance, while there is no question that the world's most developed democratic states are frequently guided by solidarity culture in shaping their behaviour toward one another, and demonstrate elements of international solidarity culture in addressing selected issues of global concern, in their relations with states that do not share some or most Western values national interests and geo-strategic considerations and concerns often prevail.

In the first post–Cold War decade, Russian foreign policy has undergone several shifts: from infatuation with the "democratic solidarity" discourse of the early 1990s, at the expense of the country's national strategic interests; to disillusionment with Western policies, fuelled by the NATO enlargement process; to a resurgence of geostrategic thinking by the mid-1990s; and, finally, to the more balanced approach of the early 2000s, generally formulated in line with the "functional cooperation" paradigm but including some elements of the "global solidarity culture".

Russia's involvement in conflicts within the CIS

Throughout the 1990s, Moscow's frequent disagreements with the United States and other Western states over regional conflicts was most commonly interpreted in the West as a manifestation of a "post-imperial syndrome" and an attempt to recover once lost geostrategic positions, seen as the main imperatives driving Russia's external behaviour. At the same time, less attention was paid to the fact that no other major country in the post–Cold War world had undergone changes as deep and profound as Russia had. Although this adaptation was a rather painful process, it may have created incentives for Russia to be better disposed to adjust to the current international realities than many of its former Western counterparts (especially the United States) that were not subject to internal or external changes of the same scale and intensity. Russia entered the twenty-first century as a regional Eurasian power, relatively weak as compared to its former Cold War Western adversaries and relatively strong as compared to most of its immediate neighbours in the post-Soviet space. It was preoccupied with its own domestic, primarily social and economic problems and confronted with remnants of local and regional instability along its periphery, particularly to the south of its borders. With a nuclear arms potential still second only to that of the United States, Russia itself could no longer politically and economically afford direct military intervention in a regional conflict outside its own territory – either unilaterally, within the Commonwealth of Independent States (CIS), or, as some would argue, even as part of a multilateral military coalition outside the CIS.

In their analyses of Russian interventions in the post-Soviet space as manifestations of Russian geostrategic thinking, most Russian and foreign authors refer to the early 1990s as the earliest and most difficult stage of the post-Soviet "transitional" period.[4] However, less attention has been paid to the fact that Russia was going through an initial stage of post-Soviet state-building, and what was interpreted as Russian "interventionism" was often a euphemism for non-controlled developments immediately following the collapse of the old Soviet system (the rapid fragmentation of the existing state and security institutions, the eruption of violent conflicts in various republics of the former USSR etc.). As demonstrated by two coup attempts (December 1991 and August 1993), the remnants of this system made themselves visible in Russia itself as much as in other post-Soviet states. One of the key remnants of the old system was the ex-Soviet armed forces, which were stationed all over the former USSR. The political command and control of these forces was not always clear; they often found themselves caught in the middle of hostilities and had to act on their own initiative.

Against this background, Russia's involvement in conflicts within and between the former Soviet republics in the early 1990s is viewed in this chapter as a largely inevitable side-effect of the earliest, most critical stage of the complex and radical transformation of the former Soviet space (and of related state-building processes in all of the "new independent states", including Russia). Overall, this transformation was relatively peaceful, as compared both to Russia's own history and to the collapse of another large multinational socialist state, Yugoslavia. The transformation processes also involved the search for Russia's new, not just post-Soviet, but also "post-imperial" national and state identity. Russia never existed in its post-Soviet borders before and, historically, Russians always thought of themselves as part of something larger than Russia itself.

It should also be stressed that, prior to the events of 11 September 2001 and the following "war on terrorism", for the world's leading powers there was hardly any direct risk to national security in ignoring unfolding post–Cold War conflicts, most of which were of relatively low intensity and of an internal character. Thus, for much of the 1990s, for both the United States and its Western partners, getting involved in most regional conflicts and crises was largely a matter of choice. In contrast, Russia could hardly afford to ignore actual or potential conflicts unfolding along its own borders, in the so-called "near abroad", even if it wanted to. The rapid decline of Russia's international capabilities and ambitions was perhaps most vividly reflected by Russia's involvement in local and regional conflicts. For post-Soviet Russia, this involvement was largely limited either to conflicts on Russia's own soil (Chechnya) or to cross-border spillover disturbances and conflicts in neighbouring or nearby CIS states (Moldova/Transdniestria, Georgia/Abkhazia, Tajikistan and so on). While Russia was still to some extent involved in conflict management efforts in more distant regions (for example, in the Balkans), such involvement increasingly became an exception, rather than the rule.

From our perspective, the cases that best illustrate Russia's involvement in and management of the CIS conflicts throughout the 1990s are the ones between Moldova and Transdniestria and between Georgia and

Abkhazia. Both conflicts go back to the early 1990s, when in the process of the disintegration of the USSR both self-proclaimed statelets (Transdniestria and Abkhazia) declared themselves sovereign republics, independent from their respective post-Soviet states (Moldova and Georgia).

An inconclusive 1992 war between Moldova and its breakaway Transdniestrian region was quelled by the intervention of Russian troops stationed in the region since Soviet times. The violent stage of the conflict ended with a Russia-mediated settlement, short of any final agreement on the region's political status. While in the following years the chances for a new breakout of hostilities were slim, little progress was achieved, despite a series of agreements negotiated under tripartite international mediation by Russia, Ukraine and the Organization for Security and Co-operation in Europe (OSCE) or the more recent mediation initiatives, such as the "five plus two" format introduced in October 2005 (Moldova, Transdniestria, the OSCE, Russia and Ukraine, with the United States and the European Union as observers).

After fierce fighting between the forces of the Republic of Georgia and of the breakaway Abkhazia in 1992/93 and several ceasefire violations, on 14 May 1994, as a result of several rounds of difficult negotiations, the Georgian and Abkhaz sides signed the Agreement on a Ceasefire and Separation of Forces in Moscow, under the auspices of the United Nations. The parties agreed to the deployment of a CIS peacekeeping force to monitor compliance with the Agreement, while the United Nations agreed to monitor implementation of the agreement and to observe the operation of the CIS force. As in the case of Moldova, Russia emerged as the main facilitator of the negotiating process, as well as the only CIS state involved in the peacekeeping mission (no other CIS state had sufficient resources or intent to sustain a peacekeeping contingent). With support from the United Nations and the OSCE, efforts to stabilize the situation and to achieve a comprehensive political settlement, including an agreement on the future political status of Abkhazia and the return of Georgian internally displaced persons, continued throughout the 1990s and early 2000s with little success.

Despite the lack of any visible progress in solving the two conflicts, they have remained effectively "frozen" throughout the decade. In contrast to the early 1990s, for the rest of the decade, the main trend in Russia's behaviour toward these (and other) conflicts on the post-Soviet space has been its slowly, but steadily increasing rationalization, coupled with its gradual, if unfinished, military withdrawal from these and most other CIS regions. Among the general factors that contributed to this process, Russia's domestic economic and security considerations played a most critical role. Since 1994, when the conflict in Chechnya came to a head on Russia's own territory, Moscow reaffirmed its support for territorial integrity of the new independent post-Soviet states. Similarly, at the 1999 OSCE Istanbul summit, Russia agreed to cut its military presence in Georgia and Moldova in exchange for the OSCE approval of more favourable flank limits in the North Caucasus, where Moscow had deployed a significant joint group of forces for an indefinite period due to the conflict in Chechnya and general instability in the region.

In contrast to Russia's domestic political, economic and security considerations, its participation in limited multilateral decision-making efforts and interaction with an even more limited OSCE presence in Moldova[5] and the United Nations[6] and OSCE missions in Georgia[7] did not appear to have played a major role in gradual rationalization and moderation of Moscow's policies in either of the "frozen" conflict zones. It often seemed that international actors were much more preoccupied with the task of speeding the withdrawal of the remnants of post-Soviet Russia's military presence from, and limiting the Russian influence in, both regions than with the root causes of violence and long-term conflict resolution efforts. This approach can be partly explained by both geostrategically and culturally motivated distrust of Russia's intentions in its "near abroad" and by a widespread view of the Russian military presence as one of the key factors exacerbating tensions rather than having a stabilizing influence throughout the CIS.

Whilst heavily criticizing Russian efforts to create some level of stability along its borders by trying to prevent large-scale internal violence in the CIS, the non-CIS international actors were consistently unwilling to take up any major responsibility in this area. During the first post–Cold War decade, major Western states and international organizations were very reluctant to commit significant resources to field operations in conflict areas. When, for instance, at the end of 2001, the withdrawal of Russia's peacekeepers from the zone of the Georgian–Abkhaz conflict seemed quite plausible, given Tbilisi's reluctance to extend their mandate, neither the OSCE nor the UN showed any enthusiasm to establish the badly needed security presence in the conflict zone to replace Russian peacekeepers.

Overall, whilst some international presence within the OSCE and/or the UN framework had been in place in both of these cases, its positive impact was limited. Rather, it was both the conflicts' internal Chisinau–Tiraspol and Tbilisi–Sukhumi dynamics and the logic of Russia's bilateral relations with Moldova and Georgia that determined the course of events in both frozen conflict zones and has so far prevented a new escalation of violence. These factors explain a somewhat different course that the developments in the two conflict zones took in the early 2000s.

In the case of the Moldova–Transdniestria dispute, there were indications of a stabilization, if not a breakthrough, in the peace process. The situation continued to stabilize and slowly improve up until the rejection by the Moldovan government in November 2003 of the Russian peace plan for this troubled region (the "Kozak" plan). Under heavy pressure from the OSCE and Western states, Moldova turned down Russia's proposal for a demilitarized "asymmetrical federation" arrangement for Moldova and its autonomous Gagauz and breakaway Transdniestria regions, despite this previously being approved by both Moldovan and Transdniestrian leaderships.[8]

By contrast, tensions between Georgia and Abkhazia never ceased. Furthermore, since the November 2003 coup in Georgia (the "revolution of roses") that forced president Eduard Shevardnadze out of office and brought to power a nationalist pro-Western leader Mikhail Saakashvili, who repeatedly threatened to use force against Georgia's breakaway regions – Abkhazia and South Ossetiya – the possibility of a renewal of full-scale hostilities became more realistic than at any time since the early 1990s.

In terms of internal political dynamics, the relatively more stable situation in the Moldova–Transdniestrian case can be explained by the fact that, as compared to the ethnic Georgian–Abkhaz conflict, there was no insuperable ethnic antagonism between the protagonists in Moldova, where multifarious social and economic contacts with the Transdniestrian region were retained throughout the 1990s. The key external explanation, however, can be found in the general context of both states' bilateral relations with Russia. Among other things, the Moldovan–Transdniestrian conflict, while important, did not appear to be directly connected to Russia's national interests, in contrast to the situation in and around Abkhazia.

Moscow's official position on Moldova's dispute with its Transdniestrian region had been ambiguous since the conflict erupted, reflecting the complex balance of forces in Russian politics and conflicting foreign policy interests. On the one hand, having prevented a full-scale massacre and further regional destabilization by directly intervening in the midst of conflict (on the Transdniestrian side, as claimed by some political forces in Moldova), Moscow had a rational interest in keeping Moldova as a sovereign and neutral state and as a CIS member and partner and tried to induce separatists in Tiraspol to make greater concessions to Chisinau. On the other hand, the Russian government for some time could not completely ignore sectors of its own public and elite opinion, calling for support to the "Russian-speaking compatriots" in Transdniestria who did not want to rejoin Moldova just to find themselves one day as part of "Greater Romania". Peace negotiations were also complicated by the linkage between a political solution to the conflict and withdrawal of the former Soviet 14th Army. The Moldovan constitution of July 1994 established the "permanent neutrality" of Moldova and prohibited the stationing of foreign troops on Moldovan territory, and Chisinau insisted that withdrawal was a precondition for a settlement. In October 1994, Russia and Moldova signed an initial agreement on withdrawal of Russian troops from Moldova within three years, but the process remained stalled for much longer by a number of factors. These factors included the intransigence of Tiraspol's regime; blocking shipments of arms and ammunition; Russia's and Ukraine's concerns about the geopolitical stability of the region, particularly in view of the pro-Romanian sympathies of parts of Moldova's elite; the inability of the Moldovan state to assure the Russian- and Ukrainian-speaking Transdniestrian minority of the central government's ability to accommodate their economic, cultural and political interests; and the lack of funding in Russia for withdrawal and/or utilization of arms, among others. In the early 2000s, the withdrawal continued, depending on the general political climate and the progress in peace talks (as of early 2007, the last removal of some of Russia's estimated 21 metric tons of munitions from Transdniestria occurred in March 2004).[9]

Against this background, it seems that it was the growing economic imperatives on both sides, as well as the "elite politics" factor in Chisinau and in Moscow, rather than international influence or pressure, that played a positive role in Moldova's peace process. The process remained blocked until the 2000 change of administration in Russia, which brought to power an increasingly pragmatic generation of leaders. This was complemented by the significant changes in Moldova's foreign and domestic policies, which occurred as a result of the Communists' victory at the February 2001 parliamentary elections (after ten years in opposition) over the pro-Western and pro-Romanian nationalist parties. Domestic political changes in Moldova, dictated, among other things, by clear economic interests (gas and electricity are delivered to Moldova by Russia and 70 per cent of the Moldavian exports go to CIS countries, especially to Russia and Ukraine), helped create a more favourable political climate for building a truly multiethnic state and engaging Transdniestria, even if not coupled by similar elite changes in Tiraspol. In April 2001, the Moldovan parliament finally ratified an intergovernmental agreement on military cooperation with Russia, signed in Moscow in July 1997. These political changes allowed Russia to begin the final stage of the complete withdrawal of its arms and military equipment from Transdniestria on 17 July 2001, in accordance with the obligations taken at the 1999 Istanbul

OSCE summit and as specified by the June 2001 trilateral agreement between the Russian Ministry of Defence, the Transdniestrian administration and the OSCE Mission.

The Transdniestrian separatist leadership repeatedly violated the terms
of an agreement and expressed its fierce opposition to Russian arms and
troop withdrawal, and even tried to physically stop the process, and in
the early 2000s, Tiraspol faced increasing isolation not just from the international community, but also from within the CIS, including from
Russia.[10] It may also be suggested that, as the Transdniestrian leadership
had no alternative to finding some form of compromise with Moldova, it
simply tried to get the most out of the arms and troop withdrawal process, both politically and financially.[11] The Transdniestrian leadership remained in the position of the main spoiler of the peace process up until
November 2003, when it actually joined the Moldovan leadership in its
initial approval of a Russia-sponsored "asymmetrical federation" peace
plan before the latter had to withdraw its initial support under heavy political pressure from the OSCE and the West in a move that effectively –
and indefinitely – blocked further progress in a peace process.

In contrast to the dispute between Moldova and Transdniestria, which
did not directly affect Russia's own security and thus left Moscow more
room for political maneuvering, its approach to the conflict between
Georgia and Abkhazia has been dominated by geostrategic concerns.
The situation in Georgia was and remained complicated by a number of
factors. While Russian peacekeepers were deployed on the confrontation
line between the conflicting sides to ensure that the armistice was respected, Russia, which borders both Abkhazia and Georgia was interested in both securing the border and keeping close economic, cultural
and security ties to both entities. While heavily criticized by Tbilisi for
providing political and economic support to Abkhazia, Russia was
viewed in Abkhazia as the main and sole guarantor of its physical survival as a nation. To complicate matters further, with the lower-scale confrontation in Chechnya still underway and particularly as the Chechen
rebels experienced greater financial, logistic and political difficulties and
had to resort to increasingly asymmetrical forms of warfare, a potential
for cross-border spillover of violence from Chechnya to the neighbouring
Chechen-populated Pankisi Gorge in Georgia, as well as in the reverse
direction, remained. This spillover effect was particularly destabilizing as
long as Georgia remained a semi-failed state that had for several years
served as a hospitable refuge and a supply route for the Chechen militants.

The gradual withdrawal of Russian arms, military equipment and bases
from Georgia, so strongly insisted on by both Tbilisi and the West, neither guaranteed progress in peace talks with Abkhazia nor prevented

the central authorities in Tbilisi from engaging in paramilitary operations in conflict zones. By the end of 2000, Russia met the deadline that had been agreed to in Istanbul for the elimination of equipment in Georgia in excess of one basic temporary deployment under the Conventional Forces in Europe Treaty. In 2001, Russia finally withdrew two of its four bases in Georgia – Vaziani, near Tbilisi (handed over on 29 June 2001), and Gudauta (Abkhazia), evacuated in late October and early November 2001.[12] In that case, Russia's international obligations were fully in concurrence with its own military and economic imperatives. While, economically, it was no longer feasible to sustain the bases anyway, from the military/geostrategic point of view Russia could literally afford the withdrawal, as it concentrated on maintaining a more strategically important base in Giumri (Armenia), with the Armenian government's consent.

The scaling back of Russia's military presence in Georgia could not and did not prevent new crises between Georgia and Abkhazia. One of these broke out in October/November 2001 as a result of Tbilisi's support for an attempted invasion of Abkhazia by Chechen rebels, joined by Georgian paramilitaries; in August 2004, tensions were simmering again, as a result of saber rattling by Georgia's new president Saakashvili, threatening a new outbreak of interethnic conflict. The lack of any progress in the peace settlement in either of Georgia's breakaway regions, despite the significant reduction of the Russian military presence, suggested that the link between that residual military presence and Georgia's internal conflicts was not as straightforward and clear as it was often presented by the Georgian government or by Western observers. The remnants of Russia's military presence in Georgia (where, as of early 2007, about 3,000 remaining personnel were in the process of leaving two bases, Batumi and Ahalkalaki)[13] turned out to be largely irrelevant to the dynamics of Georgia's internal conflicts. Rather, it was the dramatic interplay between two of the region's conflicts (in Chechnya and in Abkhazia), coupled with the ineptitude of Georgian authorities, the political and economic crisis in Georgia and the deteriorating state of Georgian–Russian relations, that led to escalations of violence in the Georgian–Abkhaz conflict in the early 2000s. According to Georgian sources, Russia, claiming that Georgia had become a hospitable refuge for retreating Chechen militants, attacked Chechen armed groups from the air on both sides of the Russian–Georgian border. Moscow's official position on the new round of the Georgian–Abkhaz conflict remained restrained, with Russian President Vladimir Putin repeatedly declaring his support for the territorial integrity of Georgia and expressing Moscow's readiness to withdraw its peacekeepers from Abkhazia – a proposal immediately rejected by Shevardnadze. The situation rapidly deteriorated as a result of a combination of impulsive nationalist policies and brinkmanship on the part of Georgia's new leader Saakashvili, who became president in January 2004. His attempts to mobilize foreign support, particularly US military support, for his aggressive plans toward Abkhazia and South Ossetiya contributed to destabilization of the situation even though they appeared inconclusive and were not met with particular enthusiasm in the West.

In terms of external involvement, the situation in Georgia presented contrasts with the case of Moldova. In Moldova, most of the non-CIS external involvement was performed by an international organization (the OSCE) and even the process of further demilitarization of Transdniestria has been thoroughly internationalized (with the OSCE and the European Union providing solid financial support for the withdrawal and utilization of the formerly Soviet weapons and other military equipment by Russia). In Georgia, the international/multilateral efforts appeared to become increasingly marginalized by the direct military involvement of the United States. In the context of rapidly deteriorating relations with Abkhazia and Russia at the end of 2001, the Georgian authorities issued a formal request to the United States for military, technical and other support under the pretext of "the need to destroy the hotbed of terrorists in the Pankisi Gorge" – a threat previously consistently denied by Tbilisi. By deploying its military personnel in Georgia as part of the "train and equip" programme, the United States effectively reconciled its newly declared priority to fight terrorism all over the world with its strategic interests in the Caucasus – in close proximity to Russia's own borders and especially to Chechnya. The US military presence, no matter how limited, became increasingly important for Tbilisi as a lever of political and direct military pressure both on Abkhazia and South Ossetia, and indirect pressure on Russia. Georgia used helicopters, provided by the United States as part of the "train and equip" programme to "fight terrorists" for flights over Abkhazia, causing new political tensions. Since the deployment of US military personnel, the Georgian side extended its traditional demands[14] and toughened its negotiating position, insisting on creating the UN interim administration in the Gali region of Abkhazia – an idea unacceptable to the Abkhaz side and not technically feasible, due to numerous security constraints. More generally, the US involvement in Georgia had a dual impact on internal conflict and conflict resolution dynamics: while it allowed Tbilisi to toughen its negotiating position, thus making it more difficult for the parties to agree to a compromise solution, it was not openly supportive of some of Saakashvili's most ambitious and belligerent rhetoric and may have played a certain role in constraining his government's behaviour.

The main paradox in applying the solidarity-versus-national interest paradigm to Russia's involvement in conflicts within CIS states is that its most "interventionist" stage – the early 1990s – coincided with the period when Russia's foreign policy elites were mired in pro-Western romanticism and sincerely believed that, as Russia was no longer an ideological rival of the West, it would be very soon admitted to the "Western club" on the basis of shared ideals of democracy and an ethically-based solidarity. By contrast, it seems that Russia's move away from interventionism, its increasingly rational behaviour in parts of the former Soviet Union and general evolution of its foreign policy toward, for instance, putting a greater emphasis on economic interests, was primarily dictated by domestic imperatives of political stabilization and economic mobilization. Achieving this ultimately depended on the very ability to finally formulate and pursue its national interests, rather than to overlook them for the sake of some abstract morally defined values, as, by the rare, almost unanimous consensus among Russian experts on foreign policy, was the case in the early 1990s.

In the late 1990s and early 2000s, the emerging understanding of Russia's national interests stemmed from the primacy of geo-economics over geopolitics and from pragmatic concerns of creating favorable conditions for its economic modernization and social development, overcoming the country's current relative weakness, avoiding unnecessary military overstretch and so on. While Russia's participation in multilateral decision-making on many issues, including resolution of conflicts over the CIS space, was generally cooperative or, at least, non-confrontational, this "functional cooperation" approach was dictated primarily by the growing pragmatism of the Russian leadership and the gradual realization of the country's real capabilities and long-term legitimate national interests, rather than by any value-based solidarity logic. Among other things, one of Russia's strongest national interests is to build and preserve a stable and peaceful political, economic and security environment along its own borders.

At the same time it has to be recognized that, with some cooperation between Russia and its Western partners on conflict management within the CIS well underway, this cooperation was generally of limited effectiveness in that it neither led to any major breakthroughs in peace processes nor significantly contributed to encouraging Russia to develop elements of a solidarity culture. Moreover, in some cases external influences, both unilaterally and multilaterally exercised, could have even made the situation worse. For example, in the early 2000s, the positions of all key external mediators on the Moldova/Transdniestria dispute appeared to be almost fully concurrent. The OSCE's rejection in November 2003 of Russia's "Kozak peace plan" (that could help resolve the Dnestr problem within the framework of a single state) led to a new impasse in the peace process. The political pressure applied on Moldovan President

Vladimir Voronin to secure rejection of a Russia-sponsored plan demonstrated that the United States and other Western states, acting through the OSCE as the Western-dominated organization, were interested only in overcoming more than a decade-long impasse in the Moldovan–Transdniestrian peace process as long as this was secured on terms dictated by the West. Otherwise, the United States and the EU states were prepared to sacrifice the peace process to the more important goal of preventing a settlement on Russia's terms, even if an agreement was initially accepted by both parties.

In the same manner, the American one-sided and unconditional support for Saakashvili's regime despite its aggressive statements on South Ossetiya and Abkhazia has proved to be counterproductive to the goal of achieving peace settlements with both statelets. It has forced the Abkhazian authorities to step up security cooperation with their South Ossetian counterparts and put their security forces on alert, and pushed both statelets closer to Russia as their only meaningful benefactor. At the same time, attempts to depict Russia's position on both conflicts as driven exclusively by anti-Western logic are hardly supported by Russia's practical behaviour vis-à-vis Moldova and particularly Georgia. It is worth remembering in this context that Moscow still does not officially recognize the breakaway regions, guided by its vital interest in safeguarding the principle of non-violation of territorial integrity of post-Soviet republics, in view of its own problems in the North Caucasus. Moscow officially sticks to this line even despite the repeated calls from both Abkhazia and South Ossetiya for a formal association with the Russian Federation and despite the fact that most of the residents of Abkhazia and South Ossetiya hold Russian citizenship. Moreover, in terms of Georgia's domestic political developments, Russia has demonstrated a relatively pragmatic approach stemming from its interpretation of Russia's national interests in that region. One of the most important interests for Russia has been to avoid further destabilization and a new civil war in that troubled country that remains on the verge of economic break-up, despite all hopes for a massive inflow of Western economic assistance in response to Tbilisi's political loyalty to the United States and NATO. In the name of that goal, Russia played a key mediating role at two critical junctures. At the peak of the November 2003 "revolution of roses" in Georgia, it was Russia's mediation that ultimately forced Shevardnadze to resign (in the form of an "honourable departure") and prevented the use of force by the former regime. Later, in May 2004, Russia refused to offer troops or arms to the leader of a fiefdom (officially, Georgia's autonomous region) of Adzharia, to resist the extension of the central government's control to that region, and facilitated a non-violent resolution of that crisis by offering Abashidze an exile in Russia.

While commonly explained by the competing geostrategic interests of Russia and Western states in the post-Soviet space, the impasse in peace processes in both regions can also at least partly be explained by an inability and/or unwillingness to consider cultural differences in approaches to conflict management demonstrated by both Russia and the West and formulated within the logic of respective "national interest cultures". While Russia often tended to view international organizations' involvement in the CIS conflict zones as nothing more than a projection of Western power and influence in general, as well as of geostrategic interests of Western powers (especially the United States), the latter have often demonstrated the lack of understanding for Russia's extremely difficult transformation process. Among other things, this approach led to overestimation of Russia's interest in keeping its military presence in both Moldova and Georgia; a suspicious or even hostile attitude to any political groups and forces within the CIS states that were not perceived as pro-Western (such as communists or post-communist socialists); overestimation of administrative capacities of central governments in both Chisinau and Tbilisi; a lack of attention to local factors driving the conflict dynamics; and the fact that even modest progress toward peaceful resolution of any of the CIS conflicts (such as in the Moldovan–Transdniestrian case in the early 2000s) has been dependent on improved bilateral relations between Russia and the respective republics' central authorities.

In sum, in the course of the 1990s, as Russia was slowly adjusting to its radically new post-Soviet and post–Cold War role and acquiring the ability to formulate and, with varying degree of effectiveness, pursue its national interests, Russia's conflict management policies in the CIS gradually became driven by "national interest" logic. It was precisely that logic that dictated Russia's increasing drive toward greater pragmatism and more rational behavioural patterns, including multilateral negotiations and mediation, involving both CIS and non-CIS states and regional and broader international organizations (the OSCE, the United Nations) in areas such as Abkhazia/Georgia and Transdniestria/Moldova. Thus, Russia's approach to conflict management efforts in those and other regions in the first years of the new century can be best described as "functional cooperation". Precisely because this approach was more clearly formulated within the "national interest" logic by the early 2000s, as compared to the early 1990s, it has led Russia to play a constructive mediating role at some critical junctures (for instance, in securing non-violent transition of power in Georgia in 2003 as a way to prevent further chaos and perhaps even its potential break-up), as it was based on a realization that stabilization of the internal political situation and prevention of re-escalation of internal conflicts in Russia's neighbouring states and other

CIS states are in Russia's own vital national interest. As long as and to the extent that other individual external players, such as the United States and other Western states, as well as broader multilateral arrangements to settle these conflicts were pursuing the same goal, Russia engaged in functional cooperation with these actors on conflict management efforts within the CIS.

Russia's involvement in conflict management outside the CIS

In contrast to Russia's role in the conflicts within or between the CIS states, the few cases of Russia's involvement in conflict management outside the CIS have largely been dependent on and, ultimately, a function of multilateral decision-making efforts. The conflict (and the search for balance) between incentives to cooperate with the international community, especially with Russia's G8 partners, on the one hand, and Russia's national interests, on the other hand, became a constant political dilemma for Moscow in any such involvement.

Russia has been the most outspoken and persistent critic of the use of force in resolving international conflicts, especially since the mid-1990s. In the post–Cold War world, military force was used or threatened mainly against anti-Western regimes – labeled as rogue states. The fact that Russia enjoyed traditionally close ties with some of these states put Moscow in a natural position of intermediary and facilitator. Sometimes it even seemed that a certain division of labour (whether deliberate or unintentional), arose when the United States (or NATO in Europe) threatened military force while Moscow was touting prospects for peace. Russia's general reluctance to sanction the unconstrained use of force in settling international conflicts was reinforced by its ability to talk to and to cooperate with the West and its most harsh opponents, reflecting a high degree of cultural relativism and flexibility, natural for a Eurasian power. This unique ability, stemming from Russia's centuries-long search for its own cultural identity, was strongly stimulated by post-Soviet de-ideologization of Russian foreign policy. A combination of the above-mentioned factors gave Russia some role in "cooperative peacemaking" in areas such as the Balkans and the Middle East, while at the same time politically tying it closer to the West.

The cases that deserve special attention in this context are those involving Russia's participation in multilateral decision-making regarding the conflicts in regions still of some, although far from critical, importance to Russia – the Balkans, the Middle East and South-west Asia. For the period of the late 1990s to the early 2000s, when Russia's policy was already mature enough not to be carried away by either the pro-Western romanticism of the early 90s (guided by what was perceived as an ethic of solidarity), or nostalgia for foreign policy Soviet-style, the cases in focus will be organized in three sub-sections: first, Russia's conflict management efforts in the late 1990s on Kosovo and Iraq, second, its support for the US-led anti-Taliban campaign in Afghanistan following the events of 11 September 2001 and, finally, Russia's position on the US-led 2003 intervention and occupation of Iraq.

Russia's policy on Kosovo and Iraq in the 1990s

During the Kosovo crisis, Russia assumed a role as one of the chief mediators because it was the only of the major European powers that was not directly involved in NATO's intervention against the Federal Republic of Yugoslavia and that enjoyed normal relations with the West and close ties to Belgrade. From the beginning of the crisis, Russia had consistently presented itself as a voice of reason, advocating a peaceful multilateral UN-based solution to the Kosovo conflict, as opposed to NATO's violent response in the form of limited, US-dominated multilateralism.[15] It was Russia's "cooperative initiative" that was required to end the quagmire for both NATO and Belgrade and to bring the peace process, at least formally, back into the UN framework (during NATO's bombing campaign, Russia, as the only major European power not drawn into the conflict directly and enjoying some leverage with Serbia, was a natural candidate to play a mediating role – primarily through Prime Minister Chernomyrdin's shuttle diplomacy).[16]

The key to understanding Russia's policy on the Kosovo crisis – a very harsh political reaction toward NATO intervention followed by the ultimate decision to find a cooperative solution within the G8 and the United Nations and to temporarily cooperate with NATO on the ground – is to realize that this policy was only remotely related to the Kosovo problem itself. The motives behind Russia's policy on Kosovo can be understood only through the prism of Moscow's complicated relations with NATO, which have become the main irritant in Russia's relations with the West, at least since the debate over the Alliance's enlargement.

Whilst much of Russia's opposition to earlier stages of NATO enlargement could be explained by a fear of the "old NATO", inherited from the Soviet era, the Alliance's military intervention against Yugoslavia made Russia deeply concerned about the "new NATO", emerging in post–Cold War Europe. This new NATO was seen as a military bloc that has lost its Cold War rationale, but re-affirmed its offensive interventionist nature by attacking a sovereign European state in the process of the Alliance's re-orientation toward "intrusive" crisis management. The parallel controversial expansion of the new NATO to areas closer to Russia's borders, potentially including the CIS countries, at a time when Russia's economy and military were in shambles, also explained the ferocity of Moscow's opposition to military action against Yugoslavia. While largely irrelevant to the real security threats faced by the West in general and the United States in particular, as ultimately demonstrated in the aftermath of the 11 September 2001 attacks, NATO enlargement retained the potential to radicalize the internal situation in politically unstable Western CIS states, such as Ukraine and Moldova, or even spark further internal splits in those countries, that would most likely drag in Russia. This was a role that Moscow did not want and could hardly afford to play. Last but not least, Moscow, facing major problems in the separatist republic of Chechnya, was highly concerned about the precedent of a military involvement by a hostile alliance on the side of separatists in the case of Kosovo.

At the same time, Russia, due to its relative political, economic and military weakness, coupled with a feeling of growing politico-military isolation in a NATO/EU-dominated Europe, could neither sacrifice relations with the West over the 1999 Kosovo crisis nor allow further marginalization of the United Nations. As a result, Moscow tried to minimize consequences of the crisis in order to escape a long-term confrontation with the West in general and with NATO in particular. So, in contrast to the general mood of the Russian people expressing broad solidarity with the Serbian people as the victims of an aggression and united in condemnation of NATO intervention in Yugoslavia, official Moscow's response to the crisis turned out to be moderate and restrained. Ultimately, the Russian state had to engage in some form of "functional cooperation" with the West and NATO over Kosovo for both tactical and strategic reasons, no matter how much domestic public opinion opposed this political choice at that time.

Was there any place for a solidarity culture, apart from these "national interest" calculations, and what kind of solidarity was it? Clearly, in Russia there was no lack of public solidarity with the people of Serbia (if not necessarily with the Serbian government). This people-to-people solidarity movement was in many ways unprecedented: apart from the countrywide mass peaceful protests and humanitarian initiatives, there was also a public campaign to send volunteers "to help defend Yugoslavia from the NATO forces".[17] Contrary to what is generally believed in the West, this solidarity did not seem to be primarily based on the former Russian empire's historical commitment to stand by the Serbs. While ethnic and religious closeness (both Russians and Serbs are Slavic peo-

ples and Eastern Orthodox Christians) did play some role, the broad solidarity movement in Russia with the Serbian people manifested in the
late 1990s had more recent roots and stemmed from a compassion for a
nation facing foreign aggression by Russia's own former Cold War adversaries and by an alliance broadly perceived in Russia as presenting the
main military threat to its security. Also, in the public discourse, some
clear, if hardly justified, parallels with and allusions to the World War II
experience were made.[18]

Thus, public solidarity with parties to the Kosovo conflict was expressed both by Russia and by its Western counterparts, but it was selective and "asymmetrical": while the Russian public's solidarity was largely
with the Serbs as "victims" of the aggressive policies and pressure by the
"neo-imperial" United States and its NATO allies, the Western public
solidarity was limited to the plight of the Kosovo Albanians as "victims"
of Serbian oppression and based on Western liberal "democratic" solidarity's emphasis on human and minority rights (while, for instance, the
plight of over 500 thousand Serbian refugees in Serbia was almost completely ignored at the time). But while in the West, the public solidarity
with the Kosovo Albanians (partly created by a one-sided media coverage of the crisis) was increasingly in line with the official policies of the
NATO states, the impact of the broad Russian public solidarity movement with the "victims of NATO aggression" on Russia's official policy
over Kosovo was very limited. This policy was driven primarily by the
long-term rational concerns over the "new NATO" threat and by realization of Russia's limited capability to respond to this threat dictating the
need to adapt to it. In sum, Russian political elites were too rational to
sincerely share the broader public solidarity attitudes let alone to use
them as a basis for strategic decision-making. This rationalism finally
made the Russian government cooperate with the West on Kosovo up
to sending a military contingent to participate in the NATO Kosovo
Force.

Such a pragmatic, non-ideological approach on the part of the Russian
government prevented any direct military involvement and dictated the
need to adjust to the NATO handling of the crisis with minimal political
losses. This approach came in sharp contrast with the much more explicit
role of ideological and value-based considerations in the United States
and NATO decision-making on Kosovo that, combined with some strategic considerations (such as the need to sustain the NATO Alliance in
the absence of its main former rationale – the Soviet threat), led the Alliance to wage war on Yugoslavia. Among other things, the value-based
approach, claimed to be pursued by NATO states, implied that a "decision taken by a serious organization by consensus among serious coun-

tries with democratic governments"[19] alone conferred sufficient legitimacy on the contemplated action and could be used as an excuse for a military intervention not authorized by the UN Security Council.

With regard to the Iraq problem in the 1990s, Russia tried to reconcile its own economic and political interests with its UN obligations, while remaining a persistent critic of US unilateralism. Whilst prior to the 11 September 2001 terrorist attacks the US could not rely for support on any allies (except the United Kingdom) for its unilateralist military strikes against Iraq, few governments, in view of the track record and semi-isolation of Baghdad's regime, openly objected to US air strikes against the Baghdad government. Of those that did, Moscow has been the most vociferous. In the 1990s, the peak of Russian criticism followed the most intensive of the US attacks against Iraq (the December 1998 Operation Desert Fox).[20]

In contrast to the Kosovo crisis and other post-Yugoslav conflicts, where Russia's primary concerns were dictated by wider security interests, particularly by the "NATO factor", the main pragmatic imperative behind Russia's policy on Iraq was economic. Prior to the US-led 2003 intervention to and occupation of Iraq, Russian companies controlled about one-third of Iraq's multibillion-dollar oil export market.[21] Trade volume between the two countries reached US$4 billion in 2001 and could grow up to 10 times that if sanctions were lifted. Russia had a US$3.5 billion, 23-year deal with Iraq to rehabilitate Iraqi oilfields, particularly the West Qurna field – one of the world's largest oil deposits.[22] Finally, the Russian government was trying to recover around $7 billion in loans made to Iraq in the 1980s mainly to pay for Soviet arms deliveries. These clear economic interests became one of the key factors that dictated Russia's consistent opposition to US strategy on Iraq that, throughout the 1990s, has been generally aimed at overthrowing Saddam Hussein. Russia feared that if Saddam were overthrown, it would have put in serious doubt the prospects of repayment of Iraq's multibillion-dollar debt to Russia and lucrative oil projects with Iraq that Moscow was keen to safeguard (this is basically what happened as a result of the US-led invasion of Iraq in March 2003).[23]

Russia's cooperation with the United Nations on Iraq and persistent opposition to US unilateral military actions against Iraq throughout the 1990s reflected not just pure economic interests related to Iraq per se, but also broader political concerns over the negative effect that the US policy had on the role and image of the United Nations in general and of the UN Security Council in particular. Russia was fully aware of its own limited leverage at the United Nations (under no circumstance could Russia push its own initiative through the Security Council, if opposed by the United States). At the same time, Moscow was still determined to use whatever leverage it had to work within the UN framework, even if at the partial expense of its economic interests (Moscow, for instance, chose not to unilaterally withdraw from the UN sanctions regime against Iraq). For Russia, working within the UN framework had its clear advantages: among other things, Moscow could still block unfavourable US-sponsored UN Security Council decisions on Iraq, particularly in the case of a serious disagreement among the Council's other members.

Russia's direct economic interests in Iraq and broader political concerns about US unilateralism in general, and its effects on the credibility of the United Nations in particular, were so important that Moscow was reluctant to change its opposition to any new sanctions or a new major US attack even in the aftermath of the attacks on 11 September. Russia expressed scepticism about the direction the United States took in its war against terrorism by singling out Iraq first as part of the "axis of evil", along with North Korea and Iran. The "axis of evil" rhetoric was seen in Russia as strategically misleading, ideologically and emotionally driven, used largely for domestic consumption and a clear manifestation of American political culture, with its missionary exceptionalism and unilateralism. In contrast, throughout the late 1990s and early 2000s up until the US occupation of Iraq, Russia's non-ideological, non-emotionally-driven, primarily economic interests in Iraq dictated the need to lift or, at least, further relieve UN sanctions against Baghdad, which in turn made cooperation with the UN on getting weapons inspectors back to Iraq and, more generally, a strongly multilateral approach to Iraqi problems an imperative for Moscow. Acting in cooperation with the UN Secretary General, the Security Council and the UN sanctions committee, Russia tried to make the best use of Iraq's readiness to resume dialogue with the United Nations and succeeded in exerting stronger pressure on Baghdad to invite UN weapons inspectors back after a three-year absence.

Cooperation with the West after 11 September

Russia's cooperation with the United States after 11 September has centred on a common interest in combating terrorism. To what extent was Russia's post–11 September cooperation with the United States driven by national interest logic? Did any genuine global solidarity with the United States play a role in improving mutual relations and facilitating Russia's cooperation with the United States on Afghanistan?

After a remarkable freezing at the end of the 1990s, US–Russian relations have clearly been on the rise since 11 September. US–Russian bilateral cooperation on combating terrorism was particularly successful, if not unprecedented. This cooperation has proved highly valuable to Russia, as perhaps for the first time since the end of the Cold War, it stemmed from the need to counter a common security threat from a radically new, truly post–Cold War type. Russia's active participation in the US-led global anti-terrorist campaign fully served Russia's national interests (as they were interpreted by the Russian government), by creating a more favourable international climate for Russia's own anti-terrorist operations in its troubled North Caucasus region and, more broadly, by allowing Moscow to avoid further marginalization, which seemed almost imminent by the end of the 1990s, and to directly associate itself with the leading world power, while surpassing cumbersome Western institutional bureaucracies such as NATO and the European Union.

The most vivid manifestation of the new favourable climate in US–Russian post–11 September relations has been Russia's cooperation with the United States during its operation in Afghanistan. Russia's main interest in Afghanistan has been the goal of rooting out terrorism there and of preventing that country from serving as a primary source of instability in a wider region that includes Central Asian states. It was these regional security concerns, coupled with the above-mentioned more general foreign policy considerations, that dictated Moscow's support for the US-led military operation launched in October 2001, as well as Russia's reserved reaction to the growth of the US military presence in Central Asia.[24] As for the many speculations about intensified US–Russian strategic rivalry in Central Asia as a result of the increased US military presence, for the Russian leadership, diminishing the United States's growing profile in the area did not appear to be a goal in itself. Rather, the US presence has been judged upon its impact on the overall security and stability of the region, which suffers more from a disturbing internal security vacuum than from any "excessive" external involvement, be it unilateral or multilateral.

It could be argued, however, that Russia's support for the US-led campaign in Afghanistan in the immediate aftermath of the 11 September attacks on the United States was also at least partly driven by "global solidarity" attitudes at the state level supported by broader public solidarity. While the need to "defend common values of the civilized world against international terrorism" was often cited as the basis of this solidarity, it could hardly be viewed as an expression of a "Western democratic solidarity culture" – rather, it stemmed from an understanding of the changing nature of security threats in an era of globalization and the common need to confront the threat of international terrorism. It is true that at that point Russia and the United States may have been primarily threatened by different types of terrorism (gradually Islamicized nationalist separatist terrorism in the case of Russia and global superterrorism in the case of the United States). At the same time, in the post–Cold War world, the distinctions between domestic and international terrorist groups do become increasingly blurred (as even groups with a localized political agenda tend to internationalize their logistical, financial and other activities), and superterrorist networks such as Al Qaeda or its successors do have a strong demonstrative impact on and may provide financial assistance to the more localized groups employing terrorist means.[25] Thus, the increasingly disturbing interrelationship between different types of terrorism *does* present a global threat. The need to respond to this and other global threats can stimulate the growth of the "global solidarity culture", even if this culture does not amount to or fit the notion of liberal democratic solidarity.

Russia and the war in Iraq

The endurance of the positive momentum created by Russia's cooperation with the United States on Afghanistan soon came under question, with sharp disagreements over the US war in Iraq. It is in Russia's position on the US-led war in Iraq that the complex mix of narrow national interests and broader normative and ideational concerns in Russian foreign policy became most evident. The Iraq crisis served for Russia, first and foremost, as a focal point for the contest between UN-centred multilateralism and US unilateralism. Russia's strong preference for multilateralism in general, and for multilateralist solutions to regional conflicts, was an integral part of its own newly acquired identity as a large regional power, strong enough to defend its sovereignty but not enough to push forward its interests if challenged by the United States and its NATO allies (as noted before, changing conceptions of Russian identity have logically altered its conception of its interests). Consequently, the United Nations, and particularly the UN Security Council, remained Russia's natural framework of choice for dealing with crises such as Iraq. It has to be noted, though, that this emphasis on UN-centred multilateralism as a general, underlying framework dominating Russia's foreign policy discourse has to be put in the context of at least two more pragmatic trends increasingly shaping Russia's policy on Iraq.

The first trend has been the growing role of geo-economics in Russia's foreign policy. In terms of the latter, Russia's direct economic losses in Iraq, as a result of the US intervention and occupation, and the limits placed by insecurity on the remaining Russian business presence, were partly compensated by Russia's financial gains from high oil prices, which were both favourable for Russian oil exporters and remained the main basis for the Putin government's economic stabilization strategy. The economic interest logic also led Russia to agree to sell part of its strategic asset Lukoil to an affiliate of the fourth-largest US oil company, Conoco-Phillips, in order to regain access to at least some of its previous contracts in Iraq.

The second pragmatic trend was dictated by Russia's new security agenda, with its focus shifting from the West to the South as the main source of potential security threats, and with its new emphasis on anti-terrorism. From Russia's perspective, not only did the Iraq war and the subsequent occupation of Iraq run against international law and serve as an extreme manifestation of US unilateralism, it also proved to be counterproductive to anti-terrorist priorities. This was because by creating more terrorism rather than less, the occupation has damaged the integrity of the "coalition against terror" and destroyed the momentum created by the rise of "global solidarity" with the United States in the immediate aftermath of the 11 September attacks (supported by and combined with self-interest security considerations on the part of most of the world's states). Even prior to the US war in Iraq, Russia had problems with the Bush administration's emphasis on the so-called "rogue states" as the primary sponsors of new forms of international terrorism and particularly on linking the Baath regime directly to Al Qaeda (Russia did not see a straightforward connection between Iraq's alleged, but never confirmed, weapons of mass destruction capability and the US charges against Baghdad as one of the major sponsors of "international terrorism"). Rather, Russia tried to draw international attention to dysfunctional and failed states and areas where the power vacuum and the lack of state control provided opportunities for transnational terrorist networks for relocation and sanctuary and where localized and transnational terrorism most easily intersect and the line between them may become increasingly blurred. This is precisely what has been happening in post-war Iraq, where the United States turned a rogue authoritarian regime into a semi-failed proxy state that became completely dependent on foreign security support, a state that invites and stimulates, rather than suppresses and prevents terrorism. Anti-terrorism concerns generated by the situation in a post-war (not pre-war) Iraq provided an additional powerful argument for Russia to support efforts to build a functional and legitimate Iraqi state as the most effective anti-terrorist strategy for a failed state. The same concerns have also made Moscow more willing or less reluctant to accept the reality of the US-dominated security presence in Iraq.[26]

Ultimately, a certain gap between Russia's UN-centred multilateralism approach (at least partly based on ideational concerns and expressed in normative categories) and the more practical dimension of its policy on Iraq dominated by economic interest and anti-terrorism considerations resulted in a compromise policy on the part of Russia, allowing accommodation of some of its economic and security interests (in the form of "functional cooperation"), while keeping political distance from the coalition.

Russia and international solidarity in the face of global challenges

Since the Soviet collapse, Russia suffered a painful erosion of its international might and prestige. It certainly took the Russian political elite some time to adapt to the loss of an empire and the sense of a "global mission" in the world, as well as to realize that Soviet-era global ambitions had led to an obvious overstretch of the country's resources. For a brief period in the early 1990s, those of Russia's post-Soviet political elites that took up the challenge of starting democratic reforms appeared to be carried away with an idealistic vision of the post–Cold War world as being guided by "democratic solidarity culture" and with ungrounded expectations of solidarity-driven behaviour on the part of its former Western adversaries. By the mid-1990s, as these false hopes did not materialize and domestic democratic reforms seemed to be mired in economic crisis, the geo-strategic political discourse was back in place. By the late 1990s–early 2000s, however, Russia was able to both overcome the idealistic vision of the "post–Cold War world" as one based on moral commitments and to realize the counterproductive nature of the narrow and "non-cooperative" geostrategic thinking contradicting Russia's own long-term national interests. In its foreign policy, the Russian state has increasingly demonstrated the "functional" approach to international cooperation.

As demonstrated by a brief outline of Russia's post-Soviet involvement in international conflict management efforts in the "far abroad", Russia was eager to play a useful instrumental role on behalf of the US-led international community in various local and regional conflicts, when strongly motivated to do so by its own national interests. While Russia's legitimate foreign policy concerns have not necessarily been in conflict with morally-defined international justice, for much of its post-Soviet history Russia simply could not afford to pursue international causes not directly serving its national interests or to be involved in managing regional crises that did not affect its own security. Up until the early 2000s, the extent to which the Russian state could play a meaningful role in addressing global challenges largely depended on and was clearly limited by its reduced economic and political potential. The disparity between Russia's real political and economic agenda and the leading international powers' global concerns was most vividly demonstrated by Russia's participation in the

G8, the group of the world's wealthiest and most powerful nations. With the exception of selected security issues, such as non-proliferation of weapons and materials of mass destruction and, since 11 September, anti-terrorism, Russia did not have much to say or offer on such "classic" global solidarity issues discussed at the G8 annual summits as, for instance, the Africa Action Plan at the 2002 Kananaskis summit, and could hardly afford to commit significant resources to these purposes. In this context, it would have been naive for the "international community" to expect the high degree of "moral awareness and solidarity" going beyond the level of rhetoric on the part of Russia in addressing issues of global concern.

As far as the role of external state actors in shaping Russia's behaviour is concerned, for the world's most developed nations, as well as the Western-dominated international organizations and financial institutions, cooperation with the Russian state seemed to work out best when guided by the same "functional cooperation" approach as the one that increasingly dominated Russia's own foreign policy. In line with this approach, the G8 partners, for instance, had repeatedly made it clear to Russia that the key to its continued economic integration (such as its quest to join the World Trade Organization) and engagement in the concert of developed and democratic states depended on the extent of its commitment to such global initiatives as the international anti-terrorism campaign.

That hardly means, though, that present Russia has not been affected by the global "solidarity culture" at all. While it was not often that post-Soviet Russia became involved in a major international undertaking, having nothing or little to do with its own national interests, some examples can be found and, interestingly, their number seems to be growing from year to year. Most of these cases fall into the category of humanitarian, economic or emergency assistance. In 2000, for instance, Russia agreed to send a small contingent to assist the UN mission in Sierra Leone where it did not have a direct interest at stake. In 2001, Russia, by many parameters a developing economy itself, in bad need of development aid and foreign economic investment and with a multibillion-dollar foreign debt, provided $472 million in assistance to the poorest developing countries and wrote off $415 million of their debts.[27] Russia had been increasingly active in providing civil emergency assistance to foreign countries, but the most significant expression of "global solidarity" on the part of the Russian government came in early 2005 as part of the global "tsunami solidarity" campaign. In addition to the Russian government's decision to allocate over US$30 million to tsunami victims, Emergencies Ministry and Defence Ministry planes have delivered dozens of tons of humanitarian aid, including medicines, food and medical and other equipment, to areas affected by the disaster, and rescuers and doctors from both ministries were sent by the government to work at the site. It should be noted that neither Russia nor the ex-USSR had ever provided such an amount of international humanitarian aid before (an amount that surpassed the contributions of some developed states).

In these and other cases, Russia's decision to provide good offices on its own or on behalf of the international community may have been at least partly guided by demonstrative ("status") purposes. Goals such as improving Russia's international image and demonstrating that it still belongs to a community of developed industrialized states and has some global role to play have, in turn, been dictated by the way the Russian leadership interpreted the country's national interests and thus have been driven by national interest logic. But this logic did not necessarily prevail on the humanitarian, economic and emergency aid issues mentioned above and was certainly supplemented by genuine "global solidarity" concerns that played no less a critical role in shaping Russia's position on these issues.

More broadly, apart from issues where the impact of "international solidarity" logic on the decision-making process is undeniable (particularly on humanitarian emergency assistance), the national interest logic and the solidarity logic do not have to be mutually exclusive, even in those policy areas where Russia has important national interests at stake. Not only can these two logics co-exist, as in the case of Russia's reaction to the US-led intervention in Iraq (motivated both by Russia's economic self-interest and its genuine concerns about the weakening of the United Nations, the violation of international norms, the increasingly "unjust" nature of the new world order and the sympathy toward the Iraqi population under foreign occupation), but they can even complement and supplement one another.

This could be further exemplified by Russia's position on international humanitarian assistance to its own troubled North Caucasus region. Russia allowed large-scale international humanitarian presence in this region, with the UN agencies playing a leading role by administrating over 80 per cent of all foreign humanitarian aid, with the help of a number of foreign and local non-governmental organizations. With the combined volume of international humanitarian assistance to the region at least comparable to the humanitarian efforts undertaken by the Russian state itself,[28] and in some cases even exceeding them,[29] Moscow's decision to allow international humanitarian involvement of that scale was partly motivated by pragmatic realist considerations, such as financial reasons. At the same time, it also demonstrated that Russia increasingly realized the growing importance of humanitarian issues on both national and international agenda and was trying to address at least the most basic humanitarian needs by providing and allowing international organizations and foreign donors to provide food, shelter, education and the right to return to thousands of internally displaced people in the North Caucasus. Thus, even if not fully shared or unconditionally accepted by Russia, issues of global concern (such as changing international perceptions of states' obligations to provide humanitarian support and basic human rights of its citizens) do affect its behaviour, directly or indirectly.

While all of the above-mentioned "global solidarity initiatives" were carried out at the state/intergovernmental level, international solidarity is not necessarily limited to that level and does not necessarily have to be connected to the state's official policy. In the Russian case in particular, the "international solidarity" attitudes, perceptions and even actions can be more closely associated with the society at large rather than the state and practiced more actively by non-governmental organizations and various public associations and groups through public contacts and public diplomacy, for instance. Moreover, in contrast to highly selective and carefully measured "state solidarity" (which is usually combined with or supplemented by national interest logic), international public solidarity is usually reciprocal and may manifest itself even on issues that remain politically controversial in terms of intergovernmental relations.

In the post–11 September world, anti-terrorism became one of the main areas where "public solidarity culture at work" has been evident, both globally (in the case of the public outrage around the world over the human costs of the 11 September terrorist attacks in the United States, the March 2004 Atocha bombings in Madrid and so on) and in a specific case of Russia. Genuine solidarity has manifested itself both in the form of the Russian public response to events abroad (such as 11 September) and in the form of public reaction in many Western states (whose governments had serious reservations and expressed concern about Russia's policy in the North Caucasus) to a series of deadly large-scale terrorist attacks in Russia, such as the October 2002 Dubrovka (Nord-Ost) hostage crisis in Moscow or the September 2004 tragedy in Beslan (North Ossetiya). These and other horrific terrorist attacks in Russia were followed not just by a wave of criticism of the policies and methods employed by the Russian state, but also by an outpouring of international public support and solidarity with the Russian people and society. International mobilization in support of the Beslan hostages and their families has been particularly extraordinary, with many Red Cross and Red Crescent Societies and ordinary citizens around the world launching fund raising campaigns on their behalf. The moral solidarity with the victims of terrorism was jointly expressed by a coalition of Russian and international non-governmental organizations (from Human Rights Watch to Moscow Helsinki Group)[30] that are known for their criticism of the Russian authorities on human rights grounds. In most of these cases, international public solidarity was also supplemented by some manifestations of solidarity on the part of the world's leading international organizations, such as the UN Security Council.

This brings us back to the need to differentiate between the limited Western-style "liberal democratic solidarity culture" and a broader and more traditional understanding of human solidarity (based on shared views on very basic humanitarian concerns and human rights, such as the right to live, get shelter and so on). Clearly, most of the above-mentioned expressions of international solidarity to and from the Russian people were based on the latter rather than the former type of solidarity. Such solidarity goes beyond the "ideal world of Western liberal values" and assumes a truly global nature, as it is formed in response to the truly global challenges.

Conclusion and recommendations

One of the main questions put forward by this volume is whether there is some role for external actors to play apart from the national interest paradigm and how the world's powers, international organizations and non-governmental organizations can help create elements of solidarity culture in the external behaviour of key regional powers, such as Russia. This task is made all the more difficult by the ambiguous policies of the world's leading Western states, which actively pursue their own national interests, often of a pure geostrategic nature, such as power projection or energy supply, while at the same time trying to satisfy the growing "international solidarity" constituency, both internationally and at home. This makes the prominence of moral considerations in the Western approach to international affairs in general and to conflict management in particular not that evident for the rest of the world. An impression of international democratic solidarity discourse being used as a cover for advancing the geostrategic interests of the Western states would not be easy to dispel.

In this context, it seems that the most effective way for external actors, such as foreign governments and intergovernmental or non-governmental organizations, to encourage the development of "solidarity culture" as a basis for cooperation with Russia is:

1. To concentrate on the common need to address global challenges, such as the global environmental crisis, humanitarian emergencies (particularly in the form of human-made and natural-disaster response) and common security challenges, such as international terrorism. Needless to say that "solidarity in response to global challenges"

would have the broadest impact if it boils down to the more traditional "solidarity culture" based on the most basic and the more traditional understanding of international solidarity encoded in the UN Charter and other key international documents and shared by most states throughout the world, rather than pushed forward by a group of like-minded Western states. In contrast to a common interest in confronting global challenges, which is a natural area for the international solidarity culture to develop in the West's relations with Russia, as well as a host of other major regional powers around the world, it is the national interest logic rather than the "solidarity culture" that will clearly dominate mutual relations on issues of strategic importance to both sides (such as international conflict management efforts in Russia's immediate CIS neighbourhood).

2. To encourage the development of solidarity culture at the non-governmental, public level, in the form of "citizen diplomacy" and the like.

3. To realize that, at the level of state policy, national interest and solidarity logic do not have to be mutually exclusive and can co-exist, as demonstrated, above all, by an uneasy combination of national interests and international solidarity in an international campaign against terrorism.

Notes

1. While frequent policy differences between Western states, particularly between the United States and European powers such as France, on issues of global and regional concern have to be kept in mind, for our purposes, the "Western community of nations" will be commonly referred to as "the West" in both political and cultural (value-based) terms.

2. For instance, up to one third of all humanitarian assistance to the victims of the conflict in Muslim-dominated Chechnya (Russia) has come from Saudi Arabia and other Muslim countries, despite the almost non-existent prospects for effectively advancing any strategic or ideological interests these states might have had in that conflict.

3. The notion of "functional cooperation" used in this chapter is a broader and more flexible term than the notion of "common", or "shared" security. "Functional cooperation" not only goes beyond more traditional security issues (and may, for instance, apply to economic cooperation) but also presents a more flexible way to distinguish between different types of "national interest culture", that is, between more unilateralist and non-cooperative approaches and "functional cooperation" approaches. While neither implies value-based "solidarity" logic, they are driven by different understandings of national interests. In practice, however, the line between them may not always be very clear and some sort of a dialectic combination of both may guide the country's foreign policy.

4. See, for instance, Roy Allison (1994) *Peacekeeping in the Soviet Successor States*, Chaillot Paper 18, Paris: Institute for Security Studies, Western European Union; Hans-Georg Ehrhart, Anna Kreikemeyer and Andrei V. Zagorski, eds (1995) *Crisis Management in the CIS: Whither Russia?*, Baden-Baden, Germany: Nomos Verlagsgesellschaft;

Elaine Holoboff (1994) "Russian Views on Military Intervention: Benevolent Peace-keeping, Monroe Doctrine, or Neo-Imperialism?" in Lawrence Freedman, ed., *Military Intervention in European Conflicts*, Cambridge, Mass.: Blackwell Publishers, pp. 154–174.

5. The OSCE mission in Moldova monitors the human rights situation in both Moldova and the Transdniestrian republic and assists the parties in the difficult negotiations by facilitating the dialogue, gathering information, supplying expertise and advice in relation to legislation and constitutional aspects, making visible the presence of the OSCE in the area and establishing contacts with all the parties to the conflict.

6. The United Nations Observer Mission in Georgia was established by Security Council resolution 858 of 24 August 1993 to verify compliance with the ceasefire agreement between the government of Georgia and the Abkhaz authorities in Georgia. The Mission's mandate was expanded following the signing by the parties of the 1994 Agreement on a Ceasefire and Separation of Forces.

7. The OSCE Mission to Georgia was established in December 1992 to promote negotiations aimed at the peaceful political settlement of the conflicts in South Ossetia and Abkhazia. The Mission also supports the UN peacemaking efforts in Abkhazia. On 15 December 1999, at the request of the government of Georgia, the Mission's mandate was expanded to include monitoring the border between Georgia and the Chechen Republic of the Russian Federation.

8. See, for instance, "Russia Unhappy with OSCE Scrapping Moldova Peace Plan", *Russia Journal*, 2 December 2003; "The Perils of Transdniestria", *Romanian Digest* 9(11), November 2004, available from http://www.hr.ro/digest/200411/digest.htm, accessed 30 May 2006. For a critique of Kozak's "federalization" peace plan, see Michael Shafir (2003) "Russia's Self-Serving Plan for Moldova's Federalization", Radio Free Europe, 24 November, available from http://www.rferl.org/newsline/2003/11/5-NOT/not-241103.asp, accessed 30 May 2006.

9. For more detail, see "Russia, West Still Split Over Georgia, Moldova", *Arms Control Today*, January/February 2007, available from http://www.armscontrol.org/act/2007_01_02/RussiaWest.asp.

10. The separatist leader Igor Smirnov's victory in the December 2001 presidential elections in the breakaway region was not recognized by any government within or outside the CIS.

11. In November 2001, Moscow, for instance, agreed to a US$100 million compensation to Tiraspol for utilized arms and equipment in the form of partial gas debt relief.

12. Georgia resisted Moscow's proposal that its base in Gudauta be transformed into a support centre for the CIS peacekeeping troops deployed in Abkhazia. Bilateral negotiations continued on the withdrawal of Russia's two remaining military bases in Georgia – the one in Batumi (Ajaria) and the other at Akhalkalaki, on the border with Armenia. The main point of contention is the time framework for withdrawal: in 2004, Russia was demanding 11 years for completing the process, as it needed to build an adequate infrastructure at home to relocate the bases, while Georgia insists that the process should take three years maximum.

13. These remnants of Russia's military presence in Georgia should not be mixed with Russia's peacekeeping presence under the CIS auspices.

14. Georgia has long demanded to extend the 24 km "security zone" along the Inguri river to include the entire Gali region of Abkhazia in its pre-war borders, to redeploy all the heavy equipment of peacekeeping contingent further on Abkhazian territory and to secure the safety of Georgian internally displaced persons' return.

15. For a discussion on this, see Ekaterina Stepanova (2002) "The Unilateral and Multilateral Use of Force by the United States: A View from Russia", in David Malone and

Yuen-Foong Khong, eds, *International Perspectives on U.S. Unilateralism and Multilateralism*, Boulder, Colo.: Lynne Rienner Publishing.

16. See Ekaterina Stepanova (2000) "Russia's Policy on the Kosovo Crisis: The Limits of 'Cooperative Peacemaking'", in Kurt R. Spillman and Joachim Krause, eds, *Kosovo: Lessons Learned for International Cooperative Security*, Bern: Peter Lang, pp. 205–230; and Ekaterina Stepanova (1999) *Explaining Russia's Dissention on Kosovo*, Program on New Approaches to Russian Security (PONARS) Policy Memo No. 57, Cambridge, Mass.: Harvard University, Davis Center for Russian Studies.

17. For more detail, see Stepanova, "Russia's Policy on the Kosovo Crisis", pp. 219–222, particularly note 21 on p. 221.

18. The former Yugoslavia was perceived in Russia as the only group of nations that were able to mount a real resistance movement in Europe and to liberate their country from the Nazis largely on their own, without direct and large-scale foreign involvement.

19. Xavier Solana quoted in Alexander Nicoll (1998) "Cracks Still Appear in NATO's Collective Will for Air Strikes", *Financial Times*, 9 October, p. 2.

20. Russia had recalled its ambassadors from the United States and the United Kingdom for the first time since the Cold War.

21. In 2001, Russia received the largest share of Iraq's contracts (worth up to US$1.3 billion) under the UN oil-for-food programme, which allowed Iraq to sell oil to buy supplies to help Iraqi civilians.

22. In December 2002, Iraq announced that it was breaking the deal with Russia's Lukoil company to rehabilitate and develop the West Curna-2 oilfield under the pretext of "non-fulfillment by Lukoil of its obligations". The real reason for breaking the contract with Lukoil might have been leaks about Lukoil's secret contacts with the United States about accommodating some of its interests in post-Saddam Iraq.

23. For more detail, see Ekaterina Stepanova (2006) "Iraq and World Order: A Russian Perspective", in Ramesh Thakur and Waheguru Pal Singh Sidhu, eds, *The Iraq Crisis and World Order: Structural, Institutional and Normative Challenges*, Tokyo: United Nations University Press, pp. 249–264.

24. On recent US–Russian cooperation on Afghanistan and counter-terrorism, see Ekaterina Stepanova (2001) "U.S.–Russia Cooperation in Afghanistan and Its Implications", *East European Constitutional Review* 10(10), Fall: 92–95; Ekaterina Stepanova (2002) "Separately Together: The U.S. and Russia's Approaches to Post-Conflict Settlement in Afghanistan", *PONARS Policy Memo No. 230*, PONARS Policy Conference, Washington, D.C.: Center for Strategic and International Studies, January, pp. 117–122; and Ekaterina Stepanova (2002) "Partners in Need: U.S.–Russia Cooperation on and Approaches to Antiterrorism", *PONARS Policy Memo No. 279*, PONARS Policy Conference, Washington, D.C.: Center for Strategic and International Studies, 6 December, pp. 187–192.

25. See, for instance, Ekaterina Stepanova (2004) "War and Peace Building", *Washington Quarterly* 27(4), Autumn: 127–136.

26. For more detail, see Stepanova, "Iraq and World Order".

27. Alexei Kudrin, the first Vice-Premier and Minister of Finance in the Russian Government, quoted by Prime-Tass News Agency, 25 June 2002.

28. By June 2000, approximately 50 per cent of all humanitarian aid to Chechnya and the neighbouring regions was provided by the international community. See Russian Ministry of Foreign Affairs Fact Sheet, 24 June 2000, available at http://www.mid.ru/mid/eurochec/ec3.htm.

29. Between August 1999 and June 2000 the Russian federal and regional state structures provided 7,740 tons of food aid to Chechnya, Ingushetia and Dagestan. In the same

period, the UNHCR provided 6,750 tons, the World Food Program 6,785 tons, the International Committee of the Red Cross 3,610 tons and the three leading foreign nongovernmental organizations 3,095 tons (overall, 2.5 times as much as the Russian state). "UN Consolidated Humanitarian Appeal for the North Caucasus (Russian Federation), Dec. 1999–Dec. 2000", Moscow: UNOCHA, July 2000, p. 20 (Russian version).
30. "Joint NGO Statement on the Beslan Hostage Tragedy", Amnesty International Press Release, 9 September 2004.

4

International intervention in Central Asia: The triumph of geopolitics?

Parviz Mullojanov

After the events of 11 September 2001, the Central Asia region (defined in this chapter as the five former Soviet republics of Kazakhstan, Uzbekistan, Kyrgyzstan, Turkmenistan and Tajikistan and including neighbouring Afghanistan) has attracted considerable attention from the international community. This is not to say that the region was ignored prior to 11 September, but it is the case that its geopolitical significance has increased enormously since the terrorist attacks on America and the Bush administration's response to these in the form of the "war on terror". The purpose of this chapter is to consider what factors explain external involvement in Central Asia. In keeping with the theme of the volume, I examine how far, if at all, solidarist sentiments and values have influenced Russian, US, Chinese, Iranian and Turkish interventionism in the region. In focusing on this question, the chapter also draws attention to the role played by international organizations and humanitarian non-governmental organizations (NGOs). I argue that whilst a culture of solidarity is less evident in interstate relations within the region, it is more evident in the practices of international organizations, and especially the activities of those humanitarians working in the region.

Against this background, this chapter will proceed by examining the foreign policies toward Central Asia of the following: Russia, the United States, Iran, Turkey and, finally, international organizations and NGOs.

National interest and international solidarity: Particular and universal ethics in international life, Coicaud and Wheeler (eds),
United Nations University Press, 2008, ISBN 978-92-808-1147-6

Russian foreign policy in Central Asia

After the meeting in Belovezhskaya Pusha where the leaders of three major Soviet republics – the Russian Federation, Belorussia and Ukraine – announced their countries' independence, the Central Asian republics had no choice but to follow their example. Nobody seriously considered the option for the Central Asian countries to leave the zone of Russian influence. Instead, the Commonwealth of Independent States (CIS) was created to keep the former Soviet republics within the Russian sphere of influence, but without Moscow incurring specific responsibility for their future economic and social development. Russian foreign policy in Central Asia can be divided up into three main periods as I discuss below.

Democratic solidarity

This stage started right after the collapse of the Soviet Union and continued approximately until the end of 1992. During this period the Russian government's attention was directed more to the West than to the rest of the former Soviet Union, and Russia gave up many of its positions in the former Soviet republics. For example, it withdrew its troops from all the republics of Central Asia except Tajikistan and Turkmenia, leaving its military equipment in the hands of the local governments. Russia also reduced, or completely withdrew, its frontier troops from the areas along the former Soviet Union's borders. This policy was implemented at the beginning of President Boris Yeltsin's term, especially in the first few months after the disintegration of the Soviet Union. It was the time when a new wave of politicians, composed of democratic leaders who played an essential role in Yeltsin's coming to power, had entered the sphere of big politics in Russia. This group of "democratic idealists" had maintained close links with democratic parties and movements in other Soviet republics since the early years of perestroika. They shared the belief that in order to move ahead it was necessary to get rid of the old Communist legacy over all of the territory of the former Soviet Union. Therefore, during this rather short period the Russian leadership (or at least a part of it) supported Central Asian pro-democratic movements and parties in their struggle against local Communist elites. This group of "democratic idealists" was strongly opposed by a wide group of "professionals" in the Ministry of Defence, Russian Frontier troops, the GRU (Foreign Intelligence Service) and the KGB who were backed by former Communist leaders. The latter group considered that a narrow definition of Russian national and geopolitical interests must be the cornerstone of the country's foreign policy. As a result, Russian foreign policy toward Central Asia in the early 1990s was rather uncertain, with different agencies and institutions holding conflicting points of view with regard to local issues – for instance in dealing with the Tajik crisis. Thus, in the course of just over one year (August 1991 to September 1992) the Russian politicians influenced by democrats rendered assistance to Tajik opposition parties despite the resistance of military and intelligence leaders who sympathized with the local pro-government coalition. During this period the Russian democrats persistently blocked all attempts by Russian troops located in Tajikistan to support the government, forcing them to observe the proclaimed "non-interference" principle.[1]

Return to geopolitical pragmatism

The second period is characterized by the rise to ascendancy of the "professional" approach. Being part of the former Soviet establishment, President Boris Yeltsin clearly understood that the only way to ensure the further strengthening of his own position in the country's leadership was to attract the support of the former bureaucratic elite. Moreover, the majority of new democrats proved to be good, charismatic leaders but rather poor administrators and officials. In the new "post-revolutionary" period, the interests of Russian statehood were perceived as demanding greater reliance on the military and security institutions. For those who controlled these organizations, international relations was viewed through the perspective of conflict and a struggle for power. There was little room for ideas of transnational solidarity.[2] As a consequence of these shifts in the internal distribution of power, the democrats lost positions of influence within the Russian government. By contrast, the position of the former Soviet *nomenklatura* and bureaucrats strengthened, and this led to a major shift in Russia's policy toward Central Asia. In the case of the Tajikistani crisis it meant a shift to the open support of pro-government forces. This made a decisive impact on the course of events and led to the military defeat of the opposition in November/December 1992.

The new team declared their foreign policy goals as promoting the region's stability,[3] protecting local Russian-speaking populations[4] and preventing the transfer of illegal drugs across the Tajik–Afghan border. However, behind these openly declared interests, geopolitical factors were the dominant ones motivating policy. First, the main task of Russian foreign policy in Central Asia is to ensure that local republics remain within its zone of influence. The majority of Russian politicians would agree with the famous statement made by former US National Security Advisor Zbigniew Brzezinski that Russia without the former Soviet republics is just a regular nation-state but Russia with them is a superpower.[5] The idea that "Russia can exist only as an empire"[6] is not a new one, but the first-wave democrats combined it with a strong anti-Communist mood and believed in the prevalence of democratic values. While dealing with former Soviet republics, their geopolitical pragmatism was too often influenced by a sense of solidarity with local democratic movements or leaders. Nowadays the same "imperial" ideas are also shared by a wide range of Russian politicians, from V. Zhirinovski, leader of local nationalists, to Anatoli Chubais, one of the authors of liberal reforms, who has invented and introduced into the Russian political science dictionary a new term – "liberal empire".[7] However, in the practice of the current political elite political pragmatism has turned into almost the only factor – an essential shift in comparison to the early period of the Yeltsin era.

Russian military and intelligence agencies have a very special interest in Central Asia. Dating from the Soviet period, the optical-electronic observation station Okno ("Window") in Tajikistan is a part of the Russian space control system; the long-distance communication post of the Russian Navy, as well as a special experimental range where rocket-torpedoes for Russian nuclear submarines are tested, is in Kyrgyzstan.[8]

A crucial consideration is maintaining continued access to oil and gas resources in Turkmenistan, Kazakstan and Uzbekistan. Today, the above-mentioned countries deliver their gas and oil products through Russian pipelines, providing an essential source of income to the Russian budget. However, this control is threatened by attempts by the major oil companies, backed by Western governments, to build new oil pipelines that would provide direct access to the oil and gas resources of the Caspian Sea. There is a project to construct a pipeline connecting Kazakhstan to Azerbaijan (on the bottom of the Caspian Sea) and from Georgia to the Turkish harbor Jaihan, which was started in 2000 by Turkey and than supported by the United States.[9] Another route, developed by the Gentagas Consortium and led by the American company Unicol, involves the construction of a pipeline from Turkmenistan to Afghanistan, ending up at the Pakistani harbor in Karachi.[10] Therefore, a key policy objective of Russia is to convince both local governments and foreign investors that the best option would be to transport oil through the territory of Russia.

Given the above considerations, it is evident that Russia's key priority is to ensure that governments in the region have a pro-Russian bias. Although Russia does not have the financial means to secure such loyalty, it still has a set of effective economic or political levers to exert pressure or simply destabilize the internal political situation in these countries. In this respect, Uzbekistan and Turkmenistan, and partly Kazakhstan, have greater ability to resist such pressure due to the existence of essential oil and gas resources, which implies the possession of financial and other capacities to minimize any external interference. As to Kyrgyzstan, and especially Tajikistan, they are subject to greater pressure due to their economic dependency. Thus, Tajikistan has about 1.5 million of its citizens working in Russia as labour migrants. If Russia closed its borders or just adopted new laws restricting this migrant flow, it would create an extremely explosive and tense social and political situation inside Tajikistan.[11]

Initially, the Russian democratic elite strongly supported the Tajik opposition, the Democratic Party of Tajikistan and the Rastokhez (Renaissance) movement. When, at the end of August 1991, Tajik democrats held a series of demonstrations demanding the resignation of Mahkamov, the First Secretary of the Communist Party of Tajikistan, nobody in Moscow tried to stop them. Mahkamov announced his resignation and the first presidential elections were scheduled for October 1991. Before the elections, Tajik democrats, together with the local Islamic Renaissance Party, organized a new series of meetings backed by senior democratic leaders from Russia. In the presidential elections, Russian democratic movements and the Russian establishment supported the candidacy of Davlat Khudonazarov of the Tajik opposition. However, he was defeated and the first President of Tajikistan was Rahmon Nabiev, supported by the pro-Communist Tajikistani alliance. The events of 1991, when the Tajik democrats established a political alliance with local Islamists, reduced support for the Tajik opposition among Russian politicians and it strengthened the positions of the "professionals" within Russian decision-making circles.

However, Russian policy over Tajikistan remained uncertain until the end of 1992. In January 1991, the Tajik opposition launched a new series of demonstrations and anti-government actions continued for three months. Tajik President Rahmon Nabiev did not have an effective means to resist the political pressure or to suppress the opposition actions: the local Ministry of the Interior was paralyzed and the Tajik army did not exist. He requested help from the Russian 20 1st Rifle Division based in Tajikistan but it refused to interfere in the internal Tajik conflict due to instructions from Moscow. At the end of April, President Nabiev was forced to accept the terms proposed by the opposition leaders: Safarali Kenjaev, the Tajik Parliament speaker was dismissed and a few main opposition leaders received some key positions in the government structure. The pro-Communist elite responded with the organization of military resistance in Kuliab province (in the south of the country) and separated from the northern Khujand province. The large-scale military clashes launched at the end of June 1992 continued for several months. During this period both the Tajik opposition leaders and their pro-Communist opponents had been applying to Russia for military and political support.

The Russian Ministry of Defence, especially the leadership of the 201st Rifle Division based in Dushanbe, Russia's intelligence services and an essential part of its establishment launched a wide campaign against the Tajik opposition both inside Tajikistan and in the Russian media. There is evidence that since the beginning of the Tajik conflict Russian military specialists, instructors and special forces groups rendered assistance to the pro-government troops, sometimes directly participating in the clashes.[12] On the other hand, the "pro-democratic" lobby inside the Russian President's office and the government continued to block any decisive action directed against the Tajik opposition.

Only at the end of October 1992 did the Russian leadership finally decide to support the pro–Communist forces in Tajikistan. The decision was made purely on the basis of Russia's geopolitical interests, given the steady pro-Russian orientation of Tajik Communists and their allies. Russia's support became a decisive factor, which completely changed the situation to the advantage of the pro-Communist forces united in the framework of the so-called Popular Front. During the Sixteenth Tajik Parliament Session, the representatives of the Southern Kuliabi clans seized power. In the ensuing military campaign, the Tajik opposition forces were defeated and ousted to the mountainous eastern regions of the republic – the main part of them moved later to Afghanistan where a network of military bases and training camps along the Tajik–Afghan border was organized.

Putin's pragmatism and Russian policies post 11 September

The third period started after Vladimir Putin came to power in 1999. The problem facing Putin was that the definition of Russia's interests under the previous government did not correspond to the economic, military and financial capacities of the Russian Federation. In the eyes of the former Soviet republics, Russian policy suffered from two crucial shortcomings: its inability to provide financial aid and large-scale investments in their economies, and its failure to provide security against the rise of Islamic fundamentalism in the region, especially the rise of the Taliban in Afghanistan. The weak hand that Russia found itself playing in the region was graphically revealed after 11 September 2001. The Bush administration requested Russia's permission to "use a few Central Asian airbases in the anti-terrorist campaign against the Taliban".[13] When Moscow said no, the Americans asked the Central Asia republics, which almost immediately responded with a resounding yes. Faced with this loss of power, Russia's difficult task is to try to limit any further damage to its position in the region. In this changed context, Russian diplomacy is becoming more and more pragmatic, sometimes even cynical, with basic norms and values being disregarded for the sake of economic and political benefits.

The best example of this was the agreement on the purchasing of Turkmenistani gas (Agreement between the Russian Federation and Turkmenistan on Cooperation in the Field of Gas Industry, 9 April 2003). Saparmurad Niazov, Turkmen President, visited Moscow to sign the documents but the agreement was vitally needed, especially for Russia. It gives Russia the opportunity to sell its own gas to Eastern and Western Europe at much higher prices.[14] After the agreement was concluded, Turkmenistan issued a decree cancelling the double citizenship law.[15] The decree was directed against the interests of the Russian minority; many Russians preferred to keep their passports as an additional guarantee of their security and human rights. However, local Russians were given two months to choose their citizenship. The dilemma facing the majority of Russians was hard – to refuse Russian citizenship or to lose their flats and homes in Turkmenistan. People started to leave the country selling their flats for nothing or just abandoning them.[16]

The Russian opposition initiated a political scandal, blaming the government for trading away the interests of Russian people living abroad. According to the opposition leaders, the action undertaken by the Turkmen leader (who had tried to adopt this law a long time ago) was a part of a bargain between the sides – a concession made by the Russian government to Mr. Niazov for the sake of getting the agreement approved.[17] On the other hand, some Russian media proposed another interpretation of the political scandal around the agreement alleging it was initiated by the leadership of Gazprom (a "natural monopoly" supposed to stay out of the agreement) when in June 2003 Turkmenbashi suddenly attempted to change the agreement terms, raising the cost of gas. The scandal suddenly stopped in the middle of June when the sides reached a compromise on prices – although the Russian minority's situation in Turkmenistan has not improved yet.

The silence of not only the Russian political elite but also the society in general regarding the rights of the Russian-speaking population in Turkmenistan is rather astonishing. It is especially striking in light of a loud propagandist campaign on the rights of Russians in the Near Baltic countries carried on for many years by a wide range of Russian political and public leaders. This is an example of a "double standard" approach when the issue of typical humanitarian character is plainly subdued to geopolitics: for the sake of geopolitical interests the rights of Russians in Turkmenistan are systematically disregarded while the rights of the Russian population in the Near Baltic area – where the human rights situation (with all its complexity) could not be compared to the one in Central Asia – is in the focus of public attention.

By 2004, only two Central Asian republics – Tajikistan and Kyrgyzstan – were considered faithful Russian strongholds in the region. According to unofficial Russian sources, "certain Western countries" promised the Tajikistani leadership about US$1 billion in aid if the Russian military presence in the country is ended.[18] In the fall of 2004, faced with the real possibility of losing its remaining strongholds in the region, Russia finally offered both republics several large-scale economic projects. The Russian government committed to invest in the few next years about US$2 billion in Tajikistan for the construction of two hydroelectric power stations and two aluminum plants and US$1.3 billion in Kyrgyzstan for the construction of a hydroelectric power station. These commitments have stopped a further decline in its influence in the region. However, the geopolitical return of Russia into the region would be temporary if the Russian government would not be able to fulfill its commitments. Thus, some falling off of relations between Russia and Tajikistan occurred in the end of 2006 caused by the delay in the construction of the Rogun Hydroelectric Power Station.

Russia's recent return into the region's economy has been caused partly by the fact that President Putin and his team managed finally to convince Russia's biggest business companies (Rusal and RAOES) to invest essential financial means in Central Asian projects. On the other hand, Russia managed to get maximum geopolitical benefit out of the recent violent events in the Uzbek city of Andijan and following the deterioration of relations between Uzbekistan and the United States (see below). Using the mechanism of the Shanghai Cooperation Organisation (SCO)[19] and especially the local regimes' fear of so-called "color revolutions",[20] the Russian leadership tries to create a durable and reliable barrier able to prevent a further rise of US influence in Central Asia.[21] Today the Russian government's efforts are directed to the further strengthening of the SCO's positions and influence in the region.

Russia also skillfully uses in its interests the increasing flow of labour migration from the Central Asian countries, especially from Tajikistan, Kyrgyzstan and Uzbekistan, to the Russian labour market. According to the new Law on Migration adopted recently by the Russian Parliament, a set of quotas on migration would be defined for all countries and major foreign sources of Russia's labour force. The quota for each country would be determined by the Russian government, which can increase or decrease it following state interests and local market needs. In fact, the provisions of the new law may be used as an extremely effective tool of exerting political pressure on "disloyal" countries whose budget depends on the means transferred by labour migrants working abroad.

The current Russian "offensive" in the region is caused by purely geopolitical reasons free from any signs of the solidarity culture or, at least, the ideology that would be attractive for local people. Russia is actually the only country that unconditionally backed the Uzbek government after the events in Andijan. In this respect, it differs essentially from the previous Russian/Soviet State policy in Central Asia, when geopolitical interests were skillfully draped with ideology. At the beginning of the last century, the Bolsheviks managed to re-establish the Russian empire using the messianic Communist ideology, which had found many supporters among the local population, as a uniting mechanism. As a result, over the decades they managed to create a wide stratum of Russia-oriented people, ranging from top-level politicians to the ordinary citizens in the region. The current Russian policy in Central Asia is shorn of such ideological pretensions and is extremely pragmatic in character.

US foreign policy in Central Asia

US involvement in Central Asia has become steadily more pronounced since the Soviet invasion of Afghanistan in 1979. At that time the United States and its allies' policy in the region was defined by a set of geopolitical interests, with the main goal being to oust the USSR from Afghanistan and overthrow the pro-Soviet government in Kabul. In the period from 1989 to 1992, mujahideen leaders in Afghanistan (mostly of Pashtun origin) received about US$5 billion in American aid. One of the major results of this policy was the rise of a network of special religious schools on Pakistani territory where Afghan refugee children were taught the most militant and radical type of Islam. According to some sources, about 500 thousand pupils studied in this school network.[22] The CIA was also engaged in recruiting thousands of mercenaries all over the Muslim world to fight against the Soviets, activities in which Osama bin Laden played a very important role. This network became the base for the establishment of the Taliban movement, which was supported by the United States until 1998.

The Clinton administration had three main reasons for supporting the Taliban. First, according to Ahmed Rashid, the United States sought to use the Taliban as a counterbalance to Iranian influence in the region. Second, the Clinton administration was influenced by American oil companies, especially Unocal. The main aim of the international consortium Gentgas, which was led by Unocal, was to secure access to the gas resources of Central Asia by constructing a pipeline from the Turkmen Davlatabad gas deposit to Multan, Pakistan. The total cost of the project is estimated to be between US$2 billion and US$3.4 billion. Third, in its dealings with Afghanistan, the United States traditionally relied on Pakistan as its main ally in the region. As a result, Washington had to take into account the position of Pakistan, which strongly supported the Taliban based on its own strategic interests. Although the Clinton administration expressed support for democracy and human rights in its general policy statements, US connivance enabled the Taliban to establish a regime that perpetrated the most appalling human rights abuses, especially against Afghan women. Washington's policy vis-à-vis the Taliban illustrated the triumph of geopolitical factors over solidarity concerns in foreign policy decision-making.[23]

The situation fundamentally changed when the Al Qaeda network, which had a secure base on Afghan soil, struck against the United States on 11 September 2001. In its military operation against the Taliban, the US was forced to rely on the Northern Alliance, despite its previous lack of support for this opposition movement.

Even now, the current government of Afghanistan is going to continue the old Pakistan-supported policy, which is intended to recreate the Pashto domination in the country. To all appearances, this political course is supported not only by Pakistan but also by the corresponding US bodies. As a result, minorities' rights in Afghanistan are as usual disregarded for the sake of geopolitical interests.

However, the major mistake is the disregard of humanitarian and social needs of the local population, the expectations and hopes for economic prosperity and security that many ordinary Afghans held for the collapse of the Taliban regime. In the course of the last few years, the economic and social life of the general populace has not improved and opposition to the pro-American government is growing today in both the north and the south of Afghanistan. The southern regions have become increasingly unstable in 2006/07, with bombs and murder almost daily fare due to the offensive of Taliban insurgents welcomed by the increasing number of local tribes.

In the north, a new political coalition called the National United Front was recently formed. It brings together a broad assortment of former mujahideen leaders from most of the groups that fought the Soviet-backed communist regime in the 1980s; in the 1990's the majority of them fought the Taliban forces. The Coalition is considered as a powerful new opposition to President Hamid Karzai – its leaders want to change the constitution, change the system of government from a presidential to a parliamentary one and ensure direct elections for mayors and governors.

The increasing lack of security makes the reconstruction of the country's economy – especially in the troubled southern provinces – almost impossible, undermining people's trust in the government and raising the number of Taliban supporters. It creates a vicious circle in the country, with the failed economy contributing to rising tensions and vice versa.

As to the former Soviet countries of Central Asia who traditionally belonged to Russia's sphere of influence, they used to be beyond the direct American attention for many years. The "red line" surrounding this zone was especially respected by the Clinton administration, where many senior officials held strong illusions in regard to the democratic potential of Russia and its positive role in the post-Soviet geopolitical zone. Russia was not considered any more as the "evil empire" but as a country that gets rid of an imperialist mentality and transforms to democracy. Moreover, at that time post-Soviet Central Asia was not considered an important region for the United States in terms of its geopolitical interests. The only interference in the region's internal affairs was the human rights monitoring conducted by US embassies and correspondent agencies; in many cases, they used to warn of local states as being basic human rights violators. However, even in such cases, Russia's opinion and positions played the decisive role. For instance, in 1992 when, after the defeat of the Tajik opposition, tens of thousands of its supporters and their family members were brutally killed or ousted to Afghanistan, nothing was seriously done to stop the violence, as the criminal military groups responsible for the mess were supported by Moscow.

The situation started to change when the Bush administration came to power. It has a much more pragmatic point of view in regard to Russia and other post-Soviet countries. Bush's closest advisors developed new foreign-policy approaches aimed to maximally "capitalize the opportunities" that appeared due to the collapse of the Soviet Union as the second world superpower. The new American doctrine was for the first time formulated in 1990 by a group of conservatives, including people who occupy top-level positions in the Bush administration, such as former official Paul Wolfowitz. The main idea of the document they developed is that, in light of the Soviet empire's disappearance, the national interest of the US is to shape, rather than react to, the rest of the world and to preclude the rise of other superpowers. This "one power idea" was forgotten for ten years but was suddenly recovered after the 11 September terrorist attack, which Condoleezza Rice called "one of those great earthquakes that clarify and sharpen".[24]

The fundamental change in American foreign and defence policy led to a reassessing of the extent, reasons and shape of US involvement in Central Asian affairs. First, the geopolitical significance of Central Asia was reassessed. In light of the new doctrine, the region is a geopolitical vacuum that could be refilled by Russia or filled by China. In either case, control of this geopolitical sphere would increase China's and Russia's capacity to claim the role of the second superpower, which is not in the interest of the United States (as defined by the Bush administration). For the United States, strategic access to the region's oil and gas resources would reduce the capacity of OPEC to dictate the oil and gas prices on the world market.

On the other hand, as Central Asia is a Muslim-populated region with a difficult demographic and economic situation and rather shaky political regimes, there is always the possibility of the establishment of an Islamic state (or a group of Islamic states) of an extremist character. The last point implies the need to support the existing Central Asian regimes, which all have selected the secular character of their statehood and declared the intention to build democracy and a free market economy in their countries.

The problem is that none of those regimes could be described as truly democratic or at least could even be seriously considered as an emerging democracy. The most shocking example is Turkmenistan, where the local president has established a political regime reminiscent of the most dismal years of Stalin's epoch. Almost all presidents of the Central Asian republics have already found ways to ensure their lifetime control on power: in Tajikistan, President Emomali Rahmonov held a referendum, the results of which would allow him to stay in power for an additional seventeen years. Uzbekistan and Turkmenistan are going to establish parliamentary republics and, naturally, the local presidents will be the parliamentary speakers for the rest of their lives.

When in 2001, in preparation for the anti-Taliban military operation, Washington concluded a series of agreements with local states to use their airbases, nobody could predict how difficult the operation would be. Therefore, Americans were generous with their promises to local leaders. Islam Karimov, the Uzbek President, was especially pleased – his country is considered to be the "anchor state" of the US in the region and was promised about US$8 billion over the course of a few years. However, as the operation was so fast and successful the promises were not met, being postponed for the indefinite future. As one local expert described the pragmatism of the American policy in the region, "Americans bought Central Asia on credit".[25]

However, since last year the local regimes' attitude toward the potential US role in the region has changed to a more suspicious one. These suspicions increased after the "rose revolution" in Georgia and the recent "orange revolution" in Ukraine. In both these revolutions, local Russia-oriented governments were overthrown and replaced by a more pro-Western leadership. There is widespread opinion in the post-Soviet countries that the local US embassies and some of the international agencies are behind the political disturbances in both of these countries. Many local experts consider that the events in Georgia, Ukraine and Kyrgyzstan are part of a larger geopolitical strategy designed in the West and intended to replace pro-Russian regimes in the post-Soviet territories. However, it is difficult to determine to what extent the anxiety of Central Asian leaders is well-founded. In any case, the "import" of a revolution from one society to another is too complicated and almost not a feasible task, especially in regard to the Central Asian countries.

It seems that US policy in Central Asia has become more complex and flexible, having two main directions: on the one hand, it is the policy of "democratic solidarity" when the locally based US embassies and related governmental agencies, such as the US Agency for International Development, render increasing and comprehensive assistance to the local NGO sector and political parties that have a democratic character. Of course, the promotion of democratic processes is arguably a manifestation of a solidarity culture. However, as the main opposition parties in Central Asia have an explicit pro-Western ideology, their coming to power would increase US influence and, correspondingly, diminish the influence of Russia. Therefore, with regard to US policy in Central Asia, it is often difficult to distinguish between the solidarity culture and the pursuit of geopolitical interests. In many cases, the democratization and civil society slogans are used as an umbrella aimed at pursuing geostrategic concerns.

On the other hand, until very recent times, US policymakers continued to cooperate with the Central Asian totalitarian regimes, such as Uzbekistan and Turkmenistan, whose immunity to "color revolution" has been obtained by brutal suppression of the opposition. The few attempts by some officials to violate the limits were therefore nipped in the bud, as was shown in November 2004 when the British Foreign Office forced the resignation of Craig Murray, the then-UK Ambassador in Tashkent. According to unofficial sources, this decision was made under the direct pressure of Washington. Up until his forced resignation, Murray was the most steadfast critic of Uzbekistan domestic policy, accusing it of violating human rights. Interviewed by the *Financial Times*, Murray accused both British and American secret services of using information that Uzbekistani law enforcement bodies obtained by torturing arrested Uzbek citizens.[26]

Washington could not completely disregard the systematic and open violation of human rights and basic democratic norms committed by Islam Karimov because the implicit, unconditional support of such an odious regime would have a negative impact on its own image. It made the United States react and, under pressure from the international community and human rights organizations, the volume of critical comments and statements made by American officials and public leaders has been increasing. Such criticism was painfully heard in Tashkent, causing the rise of smoldering discontent and irritation. The critical point was reached in May 2005 when Uzbek troops and security forces brutally suppressed the civil uprisings in Andijan city. Being overwhelmed by a new wave of criticism, Islam Karimov finally took a step that led to essential changes in the geopolitical situation in Central Asia. He launched a wide-scale anti-American campaign in the local mass media and asked the Americans to leave the airbase in Khanabad. Moreover, the Uzbek regime started a sharp 180-degree turn toward Russia in particular and toward closer cooperation within the framework of the SCO in general. It is not the first but probably the last and definitive change in its geopolitical orientation.

In this new situation, with the inclusion of almost all Central Asian republics (except Turkmenistan), the SCO has turned into the main geopolitical alliance in the region, with Russia and China having the leading role. It seems that such abrupt geopolitical changes, which essentially jeopardize the American position in the region, have taken the US government by surprise. The Americans' recent proposals to create a "new economic alliance" in the region have so far not had a positive response from local governments.[27]

In general, the Uzbek case has proven that the American geopolitical approach is more complicated and complex than the Russian or Chinese ones. Of course, the Americans' involvement in the region is also caused by very pragmatic geopolitical reasons. However, the role of principal "democracy promoter" in the world deliberately assumed by the United States implies a series of obligations, criteria and limitations to be followed while concluding alliances on the international scene. Such limitations or obligations could be overlooked – but only to a certain extent. It means that US foreign policy is influenced – to some degree – by solidarity concerns.

Iranian foreign policy in Central Asia

The collapse of the Soviet Union seemed to be a good opportunity for Iran to promote its influence in Central Asia. It supported the Tajik opposition in 1991/92, opening relations not only with local Islamist groups but also with democratic reformers. Many of the Tajik democratic and Islamic leaders used to adopt pro-Iranian positions, although many of them did that on the basis of cultural and linguistic ties. There was even a tendency among Tajik opposition leaders to speak with an Iranian accent, and the local Parliament renamed the Tajiki language as "Farsi-Tajiki". But the expectations of Iranian support were not realized and, from the beginning, support was rather limited. According to unofficial sources, the opposition received military supplies and finances but these were so limited that this did not change the situation to the advantage of the opposition troops. The reasons for this restraint in Iranian policy were purely pragmatic and dictated by the country's following geopolitical interests. First, Iran did not want to spoil relations with Russia, which, as discussed above, began after October 1992 strongly supporting the local pro-government forces. Russia is one of the most important partners of Iran in terms of the development of its nuclear programme and modernization of the Iranian army. Second, Iran considered relations with other secular and Turkic-speaking Central Asian countries more important than the ethnic affinities it felt toward Tajikistan.

On the other hand, Iran has a set of important economic reasons for keeping good relations with Kazakhstan, Uzbekistan and especially neighbouring Turkmenistan, namely, their large gas and oil resources. Moreover, Iran is strategically important because its territory is the best way for international companies to gain access to these mineral resources. Thus, Iran developed a number of projects related to the construction of pipelines and roads in the hope that it could control the access of oil from the region to the wider world. For instance, starting at the beginning of the 1990's, Iran proposed to transport the Caspian oil through its territory. The Iranians' idea was to construct a short pipeline connecting the Azerbaijan network with the Iranian one – the whole project would cost Iran only US$300,000, in comparison with the US$3 billion calculated for the alternative US- and Turkey-supported projects. Another, even less expensive option proposed by Iranians was to exchange the Caspian and Iranian oil products – the Iranians would process the transported Caspian oil (from the Central Asian area and Azerbaijan to the north of Iran) for its internal market and the Western companies would get the same amount of Iranian oil in the country's harbors. However, despite their financial attractiveness, all Iranian proposals and plans have failed because the Americans insisted on the construction of transportation routes that avoided Iran.[28]

Current Iranian policy in Central Asia is influenced by its increasing confrontation with the US and the West in general. A potential military confrontation with the United States has made the Iranian government undertake urgent steps to improve its relations with its neighbouring states, especially Turkmenistan. In the given geopolitical situation, the usual pragmatism of the Iranians has been even more increased. The slogan of Islamic solidarity is almost not used in regard to the Central Asian countries or Russia – it has given way to purely geopolitical interests. As a result, the Iranian foreign policy becomes more and more contradictory, while the "double-standard approach" is a usual practice. Thus, the Iranian mass media is overwhelmed by the news from Palestine and a sense of solidarity with the Palestinian people. At the same time, Iran continuously and almost completely disregards brutal violations of the religious and civil rights of Muslims in Central Asian countries and Russia.

Turkish foreign policy in Central Asia

At the beginning of 1992, S. Demirel, the Turkish Prime Minister, stated during a meeting with US President George W. Bush that Turkey is going to change its regional status because of its increasing capacity to define the political future of Central Asia. Later he stated, "A Turkish world from the Adriatic to the Great Chinese Wall".[29] T. Ozal, another top Turkish official, announced that the twenty-first century would be "the century of Turkey".[30] Although the future Great Empire was envisaged as a Union of Turkish states, some non-Turkish nations were also to be welcomed. For example, A. Chei, the minister responsible for relations with the CIS, welcomed Ukraine and Iran as former parts of the Ottoman Empire to join the future Turkish Union. As for the non-Turkish states of Central Asia (Afghanistan and Tajikistan), the majority of Turkish experts and politicians artificially exaggerate the proportion of the local Turkic-speaking population in order to prove "the right of local Turks" for political power.[31] The same approach was used at the beginning of the last century, when the very existence of a non-Turkish population in Central Asia was denied by the local ideologues of Pan Turkism.[32]

Besides the above-mentioned geopolitical reasons, a range of purely economic tasks dictate Turkey's involvement in the region. The primary of these is to get access to the region's rich gas and oil resources by the implementation of international projects on the construction of pipelines from Central Asia to the Caucasus and then to the Turkish harbor Jaihan. Such projects would provide Turkey with an essential source of income, thereby increasing its influence in the region.[33] Since 1992, Turkish diplomacy has made great efforts to strengthen the country's position in Central Asia. Turkish top-level officials regularly visit Central Asian countries; almost every year since 1993 leaders of Central Asia have been invited to Turkey for consultations and meetings with the Turkish leadership. The Turkish Ministry of Foreign Affairs created the "Agency of Turkish Cooperation and Development", which has representatives in all Turkish countries of the former Soviet Union. Turkish official circles directly, and in some cases indirectly, support the activities of informal organizations, public associations and foundations engaged in the implementation of joint projects in the Central Asian states. Since 1993, the Kurultai (Congress) of Turkish People is annually conducted in Ankara and other cities of Turkey where one of the main topics on the agenda is to develop ways in which to create a Turkish Union under the overall dominance of Turkey.

The Islamic associations, foundations and organizations of Turkey that wish to see the future Union based on Islamic values act to promote this goal in the region. One of the most important examples of their efforts is the creation of a network of Turkish schools in the republics of Central Asia. The founders of the network officially deny any relation of their initiative to politics. However, in 2000 the activities of the network were described by a Turkish court in the following terms: "The real goal of the school network is to prepare administrative cadres for local countries in order to ensure their sympathy to Turkey when an Islamic state will be established there".[34]

There were also expectations of economic and technical assistance from Turkey. For Uzbekistan and Kazakhstan, this was especially attractive given the Turkish model of a secular state. The majority of local Turkic-speaking states even accepted the Turkish alphabet instead of the previously used Cyrillic. However, after a while it became evident that Turkey was not economically powerful enough to meet the expectations and needs of the Central Asian countries, or to compete with Russia's influence in the region.

Moreover, Turkey's role of major promoter of a unified Turkistan is challenged today by Kazakhstan, whose financial resources and economic might have been significantly increased in the course of several years due to the rise of energy prices. In the beginning of 2007, Nursultan Nazarbaev, the Kazakh President, introduced the idea of creating a Union of Central Asian Countries, where Kazakhstan is supposed to play a leading role.

As a result, Turkey finally developed a more pragmatic approach regarding the Central Asian countries. The reasons for its involvement in the region are still the same – on the one hand, there are still so-called "ethnic solidarity" concerns considerably influenced by the ideology of pan-Turkism; on the other hand, Turkey's involvement is caused by a set of purely economic interests represented by the Turkish business circles. There is an understanding today that the dreams of a new "Ottoman Empire" are not feasible in the foreseeable future but the rise of economic, cultural and military involvement would increase Turkey's influence in the region and create conditions for closer integration with the Central Asian countries in the long run. Therefore, at the present time Turkey's engagement in the region's affairs is increasingly essential in the fields of construction, culture, economy and military. For instance, with Turkmenistan and Kazakhstan, it implements joint oil and gas projects. Turkey is also the major consumer of Turkmen cotton, while Turkish private companies have made investments into the country's textile industry.

Chinese foreign policy in Central Asia

The history of China's involvement in the Central Asian region can be divided into two phases. During the first period, which continued until the end of the 1980's, China's foreign policy was dictated mostly by ideology. It supported the Afghan mujahideen movement because of old contradictions (mostly ideological) that existed between the Soviet Union and China. The second period is the time when China returned to its traditional policy, which is almost free from the influence of the ruling Communist ideology. Its foreign policy today is much more flexible and based on a new interpretation of geopolitical interests of the country as an emerging economic and military superpower. In light of the geopolitical changes in the region (the increase of the US influence at the expense of the weakened Russian positions), Chinese policymakers have revised its significance for Central Asian countries. Currently, there are three main reasons for China's involvement in the Central Asia region.

First, there is the problem of its Western Sintszian province, where Muslims, most of Uigur origin, compose more than half of the population. The province has increasing significance for the country because of its essential mineral and oil resources and geographical location, which guarantees direct access to Central Asia. At the same time, the province is the least stable region of China. The Uigur separatist movement, whose goal is to separate the province from China and to create an independent state called Eastern Turkistan or Uiguristan, has increasing influence among local Muslims. In 1997 and 1999, anti-Chinese demonstrations and disturbances were brutally suppressed. However repressive the crackdowns, separatism, often mixed with militant Islamism, is still popular among local Uigurs. The separatist movement still has steady relations with the Taliban movement, the Islamic Movement of Uzbekistan (IMU) and Hizbi-Tahrir. There is evidence that Uigur separatists used the IMU underground networks to transport into the region weapons and military supplies.[35] Hizbi Tahrir, or the Freedom Party, was founded in the 1950s in the Middle East and is considered to be one of the most active fundamentalist Islamic organizations in the world. The party's main goal in post-Soviet Central Asia is the creation of a religious state, an Islamic caliphate, throughout the region; thousands of Muslims in Central Asia, especially in Uzbekistan, Kyrgyzstan and Tajikistan, are believed to be members. As for the Taliban movement, it used to have about 16 training camps in Afghanistan specializing in the training of

Uigur fighters. There are big Uigur communities in Kazakhstan and Kyr-gyzstan, which are the bases of an underground network having steady relations with underground groups inside the region. The separatist movement is the main concern of Chinese foreign-policymakers and they would like to see the region run by secular and stable regimes able to prevent the rise and development of militant Islamic movements.[36]

The second factor driving China's policy is its need for more and more oil and energy resources if the country is to continue to grow. Indigenous Chinese energy resources are limited and need to be supported by im-ports from abroad, which will become more and more expensive. More-over, the regular delivery of oil products to the Chinese market is already becoming a problem. Ugansk, one of the major Russian oil producing companies and considered the main exporter of oil products to China, announced the possibility of its reducing oil product exports there and to its Far East markets because of the company's financial problems. China has initiated a joint venture with Kazakhstan on the construction of a pipeline to transport oil from the rich Kazakh oil fields to China. Ad-ditionally, the Chinese government is developing railway routes and roads intended to strengthen future cooperation and trade with the Cen-tral Asian states. There are joint projects to recreate the Great Silk Road that, as in the ancient times, would connect the Far East with the rest of Eurasian continent. The Road is intended to become the principal trade route for the mutual benefit of China and Central Asian countries.

The future success of Chinese industry depends on its capacity to flood other countries' markets with cheap and low-quality products; in this re-spect the Central Asian region could turn into one of the main consumers of Chinese industrial products. Besides that, there is an industrial vacuum in the region – local industries left over from the Soviet period are in many cases paralyzed or destroyed, and the appearance of new enter-prises is a very slow and complicated process. Therefore, the region is at-tractive for small and mid-size Chinese businesses – there is almost no competition on the micro-economic level. It is also attractive from the point of view of labour migration.

Third, there are geopolitical reasons pushing greater involvement, the main one of which is the need to fill the geopolitical vacuum left after the disintegration of the Soviet Union. As an emerging superpower, China needs to extend its geopolitical space as much as possible. With regard to Central Asia, this means the inclusion of the region's territory into China's sphere of influence. China has territorial claims on almost all Central Asian countries. Since ancient times, it has claimed the region as part of its sphere of influence. During the Mao era, China claimed almost all the territory of Kyrgyzstan, a part of Kazakhstan and almost half of Tajikistan. Nowadays the current Chinese leadership has developed a more pragmatic approach toward the borders issue; a set of territorial compromises have been reached with Tajikistan and Kyrgyzstan, concluding the long-term agreements on cooperation between China and these countries.[37]

Such agreements pave the way for China's future penetration into the region. There seems little doubt that if the country's industry and economy continues to grow at the present rate for at least another decade, then China would be in a position to challenge the Russian and US positions in the Central Asia region. However, China's involvement so far is totally free from solidarity concerns even when compared to Russia's foreign policy in the region, which at least is using democratic terminology to cover its geopolitical concerns. In comparison with the United States, which promotes certain types of ideology and democratic/civic institutions in the region, China has nothing to offer to local societies except purely economic projects and cooperation in the sphere of regional security. However, even in this respect Chinese involvement in the region is still rather limited, partly because of resistance from Russia – so far the major actor in the region.

The situation started to change with the creation of the SCO in 2004. Another factor is the recent geopolitical changes in the region, including the violent events in Kyrgyzstan and Uzbekistan, that have made local regimes revise their relations with the outer world and reassess their needs and priorities for the benefit of Russia and its allies.

The SCO, in which China along with Russia plays a decisive role, creates a number of new geopolitical opportunities for the Chinese government. In the long term, the SCO could be used by the Chinese as an effective mechanism for further gradual penetration into the region. In this respect China, as an emerging superpower putting forward very pragmatic geopolitical concerns, has an increasing potential in the region.

International organization and NGO policy in Central Asia

International involvement in the region started in the early 1990s. Over those first years international agencies and especially UN-related organizations were the only foreign actors allowed, having almost unlimited access to the region, which was still considered and recognized as being within Russia's influence zone. The influence of the international organizations was therefore essential and their involvement was decisive in the solution to a number of local conflicts and problems over that period. Today, despite the appearance of a number of new geopolitical actors in the region, the role and influence of international organizations is still increasing. Their role in many local countries is underscored by the appearance and strengthening of local third-sector organizations and NGOs, which are the major outcome of many years of activity and effort on the part of the international organizations.

The activities and influence of the international organizations and NGOs have been implemented in the following main lines:

Conflict resolution and prevention

International agencies made an essential contribution to the establishment of peace in Tajikistan, as well as to the conflict resolution processes in Afghanistan and all over the region. One of the major successes of UN mediation is the Tajik Peace Treaty, signed in July 1997. The whole process of official negotiations among conflicting parties in Tajikistan was held under the auspices of the United Nations. The mediation was especially effective in promoting consensus among the involved parties and countries of the region, which had already been prepared for compromise but needed a third, neutral party to move the peace process ahead. The UN special envoys played an especially important role by leading rather than simply following the negotiation process. The UN team prepared all the draft documents of the peace agreements.[38] The United Nations and international organizations (OSCE, the International Organization for Migration, UNHCR) made possible the return of more than 100,000 Tajik refugees to their homes, from Afghanistan, Central Asian countries and Russia. More then 36,000 private houses destroyed during the civil war were rebuilt thanks to the assistance of international organizations in southern districts of Tajikistan. In the following years, international agencies monitored the situation in the above-mentioned areas, preventing and mitigating conflicts between returnees and the rest of population.

Human rights monitoring and protection: Civil society and third sector development

Monitoring human rights violations and enforcing compliance with existing UN human rights instruments is a major challenge facing humanitarian and human rights NGOs. In this field the contribution and influence of international organizations would be hard to overestimate. The permanent monitoring of human rights makes even the most odious local rulers observe certain rules and limitations (at least to a certain extent) when dealing with political oppositions, individual and minorities' rights and so on.

In the course of 10 to 15 years, the international organizations managed to create in the region a wide stratum of local NGOs and public associations, an independent (more or less) mass media and – in the majority of countries – relatively free access to information. For instance, in Tajikistan and Kyrgyzstan the first access to the Internet was provided by the international organizations (in Tajikistan by the Central Asian Development Agency in the mid-1990s).

The majority of Tajikistan's six registered parties got their registration mainly due to the backing of international organizations located in the country. Many local political leaders participated in the training and educational programmes sponsored by OSCE, the Soros Foundation, UN agencies and others aimed at promoting their political culture and skills.

Economic development promotion

International NGOs make an essential impact on the internal policies of local countries in the fields of economic and democratic development. As all Central Asian states pass through complicated transformation periods they need foreign investments, loans and assistance. Therefore they are forced to take into account the international NGOs positions and opinions while conducting both internal and foreign policies. As a result, even the presence of international NGOs in the region restrains considerably the extent of human rights violations and pushes local leadership to take some steps toward further democratization and a free market economy. For instance, the majority of economic, social and structural reforms initiated in Tajikistan over the last decade were designed with the direct involvement of international agencies and financial organizations such as the World Bank, IMF, the Asian Development Bank and UNDP, among others.

This phenomenon is especially typical for countries with dependent economies, like Tajikistan, which suffered from civil war and scarcity of resources. The Tajikistani leadership, being interested in keeping the country's positive image, makes real steps toward democracy – sometimes more real than their economically more developed neighbors. Paradoxically, the countries with less dependent economies and rich oil and gas resources like Uzbekistan and Turkmenistan are less dependent on international public opinion and consequently have much more dismal human rights violation records.

Humanitarian assistance

One of the major reasons for the involvement of humanitarian organizations is to render humanitarian assistance such as food, medicine and clothes to the people suffering from conflicts, refugees and so-called internally displaced persons. This kind of involvement was important for the local countries during their first years of transition to a market economy, when the previous mechanisms of social protection of population had been destroyed. Such assistance was and is especially crucial during emergency situations such as natural disasters or internal conflicts. As usual, such activities are not related to politics and are a pure example of humanitarian and solidarity concerns.

However, some so-called humanitarian activities are conducted by organizations of a special kind pursuing their own purposes and consequently using humanitarian activities as a cover. Such organizations are usually sponsored by foreign religious foundations and associations and at least a part of their activities is intended to spread their influence in the region by converting local people. These missionary organizations are especially successful in Kazakhstan and Kyrgyzstan and to some extent in Tajikistan but their activities are limited in Uzbekistan and Turkmenistan due to the local governments' policy.

The activities of this kind of organization are a source of increasing discontent among the local Islamic clergy, religious people and, often, ordinary Muslims. In Kyrgyzstan, where the number of converted Muslims is especially significant, inter-religious relations have became an acute issue.

In the last few years, especially after the "rose revolution" in Georgia and the "orange revolution" in Ukraine, a range of international and private organizations as well as US-related ones, plus OSCE and the Soros Foundation, are accused of rendering direct support and assistance to local pro-Western opposition groups. Today, the same range of suspicions have emerged in the Central Asia region, which is believed to be the next object of geopolitical changes in the post-Soviet territories. In spite of an absence of conditions favourable for such "democratic import", the local post-Communist ruling elites, feeling threatened, toughened their attitude toward international organizations. For example, last year Uzbekistan closed the Soros Foundation office in the country. Askar Akaev, President of Kyrgyzstan, in a speech to top military officers, stated that the political overturns in Georgia and Ukraine are "the call to take up arms for all post-Soviet countries".[39] Many politicians in Russia and Central Asian countries believe that "Ukraine ... is but the first stage of a larger scale geopolitical operation by the West aimed at changing the local regimes via revolution".[40] In their opinion, support of local NGOs by international agencies and the West is just a part of this operation.

The involvement of international agencies and humanitarian organizations in the region is often explained as being dictated by the interests of the major superpowers or so-called donor countries – the main contributors to the United Nations and other major international organizations' funds. The majority of international organizations, especially the most important of them such as the United Nations or OSCE, must at least take into account the positions and opinion of the US and other major states while conducting their policy in the region. The regions that have geopolitical significance for the major states, as usual, become attractive for the international NGOs as well.

However, it is difficult and almost impossible to determine to what extent the policy of international organizations in Central Asia is influenced by the positions of the major donor countries such as the US. Such influence could be considered essential with regard to US government-related organizations such as the National Democratic Institute but much less so with regard to UN-related agencies and especially private foundations such as the Open Society Institute. At the same time, a number of agencies have policies that are, indeed, directed almost exclusively by solidarity concerns. This is especially true in regard to a range of private foundations that are self-financing.

The international organizations' presence in the Central Asia region is especially important for local non-governmental organizations and public associations whose activities are exclusively based on external financial support. Additionally, the external involvement in Central Asian affairs, regardless of its reasons and motives, has a positive influence on the overall situation in the region. On the one hand, the international involvement essentially restrains totalitarian and authoritarian tendencies of local regimes, making them to follow certain worldwide-accepted rules and norms. On the other hand, the international involvement, especially the activities of international NGOs, promotes the democratic processes and economic reforms considerably in the majority countries of the region. In general, regardless of the above-mentioned accusations, the international organizations' policies are within the overall framework of solidarity culture and are significant for the promotion of democracy in the region.

Conclusion

The main reason for the external involvement of major states in Central Asia is national interest. States enter into the region drawn by their own unilaterally defined interests but inside the region they must take into account the positions and interests of other geopolitical actors, both domestic and foreign. As a result, they create political bloks and alliances, officially announced or not, each of them drawn by a combination of interests and concerns of the actor-members involved. This does not mean that there is no solidarity culture at work but it serves mostly as an ideological or theoretical background.

When states officially declare their political goals and interests, they use, as usual, the terminology of solidarity culture. There is a set of ideological values and norms shared or at least recognized by the majority of states and even the most odious regimes do not deny them, often openly using the democratic terminology as an umbrella. However, behind the officially declared goals could often be found a set of much more pragmatic geopolitical tasks and interests that usually are not presented officially. Thus, the United States's interference into the region is officially explained by the need to struggle against world terrorism and religious extremism but there is another task that is not openly discussed – to take advantage of the geopolitical vacuum that appeared due to the weakening of Russia's positions in Central Asia.

States' foreign policy is often under the influence of so-called "interest groups" or "lobbies" reflecting the interests of internal and international business circles or national or social groups, political movements and so on. For instance, the so-called "oil lobby" made an essential impact on US foreign policy in regard to the Taliban issue in the 1990s.

The problem is that the lobbies' interests do not correspond with the solidarity culture approach. In the majority of cases the policy implemented under the influence of such interests groups is in contradiction with basic human rights requirements and democratic norms and values. Moreover, the interests of lobbing groups very often do not coincide with the real state or society interests.

There is, however, a set of differences between the external actors' way of involvement that makes an essential impact on the overall geopolitical situation in the region. In this regard, national actors involved in the region differ essentially in terms of the proportion of solidarity and geostrategy concerns in their practice, ranging from China, Iran and Russia on one side to the United States on the other. In this regard, the external actors involved in the Central Asian region could be divided into three groups, as follows.

The first group consists of countries that use mostly the so-called "geostrategy approach". It is represented by Russia and China, whose involvement in the region bears an extremely pragmatic character almost free from solidarity concerns. In this case the slogans of democratic solidarity are used mostly as an umbrella (Russia) or such terminology is almost not used (China). Unilaterally defined national interests are the cornerstone of both countries' foreign policy. As to the interests of local partners, they are taken into account as required and as long as they are not in sharp contradiction with their own geopolitical concerns.

The second group, with a so-called "Western democracies approach", is presented in the region mostly by the United States and to some extent by EU countries, whose influence in the region is still minimal. The approach of Western countries could be characterized as a combination of both geostrategy and solidarity concerns, with the prevalence of the former. Of course, even in this case foreign policy practice has an extremely pragmatic character. However, the Western geopolitical pragmatism has certain limits due to a strong influence of democratic solidarity concerns.

There is a third group, taking a so-called "non-democratic solidarity approach", presented in the region by Iran and Turkey. The geopolitical pragmatism in both countries' foreign policy is based on an ideological background of a special character: pan-Islamism in the case of Iran and pan-Turkism in the case of Turkey. It implies the existence of so called "non-democratic" kinds of solidarity concerns in practice – mostly religious solidarity in the case of Iran (for instance, toward Shia minorities in Afghanistan) and ethnic solidarity in the case of Turkey (toward Turkic-speaking people of the region).

The differences between the groups can be illustrated by a comparison of two major geopolitical players in the region, Russia and the US. Of course, for the most part, their unilaterally defined national interests draw both countries to the region. At the same time, the major difference between them is related to the ideology that defines the practice. For Russia it is the ideology of geopolitical pragmatism aimed at recreating its superpower status.[41] It is ideology mixed with a bit of painful "imperial syndrome". This kind of sentiment is still more or less shared by an essential part of the Russian public. In this regard the Russian president, as long as he pursues this goal, is free to use every means, being backed by the majority of his people. Furthermore, as Russian civil society is weak and the mass media dependent on the government, the Russian president is more or less free from public control. In the case of Russian policy in the region, the democratic slogans and solidarity culture terminology are used only as an umbrella to cover this goal or, at least, they are no more than secondary. Russian policymakers can easily disregard the negative image of some local regimes or politicians for the sake of geopolitical interests and without serious consequences for their personal political future. While pursuing their goals inside the region, the Russians prefer to deal almost exclusively with local authorities overlooking the local third sector or even regarding it with distrust as the creature and promoter of Western influence.

As to US foreign policy, it is mostly defined by geopolitical pragmatism as well. However, it is also bound to the comprehensively developed "democratic ideology", which has actually turned into the "national (state)" ideology of the United States. It implies that as the major democracy in the world, the US assumes certain obligations to promote civil society and democratic values abroad. The democratic slogans and terminology, as well as the country's image of "principal democracy promoter", are taken seriously by the American public – moreover, there is a strong civil society, mass media and public that can effectively monitor their implementation and even influence the foreign policy issues. Thus, the pressure exerted by American feminist organizations made the Clinton administration revise its policy and attitude toward the Taliban regime in 1996.[42] Therefore, the US government's ability to overlook human rights violations in the countries it deals with is much more limited in comparison with Russia. The use of democratic solidarity slogans implies the necessity of assuming obligations to promote the formation of multiparty systems and civil society in the region as well as to support the local NGO sector. Assistance of this kind is rendered anyway, often in spite of the risk of spoiling relations with local authorities and, consequently, jeopardizing the achievement of the pursued geostrategy goals.

Since 11 September 2001, the geopolitical situation in Central Asia has been rather uncertain. It has been a shaky balance described in 2004 as "a delicate geopolitical game between the USA and Russia in the region according to the formula 'action – reaction'. Both of them are moving on the territory of the CIS countries like on a chessboard, being afraid of making a mistake that would give irreversible strategic advantage to the opposite side".[43] In other words it was actually a struggle between the "geostrategy approach" presented by Russia and the "Western democracies approach" presented by the US. The turning point was reached in May/June 2005, during and after the events in the Uzbek city Andijan when, willingly or not, the Americans were forced to criticize their ally for excessive brutality. At the same time, the Russian leadership expressed sympathy with the uncompromising position of the Uzbek government and justified the use of force during the Andijan uprising.

The following complete turn of the Uzbekistani regime toward Russia and the strengthening of SCO positions and influence among the Central Asian countries – former Soviet republics – imply that the shaky geopolitical balance in the region is finally upset in favour of Putin's government.[44] It was not an abrupt change but the result of local regimes' discontent and disappointment accumulated in the course of the last several years. The US policy in the region that promoted the local third sector and oppositional parties has contributed to cause this sense of discontent. The Central Asian authorities have learned their lesson from the recent political events in Ukraine, Georgia and especially in neighbouring Kyrgyzstan, where the local third sector and oppositional parties cherished and protected by the West have played an essential role in the local governments' overthrow. Today, local authoritarian rulers clearly understand that democratic solidarity culture in any form – even in such an incomplete and inferior form as presented by the USA and the West in general – threatens their personal positions and undermines their political future.

On the other hand, Russia and Russia-oriented alliances like the SCO are ready to promote the stability and security of local regimes in exchange for geopolitical loyalty, and do not impose democracy requirements the implementation of which would destroy the existing political order. Therefore, geopolitical domination in the post-Soviet part of the region, once again obtained by Russia, implies the triumph of geopolitical pragmatism and geostrategy concerns over democratic solidarity. In the current geopolitical situation of Central Asia, the geostrategy approach has proved to be more effective and attractive for local political elites whose major concern is to maintain power as long as possible.

History shows us, however, that military, economic or political progress cannot be sustained in the long run without taking the rights of people seriously. In comparison to Russia, whose influence in the region is increasingly bound to the destiny of local authoritarian rulers, US involvement has a better future prospect for success – not only because of the country's financial and economic resources but also because of its powerful ideological and solidarity culture used to ensure its geostrategic interests. One of the major sources of support to future US involvement into the region is the local third sector and especially oppositional political parties of a democratic character, the majority of which share the same ideological pro-Western beliefs. In this respect, the recent geostrategy triumph in Central Asia can be regarded as a rather temporary phenomenon.

Notes

1. Buri Karimov (1997) *Fariedi Solho* (*Call of the Years*), Moscow: Sov. Misl, pp. 100–110.
2. Artem Artukov (2005) "Rossia Mechtaet Postroit Dubl SSR" ("Russia's Dream Is to Build a Bubble USSR"), 4 February, available from http://www.utro.ru/articles/2005/02/04/404085.shtml, accessed 30 May 2006.
3. See "Kontsepsia Vneshei Politiki Rossiiskoi Federatsii" ("The Concept of Foreign Policy of the Russian Federation"), *Svobodnaya Misl* 21(7): 13–28, Moscow, 2002.
4. Ibid.
5. Zbigniew Brzezinski (1994) "Prezhdevremennoe Partnerstvo" ("The Premature Partnership"), *Nezavisimaya Gazeta*, 7 May, p. 4.

6. Aleksandr Prokhanov, editor in chief of *Zavtra* newspaper, quoted in Georgi Ilichev (2004) "Should Russia Be an Empire?", 10 December, available from http://www. izvestia.ru.

7. Maksim Artemov (2004) "Russia Must Be Empire without Emperor", Utro.Ru, 20 December, available from http://www.utro.ru/articles/2004/12/203881170.

8. Nabi Ziadullaev (2002) "Rossia i Problemi Natsionalnoi Bezopasnosti Juzhnikh Regionov SNG" ("Russia and Problems of National Security of Its Southern Regions"), "Rossia i Musulmanskii Mir" ("Russia and the Muslim World"), *IV RAN* (Institute of Oriental Studies of the Russian Academy of Science) *Bulletin* 119(5): 91–145.

9. A. Rashid (2005) "Islam, Neft I Novaiya Bolshaya Igra v Tsentralnoy Azii" ("Islam, Oil and a New Big Game in Central Asia"), part 1. 17 January, available from http://www.CentrAsia.org/newsA.php4?st=1105948320, accessed 30 May 2006.

10. I. I. Ivanova (2000) "Afganistan i Turtsija" ("Afghanistan and Turkey"), in A. D. Davidov, ed., *Afghanistan: Problemi Voini i Mira (Problems of War and Peace)*, Moscow: IV RAN (Institute of Oriental Studies of the Russian Academy of Science), pp. 180–185.

11. Rashid Abdullo (2004) "Visit Putina: Ozhidania I opasenia", *Asia Plus*, available from http://www.http.asia.plus.tj/inbox.

12. According to United Tajik Opposition sources, small units of the Russian special forces unofficially participated in the inter-Tajik clashes (backing the pro-government People Front) starting in the summer of 1992. However, Russian officials categorically denied these accusations. Later, from 1993 until 1997, Russian troops were mostly engaged in small-scale clashes along the Afghan-Tajik border trying to prevent (rather unsuccessfully) the penetration of Tajik mujahideen into the territory of Tajikistan. For more details on the Tajik Civil War, see V. L. Buzhkov and D. V. Mikulski, eds (1997) *Anatomia Grazhdanskoi Voini v Tadjikistane: etnosocialnya i politicheskaya borba (Anatomy of the Civil War in Tajikistan: Ethno-social Processes and Political Struggle)*, Moscow: Institute of Ethnology and Anthropology of the Russian Academy of Science – Institute of Practical Oriental Studies; Parviz Mullojanov (2001) "The Islamic Clergy in Tajikistan Since the End of the Soviet Union", in Stephane Dudoignon and Komatsu Hissao, eds, *Islamic Area Studies*, London: Kegan Paul International, pp. 221–252; Aziz Niyazi (1997) "Tadjikistan: Konflict Regionov" ("Tajikistan: Conflict of Regions"), *Vostok* 2: 94–107; Kirill Nourzhanov (1998) "Seeking Peace in Tajikistan: Who Is the Odd Man Out?", *Central Asia Monitor*, pp. 15–23; Barnett Rubin (1998) "Russian Hegemony and State Breakdown in the Periphery: Causes and Consequences of the Civil War in Tajikistan", in R. Rubin and Jack Snyder, eds, *Post-Soviet Political Order: Conflict and State Building*, London: Routledge, pp. 128–161.

13. Aleksei Aleksandrov (2002) "Amerikantsi Obzhivajut Tsentralnuju Aziju" ("Americans Take Roots in Central Asia"), *Rossia i Musulmanskii Mir (Russia and the Muslim World)*, Moscow: *IV RAN* (Institute of Oriental Studies of Russian Academy of Science) *Bulletin* 120(6): 102–112.

14. Olga Gubenko (2003) "Turkmenia i Ukraina Zastavljajut Gazprom Stroit Nevigodnii Gazoprovod" ("Turkmenia and Ukraine force Gazprom Company to Construct Unprofitable Gas Pipeline"), *Finasovie Izvestia*, available from http://www.finiz.ru/cfin/tmpl-art/id_art-616813. For more details, see Olga Gubenko (2003) "Gazprom Budet Investirovat Bolshie Dengi v Razvitie Gazotransportnoi Sisitemi Srednei Azii" ("Gazprom Company Is Going to Invest a Considerable Amount of Funds in the Development of Gas Transportation Network of Central Asia"), *Finasovie Izvestia*, 20 August, available from http://www.finiz.ru/cfin/tmpl-art/id_art-621702, accessed 30 May 2006.

15. More details are available from Novosti Mira, http://www.newsru.com/world/08jun2003/gra.html.

16. More details are available from Novosti Mira, http://www.newsru.com/world/27jun2003/konfa.html.
17. Rudolf Bessmertny (2003) "Ognivo" ("Lighter"), *Sovremennii Gorozhanin*, 10 September, available from http://urbi.ru/week/1716.html.
18. Vladimir Mukhin (2004) "No Evidence that Moscow Would Get Essential Benefits from Military and Economic Cooperation with Dushanbe", *Ferghana.Ru*, 22 October, available from http://www.fergana.ru/main.php?did=17&name_division=Аналитика&bracket_flag=1.
19. The declaration on the establishment of the Shanghai Cooperation Organisation was signed on 21 June in Shanghai. The SCO now includes Russia, China, Tajikistan, Kazakhstan, Kyrgyzstan and Uzbekistan. The SCO's proclaimed aims are strengthening of friendship and cooperation in the fields of economy, politics, defence and stability in the region and the promotion of a new rational democratic order on the international scene. For more information, see Richard W. X. Hu (2005) "China's Central Asia Policy: Making Sense of the Shanghai Cooperation Organization", in Boris Rumer, ed., *Central Asia at the End of the Transition*, New York: M. E. Sharpe Armonk, pp. 130–135.
20. The term used mostly by Russian and Central Asian mass media as a general definition of the recent geopolitical phenomenon in the post-Soviet territory – the so-called "rose revolution" in Georgia and the "orange revolution" in Ukraine.
21. D. Serov (2005) "Post-Sovetstkaya Tectralnaya Asia – Stsenarii Razvitiya" ("Post-Soviet Central Asia – Variants of Development"), *dumaem.ru*, available from http://www.Centr.Asia.org/newsA.php4.
22. Aleksei Smirnov (2001) "Boi SSHA s Sobstvennoi Teniju" ("The USA's Fighting against Its Own Shadow"), *Novie Izvestia*, Moscow, 10 October, p. 5.
23. Rashid, "Islam, Neft I Novaiya Bolshaya Igra v Tsentralnoy Azii" ("Islam, Oil and a New Big Game in Central Aisa").
24. Nicholas Lemann (2002) "The Next World Order", *New Yorker*, April 1, pp. 42–48.
25. Aleksei Aleksandrov (2002) "Amerikantsi Obzhivajut Tsentralnuju Aziju" (Americans Take Root in Central Asia), *Rossia i Musulmanskii Mir* (Russia and the Muslim World), IV RAN (Institute of Oriental Studies of Russian Academy of Science) Bulletin, 120(6): 102–112.
26. Zurab Nalbandian (2004) "Kak Vshington pitalsia uvolit britanskogo posla v Uzbekistane Kreiga Murrea" ("How the Washington Administration Attempted to Dismiss Craig Murray, British Ambassodor in Uzbekistan"), *Trud*, 9 January, p. 3.
27. P. Bikov (2005) "Tsentralnaia Azia: Konets Avtoritarnoi Stabilnosti" ("Central Asia: The End of Authoritarian Stability"), Part 1, *Central Asia*, available from http://centrasia.org/newsA.php4?st=1131089220.
28. Rashid, "Islam, Neft I Novaiya Bolshaya Igra v Tsentralnoy Azii" ("Islam, Oil and a New Big Game in Central Aisa").
29. V. Egorov (2000) "Rossija i Turtsija: Linija Protivorechii" ("Russia and Turkey: Line of Contradictions"), *Blizhni Vostok i Sovremennost*, Moscow, 9 November, pp. 320–330.
30. Ibid.
31. Ivanova, "Afganistan i Turtsija" ("Afghanistan and Turkey").
32. Rahim Masov (1997) *Istoria Topornogo Razdelenia (The History of the Clumsy Division)*, Dushanbe, Tajikistan: Irfon, pp. 15–40.
33. Rashid, "Islam, Neft I Novaiya Bolshaya Igra v Tsentralnoy Azii" ("Islam, Oil and a New Big Game in Central Aisa").
34. V. Egorov, "Rossija i Turtsija: Linija Protivorechii" ("Russia and Turkey: Line of Contradictions"); and V. Egorov (2002) "Rossia i Musulmanskii Mir" (Russia and the Muslim World), Moscow: *IV RAN* (Institute of Oriental Studies of the Russian Academy of Science) *Bulletin* 119(5): 106–108.

35. Igor Rotar (2002) "Sinszian-Yigurskii Avtonomnii Rayon (Kitai)" ("Uigur Autono-mous Region (China)"), *Rossia i Musulmanskii Mir (Russia and the Muslim World), IV RAN* (Institute of Oriental Studies of the Russian Academy of Science) *Bulletin*, Mos-cow, 119(5): 106–108.
36. Chzhao Lungen (1997) "Islamski factor v Rossisko-Kitaiskikh Otosheniyakl Strategi-cheskogo Partnerstva" (The Islamic Factor in Russian–Chinese Relations of Strategic Partnership), IDV RAN, *Express-Information Bulletin* 11: 60–70.
37. Hu, "China's Central Asia Policy".
38. For more details, see Vladimir Goryayev (2001) "Architecture of International Involve-ment at the Inter-Tajik Peace Process", in K. Abdullaev and Katherine Barnes, eds, *Politics of Compromise: The Tajikistan Peace Process, Accord* 10, London: Conciliation Resources, pp. 32–37; and Elena Rigacci Hay (2001) "Methodology of the Inter-Tajik Negotiations Process" in same, pp. 38–43.
39. Michael Meyer (2005) "Domino Theory", *Newsweek*, January 11.
40. Ibid.
41. Konstantin Siroezhkin (2005) "Russia: On the Path to Empire?", in Boris Rumer, ed., *Central Asia at the End of the Transition*, Armonk, N.Y.: M. E. Sharpe, pp. 93–130.
42. A. Rashid, "Islam, Neft I Novaiya Bolshaya Igra v Tsentralnoy Azii" (Islam, Oil and a New Big Game in Central Aisa), part 3, p. 20, available from http://www.CentrAsia.org/newsA.php4?st=1105948320.
43. Najia Badikova, "Turkmenistan: Apotheosis of Autocracy", centrasia.ru, available from http://www.CentrAsia.Ru/newsA.php4?st=1098651240.
44. Ilia Barabananov (2005) " Putin Zavel Sebe Vtorogo Batku" (Putin Found a New Lu-kashanko), *Asia Plus*, 17 November, p. 12.

5

Constructions of solidarity: The US and the EU in the Israeli–Palestinian conflict

Mira Sucharov

Arab–Israeli relations have long captured the imagination of external observers. Accordingly, many states, to the extent that their material capabilities allow and their domestic populations dictate, have involved themselves diplomatically and economically with events in the region. While these activities cannot be classified as humanitarian intervention in the conventional sense, which typically entails the use of armed force to address a humanitarian crisis in another state and which necessarily involves a bracketing of the state's self-interest in the goal of helping strangers,[1] these types of actions raise similar questions about interest and identification that have captivated those attempting to understand patterns of global intervention.[2]

Empirically speaking, these external involvements have helped to shape the course of the Arab–Israeli conflict and, more recently, the halting Israeli–Palestinian peace process, and so it is useful to uncover their determinants. At the theoretical level, one of the main questions that accompanies many efforts to understand such patterns of intervention, and that indeed guides this volume, is whether external parties are motivated by a culture of national interest or by one of solidarity. In the former, particularistic interests bring about foreign policies intended to serve the narrow interests of the actor; in the latter, the intervening polity consciously identifies with the welfare of the target population, leading to policies intended to help the other. A culture of solidarity also raises questions about the weight of sovereignty as an organizing principle of the international system – whether actors consider the primary unit of

National interest and international solidarity: Particular and universal ethics in international life, Coicaud and Wheeler (eds),
United Nations University Press, 2008, ISBN 978-92-808-1147-6

focus to be states or individuals and therefore whether, in the context of a stateless nation such as the Palestinians, the status quo is to be preserved at the expense of fundamental political change – namely the establishment of a Palestinian state alongside Israel.

Determining the causes of external involvement – specifically, whether actors are motivated by a culture of national interest or by solidarity – is particularly salient in the context of the Middle East. For the generations of Israelis and Arabs raised under the shadow of war, the security situation resembles a humanitarian problem that would lend itself to varying degrees of identification. The populations of both states have endured decades of interstate war (there have been six Arab–Israeli wars since 1948, and conflicts outside the immediate area – namely between the United States and Iraq, as well as tensions between the United States and Iran – threaten to involve the Mediterranean core) and, more recently, Israelis have been living in constant terror of Palestinian suicide bombings, whilst Palestinians in the West Bank and Gaza suffer the ongoing effects of Israeli occupation punctuated by Israeli military reprisals.

Yet the Middle East is not only a humanitarian issue, and indeed that aspect has often been ignored by third parties, particularly given that the region has historically been of crucial geopolitical importance. With one-fifth of the world's oil supply coming from the Middle East, external actors – especially the great powers – have been strongly motivated to maintain a strategic foothold in the region. Yet it is not only material interests that have driven the Western world to get involved. This point becomes obvious when one considers that, aside from the flurry of activity surrounding the US-brokered 1978 Camp David Accords, American involvement with the Israeli–Palestinian peace process intensified – rather than waned – after the Cold War had ended. An explanation resting solely on the oil question would suggest that third-party involvement in the Middle East, and particularly in the Israeli–Palestinian domain, would have weakened once spheres of influence were no longer as salient in the 1990s and beyond, and once the Arab states no longer enjoyed Soviet patronage. Yet this is not the case.

This chapter will attempt to uncover the determinants of intervention in the Israeli–Palestinian sphere by two sets of actors who have been visible to varying degrees in the conflict and peace process: the United States and the European Union. In discussing the role of these third-party involvements in structuring the conflict for Israelis and Palestinians, I will argue that a culture of solidarity generally shapes the outlook of the United States and the European Union, but that these cultures emerge from the identity of the state in question and in turn give rise to the polity's conception of the national interest. Drawing on the constructivist tradition that stresses the constitutive importance of identity, I argue that the degree to which a state understands its fate to be intertwined with that of others (a stance that represents a culture of solidarity) emerges from the overall identity of the state: how that polity views itself as a participant in the international system, and the stories that society tells about itself. That identity in turn leads to particular conceptions of the national interest; what the country cares about and what aspects of its "collective self" the polity attempts to achieve through global politics. The chapter therefore attempts an integrative view of the relationship between culture and interests.[3] The argument also opposes a strictly materialist view (i.e., one that would stress costs and benefits absent the constitutive force of identity in laying out such a calculus) as well as a view that would privilege strictly selfish, or particularistic, interests at the expense of other-regarding, or solidarity, ones. The chapter will begin with an analysis of US activities in the Israeli–Palestinian domain, followed by a discussion of the European Union's involvement in the region. It will conclude by exploring the reactions of Israelis and Palestinians to external involvement in the conflict and peace process.

The US in the Israeli–Palestinian sphere

The United States has been involved with the politics of the Middle East since President Harry Truman lent his country's recognition to Israel almost immediately upon the Jewish state's inception in May 1948. It was not until the aftermath of the Six Day War in 1967, however, when France decided to stop providing military support to Israel, that the United States became Israel's main arms supplier, in part as a response to Soviet patronage to the Arab states. Yet, while US support for Israel has not wavered, successive presidents' degrees of involvement in the Middle East has varied in form and intensity.

Since President Jimmy Carter shepherded Israel and Egypt toward a bilateral peace treaty and an attempted solution to the Palestinian question at Camp David in 1978, the post–Cold War era has signified the most direct involvement by the United States in Arab–Israeli peacemaking. The immediate wake of the Cold War saw President George Bush senior's decision to co-sponsor, along with Moscow, a jointly bilateral and multilateral framework for peace through the 1991 Madrid talks. Two years later, after little progress had been made, President Bill Clinton attempted to further the Israeli–Palestinian peace process begun at Oslo in 1993. This was a watershed in Israeli–Palestinian relations because the United States came on board only once the agreement had been reached between Israeli and Palestinian officials following eight months of secret diplomacy in Norway. While having arrived on the world stage with much fanfare, the Oslo track ultimately faltered amidst a second Palestinian Intifada (uprising) beginning in 2000, which prompted many observers to declare that "Oslo is dead."[4]

With the current Bush administration blindsided by the attacks of 11 September 2001, what was already only a limited focus on Israeli–Palestinian peacemaking has taken a back seat to the war on terrorism. This relative lack of interest in the Israeli–Palestinian core has led one observer to dub the Bush administration's posture "selective engagement", referring to the variability of American involvement in the Middle East, involvement that depends on the perceived interests and level of risk involved.

Currently, the United States has adopted a role as one of four influential would-be peacemakers in the region, as a member of the Quartet – comprising the United States, the European Union, Russia and the United Nations. Given the global scope of that group's membership, the body has been careful to put forth an even-handed approach – a "roadmap" for peace, in Quartet parlance – that stresses the need for both sides to quell the violence (the Palestinian Authority needing to reign in terrorism and Israel needing to exercise restraint in responding to terrorist attacks as well as to freeze settlement-building in the occupied territories) and reach a negotiated settlement leading to the creation of a Palestinian state.

Yet there is by no means a harmony of preferences within the US administration on the question of the Middle East. As the Quartet was being formed in 2002, Secretary of State Colin Powell was more forthright in advocating aggressive support for the creation of a Palestinian state, whilst Secretary of Defense Donald H. Rumsfeld and Vice President Dick Cheney were more hesitant to get involved in an active peacemaking role and viewed the conflict largely through the lens of America's broader war against terrorism, with Israel seen as being engaged in a similar titanic struggle.[5] More recently, the Bush administration has appeared to focus on encouraging a stable Palestinian government that can support the two-state principles outlined in the regular statements of the Quartet.[6]

Domestically, there have been natural divisions within the American political arena. While the Democrats have typically been more supportive of Israel, polls from 2006 reveal that Republicans appear to be more in step with Israel: 68 per cent of Republicans (compared to 45 per cent of Democrats) sympathize more with Israel than with the Palestinians, with 64 per cent of Republicans (compared to 39 per cent of Democrats) in favour of aligning with Israel versus neutrality.[7] These domestic political cleavages – as well as the shifting tides of party identification and foreign policy outlooks – suggest that attributing any external involvement to a crude calculation of self-interest is a risky explanation at best, given that the "national interest" can be a fluid category, with various political orientations as well as political actors harbouring different perspectives on what is best for their country.

In general, the fact that the United States emerged from the Cold War as the global hegemon certainly shaped both its motivations for involvement in the region and the effects of its interventions. While President Bush senior attempted to create and uphold a "new world order" centred around the 1991 Gulf War, the United States has found itself increasingly preoccupied not only with state-based threats emanating from Iraq, Iran and North Korea but also with warding off non-traditional challenges to America's international supremacy, most notably in the form of the ongoing terrorist threat in the form of Al Qaeda. This has meant that peacemaking roles are both less salient in the current threat environment and contingent on the American goal of maintaining an international order friendly to US interests. Unlike the European Union, which itself is an example of the culture of interstate solidarity at work in the form of a security community, the United States shares pockets of "Lockean culture" – such as the North American regional space – but these relationships are informed by stark power asymmetries.[8] Therefore, the United States has had less practice in constraining its use of power – any need to avoid alienating rival hegemons has not yet presented itself through lack of credible challengers[9] – and thus the United States is freer to structure its foreign policy decisions around unbridled self-interest. This also means that instances where the United States intervenes but where narrow American selfish interests are less obvious suggest cases where elements of a culture of solidarity may indeed be at work.

Whatever actions the United States has taken in the Arab–Israeli sphere have derived from a certain solidarity that stems from various identity-factors, discussed below, that derived in part originally from Cold War considerations but have since become entrenched organizing frameworks within American policy consciousness. Specifically, American involvement in the Middle East has been principally shaped by its support for Israel – a quasi alliance that has come to be known as the US–Israel "special relationship". However, it has also recognized that consideration must be given to the political fate of the Palestinians as a nation. In its attitudes to both the Israelis and Palestinians, we can see a central theme of solidarity and, as constructivism argues, it is this that explains how the United States conceives its interests in the region. The United States sees all individuals as deserving of fundamental political and social rights drawing from the moral and ethical principles that animate American society, namely liberty, democracy, self-determination, Judeo–Christian morality and free market capitalism. Taken together, these tenets give rise to a certain American identity and concomitantly shape US policies toward the Israeli–Palestinian conflict. What follows is an attempt to explore each of these guiding principles and the policies to which they lead.

American liberty and the war on terrorism

Under the Bush administration's National Security Strategy (NSS), released in September 2002, the United States has been engaged in a policy of aggressive deterrence to attempt to neutralize threats before they pose a security problem for the United States.[10] Accordingly, amidst claims that Saddam Hussein was stockpiling chemical and biological weapons while attempting to acquire a nuclear arsenal, the United States led a coalition to remove the Iraqi president from power in March 2003. With this new security posture has come a renewed effort to rhetorically and actively oppose terrorism in its multiple forms, a stance that places the Israeli–Palestinian nexus at the forefront of Bush's grand strategy, and that reflects one of the central founding principles of American society: an ethic of individualism and ideas about the right to "life, liberty and property" that are enshrined in the US Constitution. Emphasizing an ethic of human solidarity focusing on individual victims of terrorism, the NSS states that the "United States of America is fighting a war against terrorists of global reach. The enemy is not a single political regime or person or religion or ideology. The enemy is terrorism – premeditated, politically motivated violence perpetrated against innocents".[11]

The latest iteration of the Israeli–Palestinian conflict has seen a spate of Palestinian suicide bombings both in the occupied territories and inside pre-1967 Israel, perpetrated by the Islamic groups Hamas and Islamic Jihad, as well as by the Palestinian nationalist Al Aqsa Martyrs Brigade, a militant offshoot of the Fatah party. It is still unclear the extent to which the 11 September attacks were motivated by the Israeli–Palestinian conflict, though in their wake, Osama bin Laden declared the end of the Israeli occupation of Palestinian territories to be one of his goals.[12] And in building a case before the UN Security Council against Saddam Hussein, then-US Secretary of State Colin Powell emphasized Saddam Hussein's ties to Hamas and Islamic Jihad, and suggested – though the evidence was far from certain – that the Iraqi leader may be supporting the Al Qaeda network.[13] Thus, in attempting to broker a solution to the conflict, to the extent that the United States had been involved since the outbreak of the Intifada in September 2000, it is clearly motivated in part by a hard-line stance toward terrorism of all forms.

While astute observers have quipped that the fight against "terrorism" in the aftermath of 11 September is akin to describing the 1941 entry of the US into World War 2 – in the wake of the Japanese attack on Pearl Harbor – as a war against "air power", the United States sees itself as having to maintain a consistent stand against terrorism in all corners of the globe in order to rally support for its war against Al Qaeda. The Palestinian elections of 2006, where Hamas won a large parliamentary majority, only served to reinforce the view within the Bush administration that the Israeli–Palestinian conflict is in large part a struggle by a democracy to sustain itself among neighbours bent on its destruction.

The strategic aspects of Bush's approach are self-evident: a tough stance against Palestinian terrorism is a corollary to the overall US global posture. But it is still important to analyse how a culture of solidarity may help to shape this strategy. The best point of entry for such a discussion is through examining the fundamentally American principle of liberty and the right of the individual to life and prosperity in the context of Just War theory.[14]

Whether the aims of a particular war, or the mode of conducting war, is considered legitimate within international legal discourse has largely fallen to this set of principles that arose from medieval Christian theology and that have since formed the backbone of much of the international law governing warfare. Just War criteria comprise two main principles: *jus ad bellum* (the justness of a given war) and *jus in bello* (just conduct within war). The principle of discriminating between combatants and civilians constitutes one of the central tenets of *jus in bello*, and is where the main problem with terrorism would lie according to Just War criteria.[15] While some analysts understand terrorism to refer to any political violence conducted by non-state actors – a position that easily leads to a critique of the terrorism label by those concerned that its use perpetuates a state-centric view of the international system while delegitimizing non-state actors – it seems more accurate to define terrorism as political violence directed at civilians – that is, for the purpose of instilling fear in a population base in order to bring about policy change. According to this framework, we can see that terrorism, insofar as it intrinsically involves the deliberate targeting of civilians, whatever the political ends, clashes with one of the major tenets of Just War criteria. Therefore, we can consider the American support for Israel's struggle against terrorism to be buoyed by ethical precepts, and hence according with a culture of solidarity – in this case, for Israeli victims of terrorism. And insofar as the United States identifies with Israel in its own global battle against terrorism, this ethical motivation can indeed be considered an ethic of solidarity, yet in this case one that is tempered by the glaring inconsistencies of American inaction in Rwanda and Darfur.

Nevertheless, the organized violence that has formed the backbone of the Israeli–Palestinian conflict has taken the form not only of Palestinian terrorism but also of harsh measures undertaken by the Israeli military in response. The net result has been significant loss of life on both sides: as of the end of April 2007, Intifada casualties included 4,057 Palestinians killed by Israeli security forces, 41 Palestinians killed by Israeli civilians, 317 Palestinians killed by Palestinians, 705 Israeli civilians killed by Palestinians, and 316 Israeli security personnel killed by Palestinians.[16]

That said, while the United States expresses a desire to end the bloodshed, it is easier for the United States to lay blame on the Palestinians for the direct carnage while pointing to Israel's role in continuing settlement-building in the territories and conducting harsh reprisals, which, while not providing a generally hospitable environment for peacemaking, does not have the same alarming resonance as does the deliberate killing of civilians. This stance is particularly salient in the context of historical American strategic policy, which has seen multiple wars waged in various regions for the purpose of overturning hostile regimes, wars that have invariably involved civilian casualties, not least of which were the bombings of Hiroshima and Nagasaki in the Second World War.

American democracy, Judeo–Christian morality, and support for Israel

Two additional cultural reasons for the US's tendency to support Israel are America's commitment to democracy and a Judeo–Christian perspective that sees the Jews' restoration in the ancient Land of Israel as part of a Biblical teleology. In courting approval, Israeli leaders have often emphasized their state's role as the sole democracy in the Middle East,[17] a status that the United States cannot help but be aware of in its sustained assistance to Israel through most of the Arab–Israeli conflict. This reasoning has become increasingly attractive to a government that has come under attack by critics for its support for conservative Arab regimes, particularly in the wake of 11 September.[18] Supporting the only democracy in the Middle East has therefore lent moral credence to America's significant aid to Israel, amidst contentious domestic politics that include increasingly vocal "pro-Israel" and "pro-Arab" lobbying. Since 1985, the United States has granted US$3 billion per year to Israel in combined military and economic assistance, making the country, since 1976, the largest single recipient of American aid.[19] This is particularly salient given the American focus on democratization projects in the developing world, largely funded by the US Agency for International Development and embodied in then-National Security Advisor Anthony

Lake's strategy of "enlargement" that formed a major part of American foreign policy under the Clinton administration in the mid-1990s.

The emphasis on democracy has a clear ethical pedigree in American political culture and, since President Woodrow Wilson championed self-determination as a desirable global principle following World War 1, American foreign policy has followed accordingly. Yet the question remains whether US support for Israel in the post–Cold War era indeed results from American values – and hence a culture of "democratic solidarity" – or is simply a response to domestic politics and particularly the Israel lobby embodied in the America–Israel Public Affairs Committee (AIPAC), as some have argued.[20] Still a third reading would suggest that lobby groups such as AIPAC might simply be acting as a conduit of those values that already exist at the broader societal level. Yet a closer analysis suggests that American foreign policy toward Israel is actually conducted independently of the efforts of Israel lobbyists to encourage a closer relationship with the Jewish state. Examples include President Ronald Reagan's sale of AWACS aircraft to Saudi Arabia despite protests by AIPAC, and President Bush senior's precipitation of the 1991 loan guarantees crisis when the president threatened to withhold an American guarantee for US$10 billion in Israeli loans unless Prime Minister Yitzhak Shamir ordered a freeze on the building of Israeli settlements in the West Bank and Gaza Strip.[21]

Along with democracy as an American value that shapes US involvement in the region is the fact of Jewish sovereignty in the Land of Israel as constituting a central component of a Judeo–Christian teleology. One manifestation of the overall Judeo–Christian ethic within American society is evangelical Christianity, a religious stream that has become more prominent on the US political stage in recent years, along with the overall popularity of churchgoing in American society, at rates that differ sharply from other nominally Christian countries – particularly in Europe. That perspective sees Jewish sovereignty in Israel as integral to the Second Coming, whereby, curiously, the Jews are expected to be converted or abolished – through a "world war" if necessary, in order to establish the reign of Christ.

This narrative is only relevant, of course, to the extent that Christian-right groups in the United States hold some sway over the policy directions of their governments. And this influence is not insignificant: self-declared Christian-right voters appear to represent 11 per cent of the electorate in the United States.[22] Furthermore, this particular evangelical stream is not the only voice in American politics concerned with the links between religion and American politics. On the occasion of Martin Luther King, Jr.'s birthday, Bush stated in 2002 that "It is fitting that we honor this great American in a church because out of the church comes the notion of equality and justice".[23] Christianity is frequently invoked in presidential addresses; Bush's speech after the space-shuttle Columbia tragedy contained references to the Old Testament and to God, as when he quoted from the book of Isaiah and later stated that "The same Creator who names the stars also knows the names of the seven souls we mourn today."[24]

Partly because of this Christian narrative, however literally applied, American support for Israel has remained steady, despite occasional periods of tension, such as the 1991 loan guarantees crisis mentioned above. But even then, Bush senior declared in 1992 that "the U.S. commitment to Israel is a fundamental one".[25] Finally, from the end of the Cold War and until 1999, American public opinion exhibited little change toward Israel, and the US elite perceived the two countries as sharing an increased number of "vital interests".[26] Even during the Israel–Lebanon hostilities of 2006, a majority of Americans polled (52%) said they sided with Israel in its conflict with the Palestinians.[27] Yet this does not mean that American foreign policy exhibits no continuing differences with Israel. For the first time in the current Bush administration, the United States appears to be treading within the peace process quite independently of Israel: Secretary of State Condoleezza Rice has been holding talks with Arab foreign ministers regarding the eventual creation of a Palestinian state, despite Israel's ongoing boycott of the Hamas-majority government.[28]

The principle of self-determination and the Palestinian question

Along with the principle of democracy comes not only the desire to support an existing democracy in the Middle East (Israel), but the idea of encouraging self-determination. This latter principle points to the political status of the Palestinians as an issue in need of ameliorating, and which ultimately lends the United States a greater air of legitimacy in its Middle East involvements than were it solely concerned with the fate of Israel. A perception of even-handedness is particularly important insofar as the United States has attempted to shepherd Israel and the Palestinians along a negotiating path. And while the United States may have enjoyed the position of honest broker at certain points throughout the peace process, there are many, especially in the Muslim and Arab world, who would contest this even before recent events. Certainly, in recent years, America has been struggling to maintain that perception, particularly among the Palestinians.[29]

The contemporary manifestation of the Israeli–Arab conflict has indeed centred on the question of Palestinian autonomy, particularly since the emergence of the Oslo process in 1993 and subsequent negotiations over the political fate of the 3.5 million Palestinians in the West Bank and Gaza Strip. While the United States was slower than some other countries to voice support for the establishment of a Palestinian state, since Bush's October 2001 pronouncement supporting that goal a two-state solution has been the policy stance of the American government.[30] There is little in the way of immediate "national interest" for the United States to support the creation of a Palestinian state, particularly since the dissatisfaction experienced by the Palestinians arguably does not pose a fundamentally destabilizing force in the region, beyond the sense of personal insecurity that has gripped Israelis particularly since the onset of the second Palestinian Intifada. While securing allies in the region is certainly a consideration, the most pressing threat from the Middle East remains Al Qaeda, and it is far from clear that setting up a Palestinian state alongside Israel – rather than abolishing Israel altogether – would appease Osama bin Laden and his supporters. Rather, Bush's decision to call for a Palestinian state largely derives from an ethic of solidarity toward peoples desirous of self-determination. As then-Secretary of State Colin Powell described the president's position in April 2002: "He wanted to say to the Palestinian people that the United States has a vision for you; we will always be Israel's closest friend, we have been there from the very beginning, and we will always be there for Israel, but at the same time we recognize that a way has to be found for these two peoples to live side by side in peace behind secure and recognizable borders".[31] By 2007, the Bush administration was actively expounding its support for a Palestinian state. About an upcoming Arab summit to discuss the 2002 Arab Peace Initiative, Secretary of State Condoleezza Rice was quoted as saying, "Such bold outreach ... can hasten the day when a state called Palestine will take its rightful place in the international community."[32]

Nevertheless, as with the case of American support for a democratic Israel being a potentially useful counterpoint to what is perceived by some as the American pattern of propping up conservative Arab regimes, nurturing indigenous Palestinian democracy can also serve to limit critiques of US foreign policy as being one-sided in support of the status quo. That said, the degree to which the United States viewed Yasser Arafat as a legitimate and effective representative of the Palestinian people is subject to question amidst claims that his was a corrupt regime lacking democratic accountability. As President Bush stated in December 2002 regarding the peace process, "We must encourage the development of Palestinian institutions which are transparent, [and] which promote freedom and democracy".[33] Encouraging Palestinian reform faced at least two obstacles: the privileged position of Arafat as decades-long symbolic leader of the Palestinian people, even before his formal election to president in 1996, a race that his most dominant opposition – the Islamic movement in the form of Hamas and Islamic Jihad – chose to boycott; and the harsh Israeli crackdown on Palestinian terrorism, resulting in a Palestinian economy in shambles and the institutions of governance maimed.[34] With Mahmoud Abbas having succeeded Arafat in 2004 and having been elected Palestinian Authority president in 2005, the United States no doubt hoped that Palestinian Authority transparency and accountability would be improved. Part of the effort to encourage the spread of democracy more generally across the Arab world has taken the form of a US–Middle East Partnership Initiative involving US$1 billion in annual funding and an initial US$29 billion for related pilot projects related to "economic, political and educational opportunities" in the region; by 2007 the amount spent had reached $293 million.[35]

The American capitalist ideal and the question of oil

There remains one factor inextricably linked to historical US interest in the region: oil. Since this is a geostrategic concern *par excellence*, and hence one that would, at first glance, lend itself to assessing American involvement in the region in terms of a culture of national interest, we must consider this motivation in light of the multiple factors pointing to a culture of solidarity. The issue of maintaining access to oil is a theme that has run continually through the decades of US involvement in the Middle East, including the debate over whether the 1991 Gulf War was motivated by a US demand for oil rather than by the declared aims of collective security; and whether the recent war on Iraq was more about petroleum than about weapons of mass destruction. While the desire to secure affordable oil for Americans – as well as what some have called Americans' addiction to oil – cannot be ignored in analysing US policy, ultimately the American interest in maintaining access to the oil reserves of the Middle East can only be fully understood in the context of an ethic of capitalism. This is not to say that seeking national profit via oil-wealth is directly linked to a culture of solidarity, but rather that maintaining affordable access to the world's oil supply can be viewed as an essential task for a hegemon to undertake.[36] That is, in attempting to underwrite the rules of the international order, a global hegemon is virtually required to ensure that the primary engine of global industry is maintained; otherwise its credibility and legitimacy as leader would be cast seriously into doubt. Viewed in this way, the geopolitical stance suggested by an oil motivation is in fact shaped by a particular one (the hegemon's desire for international legitimacy) certainly linked to the national interest and perhaps partly connected to the idea of global responsibility, if not solidarity (with its global charges) per se. In constructivist terms, this means that the hegemon's *role* (an intersubjective notion that implies both the holding and prescribing of an international identity) leads it to take particular actions that both benefit it directly while indirectly sustaining the other members of the international system.

The EU and the Middle East

The nature of the European Union is an excellent example of the logic of solidarity operating at the interstate level, where political violence between its 27 member states has become unthinkable. The transformation in the character of relations among the members of the European Union has been so fundamental that against an historical background of multiple historical interstate enmities leading to and arising from two world wars has emerged what has come to be known as a security community.[37] The process of European integration has doubtless led the foreign policies of the European states to be informed by a culture of solidarity, whereby each member restrains its aggressive impulses vis-à-vis the others. The overriding question, though, is the degree to which the European Union has been able to coordinate its individual state policies so as to create a coherent set of collective foreign policies, and whether the orientation of EU foreign policy in various regions can be characterized by a culture of national interest or one of solidarity. On the former issue, there remains debate as to the degree of unity among member states' international proclivities, and it indeed remains to be seen whether the European Union is able to create a common foreign policy such that the region poses a challenge to American global hegemony.[38] Moreover, the recent attempt by the organization to draft a constitution has seen divisive debates over whether to include references to common values, and particularly to God.[39]

Nevertheless, in the sphere of Israeli–Palestinian relations the European Union has attempted to forge a set of policies with some degree of coherence. On the question of solidarity versus national interest, we can conclude that the European Union's actions are characterized by a mix of supra-national global jockeying and a playing out of internationalist values that take the form of seeking to extend European conceptions of global justice, including democracy-promotion and support for self-determination. Specifically, the European Union's activities in the Israeli–Palestinian peace process can be seen to emanate from three motivations: the desire to consolidate an independent, multi–foreign policy machinery by attempting diplomatic overtures in an external conflict, to counteract US global hegemony by wielding influence in an external

conflict with which the United States is intimately involved and to promote democracy and self-determination for the citizens of the region. The
latter two goals point to what has been seen by many as a diplomatic
stance tilted toward the Palestinians, particularly since they are the ones
who lack sovereignty. The first two of these motivations are largely geostrategic and therefore self-serving, aiming as they do to wield increasing
influence on the world stage, yet only to an extent: some would argue
that gently buffering American power can only serve to better international relations and help bring about justice for parties who may have been
forgotten by the American colossus. The third goal – specifically promoting self-determination for the Palestinians – derives from a culture
of solidarity, and indeed from a belief that the Palestinians deserve a fundamental transformation in their political status without this threatening
Israel's core values and security. What this suggests is that the interests of
the EU are primarily defined by the values of its member states: multinational autonomy coupled with the organization's own attempts at creating
a concerted foreign policy out of disparate sovereign-state proclivities
(desire to wield diplomatic influence) and self-determination (support
for a Palestinian state). Europe's attempt to counter American hegemony
– as well as to achieve what Europeans see as a just solution to the
Israeli–Palestinian conflict that might involve a settlement more favourable to the Palestinians than that which the United States has so far supported – is arguably expressed in the organization's relative criticalness
of Israel.

The initial diplomatic activities of the European Union in the Middle
East peace process grew out of the 1991 Arab–Israeli Madrid talks,
which were co-sponsored by Washington and Moscow. That conference,
established as the Cold War was ending and in part as an opportunity for
Moscow and Washington to display a degree of unprecedented diplomatic cooperation on the global stage, brought Israel together with its
Arab neighbours to negotiate a framework for bilateral as well as regional peace. While the summit opened with much fanfare, the talks ultimately achieved little. Madrid's lack of success can be attributed in part
to an Israeli government, led by Likud Prime Minister Yitzhak Shamir,
that was inhospitable to peace between Israel and the Palestinians, as
well as the lack of direct Palestinian Liberation Organization (PLO) participation: Israel stipulated that the Palestinians could participate only
within the context of a joint Jordanian–Palestinian delegation and without any PLO representation. In the event, the PLO effectively circum-
vented this demand by controlling the Jordanian–Palestinian delegation's
negotiating strategies from its own headquarters in Tunis.

In addition to the Arab–Israeli bilateral tracks, consisting of Israel negotiating separately with Egypt and the Palestinian–Jordanian delega-

tion, five working groups emerged to address broader regional issues that would be essential to any comprehensive peace in the region. These meetings became known as the "multilaterals". For the working group on regional and economic development (REDWG), the EU was invited to serve as chair, or "gavel holder". The other working groups included the environment (chaired by Japan), refugees (chaired by Canada), water resources (chaired by the United States), and arms control and regional security, chaired jointly by the US and Russia. The topic of regional and economic development, which in REDWG included issues of tourism, trade, finance and overall economic infrastructure, was particularly suited to the European Union, given its own experience of integration. As Christopher Patten, the European Union's external relations commissioner, stated in 2000, "Regional co-operation is by far the most effective means of achieving long term security. Indeed there is no better illustration of this than the experience of the EU itself throughout the second half of the 20th century."[40]

Only two years after the launch of the Madrid talks, the September 1993 Oslo agreement emerged out of secret negotiations that had taken place during much of that year between senior Israeli and PLO officials. The change of government in Israel from Shamir's Likud regime to Yitzhak Rabin's Labour government signaled a shift on the part of Israelis, generated to some extent by the protracted six-year Intifada that had ignited the occupied territories. The news of Oslo, an agreement that laid out a multi-year framework for negotiations on the evolving status of the Palestinian territories, necessarily relegated the multilateral tracks to the background, and a bilateral peace treaty between Israel and Jordan soon emerged in 1994. (Israel had already signed a peace treaty with Egypt, in 1979, following the 1978 Camp David Accords.) Oslo signified a watershed in relations between Israel and the Palestinians, because Israel had, in 1986, outlawed contacts with the PLO and had long refused to recognize the Palestinian people as a distinct nation. Whether one was for or against the parameters of the agreement, most observers felt Oslo to be a momentous occasion: it was seen as either ushering in a framework to achieve full peace between Israelis and Palestinians, or else creating an unjust formula that would prejudice a final settlement to the conflict. Either way, it was viewed to be historically significant in creating a new context within which Israeli and Palestinian politics would operate, capped by the likely establishment of a Palestinian state.

The optimism that Oslo engendered among the parties themselves, an enthusiasm that would be matched only by the receipt of the Nobel Peace Prize by Rabin, Arafat and Israeli Foreign Minister Shimon Peres, enabled the multilaterals to continue operating formally for another three years, even though bilateral peace between Israel and Jordan had already been achieved two years earlier, and even though the Israelis and Palestinians were all consumed with the halting progress of the Oslo framework, amidst accusations by each side that the other was not adhering to its commitments. In 1996, the Arab states decided to withdraw formally from the multilaterals, frustrated by lack of progress over negotiating the redeployment of Israeli troops from the West Bank town of Hebron.[41] This decision was cemented by the decision of the Arab League, in April 1997, to freeze normalization with Israel.[42] Informal contacts through the working groups continued, however, until September 2000, when the second Palestinian Intifada broke out, in the wake of the failure of Israel (under Prime Minister Ehud Barak) to reach a final agreement with Arafat over the fate of the territories, and the issues surrounding the right of return for Palestinian refugees and the status of Jerusalem. Analysts of the multilateral track note that they failed because of lack of focus, rivalry between Israel and Egypt and between the United States and the European Union, concerns of the Arab states about Israel's nuclear capabilities, and Israel's overriding focus on achieving recognition (referred to as "normalization" in Israeli diplomatic parlance) within the region.[43] Since 1996, the multilaterals have ceased to exist, and have been relegated mostly to an historical footnote for observers of the Arab–Israeli peace process.

Aside from the specific role that the European Union undertook within the multilaterals, the European Union's overall diplomatic stance toward the peace process differs significantly from that of the United States in its tilt toward changing the political status of the Palestinians. While the Bush administration did not begin talking of a Palestinian state until 2001, the European Union voiced support for such an outcome as early as 1999 in its Berlin Declaration.[44] And Bush's early-October 2001 declaration of support for a Palestinian state may have indeed been accelerated by the attacks of 11 September, as when Bush refused to answer a reporter's question to that effect.

As for what a Palestinian state would look like, the European Union declares its support for the "establishment of a democratic, viable and peaceful sovereign Palestinian State on the basis of the 1967 borders ... [with] Jerusalem as a shared capital".[45] By contrast, the United States has been more circumspect in the precise details of the solution it supports. As Bush stated in June 2002, "When the Palestinian people have new leaders, new institutions and new security arrangements with their neighbors, the United States of America will support the creation of a Palestinian state whose borders and certain aspects of its sovereignty will be provisional until resolved as part of a final settlement in the Middle East".[46] Bush's repeated call for Arafat to be replaced was at odds with European sensibilities (though was in line with the ideas of Sharon's government). While most European policymakers favour political reform in the Palestinian Authority, they were hesitant to outwardly prescribe who the leader of the Palestinians should be.

This different tack from that of the United States has enabled the European Union to provide a diplomatic counterweight to American global influence while at the same time allowing it to entrench its collective foreign-policy voice in international affairs. And while the European Union demarcates itself from US positions, the United States is concurrently trying to emphasize points of policy overlap, perhaps to diffuse whatever power competition exists. As Colin Powell remarked over a year into the Palestinian Intifada, "With the good cooperation between the United States and the European Union, it's possible certainly to have new, better results in a short period of time", and he emphasized that the United States and the European Union were united in finding a solution to the Israeli–Palestinian quagmire.[47] Finally, complicating the relationship between the European Union and the United States on the Arab–Israeli issue was the question of war with Iraq. While the United States assertively sought out allies, many European leaders found themselves hesitating to support a war that could extend American global hegemony, fuel domestic interreligious tensions or exacerbate the Israeli–Palestinian situation.[48]

The European Union has taken not only an active diplomatic role in the peace process, but a pivotal economic one as well. The European Union is currently the largest donor of non-military aid to the Middle East peace process, representing €197 million per year to the Palestinian Authority, and €630 million to Jordan, Lebanon, Syria and Egypt combined. In addition, the European Union serves as co-chair of the Ad-Hoc Liaison Committee, which serves as an umbrella organization to coordinate international donor assistance to the Palestinian Authority. From 1994 to 1998, European aid (i.e., from the European Union and from its member states) to the Palestinians, including aid directed at Palestinian refugees, totalled €2 billion;[49] by 2005, the member states donated €340 million.[50] The EU views its financial support to the Palestinian Authority as being critical to upholding one of the two main interlocutors in the faltering peace process, declaring that its budgetary contributions have "prevented the financial collapse of the PA".[51] Likewise, supporting the Palestinian Authority to the extent that it does allows the European Union to form an economic counterweight to American economic and military support for Israel. Thus, the European Union's economic activities primarily represent a culture of solidarity (with the fledgling institutions of Palestinian democracy) even in its aim to serve as a benign check on American power. However, the election of a Hamas government in 2006 and the ensuing international diplomatic and economic boycott has, in some senses, brought European foreign policy more in line with that of the United States, while at the same time hobbling the EU–PA relationship.

In terms of geopolitics, the Middle East represents a region of "vital strategic importance to the European Union", in the words of its official external relations Web site, and its activities in the peace process stem from an overall commitment to the region exemplified in a Euro-Mediterranean Partnership that emerged from a 1995 conference in Barcelona.[52] The goals of the process include promoting civil society in the target states and furthering economic links leading to the eventual establishment of a free trade zone between the European Union and the partner countries, as well as among the Mediterranean partner states themselves. Clearly, a viable solution to the Israeli–Palestinian conflict (and broader Arab–Israeli conflict) will only benefit the region economically given the substantial "peace dividend" that is likely to accrue to a resolution to the conflict in the Mediterranean core.

The European Union's resolute diplomatic support for the establishment of a Palestinian state and its significant economic contribution to the Palestinian Authority has in part led some to view EU involvement as tilted toward the Palestinians rather than the Israelis. Competing narratives inherent in any protracted conflict mean that any third party attempting diplomatic and economic involvement can fall prey to perceptions of privileging one frame of events over another. Some observers have alleged that Europe's policies are intended as a counterweight not only to American hegemony but also to historical "pro-Israel biases of the 1940s and 1950s",[53] a stance which can suggest not only a geopolitical aim of balancing American policies, but a strategy of solidarity with attempting to ensure that the parties to the Israeli–Palestinian conflict are more evenly matched. And as the peace process has unravelled under the weight of the second Intifada, the coherence in a multi-state foreign policy endeavour has weakened amidst intra-European disagreement over the most effective course for EU foreign policy. While Britain has remained closely aligned with American policy proclivities – a stance reflected in Prime Minister Tony Blair's support for the war in Iraq – other European states have parted company with the United States, and by extension Israel. France has expressed frustration with American support for Israel; Germany has recently withheld arms sales to Israel and has come out against Israel's retaliatory policies in the territories; Spain has shown more sympathy to the Palestinians of late than has the United States; and even Turkey (though not yet part of the European Union, is currently a candidate for membership) has issued statements openly critical of Israel, including a short-lived accusation that Israel is conducting "genocide". (Turkey's Prime Minister, Bulent Ecevit, withdrew the remark in the wake of Jewish–American pressure.)[54]

Response by regional actors to international involvement

Though both sets of actors – the Israelis and the Palestinians – have used the international media to attempt to transmit their frame of events to the global community, Israel and the Palestinians differ in their willingness to entertain externally imposed solutions, including possibilities for multinational observer forces to enter the region. Traditionally, Israel has accepted diplomatic intervention but not military intervention. The reasons for this stance arguably lie with the Zionist narrative, which has centred on the achievement of national "normalization". This normalization took the form of Jewish nationalism, which indeed arose in part from the many instances of persecution experienced in the face of anti-Semitism: what are generally referred to as the "push factors" of the Zionist movement. Ultimately, Zionist "normalization" referred to the desire by the Jews to achieve national sovereignty – which was formally achieved in 1948 – and for the Jewish state to take its place among the community of states – a goal that has been reached formally through international fora and informally through its many military, economic and diplomatic links, but the full extension (namely among all state members of the Arab world) has thus far eluded it.

In that "normalization" ultimately hinges on the achievement and maintenance of state sovereignty, Israel views different forms of intervention in terms of the sovereign ideal. Diplomacy easily co-exists with the notion of sovereignty – and even reinforces it insofar as most diplomatic forays are conducted by state officials. In this way, even an American mention of support for a Palestinian state became acceptable to hawkish Israelis such as then-Prime Minister Sharon, as long as the blame for the stalemate was placed on the Palestinian leadership – particularly in its inability or refusal to rein in Palestinian terrorism. Prior to his exit from the political scene, Sharon appeared to revel in the joint interests in their respective wars on terrorism that appear to be shared by the United States and Israel, as when he thanked Bush for granting Israel "the required leeway in our ongoing war on terrorism".[55]

Moreover, while various political streams within Israel place different degrees of importance on relations with the United States, successive Israeli governments have shaped their peace-process policies in part with an eye toward the effects of US involvement. For instance, as at least one account has shown, out of fear that the United States would harm the Israeli and Palestinian chances to reach a negotiated settlement in the wake of the failed 1987 London agreement, Israel chose to pursue the Oslo agreement deliberately without American help.[56]

Conversely, by definition, full-fledged military intervention infringes on state sovereignty; multinational peacekeeping forces, while typically sent with the express consent of both parties, are more in line with state sovereignty but nevertheless imply a certain inability to defend one's borders independently. In addition, Israel's typically blunt opposition to external intervention relates to its strategic goals. Israel is hesitant to withdraw completely from the West Bank, given the presence of Israeli settlements there and the strategic hinterland that the area affords, and military intervention would likely hasten the process of Israeli withdrawal. However, even diplomatic overtures by third parties are not necessarily genuinely welcomed, and may be entertained more as an attempt to project a positive international reputation than as an example of a true commitment to conflict resolution. While Likud's Prime Minister Yitzhak Shamir declared that he would not have minded dragging out the 1991 Madrid talks for ten years, Sharon has at times shown more enthusiasm for regional conference proposals – such as those suggested by Saudi Arabia and backed by the United States – than for meaningful negotiation about the most pressing outstanding issues of the conflict.[57] Nevertheless, there has been some movement within Israeli public opinion on the issue of external involvement. An April 2002 poll revealed that "about half of those asked would welcome outside involvement" in bringing about a solution to the conflict. More than one-third "favoured the deployment of an armed international force", while "a quarter said they supported the idea of a settlement imposed by the international community".[58] More recently, a former Israeli foreign minister has written that, in Gaza, "an international force can and should be deployed even before the contour of a settlement has been agreed by the parties".[59]

The Palestinians, on the other hand, have not only been generally acceptant of external diplomatic involvement, they have also been much more willing to see military intervention than has Israel. As in the Israeli case, this Palestinian orientation can be explained by the idea of sovereignty. Yet while Israel's central *raison d'état* is to maintain its sovereign status quo, the main Palestinian goal – as a stateless nation – is to achieve statehood and thus to fundamentally alter the status quo, a task that evidently cannot be achieved without external intervention of some sort. The Palestinians are therefore open to various options that would, in their assessment, hasten an Israeli withdrawal and facilitate the creation of a Palestinian state in the West Bank and Gaza Strip.

Conclusion

In exploring the determinants of involvement by the United States and the European Union in the Israeli–Palestinian conflict and peace process, this chapter has put forth an integrative view of national interest and solidarity. The identity of the state (or post-Westphalian entity, in the case of the European Union) serves to structure ideas about what constitutes the national interest, which in turn leads to policies that are largely articulated in terms of identification with the target actors. Specifically, we saw that in the case of the United States a central theme of ethical solidarity emerges that stems directly from American guiding principles: liberty (war on terrorism), democracy (support for Israel), self-determination (longstanding support for Israeli statehood and more recent support for Palestinian attempts at creating a state), divinely inspired morality (support for the State of Israel as the Jews' restoration in the Land of Israel) and, to a lesser extent, free market capitalism, specifically through an attempt to maintain access to oil – both for itself and for the other members of the international system. The motivations of the European Union involve some elements of geopolitics (particularly through attempting to consolidate the organization's foreign-policy machinery and to check the power of the United States on the global stage), yet ultimately hinge on a culture of solidarity, namely striving to assist the Palestinians in gaining self-determination, and in evening out the international playing field to ameliorate those who appear to have been neglected.

These findings suggest that national interest and solidarity may in fact be operating in tandem within foreign-policy decision contexts, and may ultimately derive from a common source: the nature of a state's identity. That is, a state's fundamental values as well as the role it perceives itself to hold within the international arena give rise to a certain view of the "national interest", which in turn structures foreign policy strategies. In the cases of the United States and the European Union, particular national values have led these international actors to develop a set of international actions that serve both to fulfill national value-imperatives while connecting with other international actors in a way that attempts to support the national goals of the latter. This suggests not only that the national interest can derive from identity, but that the moral question posed by the Babylonian Jewish sage Hillel may indeed hold resonance for global politics in the new millennium: "If I am not for myself then who is for me, but if I am only for myself, then what am I?"

Notes

1. Martha Finnemore (1998) "Constructing Norms of Humanitarian Intervention", in Peter J. Katzenstein, ed., *The Culture of National Security: Norms and Identity in World Politics*, New York: Columbia University Press, pp. 153–185; Nicholas J. Wheeler (2000) *Saving Strangers: Humanitarian Intervention in International Society*, New York: Oxford University Press.

2. There have been some instances of more formal military-intervention activity in the Middle East, in the form of UN peacekeeping throughout the decades. This chapter will not address peacekeeping specifically, as it is a UN-mandated operation, and will instead look at the diplomatic, economic and military-aid actions taken by individual sets of actors. The latter focus is a better way to measure the relative strength of geopolitics and solidarity explanations for international behaviour.

3. James Fearon and Alexander Wendt (2002) "Rationalism vs. Constructivism: A Skeptical View", and Duncan Snidal (2002) "Rational Choice and International Relations", both in Walter Carlsnaes, Thomas Risse and Beth A. Simmons, eds, *Handbook of International Relations*, London: Sage. This chapter seeks to shed further light on the continuing debate between rationality and identity, following recent explorations of rational-choice approaches that account for the role of identity in structuring the interests of cost-sensitive decision-makers.

4. See, for instance, "A History of Palestinian/Israeli Peace Agreement," CNN on-line edition, 13 September 2003, available from http://edition.cnn.com/TRANSCRIPTS/0309/13/cst.05.html; Robert Fisk (2000) "Peace is Dead: My People Will No Longer Be Victims", Fontenelles – Palestinian Archive, 8 November, available from http://home.mindspring.com/~fontenelles/fisk11-8-00.htm; and Gerald M. Steinberg (2001) "Oslo Is Dead: Time to Move On", *Jerusalem Post*, 5 October, available from http://faculty.biu.ac.il/~steing/conflict/oped/Osloisdead.htm.

5. "Home Thoughts Abroad", 27 June 2002, *Economist*, Internet edition.

6. Secretary of State Condoleezza Rice (2006) "Remarks with Palestinian Authority President Mahmoud Abbas after Their Meeting", 4 October, available from http://www.state.gov/secretary/rm/2006/73576.htm, accessed 25 March 2007.

7. Marc Ballon (2006) "Jewish Voters: Left, Left, Left, Right, Left", *St. Petersburg Times*, 29 October, available from http://www.sptimes.com/2006/10/29/Opinion/Jewish_voters_left_.shtml

8. On three types of anarchies – Hobbesian, Lockean and Kantian – see Alexander Wendt (1999) *Social Theory of International Politics*, New York: Cambridge University Press, pp. 246–312.

9. Charles A. Kupchan (1998) "After Pax Americana: Benign Power, Regional Integration, and the Sources of a Stable Multipolarity", *International Security* 23(2), Fall: 40–79.

10. As the NSS states, "Nations need not suffer an attack before they can lawfully take action to defend themselves against forces that present an imminent danger of attack". For an insightful discussion of Bush's national security strategy, see John Lewis Gaddis (2003) "A Grand Strategy of Transformation", *Foreign Policy*, January/February.

11. US Department of State (2002) "U.S. National Security Strategy: Strengthen Alliances to Defeat Global Terrorism and Work to Prevent Attacks against Us and Our Friends", available from http://www.state.gov/r/pa/ei/wh/15423.htm, accessed 17 January 2003.

12. Bin Laden stated on Al Jazeera television in October 2001 that "Neither the United States nor he who lives in the United States will enjoy security before we can see it as a reality in Palestine and before all the infidel armies leave the land of Mohammed". Whether bin Laden was referring to the West Bank and Gaza or to all of pre-1967 Israel as well remains unclear, though his statement suggests the latter. Transcript of statement available from http://news.bbc.co.uk/1/hi/world/south_asia/1585636.stm, accessed on 17 January 2003.

13. Powell presented these allegations in a 5 February 2003 address to the United Nations. For a transcript of his speech, see http://www.cnn.com/2003/US/02/05/sprj.irq.powell.transcript/index.html.

14. Jean Bethke Elshtain (2003) makes a similar argument in the context of the current war on terror in *Just War against Terror: The Burden of American Power in a Violent World*, New York: Basic Books.

15. Andrew Valls (2000) "Can Terrorism Be Justified?", in Valls, ed., *Ethics in International Affairs: Theories and Cases*, Lanham, Md.: Rowman & Littlefield Publishers.

16. B'Tselem (2007) "Statistics: Fatalities", available at http://www.btselem.org/english/statistics/Casualties.asp.

17. Benjamin Netanyahu (1993) *A Place among the Nations: Israel and the World*, New York: Bantam Books.

18. See, for instance, Stephen M. Walt (2001) "Beyond bin Laden: Reshaping U.S. Foreign Policy", *International Security* 26(3), Winter.

19. Clyde R. Mark (2002) "Israel: U.S. Foreign Assistance," Issue Brief for Congress, 21 May (Order Code IB85066), available from http://fpc.state.gov/documents/organization/10871.pdf.

20. John Mearsheimer and Stephen Walt (2006) "The Israel Lobby", *London Review of Books* 28(6), 23 March.

21. "No Schmooze with the Jews", *Economist*, Internet edition, 4 April 2002. For an account of the loan guarantees crisis, see Scott Lasensky (2002) "Underwriting Peace in the Middle East: U.S. Foreign Policy and the Limits of Economic Inducements", *Middle East Review of International Affairs*, Internet edition, 6(1), March.

22. "Many Americans Uneasy with Mix of Religion and Politics", Pew Forum on Religion and Public Life, 24 August 2006, available from http://pewforum.org/docs/index.php?DocID=153.

23. Richard W. Stevenson (2002) "Bush Invoke's Faith's Power to Cure Society's Ills", *New York Times*, Internet edition, 21 January.

24. "Transcript of Bush Speech on Shuttle Loss", *Washington Times*, Internet edition, 1 February 2003, available from http://www.washtimes.com/upi-breaking/20030201-023944-3021r.htm.

25. Israel Television Network (in Hebrew), 28 March 1992 (FBIS-NES-92-061; 30 March 1992).

26. Robert J. Lieber (2000) "U.S.–Israel Relations since 1948", in Robert O. Freedman, ed., *Israel at Fifty*, Gainesville, Fla.: University of Florida Press.

27. "American Attitudes Hold Steady in Face of Foreign Crises", Pew Research Center for the People and the Press, 17 August 2006, available from http://people-press.org/reports/display.php3?ReportID=285.

28. "Rice Begins New Mid-East Mission" (2007) BBC News, 24 March, available from http://news.bbc.co.uk/2/hi/middle_east/6490623.stm.

29. See, for instance, an article on the Palestinian Authority's Web site stating that in rejecting the Palestinian demand for a right of return, Bush had "damaged US credibility as an 'honest broker' in the peace process", "US Set to Offer Written Assurance to Jordan on Negotiations for an Eventual Israeli–Palestinian Peace Deal", Palestinian National Authority, available from http://www.pna.gov.ps/subject_details2.asp?DocId=1409.

30. Bush issued this pronouncement soon after 11 September, stating that, as long as Israel's right to exist was guaranteed, a Palestinian state has always been "part of a vision" for a peace settlement. "Bush: Palestinian State 'Part of a Vision' if Israel Respected", CNN.com, 2 October 2001, available from http://www.cnn.com/2001/US/10/02/gen.mideast.us/.

31. Colin L. Powell (2002) "Testimony before the Senate Appropriations Subcommittee on Foreign Operations, Export Financing", Washington, D.C., 24 April, available from http://www.state.gov/secretary/rm/2002/9713.htm.

32. Mark MacKinnon and Carolynne Wheeler (2007) "Arab League Meeting to Talk Israel", *Globe and Mail*, 28 March, p. A16.
33. US Department of State (2002) "President Welcomes Quartet Principals to White House", Washington D.C., 20 December, available from http://www.state.gov/p/nea/rls/rm/16177.htm.
34. Dennis Ross (2002) "Palestinians Must Accept Accountability", *Los Angeles Times*, 9 July, p. B13.
35. Office of the Spokesman, US Department of State (2002) "US–Middle East Partnership Initiative", Fact Sheet, 12 December, available from http://www.state.gov/r/pa/prs/ps/2002/15923.htm. See also http://mepi.state.gov/, accessed 25 March 2007.
36. As suggested in roundtable remarks by Michael Ignatieff, following his Sun Life Financial Public Lecture "Canada in the Age of Terror", Carleton University, Ottawa, 8 November 2002.
37. See Emanuel Adler and Michael Barnett, eds (1998) *Security Communities*, New York: Cambridge University Press.
38. Philip H. Gordon (1997) "Europe's Uncommon Foreign Policy," *International Security* 22(3), Winter.
39. Thomas Fuller (2003) "Europe Debates Whether to Admit God to Union", *New York Times*, Internet edition, 5 February.
40. Rt. Hon. Chris Patten (2000) "Statement at the Ministerial Meeting of the Multilateral Steering Group of the Middle East Peace Process", 1 February, Moscow, available from http://europa.eu.int/comm/external_relations/news/patten/speech_00_28.htm.
41. Joel Peters (1999) "Can the Multilateral Middle East Talks Be Revived?", *Middle East Review of International Affairs* 3(4), December.
42. Middle East Peace Process Multilateral Steering Group (2000) "Report from the European Union", Moscow, 31 January/1 February, available from http://www.euromed.net/eu/mepp/REDWG_Gavel_Holder_Report_Feb_2000_v2.rtf.
43. Peters, "Can the Multilateral Middle East Talks Be Revived?"; Dalia Dassa Kaye (2001) *Beyond the Handshake: Multilateral Cooperation in the Arab–Israeli Peace Process, 1991–1996*, New York: Columbia University Press.
44. Gerald M. Steinberg (1999) "The European Union and the Middle East Peace Process", Letter No. 418, Jerusalem Center for Public Affairs, November, available from http://faculty.biu.ac.il/~steing/election/jl408.htm, accessed 31 May 2006.
45. "The EU & the Middle East: Position & Background", European Union, available from http://europa.eu.int/comm/external_relations/mepp/faq/index.htm.
46. "President Bush Calls for New Palestinian Leadership", transcript of a speech by Bush, 24 June 2002, Washington, D.C., available from http://www.state.gov/p/nea/rt/13544.htm.
47. Elise Labott (2002) "Powell: US and EU United on Middle East", CNN.com, 19 December, available from http://www.cnn.com/2001/US/12/19/us.eu.mideast/index.html.
48. "You Can Be Warriors or Wimps; Or So Say the Americans", *Economist*, Internet edition, 8 August 2002.
49. "The EU and the Middle East Peace Process", European Commission, available from http://europa.eu.int/comm/external_relations/mepp/index.htm, accessed 31 May 2006.
50. "EU 'To Keep Funding' Palestinians", BBC News Online, 30 January 2006, available from http://news.bbc.co.uk/2/hi/middle_east/4663742.stm.
51. Rt. Hon. Chris Patten (2002) "Statement to the Foreign Affairs Committee on EU Budgetary Assistance to the PA", Foreign Affairs Committee of the European Parliament, Brussels, 19 June, available from http://europa.eu.int/comm/external_relations/news/patten/s02_293.htm, accessed 31 May 2006.

52. Participants in the Barcelona Process include Morocco, Algeria, Tunisia, Egypt, Israel, Jordan, the Palestinian Authority, Lebanon, Syria, Turkey, Cyprus and Malta; Libya has observer status at some meetings. "The EU's Mediterranean & Middle East Policy", European Commission, available from http://europa.eu.int/comm/external _relations/med_mideast/intro/, accessed 31 May 2006.
53. Steinberg, "The European Union and the Middle East Peace Process".
54. "Allies at Odds – All Round", *Economist*, Internet edition, 11 April 2002.
55. Robert G. Kaiser (2003) "Bush and Sharon Nearly Identical on Mideast Policy", *Washington Post*, 9 February, p. A1.
56. Jonathan Rynhold (2000) "Israeli–American Relations and the Peace Process", *Middle East Review of International Affairs* 4(2), June.
57. "His Master's Voice," *Economist*, Internet edition, 18 April 2002.
58. "An International Spectre over Sharon", *Economist*, Internet edition, 2 May 2002.
59. Shlomo Ben-Ami (2006) "UN Peacekeeping: From Lebanon to Gaza," *Bitterlemons*, 18 September, available from http://www.bitterlemons.org/previous/bl180906ed37.html#isr2.

6

Beyond geopolitics and solidarism: Interpenetrated sovereignty, transnational conflict and the United States' "Plan Colombia"

Doug Stokes[1]

It is commonly argued that the traditional geostrategic logic of "national interest" inherent within conventional forms of realist statecraft has dominated the conduct of international politics for many centuries.[2] This logic takes the bounded "nation-state" as the central unit of world politics with states acting as rational egoists seeking to maximize their national interests vis-à-vis potential rivals within an anarchic international system. Crucially, a geostrategic logic of national interest (whilst not precluding cooperative interstate behaviour so as to further a particular national interest) takes the bounded and sovereign nation-state as its central normative community. It thus operationalizes a particularistic ethic of loyalty to its own citizens, and not to citizens of other states. However, with the end of the Cold War, and the lessening of global tensions, a number of liberal theorists have posited the emergence of a new ethic of international solidarity (solidarism) based upon the responsibilities that democratic states have to those imperilled in other (often non-Western) states.[3] This solidarist ethic is rooted within a democratic universalism whereby the ethical community extends beyond a bounded "nation-state" to encompass humanity as whole, with the values of universality, equality and freedom providing the normative backdrop for the emergence of this new international liberal norm.

In relation to the central focus of this chapter, namely US foreign policy, I start with an examination of the ways in which an ethic of solidarism is said to increasingly factor within the logic of international politics in the absence of the inherent tension of the Cold War period. The

National interest and international solidarity: Particular and universal ethics in international life, Coicaud and Wheeler (eds),
United Nations University Press, 2008, ISBN 978-92-808-1147-6

end of the Cold War was optimistically trumpeted as a moment whereby Western states could export democracy and engage in humanitarian interventions throughout the global South based upon the responsibilities of those states to citizens of other states. After outlining these theoretical and normative debates this chapter then moves on to argue that inherent within both realist geostrategic and solidarist approaches to world politics there exists a contestable conception of state sovereignty. This conception operationalizes a static, ahistorical conception of sovereignty with an operative distinction between the domestic and the international. In the place of this conception I argue for a theory of contemporary sovereignty that is fundamentally interpenetrated, especially between Western and third world states. In illustrating these points the chapter provides a qualitative analysis of US counter-insurgency policy in Colombia both during and after the Cold War. I show that US intervention in Colombia (in both overt and covert forms) has long shaped both the nature of the Colombian state itself and the ways in which the Colombian state has interacted with Colombian civil society. Importantly, the United States' ongoing intervention in Colombia to allegedly fight drugs and terrorism and to stem Colombia's humanitarian crisis is contributing in fundamental ways to the perpetuation of these very crises. I conclude with an examination of the underlying interests that the United States has in Colombia and the ways in which the Colombian case study reinforces the call for a move beyond solidarism and geostrategy to a theory of transnational conflict and interpenetrated sovereignty that is more attentive to the reality of world politics.

US foreign policy after the Cold War: Solidarism, democracy and human rights

Optimistically inclined solidarist interpretations of world politics tend to be aligned quite closely with (neo-)liberal international relations theorists who stress the pacific potential of liberal capitalism and see the promotion of neo-liberal forms of governance as the best way of ameliorating conflict within an anarchic international system and preventing potential human rights abuses within non-democratic states. The assumption is that capitalism leads to both economic development and complex forms of market interdependence that "tame" the logic of conflict through the pacification of state rivalry. As such, the global promotion of liberal democracy based upon an ethic of international solidarity has been linked to the opportunities presented to US foreign policy makers by the end of the Cold War and the subsequent lessening of geostrategic tensions inherent within the bipolar conflict. John G. Ikenberry, for example, argued that although US foreign policy has allegedly had a longstanding commitment to exporting a Wilsonian liberalism premised on human rights, democracy and free trade, the end of the Cold War provided a great opportunity to pursue these liberal objectives more stridently. Ikenberry rejects pessimistic analyses that are based on a zero-sum geostrategic logic of national interest and instead argues that the "United States is seized by a robust and distinctive grand strategy" of post–Cold War liberalism.[4] In a similar vein, Tony Smith has argued against the realist presumption that the promotion of human rights and democracy should take second stage to US self-interest in international relations. Smith argues that a "national security liberalism" that supports "human rights and the establishment of democratic governments abroad", combined with US self-interest (defined as "the enhancement of American influence in the world"), may "actually serve one another far more often and importantly than most commentators on the US role in world affairs generally suppose".[5] In the place of an earlier era of geostrategic containment, Smith calls for a post–Cold War United States grand strategy to enhance democratic peace and human rights through the enlargement of democratic states throughout the world.[6]

The democratic peace thesis within the field of international relations has been crucial in theorizing this alleged new humanitarian orientation within US post–Cold War foreign policy, and international politics more broadly. Moreover, it provides the theoretical basis for practical solidarist policy prescriptions such as humanitarian forms of military intervention. The thesis argues that interstate relations between democracies within the Zone of Peace are governed by a Kantian peace whilst relations within the Zone of War are characterized by a Hobbesian struggle for survival and balance of power politics. The democratic peace posits a causal relationship between the existence of democracy and the absence of interstate war with democratic peace proponents grounding their arguments on analyses that purport to show the absence of interstate wars amongst democracies since 1815, and the essentially pacific nature of their international relations with each other.[7] Democracy promotion and humanitarian intervention have thus become one of the central justifications for the conduct of US post–Cold War foreign policy in the third world, with a number of US-led interventions justified on purely humanitarian grounds. As Michel Feher argues, US and Western European leaders "proudly associated the end of the Cold War with the advent of an increasingly cohesive international community" that was committed to "fostering democracy and preventing human rights violations, even when the latter were perpetrated by the agents of a recognized state against their own population".[8] As such, a number of post–Cold War US interventions, for example the US-led intervention in Kosovo, have been justified as necessary to both promote democracy and end human rights abuses, and as such are ostensibly indicative of the new ethic of international solidarity in practice.[9] This justification has even extended to encompass the new "war on terror" and the doctrine of pre-emptive intervention of the current Bush administration with the Anglo-American occupation of Iraq after 2003 increasingly justified as an attempt to bring democracy and a human rights-based order to the wider Middle East.

It is thus possible to identify two norms within international politics that are based on very different kinds of operating principles and which subsequently enable very different kinds of statecraft. On the one hand stands a geostrategic logic of *national interest* whereby states act purely in their perceived interests. Importantly, because of the bounded normative community inherent within this logic, states have no moral obligation to the "Other", save for when non-action toward the Other could potentially impact upon a state's rational calculation of its best interest.[10] Counterpoised to this is an ethic of solidarism based on a theory of *democratic universalism*, which takes as its normative community humanity as a whole. In relation to this ethic, solidarist states will intervene to defend "strangers" within other states when the norms and rights of those communities are in some way threatened.[11] Crucially, with the lessening of tensions at the end of the Cold War, solidarist logics have been said to increasingly factor into the norms of international statecraft, with a number of interventions (often led by the United States) said to be based upon universalist principles of an innate humanitarianism to both prevent human rights abuses against the Other and to install more humane forms of democratic governance. The central political modality of this new ethic has thus been new forms of humanitarian intervention wedded to the promotion of neo-liberal forms of democratic governance.

However, this taxonomy of "solidarist" humanitarianism versus a "geostrategic" logic of national interest has a number of inherent problems. First, both of these dual logics share the assumption of a bounded and relatively static conception of state sovereignty. Importantly, this conception of state sovereignty is not fully attentive to the variable historical forms of state sovereignty and in particular the interpenetrated nature of state sovereignty between the first and third worlds (where the vast majority of so-called humanitarian interventions take place). Specifically, it is arguable that the principal historical state form of the international system has been imperial with the vast majority of third world states coming into existence through processes of both imperial expansion and contraction.[12]

By extension it is no exaggeration to say that the principal geo-political form of the world system today is that of US Empire that has both formal and informal aspects. That is, US Empire is formal in the sense that sometimes it becomes necessary to revert to the more territorialist mode of empire principally reliant on occupation and territorial control of subject nations (for example, post–11 September Iraq, which was itself a creation of an earlier Empire, Great Britain in 1921). Conjunctural factors that may lead to this include the stabilization of pro–United States internal social forces or the consolidation of weak states until "satisfactory" arrangements are in place for US force withdrawal. However, US Empire also has a very large informal component in the sense that the US state dominates so-called multilateral institutions of global governance whilst retaining the capacity to structure the strategic, political and economic contexts and options of other states (both Western and non-Western). Importantly, the US state also relies upon global "financial capital" dominated by Wall Street and US banks to discipline recalcitrant states (through capital flight, negative credit ratings and so on) whilst enjoying the enormous structural power that accrues to the US state as a result of the dollarization of the global political economy.[13] Crucially then, it is arguable that the implicit assumption of bounded sovereignty and statehood inherent within the geostrategic and solidarist approaches ignores both the imperial penetration of third world sovereignties and the historical and ongoing constitution of third world statehood within the context of contemporary forms of global Empire.

In relation to the early development of the US state's imperial role, George Kennan, one of the central architects of US post-war policy, cynically captured the imperial role of the US state in a top secret planning document in 1948. Kennan argued that the US has

> about 50% of the world's wealth, but only 6.3% of its population.... In this situation, we cannot fail to be the object of envy and resentment. Our real task in the coming period is to devise a pattern of relationships that will permit us to maintain this position of disparity.[14]

In devising "a pattern of relationships", US planners constructed a liberal international economic order integrated with (and largely beneficial to) other leading powers under the tutelage of the US state, or what Geir Lundestad has termed "Empire by invitation" in relation to the major European capitalist powers.[15] The massive levels of post-war US foreign direct investment into Japan and Europe coupled with the US state's strategic dominance of collective security arrangements further integrated the leading powers into a common "informal American Empire"[16] and it was in this way that the US state was internationalized in its global relations and subsequent obligations. Henry Kissinger captured this new reality in the early 1970s when he argued that the "United

States [had] global interests and responsibilities" whilst "our European allies" merely "have regional interests".[17]

If the "soft power"[18] and forms of multilateral coordination of US Empire were felt most keenly amongst the Japanese and European states, in the third world it was another story entirely. Given the ferment developed as a result of rapid decolonization and massive class disparities coupled with the often narrow social base of a number of third world states, US Empire frequently fell back on tried and trusted modes of co-ercive statecraft. However, unlike earlier eras of Empires that sought to "physicalize" their rule through territorial acquisition and control, the US state principally sought to act through pre-existing state structures and local ruling classes. Indigenous pro-US elites both ensured internal "stability" through the containment of potentially inimical social forces and were externally responsive to the wider requirements of the US imperial state and the capitalist global political economy.[19] Third world militaries, trained and funded by the United States, became central con-duits through which US power extended to underwrite and police the burgeoning US Empire in the third world, and these forces provided a bulwark against varying forms of internal reformism, with a wide range of oppositional social forces refracted through the lens of Cold War anti-communism. In Latin America alone, one of the United States' counter-insurgency training academies, the School of the Americas, had trained over 40,000 Latin American military personnel by the end of the Cold War.[20] Kennan explained that in dealing with dissent during the Cold War, the final answer "may be an unpleasant one" but the United States "should not hesitate before police repression by the local govern-ment".[21] The human cost of this support was enormous, with all but 200,000 of the 20 million people that died in wars between 1945 and 1990 dying in the third world.[22] In short, imperial forms of statecraft were crucial to the processes of third world state formation and sover-eignty.

Crucially, contemporary forms of statecraft can still be said to be (neo-)imperial insofar as third world states are still articulated to an asym-metric global political economy and forms of transnational governance dominated by the core capitalist states under the aegis of American Empire. As such, contemporary forms of state sovereignty (in practice if not in theory) are fully imbricated. In the face of this historicization then, both the geostrategic and solidarist logics of international statecraft presuppose a contestable conceptualization of the state. Concomitantly, they also operationalize a notion of state sovereignty that takes the state as a juridically and nationally grounded pre-given, with a strict separation between the domestic and the international. This static and under-historicized conception ignores the variability of state sovereignty and state formation and serves to invisibilize the imperial character and constitution of both first world and third world states. Crucially, it is also not sufficiently attentive to the often covert forms of imperial statecraft that have served to further imbricate the mutually constitutive "sovereignties" of both first and third world nations and the role that core imperial states play in generating and perpetuating humanitarian crises in the global South. So called "failed" or "rogue" states that provide the deliberative moment between a logic of geostrategy or solidarism thus must be historicized and understood as part of this wider framing. In the place of the geostrategic/solidarist dyad, then, I would instead argue for a conception of sovereignty as intrinsically interpenetrated, which I believe is more attentive to the historically variable nature of state sovereignty within the global political economy.

In the next part of this chapter, I flesh out some of these theoretical points with an examination of the role played by the US state in Colombia. In particular I focus on Plan Colombia, which was a US$1.3 billion US aid package to Colombia in 2000 that radically increased the ongoing humanitarian crisis in Colombia. However, before we examine Plan Colombia we must go over the earlier period of US–Colombia relations to provide an historical context.

Understanding US intervention in Colombia during the Cold War

The interpenetrated nature of US–Colombian relations and the role of the US state within Colombian state formation was clear from the outset of the early Cold War period. Following a decade of civil war in Colombia during the 1950s, there were growing US concerns about armed peasant "enclaves" throughout Colombia's southern regions. A 1959 memo from Roy Rubottom, US Assistant Secretary of State for Inter-American Affairs, outlined the rationale for the provision of US counterinsurgency (CI) training for Colombia. The memo argued that although "it would be difficult to make the finding of present Communist danger in the Colombian guerrilla situation" the "continuance of unsettled conditions in Colombia contributes to Communist objectives" and threatens the "establishment of a pro-US, free enterprise democracy".[23] Colombia was one of the largest recipients of US foreign direct investment in South America. Of the US$399 million of US foreign direct investment in Colombia in 1959, the vast majority was in oil (US$225 million), followed by manufacturing, public utilities and trade.[24] Colombia's close proximity to the Panama Canal also worried US planners in the early years of US

CI assistance: instability near the canal zone could potentially impact upon world trade and US strategic access. In 1960, Colonel Edward Lansdale, US Assistant Secretary of Defense for Special Operations, argued that the United States should "undertake assistance to Colombia to correct the situation of political insurrection" near the canal zone, a "place so vital to our own national security".[25]

Internal US documentation related to US CI training reveals the American state's active promotion of the widespread surveillance and policing of progressive elements in civil society so as to prevent the "subversion" of socio-economic relations. This form of US intervention had major ramifications on the Colombian state's relations to civil society. For example, one manual used to train Colombian CI forces told them to ask: "Are there any legal political organizations which may be a front for insurgent activities? Is the public education system vulnerable to infiltration by insurgent agents? What is the influence of politics on teachers, textbooks, and students, conversely, what influence does the education system exercise on politics?"[26] They then were told to ask what "is the nature of the labor organizations; what relationship exists between these organizations, the government, and the insurgents?" In outlining targets for CI intelligence operations the manual identified a number of different occupational categories and generic social identities. These included "merchants" and "bar owners and bar girls" and "ordinary citizens who are typical members of organizations or associations which ... play an important role in the local society". In particular, US-backed CI forces were to concentrate on "leaders of Dissident groups (minorities, religious sects, labor unions, political factions) who may be able to identify insurgent personnel, their methods of operation, and local agencies the insurgents hope to exploit". In an overt indication of the equation of labour movements with subversion the manual then went on to state that insurgent forces typically try to work with labour unions and union leaders so as to determine "the principal causes of discontent which can best be exploited to overthrow the established government [and] recruit loyal supporters". The manual stated that organizations that stress "immediate social, political, or economic reform may be an indication that the insurgents have gained a significant degree of control", and moved on to detail a series of what it terms "Insurgent Activity Indicators":

Refusal of peasants to pay rent, taxes, or loan payments or unusual difficulty in their collection. Increase in the number of entertainers with a political message. Discrediting the judicial system and police organizations. Characterization of the armed forces as the enemy of the people. Appearance of questionable doctrine in the educational system. Appearance of many new members in established organizations such as labor organizations. Increased unrest among laborers. Increased student activity against the government and its police, or against minority groups, foreigners and the like. An increased number of articles or advertisements in newspapers criticizing the government. Strikes or work stoppages called to protest government actions. Increase of petitions demanding government redress of grievances. Proliferation of slogans pinpointing specific grievances. Initiation of letterwriting campaigns to newspapers and government officials deploring undesirable conditions and blaming individuals in power.[27]

US CI strategy was thus directly at odds with broad swathes of democratic activity and served to entrench and reproduce a particular kind of political stability in Colombia. Central to this security posture was the secret advocacy of state terrorism and the development of covert paramilitary networks. In 1962, General William Yarborough, the head of a US Army Special Warfare team that provided the initial blueprint for the reorientation of the Colombian military for CI, stated that:

> It is the considered opinion of the survey team that a concerted country team effort should be made now to select civilian and military personnel for clandestine training in resistance operations in case they are needed later. This should be done with a view toward development of a civil and military structure for exploitation in the event that the Colombian internal security system deteriorates further. This structure should be used to pressure toward reforms known to be needed, perform counter-agent and counter-propaganda functions and as necessary execute paramilitary, sabotage and/or terrorist activities against known communist proponents. It should be backed by the United States.... The apparatus should be charged with clandestine execution of plans developed by the United States Government toward defined objectives in the political, economic and military fields. This would permit passing to the offensive in all fields of endeavor rather than depending on the Colombians to find their own solution.[28]

US policy was thus instrumental in shaping the explicit posture of the Colombian military and state and civil society relations during the Cold War. Crucially, this form of covert interventionism had a significant impact on both the nature of the Colombian conflict throughout the Cold War period and on the way the conflict is playing itself out today. Whilst an examination of US policy throughout the Cold War period is beyond the scope of this chapter,[29] as I now go on to show, the US has continued to pursue a CI strategy in Colombia as part of its allegedly counter-drug Plan Colombia, a US$1.3 billion US military aid plan for the Colombian military in 2000. Although Colombia had continued to receive substantial US military aid and training throughout the post Cold War, Plan Colombia made the Colombian military the third largest recipient of US military aid in the world and the largest by far in Latin America. The United

States argued that Plan Colombia had two primary objectives. These were the eradication of Colombia's coca plantations that supply the majority of cocaine to US markets and the promotion of human rights. Plan Colombia was thus justified using both a geostrategic (war on drugs) and a solidarist (human rights) logic. I now turn to examine each of these justifications in turn.

Plan Colombia: A humanitarian intervention?

Plan Colombia was said to be a humanitarian intervention in two main ways. First, Plan Colombia was designed to establish a secure environment free from non-state armed actors. Second, US military aid and training was alleged to lead to a professionalization of the Colombian military. Moreover, US military aid and training was subject to the Leahy Law, which is supposed to ensure that US military aid does not go to any human rights abusers. In relation to securing an environment for Colombia's civilian population free from armed actors, US President Bill Clinton's Assistant Secretary of State of the Western Hemisphere Affairs Bureau, Peter F. Romero, argued that

> Colombia must re-establish authority over narcotics producing 'sanctuaries'.... Any comprehensive solution to Colombia's problems must include the re-establishment of government authority over these lawless areas. To achieve this, we propose to give the GOC [government of Colombia] the air mobility to reach deep into these lawless zones and establish a secure environment for GOC officials and NGOs to extend basic services to these long deprived areas.[30]

This was supposed to establish a secure environment for officials and non-governmental organizations to provide essential services as a prerequisite for encouraging economic growth and inward investment. General Charles Wilhelm, Commander-in-Chief of the U.S. Southern Command, stated, "While I share the widely held opinion that the ultimate solution to Colombia's internal problems lies in negotiations, I am convinced that success on the battlefield provides the leverage that is a precondition for meaningful and productive negotiations".[31] The underlying rationale is the perception that rebel-held territory provides a safe haven for drugs production and the recruitment of cadres for the guerrilla movements. The pre-existence of the FARC (Revolutionary Armed Forces of Columbia) zones of control requires a military solution both to extend the rule of law (and thus bring these areas under control) and to weaken the insurgents' power and bring them to the negotiating table.

The second main way in which Plan Colombia was said to be a form of humanitarian intervention was the role played by US military aid and training to professionalize the Colombian military. This was principally done through the allegedly strict conditionalities attached to US military aid and training. For example, US military aid and training was subject to the Leahy Law, whereby "all assistance to the Colombian armed forces is contingent upon human rights screening. No assistance will be provided to any unit of the Colombian military for which there is credible evidence of serious human rights violations by its members".[32] The United States argued that this will ensure that US equipment and training will not be directed toward any members of the Colombian military involved in gross human rights violations. Furthermore, a US–Colombian End Use Monitoring Agreement of August 1997 provided for the screening of unit members for past corruption. The agreement also required Colombia's Defence Ministry to submit certification of ongoing investigations of alleged human rights abusers within Colombian military units every six months. In 1998 the United States refused assistance to three Colombian military units on the basis of their human rights record.[33] The United States thus argues that its military aid is conditional on human rights screening and will serve to professionalize the Colombian military.

Despite these arguments, the Colombian military has one of the worst human rights records in the western hemisphere and has continued to maintain strong links with the paramilitary umbrella organization euphemistically named the United Self Defence Forces of Colombia (AUC). Furthermore, there is a pervasive culture of impunity, as a result of which members of the Colombian military shown to have committed human rights violations are rarely brought to justice.[34] Far from bringing security to what Romero calls "lawless zones", the Colombian military have continued to bring lawlessness and murder to the peasant inhabitants of Colombia, as reported by international and Colombian human rights organizations.[35] Although the Leahy Law is intended to address the issue of military human rights abuse by refusing to supply, train or equip any army unit where collusion with paramilitaries can be proven to have taken place, there are dangerous weaknesses in the implementation of this law that render it effectively useless.

First, instead of vetting older units in the Colombian military for soldiers who have committed human rights violations, "counter-narcotics" units are being formed from scratch. In this way, the emphasis in the Colombian military is on forming newly vetted units rather than investigating the "bad apples" in the older units. Second, a soldier from a disbanded unit can still receive training if his personal record is clean. He can then go back to his unit and pass on training. In effect this means that tainted soldiers within banned units can still receive training as long as they are not present initially when US military advisers are giving it. Third, the Leahy Law relies on a large amount of transparency on the part of the United States. Every year the United States publishes the Foreign Military Training Report (FMTR). The Center for International Policy regularly monitors the FMTR and publishes research findings based on its information. They have shown that between 1999 and 2002 the United States increased the classification of information contained in the FMTR. This prevented "all without classified access from monitoring implementation of the 'Leahy Law' human rights restrictions", which had in reports prior to the increased classification shown that "vetted individuals from Colombian Army brigades banned from receiving unit-level assistance were being trained" in direct contravention of the Leahy Law.[36] The classification of the FMTR thus made it "impossible to oversee the US government's implementation of the Leahy Amendment" during the crucial period of US military aid escalation under Plan Colombia.[37]

Fourth, whilst the Leahy Law encompasses most forms of military funding, the version of Leahy on Defense Department-funded aid, for example, section 1004, is much weaker than State Department International Narcotic Control funding channels. Moreover, monitoring of section 1004 funding does not apply to military exercises, arms sales and some forms of intelligence sharing.[38] Fifth, in implementing human rights vetting in Colombia, the United States solicits a list from the Colombian Defence Ministry of Colombian military personnel deemed to be free of human rights violations. However, in determining whether a potential trainee meets this criterion, the Colombian Defence Ministry checks both the Colombian court system and Colombia's Internal Affairs Agency. Importantly, this review ignores cases where credible evidence exists but has not yet resulted in any formal charges against the named individual. Human Rights Watch notes that formal charges often take years to be filed under the Colombian judicial system largely because of underfunding and understaffing (which in itself gives an indication of institutional priorities).[39] When we couple this with the climate of fear that exists in Colombia and the frequent targeting of civilians who have accused Colombian military personnel of human rights abuses, this represents a serious weakness in US human rights monitoring in Colombia.

Lastly, the use of private contractors by Washington obscures legal oversight and end-use monitoring of training and arms. US mercenary companies like DynCorp and Military Professional Resources, Inc. (MPRI) have provided logistical support and training to the Colombian military. These private contractors maintain databases of thousands of former US military and intelligence operatives who can be called upon for temporary assignment in the field.[40] This "public–private partnership" is convenient in a number of ways. It allows Washington to deploy military know-how in pursuing strategic objectives whilst avoiding congressional caps on official military personnel overseas. Privately outsourced contractors also circumnavigate the potential negative media coverage of US military casualties, and thus lessen governmental exposure risks. Also, private contractors are only accountable to the company that employs them. Thus, if anyone is involved in actions that may generate negative publicity, Washington can plausibly deny responsibility. Myles Frechette, the former US ambassador to Colombia, outlined the utility of using private mercenaries when he argued that it is "very handy to have an outfit not part of the US Armed Forces. Obviously, if anybody gets killed or whatever, you can say its not a member of the armed forces".[41] This public–private partnership has thus seriously weakened the transparent operation of the Leahy Law, which covers only public money and the use of official US soldiers and equipment, and provides a high level of "plausible deniability" for Washington.

In 2000, the Senate Appropriations Committee attempted to address some of these flaws by attaching six conditions to Plan Colombia. These included a more rigorous assessment of the prosecution of Colombian military personnel who are believed to have committed human rights violations, the prosecution of paramilitary groups and the cooperation of the Colombian military with civilian authorities investigating human rights violations. A clause attached to these conditions, however, allowed the President to waive them if it was considered to be in the US national interest to do so. On 22 August 2000, US President Bill Clinton signed a presidential waiver excluding the human rights considerations within Plan Colombia. The reason given for the waiver was the threat to US national security from drug trafficking.[42] Although Clinton maintained that he could certify Colombia on one of the seven conditions, that of bringing to the civil courts military personnel who have committed gross violations of human rights, a report disputes the effective implementation of even this basic safeguard. The report, prepared by Amnesty International, Human Rights Watch and the Washington Office on Latin America, argues that the Colombian government has "been unwilling to take affirmative measures needed to address impunity, it has also worked to block legislation designed to implement measures that would ensure human rights violations are tried within the civilian court system".[43] The areas outlined above represent a serious weakening of the intent of the Leahy Law and, as argued, the good intentions of the Leahy Law could see a lessening of emphasis on the bringing to justice of human rights abusers in the Colombian military in favour of forming US-friendly vetted units with little to no capacity of holding Colombian recipients of US military aid and training accountable due to US-imposed secrecy and outsourcing. I now turn to consider the argument that Plan Colombia was also part of the United States' so-called "war on drugs".

Geopolitics and the war on drugs in Colombia

The use of the Colombian military as part of the United States' "war on drugs" has been justified as a necessary response to the continued and deepening ties between the FARC insurgents concentrated in Colombia's south and international drug trafficking. The United States has argued that an aggressive supply-side destruction of coca plantations and military engagement with Colombia's "narco-guerrillas" formed the primary component of Plan Colombia and it is this justification that most closely resembles the more familiar logic of national interest. The major US and Colombian military initiative under Plan Colombia was the formation of two 950-man counter-narcotics divisions and additional funding for another division. The counter-narcotic units were said to be trained and equipped for a southern push into the Putumayo region of Colombia. The United States argued that this was where the majority of peasant coca cultivation took place and therefore where the counter-narcotic operations should concentrate. The FARC have long been active in this region, therefore the United States argued that the rebels have a vested interest in the coca trade and in protecting it from being destroyed. The strategic logic undergirding the US justification was thus the necessity for the counter-narcotic units to be highly trained and equipped to deal with potential clashes with rebel forces whilst undertaking their primary mission of drug interdiction and eradication activity. To this end the United States supplied the Colombian military with 30 Black Hawk helicopters and 33 UH-1N helicopters. The United States also provided a US$28 million upgrade to radar facilities in Colombia as well as sharing intelligence on guerrilla activity in the southern areas. A river interdiction programme will be deployed along the rivers on the Ecuadorian border to the south in conjunction with an upgrade to the A-37 aircraft used by the Colombian air force.[44] The US Department of Defence maintained that there are approximately 250 to 300 US military personnel and 400 to 500 private mercenary contractors in Colombia at any one time during the implementation of Plan Colombia. Typically these units are made up of US Special Forces and US Navy Seals or retired US military or intelligence operatives. In sum, the United States argued that the FARC narco-guerrillas make huge profits from the drug trade and have used those profits to wage a war against the democratically elected Colombian government. Accordingly, under Plan Colombia the eradication of the coca fields comes first, and any engagement with the rebels is secondary and subordinate to the primary military objective of coca eradication. Central to the southern push against the FARC were the claims that the FARC were the biggest drug traffickers within Colombia.

In the South, there is a pattern of small-scale coca cultivation by peasants displaced through the decades of civil war and unequal landholding.[45] Whilst this southern area hosts significant coca cultivation, the activity is by no means concentrated solely here. For example, in 2001 coca cultivation was relatively diversified throughout Colombia, with coca concentrations in eastern and western Colombia, as well as in the paramilitary strongholds in Colombia's northern departments.[46] Aside from the geographical areas where coca is grown, however, are the more important trafficking networks that are concentrated in the north of Colombia. These are in turn run, protected and sustained by Colombia's narco-mafia and their paramilitary armies. It is these trafficking networks that are responsible for transhipment into US markets and laundering efforts into both Colombian and international financial networks. Fascinatingly, the United States completely ignored these in Plan Colombia, and continued to insist both on its southern push against the FARC and that this push is driven by counternarcotic concerns.

However, James Milford, the former Deputy Administrator with the United States' central drug eradication body, the Drug Enforcement Administration (DEA), argued that Carlos Castano, who headed the paramilitary umbrella group AUC at the time of Plan Colombia's implementation was a "major cocaine trafficker in his own right" and had close links to the North Valle drug syndicate, which was "among the most powerful drug trafficking groups in Colombia".[47] Donnie Marshall, the former Administrator of the DEA, confirmed that right-wing paramilitary groups "raise funds through extortion, or by protecting laboratory operations in northern and central Colombia. The Carlos Castano organization and possibly other paramilitary groups appear to be directly involved in processing cocaine. At least one of these paramilitary groups appears to be involved in exporting cocaine from Colombia."[48]

Unlike the AUC, the FARC operated a taxation system on the coca trade. This taxation system, rather than drug cultivation, trafficking and transhipment, was confirmed by the DEA. Milford argued "there is little to indicate the insurgent groups are trafficking in cocaine themselves, either by producing cocaine ... and selling it to Mexican syndicates, or by establishing their own distribution networks in the United States".[49] Instead, he continued that "the FARC controls certain areas of Colombia and the FARC in those regions generate revenue by 'taxing' local drug related activities". Nonetheless, as Marshall says, "there is no corroborated information that the FARC is involved directly in the shipment of drugs from Colombia to international markets".[50] This view has been confirmed by the United Nations. Klaus Nyholm, the Director of the United Nations Drug Control Programme (UNDCP) argued that in 2000 the "guerrillas are something different than the traffickers, the local fronts are quite autonomous. But in some areas, they're not involved at all. And in others, they actively tell the farmers not to grow coca". In the rebels' former demilitarized zone, Nyholm stated, "drug cultivation has not increased or decreased" once "FARC took control".[51] Indeed, Nyholm pointed out that in 1999 the FARC were cooperating with a US$6 million UN project to replace coca crops with new forms of legal alternative development.[52] Nyholm confirmed this in 2003 when he argued that "the paramilitary relation with drug trafficking undoubtedly is much more intimate" than FARC's. He continued, "many of the paramilitary bands started as the drug traffickers' hired guns. They are more autonomous now, but have maintained their close relations with the drug traffickers. In some of the coastal towns it can, in fact, sometimes be hard to tell whether a man is a paramilitary chief, a big coca planter, a cocaine lab owner, a rancher, or a local politician. He may be all five things at a time".[53] Nyholm's analysis thus confirms DEA's analysis: namely, throughout the time period of Plan Colombia's implementation, the guerillas were involved in some aspects of the coca trade and raised funds through a generic taxation system. The Colombian government has also alleged that FARC have traded cocaine for guns with Brazilian drug traffickers.[54] However, FARC are "bit part" players in comparison to the paramilitary networks and the cocaine barons that these paramilitaries protect. Both the United States' own agencies and the UN have consistently reported over a number of years that the paramilitaries are far more heavily involved than FARC in drug cultivation, refinement and transhipment to the United States. Castano admitted as much when he stated that drug trafficking and drug traffickers financed 70 per cent of his organization's operations.[55] Instead of the term "narco-guerrilla", a more suitable phrase would be "narco-paramilitary". However, this is a term conspicuous by its absence under Plan Colombia and the United States continued to gear Colombian military strategy toward, and supply the arms exclusively for, an intensified CI campaign against FARC and their alleged civilian sympathizers. In short, the "war on drugs" component of Plan Colombia was actually a "war on drugs that some FARC fronts tax" that sidestepped the paramilitaries' deep involvement in drug trafficking to US markets.

Why did the United States emphasise FARC's alleged links to international drug trafficking under Plan Colombia and yet largely ignore the well-documented role of the paramilitaries in the cultivation and transhipment of drugs? As we saw earlier, the United States was instrumental in setting up and institutionalizing a CI framework for the Colombian military that from its very inception developed and then incorporated paramilitary networks. Whilst these networks were closely tied with the Colombian military, they have also historically aligned themselves with local sections of the Colombian ruling class, especially in Colombia's rural areas. For example, a number of paramilitary groups have acted as the private armies of large landholders and cattle ranchers and, during the 1980s, as the private militias of local criminal mafias intimately involved in the drug trade. Indeed, the US State Department has noted that although "AUC increasingly tried to depict itself as an autonomous organization with a political agenda" it was in practice "a mercenary vigilante force, financed by criminal activities" and essentially remained "the paid private" army of "narcotics traffickers or large landowners".[56] However, as with all armies, the narco-paramilitaries need funding for equipment, training, weaponry and so on. The historical record shows that the United States has backed actors and organizations involved in drug trafficking so as to further strategic and/or political objectives such as CI campaigns.[57] The most notable instance of this in Latin America was during the US-backed Contra war in Nicaragua during the 1980s. In 1989, the Senate Subcommittee on Terrorism, Narcotics, and International Operations, the "Kerry Committee", concluded a three-year investigation of Contra involvement with drugs by observing that "one or another agency of the US government had information regarding the involvement [in drug smuggling] either while it was occurring, or immediately thereafter.... Senior US policy makers were not immune to the idea that drug money was a perfect solution to the Contras' funding problems".[58] Given the evidence of the United States' clear knowledge of paramilitary involvement in drugs, it is apparent that the United States is willing to turn a blind eye to paramilitary drug involvement so long as they co-operate with the wider US objective of CI. In the aftermath of 11 September, however, an explicit counterterror orientation has developed within US policy.

After 11 September: From drugs to terror

The primary means for the US war on terror in Colombia has been the continued substantial funding of the Colombian military but a shift from the language of counter-narcotics to counterterrorism. US Senator John McCain argued, "American policy has dispensed with the illusion that the Colombian government is fighting two separate wars, one against drug trafficking and another against domestic terrorists". Tellingly, he continued that the United States has now abandoned "any fictional

distinctions between counter-narcotic and counter-insurgency operations".[59] Thus, in the aftermath of 11 September the United States has
dropped the pretence that its military assistance has been driven solely
by counter-narcotics and human rights concerns and has now started
overtly to couch its funding in terms of an overt strategy of counterterrorism targeted against FARC, who are now being linked to international
terrorism as well as drug trafficking, and human rights abuses. For example, former US Attorney General John Ashcroft designated FARC the
"most dangerous international terrorist group based in the Western
Hemisphere".[60] The Bush administration's 2003 aid package for the
Colombian military, which was called the Andean Regional Initiative
(ARI), allocated approximately US$538 million for funding year 2003.
The 2003 ARI package also contained almost identical human-rights
text to that found in Plan Colombia but softened some of the language
used to monitor Colombian military collaboration with paramilitary
forces. For example, whereas Plan Colombia specified that the Colombian military must be "vigorously prosecuting in the civilian courts"
paramilitary leaders and their military collaborators, the ARI calls for
"effective measures to sever links" between the armed forces and
the paramilitaries. Similarly, Colombian military efforts at "cooperating
fully" with ending collusion now merely call for "cooperation".[61] The
ARI has thus maintained the high levels of US funding for the Colombian military, whilst decreasing the requirements on Colombia to comply
with basic safeguards on human rights.

The ARI also contains a component that sent US$98 million to a new
Colombian military unit trained to protect the 500-mile-long Caño Limón
pipeline owned by the US multinational oil corporation Occidental Petroleum. This money was used to train approximately 4,000 Colombian
military personnel, and has been overtly couched in terms of counter-
insurgency training (in addition to an initial US$6 million for a "pipeline
protection" brigade sent in the 2002 appropriations request). The pipeline money forms part of the overall US$538 million contained within
the 2003 ARI. Originally, the pipeline money was to be sent outside of
the ARI and was instead to go through Foreign Military Funding (FMF)
channels, which have not been used to send money to the Colombian military since the end of the Cold War. The logic undergirding this decision
was that publicly the United States wished to maintain a strict separation
between its counter-drug assistance sent under the ARI and outright CI
assistance sent under FMF, which is generally considered to be all-
purpose, non-drug military aid. However, due to US concerns about
Colombia's delayed signing of an Article 98 agreement exempting US
personnel from being prosecuted by the International Criminal Court for
possible human rights violations, the money ended up being sent under

the ARI, which is unaffected by Article 98 considerations. This further underscores the interchangeability of alleged US counter-drug assistance (ARI) and US CI assistance (FMF), which is supposedly technically separate. Former US Ambassador to Colombia Anne Paterson stated that the pipeline "lost $500 million in revenue because of attacks" in 2001. In response, US Special Forces have been training Colombian CI units along the pipeline. The US$98 million contained within the ARI allowed Colombia to purchase helicopters and the US to continue training the Colombian military.[62] The money will concentrate on training troops to clear rebels from the oil-rich Arauca region near the northeastern border with Venezuela.

In sum, the major difference between Plan Colombia and the ARI has been the stated rationales of US intervention, which have switched from a pretext of counter-drugs to counter-drugs and counterterrorism. Thus, the post–11 September environment has seen the escalation of the United States' publicly stated commitment to Colombia as part of its global "war on terror". Asa Hutchinson, a former director of the DEA, stated that the United States has "demonstrated that drug traffickers and terrorists work out of the same jungle, they plan in the same cave, and they train in the same desert".[63] However, whilst the United States has publicly declared its support for a new war on terrorism in Colombia, it has long acted to make the principal terrorists more effective as part of its continued CI campaign against FARC and Colombian civil society. This is made clearer by the fact that in 1991 US Department of Defense and CIA advisers travelled to Colombia to reshape Colombian military intelligence networks. This restructuring was kept secret and again was supposedly designed to aid the Colombian military in their counter-narcotics efforts. However, Human Rights Watch obtained a copy of the order, which was confirmed as authentic by then-Colombian Defence Minister Rafael Pardo.[64] Nowhere within the order (named Order 200-05/91) is any mention made of drugs. Instead, the secret reorganization focussed solely on combating what was called "escalating terrorism by armed subversion" through the creation of what Human Rights Watch characterized as a "secret network that relied on paramilitaries not only for intelligence, but to carry out murder".[65] The reorganization solidified linkages between the Colombian military and paramilitary networks and further entrenched the covert nature of paramilitary networks with all "written material" to be "removed" and any "open contacts and interaction with military installations" to be avoided by paramilitaries. The handling of the networks was to be conducted covertly, which allowed for the "necessary flexibility to cover targets of interest".[66] Once the reorganization was complete, paramilitary violence "dramatically increased"[67] in Colombia, with the victims primarily trade unionists, journalists, teachers, human rights workers and the poor. Thus, the United States further incorporated the principal terrorist networks into the prevailing Colombian CI strategy and sought to further obscure the linkages by making the relationship more covert.

This reorganization proved remarkably effective. In 2001, a year after the implementation of Plan Colombia, Amnesty International documented the ongoing collusion between paramilitary forces and the Colombian military whereby in "areas of long-standing paramilitary activity, reliable and abundant information shows that the security forces continued to allow paramilitary operations with little or no evidence of actions taken to curtail such activity". Actions taken by the Colombian government to combat paramilitary forces are non-existent despite claims to the contrary. Amnesty International continues that one Colombian military unit set up specifically to deal with paramilitarism was no more than a "paper tiger", with the official Colombian government office that allegedly monitors paramilitary massacres "a public relations mouthpiece for the government".[68] Although this chapter is primarily concerned with the earlier implementation of US military assistance to Colombia, this high level collusion continues to exist between the Colombian military and paramilitary forces to the extent that senior members of the current Colombian Presidents administration, including a former security police chief, have been charged with collusion with paramilitary forces.[69] What conclusions can be drawn from this account? I now go on to link my earlier theoretical arguments with the empirical material examined above.

Beyond geopolitics and solidarism: Interpenetrated sovereignty and transnational conflict

Static and ahistorical notions of state sovereignty are clearly not sufficient for understanding the nature of US–Colombian state-to-state relations. At the very beginning of the United States' CI assistance for the Colombian state, there were very conscious and clear attempts to influence the forms and ways in which the Colombian state interacted with Colombian civil society. For example, a very early US CI assessment of the Colombian military argued that

> From the beginning it was considered that in order to adequately influence and capture the minds of present and future [Colombian] Armed Forces leaders, with the objective of orientating them to western democratic concepts and precepts ... an approximate total of 225,000 copies of direct anti-communist type of literature and security was distributed to the Armed Forces units and personnel as well as civilians during various civic action "Jornadas" of many military units.[70]

Moreover, US–Colombian interaction has continued to shape the nature and form of the Colombian state. At issue then is a challenge to the deliberative moment in both the solidarist and geostrategic approaches to world politics and (non-)intervention insofar as both presume that the (invariably non-Western) State A that is subject to potential intervention is somehow free from ongoing forms of intervention from State B (invariably Western core powers). This in turn often erases forms of covert statecraft and, most importantly, the centrality of imperial statecraft to ongoing forms of humanitarian crisis in the global South. For example, in the Colombian case examined above, most conventional analysis combined with the discourses of US policymakers themselves portrays the United States as both a moral agent in relation to the Colombian crisis and as somehow an actor distinct from the ongoing humanitarian crisis in Colombia today. As the empirical material shows, however, the United States has long been active in Colombia and was instrumental in setting up, indirectly funding and perpetuating the paramilitary networks that are today the largest abusers of human rights in Colombia. In essence, then, when the United States declares its intention to intervene to stem the humanitarian crisis in Colombia, the United States is, in a very real sense, deeply implicated within the very conditions that provide the conditions of possibility for the crisis in the first place. It is wholly naive to assume that moral rhetoric alone is a sufficient condition for the assessment of whether a state is acting out of a logic of international solidarity and in the worst case can act as a smokescreen that legitimates contemporary forms of imperialism.

Second, when one examines the actual reasons for US intervention in Colombia it becomes clear that the principal form of solidarity taking place is actually what would be more accurately called "transnational class solidarity" based upon the globalizing logic of contemporary capitalism and its concomitant political forms. That is, US intervention is designed to both secure the interests of (primarily) US capital and the transnationally orientated sectors of Colombia's increasingly globalized capital and ruling class, whilst underwriting the political and strategic conditions necessary for the continued viability of the central conduit of imperial rule, the Colombian state. In its most direct sense in Colombia this has involved the "stabilization" of the Colombian state in the face of both armed and unarmed social forces. The paramilitaries have formed the central coercive means for this pacification process as the recent case of US multinationals directly sponsoring paramilitary "death squads" goes to prove.[71] In essence then, the political, economic and strategic contexts of US intervention are internally conjoined and this is illustrated most clearly by the often frank admissions of senior US planners.

For example, General Peter Pace, Commander in Chief of the US Southern Command under the Clinton Administration, and thus responsible for implementing US security assistance programmes throughout Latin America, argued that vital US national interests, which he defined as "those of broad, over-riding importance to the survival, safety and vitality of our nation", included the maintenance of stability and unhindered access to Latin American markets by US transnationals in the post–Cold War period. Noting that "our trade within the Americas represents approximately 46 percent of all US exports, and we expect this percentage to increase in the future", Pace went on to explain that underlying the US military's role in Colombia was the need to maintain a "continued stability required for access to markets ... which is critical to the continued economic expansion and prosperity of the United States". US security assistance to the Colombian military was necessary because any "loss of our Caribbean and Latin American markets would seriously damage the health of the US economy".[72] Moreover, US strategic concerns over South American oil are also crucial. Marc Grossman, former US Undersecretary of State for Political Affairs, underscored the crucial role that economic interests play in driving US intervention in Colombia, when he stated that the Colombian insurgents

represent a danger to the $4.3 billion in direct U.S. investment in Colombia. They regularly attack U.S. interests, including the railway used by the Drummond Coal Mining facility and Occidental Petroleum's stake in the Caño Limón oil pipeline. Terrorist attacks on the Caño Limón pipeline also pose a threat to U.S. energy security. Colombia supplied 3% of U.S. oil imports in 2001, and possesses substantial potential oil and natural gas reserves.[73]

The wider strategic considerations that link US CI in Colombia with US access to South American oil grow out of fears of regional instability generated by FARC. General Pace had already made this clear before the election of George W. Bush and before 11 September. He started by explaining how important South American oil is to the United States, arguing that there is a "common misperception" that the United States "is completely dependent on the Middle East" for oil, when in fact Venezuela provides "15%–19% of our imported oil in any given month". Pace then went on to note that the "internal conflict in Colombia poses a direct threat to regional stability" and US oil interests, with "Venezuela, Ecuador, and Panama" the "most vulnerable to destabilization due to Colombian insurgent activity along their borders".[74] Of course, unhindered access to South American oil became an even more pressing concern for US planners after the 11 September attacks, and this concern can only increase in the context of the continuing instability generated by the quagmire in Iraq. The former US Ambassador to Colombia, Anne Patterson, explained, "after September 11, the issue of oil security has become a priority for the United States", especially as the "traditional oil sources for the United States" in the Middle East have become even "less secure". By sourcing US energy needs from Colombia, which "after Mexico and Venezuela" is "the most important oil country in the region", the US would have "a small margin to work with" in the face of a crisis and could "avoid [oil] price speculation".[75] It is clear then that in the case of US–Colombia relations, US intervention is a form of transnational class solidarity designed to insulate the Colombian state and ruling class from a wide range of both armed and unarmed social forces. This is illustrated most clearly by the targets of US-backed Colombian CI forces. For example, in 2000, over 8,000 political assassinations were committed in Colombia, with 80 per cent of these murders committed by paramilitary groups allied to the Colombian military. In an extensive report on human rights in Colombia the UN notes that in 2004 its "office ... [has] continued to receive complaints about human rights violations implying the direct responsibility ... of the security forces.... Many of the violations, due to their serious, massive or systematic nature, constitute crimes against humanity and are susceptible to trial by the International Criminal Court".[76]

Conclusion

What conclusions can we draw from both the theoretical claims and the empirical material examined above? It is clear that the notion that contemporary world politics is characterized by sovereign states with a strict separation between the domestic and international is not sustainable in today's globalized world. In this chapter I have instead argued for a theory of interpenetrated sovereignty and transnational conflict that calls for a sensitivity to the myriad ways in which core states within the world system can and do interpenetrate the sovereignties of non-core states. This is done in a number of ways, including through the international institutions of global neo-liberal governance such as the IMF, World Bank and so on, or in more covert and coercive ways such as global military aid and training programmes. Importantly, it is necessary to historicize state relations so as to examine and investigate the ways in which the central actors in any humanitarian crisis may be fundamentally implicated within the very crisis that those same actors claim to be acting against. In the case of Colombia, it is obvious that the United States is fundamentally bound up with the ongoing humanitarian crisis there, one in which it now claims to be acting to stem. Ironically, the United States can be said to be acting from a form of solidarity: one of transnational class solidarity that ties the interests of the Colombian and US ruling classes together. Simply stated, these interests involve the preservation of Colombia as a pro-United States state, the effective incorporation of Colombia as a stable circuit within the global circulation of capital and the destruction of both armed and unarmed social forces that threaten these interests. The ongoing and massive levels of US military aid and training, combined with the United States' covert policy of backing Colombian state violence, remains consistent with earlier US Cold War objectives. In the midst of these processes a human tragedy continues to unfold. Within Colombia, according to the UN, there are thousands of politically motivated murders every year, some of the highest levels of internal displacement in the world, the widespread use of "child soldiers" by both paramilitary and guerrilla groups, regular and systematic sexualized violence against women and the ongoing "social cleansing" of civilians considered inimical to all of the major armed actors in Colombia. As scholars, it is imperative that we both theoretically and empirically interrogate the justifications given for various forms of intervention and, acting from a sense of common humanity and solidarity, hold our states to account if we find a disparity between liberal rhetoric and geostrategic reality.

Notes

1. I thank Nick Wheeler for helpful comments on an earlier draft of this chapter.
2. Hans J. Morgenthau (1978) *Politics among Nations: The Struggle for Power and Peace*, New York: Alfred A. Knopf.
3. Nicholas J. Wheeler (2000) *Saving Strangers: Humanitarian Intervention in International Society*, Oxford: Oxford University Press.
4. G. John Ikenberry (2000) "America's Liberal Grand Strategy: Democracy and National Security in the Post-War Era", in Michael Cox, Takashi Inoguchi and G. John Ikenberry, eds, *American Democracy Promotion: Impulses, Strategies, and Impacts*, Oxford: Oxford University Press, p. 104.
5. Tony Smith (2000) "National Security Liberalism and American Foreign Policy", in Cox et al., *American Democracy Promotion*, p. 85.
6. Cf Fareed Samaria (1997) "The Delusion of Impartial Intervention", *Foreign Affairs* 76(6): 22–43.
7. See Michael Doyle (1996) "Kant, Liberal Legacies, and Foreign Affairs", in Michael E. Brown, Sean M. Lynn-Jones and Steven E. Miller, eds, *Debating the Democratic Peace: An International Security Reader*, London: MIT Press, pp. 3–57; Bruce Russet (1996) "The Fact of Democratic Peace", in Brown et al., *Debating the Democratic Peace*, pp. 58–81. For an excellent set of critical interpretations of the Democratic Peace thesis see Mark Laffey and Tarak Barkawi (2001) *Democracy, Liberalism and War: Rethinking the Democratic Peace Debate*, Boulder, Colo.: Lynne Rienner Press; Tarak Barkawi and Mark Laffey (1999) "The Imperial Peace: Democracy, Force, and Globalization", in *European Journal of International Relations* 5(4): 403–434.

8. Michel Feher (2001) *Powerless by Design: The Age of the International Community*, Durham, N.C.: Duke University Press, p. 32.

9. Robert C. DiPrizio (2002) *Armed Humanitarians: U.S. Interventions from Northern Iraq to Kosovo*, Baltimore, Md.: The Johns Hopkins University Press; Cf Noam Chomsky (1999) *The New Military Humanism*, Monroe, Maine: Common Courage Press.

10. For an interesting poststructuralist perspective on our ethical duty toward the Other see David Campbell (1998) "Why Fight: Humanitarianism, Principles and Post-Structuralism", *Millennium: Journal of International Studies* 27(3): 197–221.

11. See Wheeler, *Saving Strangers*, for more on this.

12. Barkawi and Laffey "The Imperial Peace".

13. For more on this see my "The Heart of Empire? Theorizing US Empire in an Era of Transnational Capitalism", *Third World Quarterly* 26(2) (2005); Leo Panitch and Sam Gindin (2003) *Global Capitalism and American Empire*, London: Merlin Press; G. John Ikenberry (2002) "America's Imperial Ambition", *Foreign Affairs*, September/October; Richard N. Haass (2000) "Imperial America", *Foreign Affairs*, 11 November; Michael Cox (2003) "The Empire's Back in Town; or, America's Imperial Temptation – Again", *Millennium* 32(1). On the role that Wall Street and the dollarization of the global political economy play in maintaining US primacy within the world system see the excellent Peter Gowan (1999) *The Global Gamble: Washington's Faustian Bid for World Dominance*, London: Verso.

14. George Kennan (1976) *Foreign Relations of the United States, 1948*, Report by the Policy Planning Staff, Washington, D.C.: General Printing Office, pp. 524–525.

15. Geir Lundestad (1999) "Empire by Invitation in the American Century", in Michael J. Hogan, ed., *The Ambiguous Legacy: U.S. Foreign Relations in the "American Century"*, Cambridge: Cambridge University Press, pp. 52–91.

16. Panitch and Gindin, *Global Capitalism and American Empire*.

17. Henry Kissinger quoted in Seymour M. Hersh (1983) *The Price of Power: Kissinger in the Nixon White House*, London: Simon & Schuster, p. 636.

18. Joseph S. Nye, Jr. (2003) *The Paradox of American Power: Why the World's Only Superpower Can't Go It Alone*, Oxford: Oxford University Press.

19. James Petras and Morris Morley (1981) "The U.S. Imperial State", in James Petras, with Morris H. Morley, Peter DeWitt and A. Eugene Havens, *Class, State, and Power in the Third World*, Montclair, N.J.: Allanheld, Osmun and Co.

20. Jack Nelson-Pallmeyer (1997) *School of Assassins*, New York: Orbis Books. For more on the global reach of US military power see Lora Lumpe (2002) "Foreign Military Training: Global Reach, Global Power, and Oversight Issues", *Foreign Policy in Focus*, May, available from http://www.fpif.org/papers/miltrain/index.html, accessed 31 May 2006. See also Chalmers Johnson (2004) "The Arithmetic of America's Military Bases Abroad: What Does It All Add Up To?", *History News Network*, 19 January, available from http://hnn.us/articles/3097.html, accessed 31 May 2006.

21. George Kennan quoted in David F. Schmitz (1999) *Thank God They're On Our Side: The United States and Right-Wing Dictatorships 1921–1965*, Chapel Hill, N.C.: University of North Carolina Press, p. 149.

22. David Painter (1995) "Explaining US Relations with the Third World", *Diplomatic History* 19(3): 525.

23. Roy Rubottom (1959) "Subject: President Lleras' Appeal for Aid in Suppressing Colombian Guerrilla Warfare Activities", July 21, available from http://www.icdc.com/~paulwolf/colombia/rubottom21jul1959a.jpg, accessed 31 May 2006.

24. Stephen J. Randall (1992) *Colombia and the United States: Hegemony and Interdependence*, Athens, Ga.: University of Georgia Press, 1992, p. 241.

25. US Department of State (1960) "Preliminary Report, Colombia Survey Team, Colonel Lansdale", 23 February, available from http://www.icdc.com/~paulwolf/colombia/lansdale23feb1960a.jpg, accessed 31 May 2006.
26. This and the following quòtes are from US Department of the Army (1970) *Stability Operations–Intelligence*, FM 30-21, pp. 73–78.
27. Ibid., pp. E1–E7.
28. William Yarborough (1962) *Subject: Visit to Colombia, South America, by a Team from Special Warfare Center, Fort Bragg*, Supplement, *Colombian Survey Report*. 26 February, available from http://www.icdc.com/~paulwolf/colombia/surveyteam26feb1962.htm, accessed 31 May 2006.
29. See my *America's Other War: Terrorizing Colombia*, London: Zed Books (2004), for a comprehensive analysis of US policy toward Colombia both during and after the Cold War period.
30. Peter F. Romero (2000) "Statement before the House Subcommittee of Criminal Justice, Drug Policy, and Human Resources", Washington D.C., 15 February, available from http://www.state.gov/www.policy_remarks/2000/000215_romero_colombia.html, accessed 31 May 2006.
31. Washington File, Press and Culture Section, US Department of State (2000) "General Wilhelm Testifies on Proposed U.S. Aid to Colombia", 15 February, available from http://ns.usembassy.ro/USIS/Washington-File/200/00-02-15/eur215.htm, accessed 31 May 2006.
32. US Department of State Bureau of Western Hemisphere Affairs Fact Sheet, 28 March 2000.
33. Center for International Policy (2005) *Colombia Country Overview*, 12 February, available from http://www.ciponline.org/facts/co.htm, accessed 31 May 2006.
34. Javier Giraldo (1996) *Colombia the Genocidal Democracy*, Monroe, Maine: Common Courage Press, pp. 66–74.
35. Joint Report prepared by Amnesty International, Human Rights Watch and the Washington Office on Latin America (n.d.) *Colombia Certification*, available from http://www.hrw.org/campaigns/colombia/certification.htm, accessed 31 May 2006.
36. Centre for International Policy (n.d.) *Training: Findings and Recommendations*, available from http://www.ciponline.org/facts/traifind.htm, accessed 31 May 2006.
37. Centre for International Policy (n.d.) *The Foreign Military Training Report*, available from http://www.ciponline.org/facts/fmtr.htm, accessed 31 May 2006.
38. Adam Isacson, Center for International Policy, private correspondence with author, 3 March 2003.
39. Human Rights Watch (2001) *The "Sixth Division": Military and Paramilitary Ties and US Policy in Colombia, Appendix Four, US Human Rights Vetting*, September, available from http://www.hrw.org/reports/2001/colombia/app4.htm, accessed 31 May 2006.
40. Tod Robberson (2000) "Contractors Playing Increasing Role in U.S. Drug War", *Dallas Morning News*, 27 February, available from http://www.colombiasupport.net/200002/dmn-contractors-0227.html.
41. Paul de la Garza and David Adams (2002) "Special Report: The War in Columbia", *St Petersburg Times*, 3 December.
42. Richard Boucher (2000) "Plan Colombia Certification Requirements", press statement, 23 August, available from http://secretary.state.gov/www/briefings/statements/2000/ps000823.html.
43. Amnesty International et al., *Colombia Certification*.
44. Rand Beers, US Assistant Secretary for International Narcotics and Law Enforcement Affairs (2000) "Remarks before the Western Hemisphere, Peace Corps, Narcotics and

Terrorism Subcommittee", Washington, D.C., 25 February, available from http://www.state.gov/www/policy_remarks/2000/000225_beers_sfrc.html, accessed 31 May 2006.

45. Adam Isacson (2000) *Getting in Deeper: The United States' Growing Involvement in Columbia's Conflict*, Washington, D.C.: Center for International Policy, available from http://www.ciponline.org/coipr/coipr002.htm.

46. Center for International Policy (2003) *The "War on Drugs" Meets the "War on Terror"*, February, available from http://ciponline.org/colombia/0302ipr.htm, accessed 31 May 2006.

47. James Milford (1997) "DEA Congressional testimony", House International Relations Committee, Subcommittee on the Western Hemisphere, 16 July, available from http://www.usdoj.gov/dea/pubs/cngrtest/ct970716.htm, accessed 31 May 2006.

48. "Statement of Donnie R. Marshall", DEA Congressional Testimony, Senate Caucus on International Narcotics Control, 28 February 2001, available from http://www.usdoj.gov/dea/pubs/cngrtest/ct022801.htm, accessed 31 May 2006.

49. Milford, "DEA Congressional testimony".

50. Marshall, "Statement of Donnie R. Marshall".

51. *Washington Post*, 10 April 2000.

52. Associated Press, 6 August 1999.

53. Correspondence conducted by author with Klaus Nyholm, 23 January 2003.

54. Carmen J. Gentile (2005) "Drug Smugglers, Rebels Rejoin Hands", *Washington Times*, April 26.

55. US Drug Enforcement Administration (2003) "Drugs and Terrorism a Dangerous Mixture, DEA Official Tells Senate Judiciary Committee", press release, Washington, D.C.: US DEA.

56. US State Department (2001) *Colombia: Country Reports on Human Rights Practices*, available from http://www.state.gov/g/drl/rls/hrrpt/2001/wha/8326.htm, accessed 31 May 2006.

57. For an overview of CIA involvement with drugs from the Second World War onwards see Alfred W. McCoy (1991) *The Politics of Heroin: CIA Complicity in the Global Drug Trade*, New York: Harper and Row; see also Peter Dale Scott and Jonathon Marshall (1992) *Cocaine Politics: Drugs, Armies, and the CIA in Central America*, Berkeley, Calif.: University of California Press for an excellent overview of CIA involvement in the drug trade during the US-backed Contra war in Nicaragua. For an older study on the global trade in opium see Catherine Lamour and Michel R. Lamberti (1972) *The Second Opium War*, London: Penguin Books.

58. Senate Committee on Foreign Relations, Subcommittee on Terrorism, Narcotics and International Operations (1989) *Drugs, Law Enforcement and Foreign Policy*, June, available from http://ciadrugs.homestead.com/files/index.html, accessed 31 May 2006.

59. John McCain (2002) "Speech by Senator John McCain (R-Arizona)", 6 June, available from http://www.ciponline.org/colombia/02060604.htm, accessed 31 May 2006.

60. John Ashcroft (2002) "Prepared Remarks of Attorney General John Ashcroft", Drug Enforcement Administration, 19 March, available from http://www.ciponline.org/colombia/02031903.htm, accessed 31 May 2006.

61. For more detail, see Center for International Policy (2001) "Relevant Excerpts from Conference Report on H.R. 2506, the Foreign Operations Appropriations Bill", available from http://www.ciponline.org/colombia/121901.htm, accessed 31 May 2006.

62. Anne W. Patterson (2002) "Remarks by Ambassador Anne W. Patterson at the CSIS Conference", Washington, D.C., 8 October, available from http://usembassy.state.gov/posts/co1/wwwsa034.shtml, accessed 31 May 2006.

63. Asa Hutchinson (2002), *News 24*, 7 November, available from http://www.news24.com/News24/World/0,1113,2-10_1281687,00.html, accessed 31 May 2006.

64. Human Rights Watch/Americas Human Rights Watch Arms Project (1996) *Colombia's Killer Networks: The Military–Paramilitary Partnership and the United States*, London: Human Rights Watch, p. 29.

65. Ibid., pp. 28–29. In the same report, Human Rights Watch have provided the original documents of the order in both Spanish and English. See pp. 105–150.

66. Ibid., p. 30.

67. Ibid., pp. 38–39.

68. Amnesty International USA (2001) "Human Rights and USA Military Aid to Colombia II", 1 January, available from http://web.amnesty.org/ai.nsf/Recent/AMR230042001!Open, accessed 31 May 2006.

69. Reuters News, 12 March 2007, available from http://www.alertnet.org/thenews/newsdesk/N12382905.htm, accessed 23 March 2007.

70. *USARMIS Intelligence Effort in Colombia (1961–1965)*, circa 1965, available from http://www.icdc.com/~paulwolf/colombia/g21965tabfb.jpg, accessed 31 May 2006.

71. Associated Press (2007) "Drummond Denies Colluding with Far-Right Death Squads to Kill Columbia Unionists", 22 March, available from http://www.iht.com/articles/ap/2007/03/23/america/LA-GEN-Colombia-Drummond-Paramilitaries.php, accessed 23 March 2007.

72. Peter Pace (2000) "Advance Questions for Lieutenant General Peter Pace, Defense Reforms", United States Senate Committee on Armed Services, available from http://www.senate.gov/~armed_services/statemnt/2000/000906pp.pdf, accessed 31 May 2006.

73. Marc Grossman (2002) "Testimony of Ambassador Marc Grossman before the House Appropriations Committee's Subcommittee on Foreign Operations", 10 April, available from http://www.ciponline.org/colombia/02041001.htm, accessed 31 May 2006.

74. Pace, "Advance Questions for Lieutenant General Peter Pace".

75. Interview of Anne Patterson, US Ambassador to Columbia (2002) *El Tiempo* (Columbia), 10 February, available from http://www.ciponline.org/colombia/02021001.htm, accessed 31 May 2006.

76. United Nations High Commissioner for Human Rights (2004) *The Human Rights Situation in Colombia*, Geneva: UNHCHR, 17 February, p. 21, available from http://www.unhchr.ch/Huridocda/Huridoca.nsf/0/eff9a19d63a12a70c1256e5b003f4925/$FILE/G0410993.pdf.

Part III

Toward an ethics of human solidarity

7

An intersection of interests and values: US foreign policy toward Africa

Timothy W. Docking

The end of the Cold War had serious repercussions on American foreign policy toward Africa. Indeed, the collapse of Soviet communism effectively brought an end to America's bedrock "containment strategy", designed to halt the spread of communism and contain Soviet expansion around the world. In Africa, the logic of containment served as the rationale behind two frequently followed US policy courses during the Cold War: blind support for pro-Western regimes, and the sponsorship of proxy wars against pro-Soviet forces.

The end of the Soviet threat in the late 1980s thus led to a re-evaluation of the geostrategic, or realist approach to international relations – based squarely on national interest – that had guided American policies toward Africa for 40 years. The prospect of a changed US foreign policy calculus toward Africa was greeted with early enthusiasm by American activists, scholars and policymakers alike, many of whom hoped that the end of the Cold War would usher in an era of enlightened US foreign policy toward Africa based on principles of international solidarity. Former Assistant Secretary of State for African Affairs, Herman Cohen, perhaps best recalled the optimistic mood among Africa watchers in the United States at this time:

> When I took charge of the State Department's Bureau of African Affairs in March 1989 ... the shackles of the East–West struggle no longer bound our hands in Africa. The teams of Foreign Service officers I had assembled to help manage the bureau were all veterans of the days when we helped sleazy African dictators principally because they were deemed "pro-west." Now at last we

National interest and international solidarity: Particular and universal ethics in international life, Coicaud and Wheeler (eds),
United Nations University Press, 2008, ISBN 978-92-808-1147-6

had a great opportunity to formulate new policies unencumbered by the "communist menace."[1]

Indeed, the era of blind American support for anti-communist dictators and destructive proxy wars quickly, and mercifully, came to a close at the end of the 1980s. However, the much-hoped-for era of creative and constructive US diplomacy toward Africa was slow to dawn.

In practice, new post–Cold War American policy toward Africa had a mixed impact. As the perceived utility of pro-West dictators – such as President Samuel Doe in Liberia and President Mobutu Sese Seko in Zaire – faded, Washington effectively cast the motley crew aside by dramatically reducing assistance and by pressing for socio-economic reform. With the Soviet threat gone, financial, military and diplomatic support for African dictators no longer made geopolitical sense, nor was such policy politically tenable. Yet the withdrawal of support for US clients in Africa at the end of the 1980s had serious repercussions, often unleashing the destructive forces of civil war – conflicts in which the United States was unwilling to engage. Creative and constructive US policies designed to soften the often-devastating effects of African regime change during the 1990s were in short supply throughout the tumultuous decade.

Thus, while the "communist menace" had dried up, geostrategic imperatives of national interest continued to hold sway over suggestions to move toward new foreign policy approaches, based more on Africa's needs and notions of international solidarity. In fact, Washington failed to see how the fallout from the collapse of Cold War competition in Africa affected US national interests. By the early 1990s, Africans across the region could be heard using an adage to describe their emerging geopolitical reality: "When the elephants fight the grass gets trampled; but when elephants make love, the grass also gets trampled."

During the 1990s, such pessimism about Africa's future turned out to be well founded. The decade would be punctuated by crisis across sub-Saharan Africa, including the 1994 Rwandan genocide; the development of regional wars in Western, Central and the Horn of Africa; the growth of poverty; the fall of overseas development assistance; and the explosion of an AIDS epidemic.

Looking back on this period, US policy toward Africa is perhaps best characterized as long on rhetoric and short on effective action.[2] By the end of the 1990s, the twin scourges of disease and violent conflict on the African continent had grown so large, they could no longer be ignored. Some signs of a new US foreign policy toward Africa – based more on international solidarity and responsiveness to moral imperatives than hard-line geopolitics – finally emerged in 2001. Yet it was the transformative events of 11 September that finally shocked the sluggish US foreign policy establishment and led to a convergence of thinking about US national interest and concerns for international solidarity. While early signs suggest US–African relations have entered a new era, it is unclear how strong Washington's commitment is to solving Africa's manifold problems.

Evolution of American foreign policy toward Africa

US foreign policy toward sub-Saharan Africa has never received the serious and sustained attention given to other parts of the world by Washington policymakers. The often-cited starting point of America's Africa policy is the creation of the US State Department's Bureau of African Affairs in 1958. The "Africa Bureau" was created in anticipation of the ending of colonial rule on the continent and the wave of independent African states that was to follow. Central to its mission was policy formation to address the growing forces of nationalism on the continent and, thus, mounting concerns for containing the spread of communism in the developing world.

Speaking on these emerging dynamics in 1957, Senator John F. Kennedy described the way his future administration, and many that followed, would come to view black Africa when he warned, "The only real question is whether these new [African] nations will look West or East – to Moscow or Washington – for sympathy, help, and guidance in their effort to recapitulate, in a few decades, the entire history of modern Europe and America."[3] Kennedy's view of Africa was widely shared by policymakers from across the political spectrum in Washington. Thus, two themes came to characterize US policy toward Africa during the Cold War: At the foundation of all policy decisions was a preoccupation with containment and support for anti-communists.

Analysts generally agree that during the Cold War these two themes carried overwhelming weight in policy matters regardless of who controlled the White House.[4] For this reason, throughout the Cold War US policy toward Africa can best be described as crisis driven and marked by continuity rather than change. Indeed, US policymakers concluded that the communist threat and the resulting geostrategic importance of the African continent left no room for other policy initiatives.[5]

The emergence of dozens of newly independent states in sub-Saharan Africa during the early 1960s coincided with heightening East–West tensions and a growing international debate over capitalist and socialist models of development. This debate and the concomitant growth of the Cold War rivalry had a profound impact on Africa's position in the international system as both sides adopted a zero-sum game mentality. The impoverished African states quickly learned how to exploit this geopolit-ical tension to maximize military and economic support from one side or the other.

The fall of American-supported regimes in Viet Nam and Cambodia in the early 1970s, and the subsequent perceived weakening of US interna-tional resolve, led to a period of Soviet "adventurism" in Africa and to heightened East–West competition on the continent. Proxy wars in Mo-zambique and Angola and Cold War stalemates in the strategically lo-cated Horn of Africa led to decades-long civil wars and a proliferation of arms. More insidiously, Moscow and Washington propped up friendly dictatorships across the continent that were corrupt, repressive and hated by their people.

A generation of 1960s era nationalist leaders was ushered out of presi-dential palaces across sub-Saharan Africa at the barrel of the gun, as the *coup d'état* became the most common form of regime change. Military strong men, desperate for foreign patronage and largesse were to follow. The Carter administration (1976–1980), with its emphasis on linking hu-man rights to US foreign policy, initially gave hope to would-be African reformers. However, Cold War-induced geostrategic concerns in Africa trumped Carter's human rights rhetoric, and the status quo was main-tained in American foreign policy toward the continent.

In the 1980s, US President Ronald Reagan's policy of actively turning back Soviet communism, instead of containing it, led to increased support for US clients in Africa. Most notable was the administration's support for so called "freedom fighters" like Jonas Savimbi in Angola. Known as "constructive engagement", American policy toward Africa during this era was designed to achieve independence for Namibia, to drive back Cuban forces in Angola and to gradually resolve the apartheid problem in South Africa. Central to this complicated and ambitious set of geostrategic objectives was limiting Soviet advances in southern Af-rica. Largely successful in its goals, America's "constructive engage-ment" in southern Africa would be one of the last purely geostrategic policies toward sub-Saharan Africa.[6]

With the end of the Cold War in 1989, the preeminent US strategic calculus – containment – disappeared. While segments of civil society, Congress and the US administration maintained interest in sub-Saharan Africa, the driving rationale behind America's Africa policy was gone. In the United States, only narrow, disparate and limited concern for the plight of Africa remained. Thus, religious organizations such as World Vision, non-governmental organizations such as Africare and groups such as the Congressional Black Caucus occasionally banded together to draw attention to the African continent's humanitarian needs at times of drought or violent conflict. Branches of the US government also maintained limited interest in Africa. Economic links with the continent were at the heart of the US Commerce Department's interests in Africa, especially access to largely untapped markets of the region's 700 million inhabitants and to oil and mineral reserves. In the US Department of Defense, military cooperation and the strategic importance of the region's proximity to the Middle East remained the primary preoccupation, while the Department of State focused on political linkages with the region, whose 48 states represented the largest regional voting block at the United Nations.

But none of these concerns were preeminent at the end of the Cold War and what strategic importance the region once had for the United States largely vanished when the Soviet Union crumbled. The overall response in Washington and within the George H. W. Bush and Clinton administrations to the end of the Cold War was to disengage from the continent and channel what resources they could skim from the meager appropriations for African affairs to the newly independent states in Europe.

The most tangible consequence the end of the Cold War had on Africa was to effectively strip African leaders of the leverage they used so readily to exact support from the super powers in return for loyalty in the East–West, Cold War struggle. In many cases the end of superpower backing in Africa meant the end of support of certain regimes, and ushered in an era of increased violent conflict, regime change and state collapse in Africa during the 1990s. Perhaps the quintessential example of this phenomenon was the end of US support for the long-time Zairian strongman Mobutu Sese Seko and the spiral of chaos in Zaire that ensued.

Mobutu learned the utility of being an anti-communist and a friend to the United States early in his nation's history. The Congo's first post-independence leader, Prime Minister Patrice Lumumba, alienated the United States and eventually called on the Soviets for help in the power struggle that enveloped the nation following independence in 1960. This move confirmed the American fears of Lumumba's radical socialist leanings and led to his (Western-backed) assassination in January 1961. The United States backed Mobutu, a young military officer, whose loyalty to the United States won him the support he needed to stay in power and oversee a highly kleptocratic and predatory regime for over 35 years. At the close of the Cold War, however, Mobutu's utility as an anti-communist vanished and he quickly became a liability and embarrassment to his international backers – principally the United States. When the winds of democracy blew across the continent following the collapse of the Berlin Wall in 1989, Mobutu resisted calls from his people to liberalize Zaire's political system and foreign support dried up. His regime eventually fell in ignominious defeat to the rebel leader Laurent-Désiré Kabila in 1997 and Mobutu died of cancer in exile soon afterward.

Mobutu's story may be the most colorful and well known of internationally backed despots who fell at the end of the Cold War but there were many. The first test of America's new approach to Africa in the post–Cold War era was in Liberia. This small West African nation founded in the early nineteenth century by the American Colonization Society and freed American slaves had a long and close relationship with the United States. Along with the historical ties between the two nations, Liberia's firm support for US foreign policies over the years had led to a "special relationship" in which the United States rewarded Liberia with a disproportionate amount of foreign assistance. As a key Cold War ally on the African continent, the United States actively supported Liberia's leaders regardless of their authoritarian excesses, including high corruption, human rights abuses and blatant electoral fraud. Among these leaders was Samuel Doe, a young, uneducated and low-ranking military officer who seized power following a military coup in 1980. In return for US support during the 1980s, Doe granted special deployment rights to the US military, enabling it to deploy forces to Roberts Field International Airport and the Port on Monrovia with only 24 hours' notice.[7] These bases were important transit sites as the United States channeled weapons to the Savimbi-led UNITA rebels fighting the Cuban-backed Marxist government in Angola. Liberia also housed an important Voice of America relay station; a CIA-operated African telecommunications office and diplomatic relay station; and a US Coast Guard-operated "Omega" navigational station, housing a vital link in its Atlantic Ocean ship and aircraft transit system.[8] During the Cold War, strategic assets such as those in Liberia during the 1980s trumped all other considerations when policymakers in Washington considered bilateral relations. Former Assistant Secretary of State for African Affairs (1981–1988) Chester Crocker perhaps best sums up America's geostrategic point-of-view toward Liberia (and toward Africa more broadly) during the Cold War:

> I would never in a million years tell you I was seeking what was in the best interests of Liberia, I was protecting interests in Washington. The taxpayers paid me to protect the interests of the U.S., and rightly so.[9]

Yet when a civil war broke out in Liberia in December 1989, the Cold War was effectively over. Faced with a decision to once again prop up an odious African client government and protect American Cold War assets, the United States ignored opportunities to mitigate the conflict, and instead chose to watch from a distance as Liberia descended into a vicious civil war that effectively destroyed the country and created a zone of instability and state collapse that spread to neighbouring Sierra Leone and the Ivory Coast and continues to affect West Africa today. The case of the Liberian civil war (1989–1997) perhaps best illustrates the changing nature of America's policy responses to Africa in the post–Cold War era.

The Bush Administration's choice to remain on the sidelines as events spun out of control in Liberia in 1989/90 must also be seen in the context of other geopolitical events unfolding at that time. At the outset of the Liberian crisis, the US administration was planning to invade Panama. The military mission, "Operation Just Cause" (20 December 1989–31 January 1990), and the resulting loss of 23 American soldiers, clearly served as a further brake on any proposal to intervene militarily in Liberia. Other events, such as the first Gulf War, "Operation Desert Storm", in 1991, also distracted policymakers from the crisis in Liberia and generally pushed African affairs further down the list of foreign policy priorities. Further contributing to American inaction in Liberia was the absence of strong and coordinated political pressure groups in the United States, a lack of media coverage and a general ignorance about the region among the American public.

In any case, the US proclivity to "cut and run" from Africa's problems following the end of the Cold War came to characterize most US policy decisions toward the continent throughout the 1990s. Washington's refusal to play a constructive role in Africa's more thorny problems – like helping to mitigate the chaos that ensued as Africa's patronless Cold War puppets, including Doe and Mobutu, were toppled – led a number of analysts to label America's new Africa policy as one of "cynical disengagement". These critics maintained that the changing US approach toward Africa amounted to a de facto policy of disengagement that was based on three principles:

1) Do not spend much money on Africa unless Congress makes you;
2) Do not let African issues complicate policy toward other, more important parts of the world; and
3) Do not take stands [in Africa] that might create political controversies in the United States.[10]

However, even though US relations with Africa throughout the decade of the 1990s were based primarily on geostrategic tenets – reflected in the Zaire and Liberia cases – a detailed review of American actions on the continent during this period reveals a somewhat more nuanced and mixed picture, one that includes glimpses of international solidarity as the driving force behind certain US policy decisions.

US humanitarian mission to Somalia

America's cynical decision to ignore the unfolding humanitarian tragedy and civil war in Liberia in the early 1990s led many analysts to conclude that the United States was set to disengage from the continent following the end of the Cold War. This is perhaps why it came as such a surprise a few years later, in December 1992, when the United States deployed an armed humanitarian mission to Africa to feed hundreds of thousands of starving Somalis. The events that unfolded in Somalia over the following year, however, would profoundly influence American policy toward the region for years to come.

By the time the former American-client President Said Barre was overthrown in 1991, Somalia had fallen into chaos. Full-scale civil war gripped the nation. As warring clans battled for supremacy, Somalis became pawns in turf wars, their fates held in the hands of cruel warlords. By 1992, images of the humanitarian devastation caused by the war were aired on television in the United States, and pressure grew in Washington to respond to the growing famine in Somalia. An airlift of food to the worst-affected areas of southern Somalia proved insufficient to stem the rising tide of starvation. By the summer of 1992 it was estimated that 5,000 Somalis were dying of starvation per week. When negotiations with warlords, whose armed men controlled stockpiles of grain locked in Mogadishu warehouses, proved fruitless, President Bush ordered the military to intervene in Operation Restore Hope.

Within the terms of reference for the operation it was made clear that the sole US mission in Somalia would be to break the hunger cycle there. In short, the US mandate in Somalia was humanitarian and thus, argued the Bush administration, presented a low risk to American soldiers.[11] The armed humanitarian intervention to Somalia began in December 1992 with the US-led United Task Force (UNITAF). These forces soon opened up humanitarian corridors to the worst-affected areas, providing food to thousands of starving Somalis. The early success of this mission to feed Somalis was unassailable. But the mission took a turn for the worse in June 1993.

In May of that year, the United Nations assumed control of the mission, henceforth known as United Nations Operation in Somalia II (UNOSOM II). A few weeks later a fierce battle between Pakistani peacekeepers and forces loyal to warlord Mohamed Farah Aidid led to the deaths of 24 Pakistanis. The United Nations reacted with UN Security Council Resolution 837 on June 6, condemning the attack and asking the secretary general – under Chapter VII of the UN Charter, authorizing the use of deadly force – to take "all necessary measures" against those responsible for killing the peacekeepers, including arrest, detention, trial and punishment.[12]

By mid-June, a US$25,000 bounty was placed on Aidid and by August American Special Forces were sent to Somalia to hunt him down. In October, a failed attempt to capture Aidid by US forces led to the deaths of 18 American soldiers in Mogadishu. This event, notoriously remembered as "Black Hawk Down", and the television images beamed around the world of a dead American soldier being dragged through the streets of the Somali capital before cheering crowds, led onlookers to conclude that the US-led humanitarian intervention into Somalia was a failure. Indeed, the success of the original mission to feed Somalis was totally overshadowed in the United States as critics of the mission lashed out at the White House and military planners for the disaster and branded the mission to Somalia, "a naïve attempt to implement benevolent interventionism in a marginal third world state [that was] doomed to failure".[13] The loss of American lives in Somalia at the hands of armed gangs thus became a sort of syndrome; Black Hawk Down traumatized the nation, causing policymakers to pull back from engaging in humanitarian crises in regions not considered to be of vital national importance and marked a turning point in American foreign policy that would effectively rule out the possibility of future US participation in armed missions to Africa. Wary and under intense pressure at home for undertaking an ill-defined mission in an "African backwater", the young and untried Clinton administration beat a hasty retreat from Somalia, removing all its forces from UNOSOM II by March 1994.

The trauma experienced by the United States in Somalia had a profound impact on the trajectory of US and Western relations with Africa. Acts of solidarity, like the US-led mission to feed starving Somalis, were shown to have limits and henceforth would have to overcome deep scepticism by policymakers, the military planners and the general American public alike. Even the mention of putting "American boots" on African soil became taboo in Washington policymaking circles. And it was only a matter of months before the ramifications of this new reluctance to engage in Africa would become horrifically clear.

Cynical disengagement in Rwanda

We now know that from the outset of the massacres in Rwanda, which began on 6 April 1994, the US government understood the genocidal aims of Hutu extremists.[14] Despite the Clinton administration's claims of being slow to understand the breathtaking scope of the violence in

Rwanda, shortly after the killings began powerful evidence emerged that the unfolding events were in fact a state-organized genocide of ethnically Tutsi and moderate Hutu populations. Yet, in response to the unfolding horror, the administration adopted a policy of staying out of Rwanda. As Samantha Power writes, the United States

> led a successful effort to remove most of the UN peacekeepers that were already in Rwanda. It aggressively worked to block the subsequent authorization of UN reinforcements. It refused to use its technology to jam radio broadcasts that were a crucial instrument in the coordination and perpetuation of the genocide. And even as, on average, 8,000 Rwandans were being butchered each day, U.S. officials shunned the term "genocide," for fear of being obliged to act. The United States in fact did virtually nothing "to try to limit what occurred." Indeed, staying out of Rwanda was an explicit U.S. policy objective.[15]

The Clinton administration's shameful response to the Rwandan genocide was mirrored in many ways by European and African onlookers: no state, or grouping of states, was willing to step into the void and help Rwandans in their time of need. The consequences in humanitarian terms are well known: close to one million killed during the narrow period of the genocide, and millions more perished in the Democratic Republic of the Congo (DRC) in the years that followed as fighting and instability spilled over Rwanda's borders to affect the entire central African region.[16]

While it is impossible to identify one causal variable that led the United States to make the policy choices it did in 1994, the "Somalia syndrome" clearly contributed to the administration's failure to act. At the time of the genocide, the Clinton administration was putting the finishing touches on its new policy of US military involvement in multilateral peace operations, known as Presidential Decision Directive 25 (PDD-25). PDD-25 largely followed on the precedent established by General Colin Powell. The "Powell Doctrine" attempted to build on the lessons learned from US involvement in Viet Nam. Thus, Powell dictated a rigorous set of conditions to be met prior to undertaking military action. Essentially, the Powell Doctrine held that for any military intervention, policymakers must have a clear political objective and stick to it; use decisive force in achieving its goals; and have a clear exit strategy.

PDD-25's criteria for US involvement in peacekeeping missions therefore was largely a revival of the Powell Doctrine.[17] All told, the new policy laid out a restrictive checklist of numerous conditions that must be met before American forces can be deployed in a potentially violent situation. Essentially, the doctrine expresses that military action should be used only as a last resort and only if there is a clear risk to national security by the intended target; that force, when used, should be overwhelming and disproportionate to the force used by the enemy; there must be strong support for the campaign by the general public; and there must be a clear exit strategy from the conflict in which the military is engaged.

As one congressman later explained, PDD-25 tried to satisfy the administration's desire for "zero degree of involvement, and zero degree of risk, and zero degree of pain and confusion".[18] The approval of PDD-25 in 1994 removed henceforth all likelihood of American forces participating in missions to Africa. Thus, with the end of support for Africa's client strong men, and with military intervention effectively removed as an option to stop the spread of the ensuing chaos, US policy toward the continent during the Clinton administration was confined to minor initiatives designed to spread socio-economic liberalization.

Africa in the New World Order

Shortly after the collapse of the Berlin Wall, the Bush administration affirmed that the so-called "New World Order" would be based on the spread of free trade and democratization. Bush's doctrine of global socio-economic liberalization emphasized the renewed importance of the United Nations as an arbiter of international disputes, and the body henceforth charged with policing the world. The new importance placed on American solidarity with democratic states was maintained during the Clinton administration and became the centrepiece of US policy to sub-Saharan Africa during the 1990s. At this time, emphasis was thus put on policies aimed at political and economic liberalization. "Free and fair elections" became a condition for favourable relations with the United States. Perhaps even more significant, however, was the emphasis the Clinton administration placed on the growth of civil society in Africa.

Indeed, in Africa during the 1990s US policy aimed at circumventing "the corrupt African state" (symbolized by despots like Mobutu and Doe) by channeling increased foreign aid and technical assistance directly to the perceived building blocks of African democracies – civil society organizations. By the mid-1990s the promotion of civil society in Africa was central to the American international development mission. In theory, policymakers argued, the growth of civil society will create a platform for nascent democracies, thus enhancing the process of democratization on the continent. But the effects of this approach were mixed. In addition to strengthening the capacity of some elements of African civil society, direct foreign assistance to Africa's grassroots paradoxically undermined the development of Africa's weak states by creating "quasi civil society" (neither Hegelian nor Tocquevillian in nature) that was profoundly affected by, and dependent upon, the international community. Support for Africa's new Western-sponsored civil society primarily benefited Western and local non-governmental organizations (NGOs), who received a significant upsurge in funding during this period. Indeed, the African NGO sector quickly became the most visible sign of the privatization of North–South relations.

In practice, leaders of Africa's emerging "civil society" organizations were often unemployed teachers or health care workers, from the narrow class of educated Africans who were able to effectively speak the language (both literally and figuratively) of Western donors. In some cases this group represented African voices and locally based concerns – from peasant farmers' unions to women's groups. But many of these organizations were nothing more than "NGOs on paper", that is, individuals or small groups of elites looking to capitalize on the West's newfound interest in Africa's non-state actors. Often with their backs turned to the masses and, thus, out of touch with village life or the socio-economic problems they professed to master, the primary goal of these groups was to respond to the perceived interests of international donors in order to capture financial support.

The new international focus on civil society in Africa during the 1990s therefore had mixed results. On the one hand, international financing and technical training was responsible for the emergence and development of a number of people-based interest groups, many of whom owe their operational capability in accounting, communications and strategic planning to the well-intentioned Western assistance they received. On the other hand, the effects of Western "assistance" are also responsible for the creation of elite-driven, inorganic structures that are as detached from the needs of Africa's masses as are policymakers in Washington, Paris or London. Even worse, by circumventing the corrupt African state during this era and directing resources to civil society organizations, cash-strapped governments across Africa often found themselves in competition with their relatively well-heeled domestic NGOs. One ironic consequence of this phenomenon was that well-trained (often in the West), high-ranking government officials could often find better salaries, training opportunities and other perks working for newly created, Western-financed organizations than they could find working in the high echelons of their own governments.

The resulting "internal brain drain" in some cases further sapped desperately needed human capital away from the struggling governments Western policymakers intended to help. Moreover, this dynamic has created a competitive relationship – not based on ideas as one might hope, but surrounding access to foreign resources – between governmental and non-governmental spheres in African capitals across the region, in many

ways further subverting the original rationale used for targeting civil society with foreign aid.[19]

Paradoxically, in many cases the resulting tension between states and
Africa's Western-backed civil society failed to strengthen democracy as
intended, and by the end of the decade the Clinton administration's
policy of democratization in Africa had little to show for itself. While
dozens of states staged elections and national conferences during this period, many of these were designed by African elites for international,
not domestic, consumption. That is, African leaders, chided by the West,
quickly realized the symbolic importance of democratic elections in the
American-led, post–Cold War Africa. These leaders thus set out to
achieve democratic legitimacy, most often by staging political contests.
But by the end of the decade it was clear that in the majority of these
cases elections were little more than window dressing, as dictators such
as Omar Bongo in Gabon, Paul Biya in Cameroon and Robert Mugabe
in Zimbabwe rigged elections and used the ballot box as a tool in attempts to legitimize their regimes and retrench themselves at the helm
of power. As the unintended consequences of these US policies grow
more evident, they will stand as a reminder of both the challenges
Western policymakers face as they attempt to engineer social transformation in Africa, and the limits of international democratic solidarity in developing nations.

Overview of American foreign policy toward Africa during the tumultuous 1990s

The 2003 United Nations Human Development Report on international
progress toward the Millennium Development Goals paints a stark picture of the effects that the tumultuous decade of the 1990s had on sub-
Saharan Africa. With regards to HIV/AIDS: the number of cases in the
region grew from 7 million in 1990 to 25 million in 2000;[20] average per
capita income growth fell by 0.4 per cent during the decade while the
number of people living on less than US$1/day rose from 47 per cent to
49 per cent during the same period;[21] and net per capita receipts of overseas development assistance decreased from 6.13 per cent of gross domestic product in 1990 to 4.55 per cent in 2001.[22] The decade of the
1990s further witnessed a fall in global commodity prices, a rise in foreign
debt and an explosion of violent conflict on the African continent.

Despite the grim developments in Africa during this period, the
United States largely turned away from the continent, cutting back on
security-oriented programmes, scaling back funding to the US Agency for

International Development (USAID) and trimming resources for African affairs in the State Department.[23]

Perhaps the one hopeful development to emerge on the continent during the 1990s was the growth of democratic governance in a number of states. In Benin, Ghana, Lesotho, Mali, Mozambique and Tanzania, the roots of democracy began to take hold. In all of these cases, the United States played a role. Most often in the form of technical assistance and training carried out by the International Republican Institute and the National Democratic Institute – congressionally funded groups that aim to promote democratic governance throughout the world. Perhaps nowhere was democratic change in Africa more dramatic during this period than in South Africa.

South Africa's transition from apartheid rule to democracy in the 1990s is an oft-cited success story in American diplomacy. The case represents an instance when the United States transcended its broad policy prescriptions toward sub-Saharan Africa of simply supporting civil society organizations, staging elections and declaring elections "free and fair" or "corrupt". In South Africa, the United States successfully waged a concerted and sustained diplomatic effort to help usher in the democratic transition. These efforts, however, were years in the making and involved numerous domestic and international actors who worked assiduously to undermine the foundations of apartheid, primarily through economic and diplomatic pressure, while at the same time strengthening its opposition, both in exile and on the ground in South Africa. Thus, the fall of the apartheid system and the election of Nelson Mandela in 1994 – an unimaginable scenario just a few years prior – was an organic phenomenon, fostered by the United States and the international community writ large.[24]

The South Africa case is instructive for a number of reasons. It demonstrates a responsiveness by Washington policymakers to US domestic concerns for a peaceful transition in South Africa; it shows the helpful role American diplomats can play in conflict prevention while acting behind the scenes instead of in the lead; and it demonstrates that despite the end of the Cold War and the subsequent fading of South Africa's geostrategic importance, the United States was still willing to act in solidarity with the African people.[25]

Yet more often than not during the post–Cold War era, national interests, rather than concern for the plight of a nation or a specific group, have dominated US policy toward Africa. The United States failed to engage in the brutal and expanding Liberian civil war in the early 1990s and continued to stand on the sidelines as the fighting spread into neighbouring Sierra Leone. America's unwillingness to take a leadership role or to otherwise invest heavily in African conflict resolution during the 1990s was repeated in numerous African zones of conflict. As parts of the sub-

Saharan region descended into anarchy (Rwanda, Somalia, Liberia, Sierra Leone, Zaire) and violent conflict (Ethiopia, Eritrea, Guinea Bissau, Congo-Brazzaville), and as decades-old conflicts persisted (Angola, Sudan), the United States rarely strayed from its risk-averse, realist policy prescriptions. Across the region, Washington failed to see a connection between proliferating war and US national interests. Instead, time after time the government failed to exhibit political will to act in Africa, clearly reflecting a risk-averse, post-PDD-25 reality.

American inaction during the 1990s resulted in a de facto policy of "cynical neglect" toward the African continent. The Clinton administration in particular often masked this fact in a profusion of unsupported rhetoric condemning the destructive forces tearing the continent apart while doing little to mitigate the growing hardships.

Toward intersecting interests: US foreign policy toward Africa in the twenty-first century

The low priority that Africa has occupied in American foreign policy was perhaps never more evident than in the second debate between Al Gore and George W. Bush during the 2000 presidential campaign. Asked if in hindsight the Clinton administration made a mistake by not intervening in the 1994 Rwandan genocide, both candidates affirmed that the administration "did the right thing". Giving further indication of his low view of Africa, Bush then went on to list his four regional foreign policy priorities if elected president: "the Middle East ... Europe, the Far East and our own hemisphere". Needless to say, many Africa watchers in the United States saw the subsequent Bush victory as bad news for the continent.

Following the 11 September terrorist attacks, Africa watchers were quick to point out that Osama bin Laden had not only dealt a blow to the United States, he also indirectly struck a blow against sub-Saharan Africa. The pundits agreed that the increased US and Western focus on Afghanistan and the Middle East and the war on terrorism would inevitably mean less international attention on the many destructive forces plaguing Africa.

Indeed, the shock and horror of the terrorist attacks and the declaration of war against Al Qaeda by the United States at first seemed to signal the inevitable further marginalization of sub-Saharan Africa in America's foreign policy priorities. At the Department of State in Washington, Africa specialists were pulled off their portfolios in the wake of the disaster to work on Afghanistan; Department of Defense military training missions to Africa were placed on indefinite hold as US Special Forces received new assignments; and American diplomats limited US visas to Africans and hunkered down in their fortress-like embassies to guard against further suicide bombings like those that hit the embassies in Nairobi, Kenya, and Dar es Salaam, Tanzania, in the summer of 1998.

Perhaps the best illustration of the region's apparent declining importance on the international scene during the aftermath of the 11 September attacks was the complete drying up of donations to the United Nations' Global Fund to Fight AIDS, Tuberculosis and Malaria. Between June 2001, when the Global Fund was created, and August that same year, US$1.5 billion was pledged by international donors primarily concerned about the devastating effects of HIV/AIDS in Africa. The great momentum built up by the Global Fund during its first summer, however, was lost when the hijacked planes hit the World Trade Center and the Pentagon. Over the next three months less than US$10,000 was pledged to the Fund.[26]

Soon after the attacks, a series of articles began to appear in American newspapers documenting the presence of terrorist financing activities in sub-Saharan Africa. Strong evidence emerged that Al Qaeda and Hezbollah were operating in the region, laundering funds and making millions from the illicit trade in "conflict diamonds" from Sierra Leone, Liberia, the DRC and Angola; the sale of Tanzanite gem stones mined in Tanzania; and through financial networks based in Somalia.[27] Furthermore, rumours began to circulate about possible safe havens for Al Qaeda fighters and Osama bin Laden himself in the stateless societies of Somalia and the DRC. Each of these reports made a link between one or more of Africa's weak and chaotic states and the life sustaining financial networks of terrorist organizations. It soon became apparent, and accepted in Washington policy circles, that the poor, weak and disorganized states of sub-Saharan Africa are fertile ground for criminal and terrorist organizations such as Al Qaeda to conduct illicit business.[28] In Washington's think tank community, experts agreed about the new-found strategic importance of poor and failing states and the pressing need to "drain the swamps" where terrorists live became cliché. Links between Al Qaeda and the attacks on the USS Cole in Yemen (October 2000) and US embassies in Kenya and Tanzania (August 1998), as well as the terrorist group's former presence in Sudan, were soon highlighted, as were the region's slack border controls, corrupt and poorly trained police officers and pockets of religious extremists that present favourable conditions for the penetration of terrorists and criminal networks.

In one of the more vivid illustrations of the newfound (post–11 September) strategic importance of poor, feeble, third world states, Congressman Jim Kolbe, former chair of the House Appropriations subcommittee on Foreign Aid, stated, "We need to start thinking of the foreign assistance budget as part of the national security budget."[29] Kolbe was not alone in asserting that desperate poverty and the conditions of hopelessness, frustration and oppression can ultimately produce radicalism or provide a "growth medium" for radical groups like Al Qaeda. Indeed, today it is accepted in Washington policy circles that such desperate conditions can pose a long-term national security threat to rich countries like the United States.

One year after the 11 September attacks, the themes of underdevelopment, weak states and terrorism were all emphasized in President Bush's "National Security Strategy of the United States of America", a comprehensive overview of national security concerns along with their rationale and a strategy to defend US national interests. The 2002 National Security Strategy (NSS) acknowledges and repeatedly identifies the new threats to national security emerging from Africa, primarily in the form of weak and collapsed states:

> The events of September 11, 2001, taught us that weak states, like Afghanistan, can pose as great a danger to our national interests as strong states. Poverty does not make poor people into terrorists and murderers. Yet poverty, weak institutions, and corruption can make weak states vulnerable to terrorist networks and drug cartels within their borders.[30]

Throughout the NSS the Bush administration points to the threats posed by failed states and the imperative to "help strengthen Africa's fragile states". The document thus clarifies the administration's growing appreciation of the emerging nexus between African development and US national security. Indeed, it states, "America is now threatened less by conquering states than we are by failing ones."

Ironically, it now appears that contrary to initial fears that the 11 September terrorist attacks would have a negative effect on US relations with Africa – events that so clearly seemed to presage a new era of increased US indifference toward the continent – the terrorist attacks now seem to have opened the administration's eyes to Africa's strategic relevance. Africa is clearly on the Bush White House agenda. Even prior to the terrorist attacks of 2001, and just four months after taking office, Colin Powell made his first major trip as Secretary of State to sub-Saharan Africa. During the trip, Powell made a public commitment that the Bush Administration would engage on two principal issues in Africa, AIDS and the Sudanese civil war. Upon the Secretary's return to Washington in May 2001, the administration put forward concrete policy measures aimed at combating the AIDS epidemic and bringing an end to the 18-year civil war in Sudan: announcing the appointment of former Senator John Danforth as the president's Special Envoy to Sudan and a commitment of US$500 million to the Global Fund to Fight AIDS, Tuberculosis and Malaria.

Even after the terrorist attacks, the administration continued to send a steady stream of top-ranking officials to Africa, including Robert Zoellick, who in February 2002 became the first US Trade Representative ever to visit Africa, and Treasury Secretary Paul O'Neill, whose May 2002 visit with rock star and social activist Bono attracted widespread media attention and opened a discourse in the US policy community about how best to allocate overseas development assistance. Secretary of Health and Human Services Tommy Thompson and Powell (for a second time) visited Africa in 2002 and, despite a host of competing foreign policy priorities, President Bush traveled to sub-Saharan Africa for a week in July 2003.

But it has not simply been lofty rhetoric or the parade of high-ranking US officials to Africa that suggest this administration's interest in African affairs. In March 2002, at the United Nations "International Conference in Financing for Development", held in Monterrey, Mexico, President Bush announced his plans for increasing development assistance to poor countries through the Millennium Challenge Account (MCA). The MCA has added billions of dollars to US overseas development assistance (ODA) since its creation in 2004 with global obligations of more than US$3 billion, approximately US$2 billion going to sub-Saharan Africa. The innovative approach weaved into the MCA calls for funds to be allocated according to state performance instead of perceived state need. Therefore, the money will be earmarked for developing nations that demonstrate a strong commitment to good governance, sound economic policies, improved health care systems and better education for their people. The MCA represents a 50 per cent increase in ODA, and could potentially double the amount of foreign aid given to countries in sub-Saharan Africa. When fully funded, the MCA will represent the biggest increase in ODA since the Marshall Plan, further illustrating, at least in part, the growing appreciation in the US government of how political decay and underdevelopment in Africa and around the world can impact national security.[31]

Perhaps most significantly was the announcement in the president's January 2003 State of the Union address to the nation announcing the administration's "Emergency Plan for AIDS Relief". President Bush called the plan, designed to confront the spread of AIDS in Africa, "A work of mercy beyond all current international efforts to help the people of Africa". The US$15 billion, five-year programme is providing for the prevention, treatment and care of millions of Africans affected by HIV/AIDS.

While these ambitious new programmes signal a new appreciation for geopolitical importance of the 48 sub-Saharan states, they also represent a new appreciation for the level of suffering, poverty and underdevelopment that seize the African continent. Far from ignoring the plight of Africans, as was suggested he would do during the 2000 presidential debates, George W. Bush has demonstrated a new level of solidarity with the African people that has yet to be fully appreciated. Clearly, this is a solidarity with limitations: the administration's reluctance to send peacekeepers to Liberia in the summer of 2003 despite tragic circumstances on the ground and significant international pressure is a case in point. Some have argued America's reluctance to send troops to Darfur, Sudan, despite concerns of a genocide is another case when the United States failed to act in solidarity with Africans. Yet, far from belying America's growing interest in Africa, these examples underscore the nature of the evolving relationship: a selective partnership based on mutual concerns, shared norms and self-interest to improve the lives of people in the poorest, most conflict-torn region on earth. The policy is not based on realism or solidarity but on what might be termed "enlightened self-interest", which aims to address both the challenging strategic realities and moral imperatives of the time.

Conclusion

Since its independence from colonial rule, Africa has been seen in Washington as a foreign policy backwater. During the Cold War, Republican and Democratic administrations alike pursued a limited approach to the continent, hoping to contain the spread of Soviet communism in Africa by propping up pro-American regimes and anti-communist fighting forces. Geostrategic concerns were at the forefront of American thinking toward the continent. The end of the East–West struggle in the late-1980s brought with it an end to what limited strategic relevance Africa held in Washington. While many onlookers hoped the end of Cold War containment policies in Africa would unshackle the hands of US decision makers – and usher in an era of far-sighted, constructive engagement with the poorest region on earth – they were quickly disappointed. US engagement in the region continued to be limited and inconsistent and, following the death of American soldiers in Mogadishu in October 1993, extremely risk-averse.

The subsequent adoption of PDD-25, which created a set of conditions for US policymakers to adhere to prior to deploying US troops unilaterally or in multilateral peacekeeping missions – conditions so conservative that they effectively removed all possibility of US military operations in sub-Saharan Africa – once again removed a key tool of policymakers concerned with promoting stability, preserving democracy and fostering economic development. By the time of the Rwanda genocide in April and May 1994, the hopes of Afro-optimists that the 1990s would mark a period of African renaissance, and of US solidarity with the continent, appeared dashed. By the end of the twentieth century the continent was being torn apart by violent conflict, deepening poverty and the AIDS epidemic. While the impact of a decade-long programme of democratization on sub-Saharan Africa's 48 states would be hard to measure, several successful transitions from dictatorship to democracy occurred. Nevertheless, these developments were largely overshadowed by other deteriorating socio-economic conditions over the same period.

Although the 1990s was not an era of enlightened policy formation toward Africa, the end of the Cold War did usher in a new era of US–African relations. The shift was not dramatic, yet several important developments, based largely on the principles of international solidarity, did occur, including the humanitarian mission to Somalia; concerted American diplomatic activity in South Africa; and the new emphasis placed on institution building and democratization across the continent. Today these acts of American solidarity toward the continent are accelerating, as witnessed by a new willingness of the US government to help Africans combat AIDS, alleviate poverty and end some of Africa's worst conflicts.

In many ways, the current policy initiatives can be seen as based on international solidarity, aimed at the well-being and socio-economic development of Africans. Yet, as the crisis in Darfur illustrates, these policies have limits and must also be seen in terms of American self-interest. Indeed, the catastrophic declines suffered across the sub-Saharan region during the last decade produced a socio-economic setting so blighted that the United States could no longer look away. Moral and strategic imperatives have combined to dictate a more proactive American role in the region.

If the events of 11 September 2001 taught American policymakers anything, it is that collapsed states, such as Afghanistan, matter, and that poverty and the spread of hardship, disease and corruption can contribute to the spread of radicalism and anti-Americanism. While it is well known that poor people are not necessarily violent people, it also now accepted that the radical and criminal groups are more successful in spreading their ideology, transiting materials and harbouring resources in weak, corrupt and stateless societies.

This chapter has considered MCA, democracy-building efforts, the mission to bring peace to southern Sudan and America's commitment to fight AIDS in Africa. While the moral justification for such policies is clear, so too are the self-interested motives that lay behind these policy moves.[32]

At the beginning of the twenty-first century, the nature of Africa's grave socio-economic predicament is clear to the international community. So too are the risks these threats pose to Africans and the world at large. In response, it is not surprising that the developed world is showing growing concern and commitment to enact policies based on international solidarity. The Africa Action Plan introduced at the 2002 G7 meetings in Kananaskis, Canada was a clear expression of worldwide concern for the continent. So too is the UN Global Fund to Fight Malaria, Tuberculosis and AIDS, the 2005 G8 Gleneagles Summit focusing on African development, and the on-going Doha (development) round of the World Trade Organization talks.

Along with the United Kingdom, the United States has in many ways taken a lead in Africa, contributing both its financial and diplomatic weight to the success of new initiatives. It is hoped that an evolving American policy toward Africa, unshackled from the geopolitical chains of the cold war and conscious of the African predicament, will act more in solidarity with the continent.

Whether this vision of a new, more enlightened, era of American foreign policy toward Africa will indeed take root is unclear. Several factors threaten the positive trajectory that US–African relations are currently on. The emergence of powerful non-state actors as a principal threat to US interests around the world, especially the threat of Islamism, carries the principal risk of undermining solidarity and policies to the region based on enlightened self-interested. Should the region actually become a breeding ground for radical Islam, realist policies based on a "green menace" (the colour of the Islamic movement) could emerge and mirror those policies designed 40 years ago in the United States to combat the "red menace" of the Cold War. Geopolitical concerns over "Africa as a terrorist haven" however, should further engage the United States and the rest of the West in an enlightened and concerted effort to advance and strengthen the socio-economic environment in which Africans live.

Notes

1. Herman J. Cohen (2000) *Intervening in Africa: Superpower Peacemaking in a Troubled Continent*, New York: St. Martin's Press, p. 1.
2. Stephen Morrison and Jennifer G. Cooke, eds (2001) *Africa Policy in the Clinton Years: Critical Choices for the Bush Administration*, Washington, D.C.: Center for Strategic and International Studies.

3. Cited in Peter J. Schraeder (1996) "Removing the Shackles? US Foreign Policy Toward Africa after the End of the Cold War", in Edmond J. Keller and Donald Rothchild, eds, *Africa in the New International Order*, Boulder, Colo.: Lynne Rienner, p. 191.

4. Ibid., p. 187.

5. Peter J. Schraeder (1994) *United States Foreign Policy toward Africa: Incrementalism, Crisis and Change*, Cambridge: Cambridge University Press.

6. For a first-hand account of US policy toward Africa during the 1980s, see Chester A. Crocker (1993) *High Noon in Southern Africa: Making Peace in a Rough Neighborhood*, New York: W.W. Norton.

7. Cohen, *Intervening in Africa*, p. 127.

8. Ibid., p. 134.

9. Quoted in Bill Berkeley (2001) *The Graves Are Not Yet Full: Race, Tribe and Power in the Heart of Africa*, New York: Basic Books, pp. 74–75.

10. Michael Clough (1992) "The United States and Africa: The Policy of Cynical Disengagement", *Current History* 91(565), May, pp. 193–198.

11. Cohen, *Intervening in Africa*, p. 214.

12. James L. Woods (1997) "U.S. Government Decisionmaking Processes During Humanitarian Operations in Somalia", in Walter Clarke and Jeffrey Herbst, eds, *Learning from Somalia: The Lessons of Armed Humanitarian Intervention*, Boulder, Colo.: Westview Press, pp. 151–172.

13. James L. Woods cited in Walter Clarke (1997) "Failed Visions and Uncertain Mandates in Somalia", in Walter Clarke and Jeffrey Herbst, eds, *Learning from Somalia: The Lessons of Armed Humanitarian Intervention*, Boulder, Colo.: Westview Press, pp. 3–19.

14. Samantha Power (2001) "Bystanders to Genocide: Why the United States Let the Rwandan Tragedy Happen", *Atlantic Monthly* 288(2): 84–108.

15. Ibid.

16. International Rescue Committee (2001) "Mortality Study, Eastern Democratic Republic of the Congo: February–April, 2001", report, Washington, D.C.: International Rescue Committee.

17. Office of the Press Secretary (1994) "President Clinton Signs New Peacekeeping Policy", press release, Washington, D.C.: The White House, 6 May, available from http://www.fas.org/irp/offdocs/pdd25.htm, accessed 30 May 2006.

18. US Representative David Obey cited in Power, "Bystanders to Genocide".

19. Timothy W. Docking (2005) "International Influence on Civil Society in Mali", in James Igoe and Tim Kelsell, eds, *Between a Rock and a Hard Place: African NGOs, Donors, and the State*, Durham, N.C.: Carolina Academic Press.

20. "Millennium Development Goals: A Compact among Nations to End Human Poverty", *Human Development Report 2003*, New York: Oxford University Press, p. 43.

21. Ibid., p. 41.

22. Ibid., p. 147.

23. See a description of US allocations to Africa in the 1990s in Congressional Research Service (2003) "Africa: Foreign Assistance Issues", CRS Issue Brief for Congress, Washington, D.C.: Library of Congress, September 5.

24. See an account of this important period in US–South African relations in Princeton N. Lyman (2002) *Partner to History: The U.S. Role in South Africa's Transition to Democracy*, Washington, D.C.: US Institute of Peace.

25. The domestic debate over sanctions against the South African government during the 1980s was perhaps the biggest coordinated public expression of domestic concern and solidarity for a foreign people since protests over the Viet Nam War.

26. "Pledges to the Global Fund to Fight AIDS, Tuberculosis and Malaria", available from http://www.theglobalfund.org/en/, accessed 30 May 2006.

27. Douglas Farah (2001) "Al Qaeda Cash Tied to Diamond Trade: Sale of Gems From Sierra Leone", *Washington Post*, 2 November, p. A1; "Terrorist Links to Trade in Tanzanite Sales in East Africa", *Wall Street Journal*, 16 November 2001, p. A1; Douglas Farah (2001) "Digging Up Congo's Dirty Gems: Officials Say Diamond Trade Funds Radical Islamic Groups", *Washington Post*, 30 December, p. A1.
28. Timothy W. Docking (2001) "Terrorism's Africa Link", editorial, *Christian Science Monitor*, 14 November, p. 9.
29. Jim Kolbe (2002) "Does Aid Help?", editorial, *Washington Post*, 9 February, p. A26.
30. "The National Security Strategy of the United States of America", Washington, D.C.: The White House, September 2002, available from http://www.whitehouse.gov/nsc/nss.pdf, accessed 30 May 2006.
31. See an analysis of MCA by the Center for Global Development, available through www.cgdev.org.
32. National Intelligence Council (2002) "The Next Wave of HIV/AIDS: Nigeria, Ethiopia, Russia, India, and China", McLean, Va.: National Intelligence Council, September.

8

Geopolitics and solidarity on the borders of Europe: The Yugoslav wars of succession

Alex J. Bellamy[1]

On 27 June 1991, Slovene territorial defence forces shot down a Yugo-slav military helicopter, killing the pilot and mechanic.[2] This was the first act of military defiance that would become known as the Yugoslav wars of succession. They would last another eight years; claim the lives of over a quarter of a million people; provoke the first use of force in anger by NATO; become an OSCE mission larger than all of that organization's other missions combined; and involve a series of UN peacekeeping oper-ations and an EU "stability pact" comprising significant financial assis-tance tied to political conditionality. In the summer of 1991, a "troika" of EC foreign ministers took the lead in attempting to broker an agree-ment between the Slovenes, Croats and Yugoslav authorities. Jacques Poos, the Luxembourg Foreign Minister who initially led the troika, infa-mously declared that the "hour of Europe had dawned".[3] Poos lived to regret those words as they were frequently used to deride the EC's feeble response to the break-up of Yugoslavia and the atrocities that accompa-nied it.[4]

That failure was caused by three principal factors. First, there was little agreement amongst the North Atlantic allies (let alone beyond it) about whether Europe had a responsibility to protect human rights in the Bal-kans. Some states, most notably the United Kingdom and United States at this point, insisted that Yugoslav sovereignty should be privileged over humanitarian concerns, using strategic arguments to support their case.[5] Second, even if there had been agreement about the best way to proceed, the European security community lacked a centralized decision-making

National interest and international solidarity: Particular and universal ethics in international life, Coicaud and Wheeler (eds),
United Nations University Press, 2008, ISBN 978-92-808-1147-6

capability.[6] Reportedly, some foreign ministries were not fully briefed on the EC troika's mission.[7] Finally, although France and Germany were eager to protect human rights in 1991 they lacked the will or capacity to do anything other than contingency planning, whilst states such as the United Kingdom and United States had grave misgivings about using force in the Balkans.[8] In other words, although Europe exhibited a significant level of internal solidarity at the interstate level, it lacked solidarity with those beyond its borders. National interests, including an overriding concern not to incur casualties, and concerns about order took precedence over a common perspective. Thus, an ethic of solidarity with the people of Slovenia, Croatia and Bosnia and Herzegovina (BiH) was not widely evident except in the consistent position taken by Germany, and occasionally by Austria and France.

With hindsight, Poos's comments may be more kindly interpreted as premature rather than categorically wrong. Eight years later, NATO – a military alliance comprising most but not all of the European Community's members – intervened in Kosovo to halt the ethnic cleansing of Kosovar Albanians by Serbian forces and local Serb militia. In that case, NATO was criticized in some quarters for acting pre-emptively. The Alliance's critics argued that the situation in Kosovo did not amount to a "supreme humanitarian emergency"[9] and that the humanitarian crisis was in fact heightened, if not caused, by NATO's precipitous actions.[10] Despite these criticisms, there was quite a high degree of consensus within Europe about the need to use force to avert a tragedy in Kosovo. All 19 NATO members agreed to act, and of those only Italy and Greece had serious misgivings and, whilst the German government became an ardent supporter of intervention in 1999, German society was divided on the issue.[11] Whilst Russia, China and many members of the Non-Aligned Movement all rejected the idea that state sovereignty could be overridden to protect gross abuses of human rights, such arguments inhabited the fringes of debate in Europe.[12]

In an earlier work, I argued that three interlinked factors help to explain the activism that accompanied Europe's response to the Kosovo crisis after 1998.[13] The first was genuine humanitarian concern, or what I labelled the "Srebrenica syndrome". European leaders feared that, left unchecked, the violence in Kosovo would escalate to Srebrenica proportions, something that these leaders deemed intolerable on their borders. As Tony Blair put it, prior to the Rambouillet summit in February 1999, "I will not ignore war and instability in Europe". Referring explicitly to BiH, he continued, "I do not want to see such atrocities committed again, and again and again".[14] Similarly, the governments of Italy, France and Germany all pointed to the idea that Serbian activities in Kosovo were especially deplorable because they contravened European norms of

behaviour.[15] The second factor was parochial national interests and a desire to avoid a large flow of refugees from Kosovo into Western Europe.
As Jim Whitman has ably demonstrated, European domestic politics in
the lead-up intervention exhibited significant fear of a "flood" of Albanian refugees that would create yet more stress for European welfare
states.[16] Many states therefore saw early action in Kosovo as a useful
way of reducing the probable number of Albanian asylum seekers by
both remedying the cause of flight and providing temporary refuge close
to Kosovo's borders. The third factor was geopolitical concern based on
the lingering belief that, left unchecked, a local conflict in the southern
Balkans would escalate. A resulting general Balkan war would pit states
such as Macedonia and Albania against one another and could ultimately
destroy the Western alliance by drawing Greece and Turkey in on different sides. This "Balkanist" view was pervasive in Western academic
and policymaking circles. For instance, Misha Glenny argued that the
southern part of former Yugoslavia remained a strategically vital connection between East and West, claimed by the region's "four wolves"
(Greece, Bulgaria, Serbia and Albania).[17] Similarly, David Owen – one
of the European Community's mediators during the Bosnian war –
proposed a nineteenth-century style carve-up of Kosovo in order to prevent the conflict's escalation.[18]

There was therefore a marked difference between the interplay of
solidarity and interests in the European response to the break-up of Yugoslavia in 1991 and the response to the 1998/99 crisis in Kosovo. This
chapter attempts to chart the shift in the relationship between interests
and solidarity from 1991, when perceived geopolitical and domestic political concerns overrode concerns about the emerging humanitarian disaster in Yugoslavia, to the post-Kosovo era in which interests and solidarity
appeared more closely aligned. I argue that by 1999, European states in
general recognized that humanitarian concerns and national interests
were both satisfied by policy responses to the crisis in Kosovo that aimed
to end the humanitarian emergency and create a liberal democratic society there.[19] The convergence of national interests and solidarity was produced, on the one hand, by the transformation of the European security
community into a solidarist community that extended into central, eastern and southern Europe and, on the other hand, by processes of social
learning from the experience in Bosnia.[20] Importantly, however, the level
of commitment remained constrained by a persistent determination to
limit casualties, which at least partly accounts for NATO's decision to
limit its intervention in Kosovo to air strikes. As Ignatieff put it, the commitment to solidarity in Kosovo was "intense but also shallow".[21]

This presents us with two questions. First, what do I mean by the terms
"security community" and "solidarist community"? Second, how do these

different types of community relate to their neighbours? According to Adler and Barnett, security communities are communities comprising sovereign entities that enjoy "dependable expectations of peaceful change".[22] I follow Adler and Barnett by distinguishing between two *types* of community and three *stages of development*. The two types are "loosely" and "tightly" coupled. In a loosely coupled security community, sovereign states maintain dependable expectations of peaceful change and little more.[23] According to Adler and Barnett, tightly coupled security communities place more demands on the constituent units in at least two ways. First, such communities exhibit a degree of "mutual aid". Second, they maintain a framework of governance. Each of these two types of security community may pass through three stages of development: "nascent", "ascendant" and "mature". In nascent security communities, states begin to consider how they might coordinate their activities in order to increase their mutual security, reduce transaction costs or create the potential for further interaction in the future. Such activities are usually informed by a combination of self-interested calculations by states and "cultural, political, social and ideological homogeneity".[24] Ascendant security communities display "increasingly dense networks; new institutions and organizations that reflect either tighter military coordination and cooperation and/or decreased fear that the other represents a threat".[25] There is a deepening of mutual trust and emergence of collective identities, and the building of institutions leads to increased social interaction, promoting shared identities that in turn help to create common interests. When a security community matures, mutual aid and consultation become a matter of habit. A mature security community comes about when the norms at its heart become embedded or internalized by its member states. Mature security communities may develop political agency in their own right and the transnational institutions housed within them may create rules and generally accepted social knowledge.[26]

What I describe as a solidarist community is a further development of a tightly coupled mature security community.[27] It comprises all the elements of a tightly coupled mature security community but also exhibits a high degree of solidarity within the non-state sector as well.[28] Regional solidarist communities encompass the three elements of solidarism identified by Barry Buzan: shared rules guiding not only the relationship between the constituent units but also the relationship between those units and individuals, legitimate processes for enforcing those rules and expectations about the homogenization of the constituent units.[29] Importantly, a solidarist community is premised on the idea that order and justice within the community are interdependent. The overall goals of the community can be achieved only if its basic values are upheld. In the

European case, those basic values are closely aligned with values of liberal human rights and democracy, but it is important to stress that a solidarist community need not be premised on these values. The pivotal difference between a mature tightly coupled security community and a solidarist community is that those values guide not only the way that the member states relate to one another, but – crucially – also create expectations about how the states relate to their citizens. Within a solidarist community, states are not free to treat their citizens however they like, and citizens are able to lodge claims against their states in bodies that sit above the sovereign and are accepted as authoritative by the sovereign.

The second question is how do these different types of community relate to their neighbours? My starting point is to reiterate the view that, like security communities, solidarist communities are spatially bounded, not global. Levels of global solidarity are uneven. Within some regions, as Adler and Barnett suggest, states form tightly coupled communities predicated on shared identities, interests and solidarity.[30] As such communities mature, their relationship with those on their borders begins to change in important ways. Not least, the boundaries between "insiders" and "outsiders" become more blurred as institutional, epistemic and transversal networks reach across them.[31] As they mature and/or become more tightly coupled, solidarist communities and their neighbours become socialized into regional patterns of solidarist expectations. In this chapter, I argue that a regional solidarist community such as this developed in Europe during the 1990s.[32] This shaped Europe's expectations about legitimate conduct in its border regions and created a heightened sense of both interstate and transversal solidarity between the Balkans and the West.[33] It is important, however, to remember the regional limits of this community. In the Kosovo case, shared expectations and solidarity framed a particular discourse about the relationship between sovereignty and human rights that resonated within Europe, but whose resonance diminished the further one moved away from this "thick" regional solidarist community.

This chapter is organized into three snapshots of the international engagement with the former Yugoslavia since 1991. Each is a necessarily simplified discussion of European engagement focusing in particular on the shifting relationship between solidarity and national interests and the meanings attached to those terms. The first section discusses the response to the first signs of Yugoslavia's break-up in 1991 – the declarations of independence, the "phoney war" in Slovenia and the attacks on Vukovar and Dubrovnik – focusing in particular on the debate about whether to dispatch a UN or Western European Union (WEU) force to the region and the question of recognition. The second part evaluates the contrasting positions of European states and the United States on how best to respond to BiH. Prior to the Srebrenica massacre in July 1995, the response of most states was primarily driven by parochialism but the "shock" of Srebrenica led to the forging of a European consensus based on US leadership. The third part addresses NATO's intervention in Kosovo and demonstrates how Europe's transformation led to the question of intervention being placed on the agenda, and being widely accepted, at a very early stage in the crisis.

Slovenia and Croatia

On 27 September 1990, the Slovene assembly declared that laws promulgated by Yugoslavia would no longer be applied in Slovenia and on 23 December 88.5 per cent of Slovenes voted in favour of independence from Yugoslavia.[34] A day earlier, the Croatian assembly joined Slovenia by proclaiming Croatia's sovereignty.[35] With a few notable exceptions (Austria, for instance), Europe initially responded by rejecting Slovene and Croatian claims and insisting upon the maintenance of Yugoslavia's territorial integrity. For most states, the assertions of independence were precipitous and potentially dangerous. From this perspective, which remained prevalent until late 1991 at least – and well beyond 1992 for some states, such as the United Kingdom – the geopolitical harm that could be wrought by Slovene and Croatian secession far outweighed the value of the human rights and self-determination arguments being put forward by the secessionists. Roland Dumas, the French foreign minister, demonstrated the prevailing view when he argued that although he understood Slovene and Croatian aspirations for liberty it was important to remember that demands for liberty were constrained by the countervailing demands of international order, which clearly rejected secession.[36]

Fissures began to appear in this consensus in June 1991 as it became clear that Yugoslavia's republican leaders would not be able to resolve their constitutional differences. A Slovene–Croatian plan for a confederal Yugoslavia was rejected by Slobodan Milošević and evidence began to emerge that the Yugoslav authorities were planning to use force to halt the secessions. Also in that month, Croatia began planning its defence against an expected attack by the Yugoslav People's Army (JNA).[37] The war began on 27 June when it became clear that Slovene territorial defence forces would resist JNA attempts to impose martial law on the republic to prevent its march to independence. By October, though the "war" in Slovenia was over, Serb militias had begun seizing land in Croatia and the JNA had laid siege to Vukovar and Dubrovnik.

The political leaders of Germany, Austria and Italy became more sympathetic to the plight of Slovenia and Croatia. Austria argued that Yugoslavia had always been an "artificial" state and that Slovenia and Croatia's claim to independence was a legitimate exercise of their human rights. Moreover, Foreign Minister Alois Mock argued that failure to rec-ognize those rights would lead to war and instability in the Balkans.[38] Germany held a similar position. Hans-Dietrich Genscher argued that the European Community should put pressure on Milošević to accept a negotiated settlement based on the confederal plan and prevent the JNA from using force. Indeed, it was not until the destruction of Du-brovnik and Vukovar that Germany began demanding independence for Slovenia and Croatia. Although critics have argued that this position was based on self-interest, a view expressed at length by Karadžić apologist John Zametica,[39] considered more closely, the Austro-German position contained a mix of national interests and solidarist concern. In short, Genscher and others believed that the denial of fundamental human rights was destabilizing and that there was therefore a synergy between geopolitical interests and support for human rights in the Balkans.[40]

At the other end of the spectrum, the United States, United Kingdom and Soviet Union insisted that geopolitical concerns were paramount and that conflict avoidance was best served by appeasing the Yugoslav gov-ernment. In particular, there were concerns that the conflict could spread and engulf all of southeast Europe and that it could set a dangerous pre-cedent for the Soviet Union, whose impending demise was by now widely foretold. During a visit to Belgrade in April 1991, Mikhail Gorbachev's Foreign Minister insisted that Moscow considered Yugoslavia's territorial integrity "one of the essential preconditions for the stability of Eu-rope".[41] For its part, the United States also remained committed to pre-serving Yugoslavia. Deputy Secretary of State Lawrence Eagleburger – a personal friend of Milošević – endorsed both the Milošević (Serbia) and Marković (Yugoslavia) regimes and insisted that Yugoslavia remain united.[42] Similarly, Lord Carrington, the United Kingdom's chief negoti-ator for the Balkans, insisted that unity was the only way forward and placed the blame for the outbreak of war squarely at the feet of Croatia and Germany.[43] This position reflected the majority view in the Euro-pean security community, as was demonstrated on 23 June when the European Community voted to support the American position not to rec-ognize the independence of Slovenia and Croatia.[44] These states rejected the idea that geopolitical concerns and solidarity were interdependent and argued that their national interest demanded that the preservation of Yugoslavia take precedence over the human rights of Croats and Slov-enes.

Unsurprisingly, these fissures produced the lukewarm response to the outbreak of violence described at the beginning of this chapter. Under German leadership, the European Community responded swiftly to the outbreak of violence in Slovenia by despatching its troika to negotiate a settlement between Slovenia and the JNA. On 5 July, the troika succeeded in negotiating an end to the hostilities in Slovenia and on 18 July the JNA promised to withdraw from Slovenia. Although much lauded at the time, this was a pyrrhic diplomatic victory brought about by the fact that Milošević was happy to let Slovenia go because, having no significant Serbian community, it did not figure in his plans for a Serb-dominated Yugoslavia.[45] In August 1991, the Krajina Serbs backed by the JNA launched a series of attacks in Croatia and proclaimed their right to independence. JNA forces bombarded Dubrovnik and Vukovar and the term "ethnic cleansing" was first used to describe the Serbian strategy of using terror to drive Croats from their homes.

The violence in Croatia in the second half of 1991 had a significant impact on the positions adopted by European states. Crucially, one of the drivers of that change was the emergence of a sense of solidarity with the Croatian plight within European societies. Eurobarometer polls taken in September 1991 showed that, on average, 68 per cent of Europeans believed that respect for democracy and human rights in Yugoslavia was more important than maintaining Yugoslavia's territorial integrity. That figure was highest in Albania (85%), the Netherlands (76%), Ireland (74%), France, Belgium and the United Kingdom (73% each), and lowest in Russia (45%),[46] Greece (36%) and Romania (33%).[47] However, there remained no consensus about how to proceed. The United States, United Kingdom and Soviet Union in particular continued to insist upon a negotiated settlement based on some form of reconstituted Yugoslavia. The European Community dispatched monitors to negotiate and observe ceasefire agreements, more than a dozen of which failed. As I noted at the beginning of the chapter, a Franco–German-led plan to deploy a WEU peace mission was rejected by their allies. In November 1991, Germany decided to break ranks with the European Community and called for the immediate recognition of Slovenia and Croatia. After its calls were rejected, Germany insisted that it would unilaterally recognize the two republics. The British argued that such a move would derail the peace process but grudgingly accepted the move once it became clear that Germany would press ahead with its recognition regardless of the British position. Moreover, given the swing in European public opinion it had become very difficult for the United Kingdom to continue stalling international engagement with the unfolding crisis.

The European Community formally recognized Slovenia and Croatia on 15 January 1992. At the same time, it handed over the primary role in the peace process to the United Nations. Former US Secretary of State Cyrus Vance negotiated a series of deals with the Croatian government, the Croatian Serb militia and the Serbian government that paved the way for the deployment of the United Nations Protection Force

(UNPROFOR). UNPROFOR was to be a traditional-style peacekeeping mission deployed in a demilitarized zone between Serb and Croatian forces in Croatia to observe the ceasefire that Vance had negotiated.[48]

From this brief overview of the Euro-Atlantic region's first responses to the break-up of Yugoslavia we can discern five key trends. First, at the level of state-to-state relations, solidarity and human rights considerations played a minimal role. States were generally very sceptical about Austrian and German arguments, and there was widespread belief, particularly in the United Kingdom, that these two governments were using human rights arguments to justify a policy position motivated by self-interest. As Conversi has shown, however, the German position derived from the view that long-term stability rested on the satisfaction of fundamental rights. Indeed, it could be argued that predominant ideas about German identity were creating a conception of interests that were very different from those of the other major European states.[49] Second, for most policymakers, imperatives of order and justice collided with one another, and there was widespread consensus that the former should take precedence over the latter. Third, the change of direction in the second half of 1991 was in many ways forced upon reluctant leaders by a combination of the changing facts on the ground in Croatia and the increase of expressions of solidarity toward Croatia's plight by societies in Western Europe. The sensitization of European publics to the human suffering in the Balkans made it more difficult, rhetorically at least, for political leaders to trade human rights for geopolitical stability. However, this change of emphasis did little to alter the fact that most states continued to prioritize containment and order over justice. Fourth, although the European Community embarked on a collective diplomatic mission, disagreement about the relative values of order and solidarity suggests that the organization was not yet a solidarist community and its inability to act or to invoke allied agencies such as NATO suggests that it lacked at least military agency in world politics. Finally, it is intriguing to note that the arguments used to reject intervention in 1991 (order, interests, law) were precisely the arguments used to justify intervention in 1999. The next section attempts to unravel the beginning of this transformation with the engagement with BiH between 1992 and 1995.

Bosnia and Herzegovina

The pattern of interaction set by Europe's response to the initial break-up of Yugoslavia continued to shape attitudes toward BiH until 1995. Although the transformation of that attitude was gradual, the massacre at Srebrenica and collapse of the "safe areas" policy proved to be an important watershed. Not least, as the United Kingdom and France contemplated the unravelling of their peace mission to BiH in the summer of 1995, one option that was widely touted in British government circles – withdrawal and disengagement – was a political non-starter because of the high degree of concern expressed by the societies of Europe toward the victims of war in BiH. Through the media and public protests, British, German, French, Italian and other societies demanded that their governments act to bring the bloodshed to a halt.[50] Thus, in the aftermath of Srebrenica the British and French altered the nature of their engagement on the ground in BiH toward a strategy based on a more "robust" defence of human rights and the United Kingdom stopped opposing US demands for air strikes against the Bosnian Serbs.[51]

Following the EC decision to recognize republics whose citizens demonstrated a clear desire for independence and whose governments met certain basic human rights criteria, the Bosnian government held a referendum on independence in early March 1992. The vote was boycotted by Karadžić's nationalist Serb party, but of the 64 per cent of the population that did vote, there was almost unanimous support for independence.[52] Almost immediately, Serb militias – armed and organized by the JNA and their supporters in Serbia – began mobilizing. Karadžić denounced the vote and proclaimed that the Bosnian Serb people would wage war to preserve their "right" to statehood.[53] In early April, Arkan's paramilitary teams arrived in northeast BiH having recently concluded their ethnic cleansing of Vukovar. On 4 April they began their spree of ethnic cleansing in Bijelina, a predominantly Muslim town that had hitherto entirely escaped the turmoil of Yugoslavia's collapse. An estimated 100 Muslim civilians were killed. In the second week of April, Arkan's "tigers" joined forces with other Serb paramilitary organizations and JNA artillery units to widen their attacks to Zvornik, Visegrad and Foca.[54] During this time, the UN force set up to monitor the "peace" in Croatia had still not fully deployed owing to disagreements about who would pay for the mission, what its rules of engagement would be and who would command it.[55]

By June/July 1992, international society was confronting a major humanitarian catastrophe in BiH. The death toll by now was climbing to 50,000 (it would reach 250,000 by war's end) and more than half a million people had been displaced, primarily by Serbian ethnic cleansing. Once again, however, European responses to the tragedy were characterized by disagreement over the relative values of geopolitical order, self-interest and human rights. The British view was that the war was in part caused by the precipitous decision to recognize BiH as a sovereign state. This had led to a "breakdown of law and order" in which all sides were equally to blame. The Bosnian crisis was regarded as an "external"

problem and treated as such.[56] Although the United Kingdom was prepared to contribute troops to UNPROFOR it was unwilling to countenance the use of force. From 1993 onwards, the United Kingdom used
its contribution to UNPROFOR to argue that using force against the
Bosnian Serbs would place British forces in danger. This caused a major
rift between the United Kingdom and the new Clinton administration in
the United States, which advocated air strikes against Bosnian Serb
forces. Relations soured further in 1994 when it emerged that British
peacekeepers were being ordered to obstruct US efforts to find legitimate
military targets to attack.[57] Moreover, because the UK believed the war
to be a product of ancient ethnic hatreds[58] and the hasty recognition of
BiH, it insisted that an arms embargo (Security Council Resolution 713)
be maintained against the protests of the Bosnian government and the
United States. The British Foreign Minister, Douglas Hurd, famously
argued that lifting the arms embargo would only create a "level killing
field".[59]

At the other end of the spectrum, the new Clinton administration attempted to craft a very different response. Bush Senior's response to the
Bosnian conflict had been very similar to his policy on Croatia and
Slovenia. As James Baker put it, "we don't have a dog in that fight".[60]
Candidate Clinton had sharply criticized Bush's inaction over BiH. He
insisted that the United States could not "turn its back on violations of
basic human rights for political convenience" and advocated the use
of air power to ensure the delivery of humanitarian aid, and the lifting
of the arms embargo to allow the Bosnian government to organize its
own defence.[61] Once in office, however, Clinton was constrained in a
number of ways. First, with on-going commitments that went very badly
in Somalia, Clinton was reluctant to place Americans in harm's way to
save Bosnians. Second, it was not at all clear precisely how air strikes
could be used to secure the delivery of humanitarian aid. Third, although
hawks such as Germany and Austria supported the idea in principle,
Clinton soon found that there was little agreement amongst the Western
allies about the use of force.[62]

The upshot of this was that UNPROFOR was given the task of supporting the delivery of humanitarian aid in BiH, though peacekeepers
were given little or no guidance about how precisely they were to go
about doing this in a context where there was no peace to keep and
no consensus about whether they could use force to accomplish their
goals.[63] This became particularly problematic as all the belligerents
(especially the Bosnian Serbs) attempted to control the flow of aid
throughout the country and as it became apparent that the presence of
UN peacekeepers was not restraining the level of violence or preventing
the deliberate targeting of civilians. UNPROFOR peacekeepers lacked

both the mandate and means to either guarantee the delivery of aid or prevent the most egregious abuse of human rights. Indeed, in many cases these two roles collided. Peacekeepers were often obliged to cooperate with local military leaders to get aid through and that involved providing material, financial and political assistance to human rights abusers.[64] The Security Council attempted to remedy these problems in October 1992 by creating a "no-fly zone", but this had little discernible impact on the humanitarian conditions inside BiH.

In 1993, mounting public pressure for action persuaded states such as the United Kingdom and France to search for alternative strategies. The humanitarian crises continued to worsen and in spring 1993 the Vance-Owen peace plan, which called for the cantonization of BiH along ethnic lines, was rejected by the Bosnian Serb assembly.[65] The plan was predicated on the realist view that ethnic partition and population transfers would be the most effective way of maintaining geopolitical order in the region.[66] Once again international divisions came to the fore. David Owen, one of the plan's architects, insisted that it failed because the United States failed to support it.[67] Certainly, Clinton's position was particularly vexatious. On the one hand, the United States was deeply uncomfortable with the plan, believing that it rewarded ethnic cleansing and bought short-term stability at the cost of fundamental human rights. On the other hand, it was unwilling to either place Americans in harm's way to protect human rights or to take the diplomatic lead. Ultimately, the plan failed because the Bosnian Serb assembly rejected it and no one was prepared to coerce them to accept it. Some states were simply unwilling to use force (the United Kingdom) and others (notably the United States and Germany) were not persuaded by the ethical veracity of the plan.

A compromise was reached in the so-called "safe areas" policy. The safe areas idea had its roots in an Austrian proposal to create "protected zones" in BiH.[68] Alois Mock, the Austrian Foreign Minister, argued that such zones did not require the consent of the Bosnian Serb leadership and would be protected by international forces that had the capacity and mandate to defend them. Although the Austrian proposal won support from within the Non-Aligned Movement, Vance and Owen argued that consent was vital and unlikely to be forthcoming, and the permanent members of the Security Council remained "cool" on the initiative.[69] The strategy remained on the table, lacking the crucial support it needed, until the crisis in Srebrenica forced the Security Council's hand. In the informal consultations prior to the passage of Resolution 819, adopted in April 2003 and creating a "safe area" in Srebrenica, there was a broad solidarist consensus that the United Nations should act to protect the victims of ethnic cleansing. However, although some Security Council members – most notably Venezuela, Morocco and Pakistan – viewed the policy as a prelude to broader enforcement action aimed at protecting the Bosnian Muslims, key UNPROFOR troop contributors (especially the United Kingdom, France and Spain) were concerned about the potential loss of Serbian consent and the danger of UNPROFOR crossing the "Mogadishu line" into enforcement.[70] The result was an ultimately unworkable compromise. On the one hand, the safe areas policy contained a commitment to solidarism by aiming, rhetorically at least, to create "zones of peace" that would be "free of armed attack" and would allow the safe delivery of humanitarian aid and the protection of human rights.[71] On the other hand, those glimmers of solidarity were overridden by the lingering geopolitical belief (evident in responses to the initial break-up of Yugoslavia) in the importance of containment and the primacy of protecting forces deployed with UNPROFOR. As a result, the "safe areas" mandate provided only for the use of force to protect UN personnel (rather than the people sheltering within the safe areas). Moreover, member states were unwilling to support their solidarist rhetoric with material commitments. Although the UN secretariat estimated that 34,000 extra troops would be needed to fulfil the mandate, key Western states described this estimation as "excessive" and the Security Council authorized only an additional 7,600. France and the United Kingdom refused to extend their missions and Spain, the United States, Norway, Sweden, Russia and Canada all refused to contribute forces to the safe areas policy.[72] In the end, only around 3,500 extra troops were contributed to UNPROFOR to carry out the safe areas policy whilst the policy itself was extended to six towns: Sarajevo, Srebrenica, Gorazde, Bihac, Tuzla and Zepa.

The safe areas policy dramatically collapsed in the summer of 1995. Because UNPROFOR lacked both the mandate and means to ensure the delivery of humanitarian aid to the safe areas, besieged towns like Bihac, Gorazde and Srebrenica were dependent on the goodwill of the Bosnian Serb leadership for supplies. Throughout 1994 and 1995, conditions in the safe areas deteriorated as malnutrition and disease set in and the Serbs maintained their sieges because the safe areas had not been fully demilitarized as demanded by the Security Council. Then, in June/July 1995, the Bosnian Serb army decided to strengthen its position at the negotiating table by seizing the safe areas. In early July, Ratko Mladić's forces overran Srebrenica and massacred over 7,500 people in an orgy of violence. The safe area of Zepa also fell and two other safe areas, Gorazde and Bihac, came close to collapsing.[73] This prompted a significant rethink in policy. The United Kingdom and France created and deployed a rapid reaction force with robust rules of engagement and significant military capabilities.[74] After consistent pressure from the United States, on 30 August 1995 NATO launched Operation Deliberate Force, a sustained air and artillery campaign against the Bosnian Serbs. Within four months, the Bosnian war came to an end with the conclusion of the Dayton peace accords.[75]

This policy shift in the summer of 1995 reflected a subtle change in the way that geopolitical interests were understood by key European states. France and the United Kingdom (grudgingly in the latter case) began to accept the German view that long-term political stability in the Balkans could be achieved only in one of two ways: first, by continuing to appease the Serbs and turning a blind eye to their increasingly blatant strategy of war crimes – a position that was highly unpopular among European societies and politically unfeasible after Srebrenica; second, by acknowledging that basic rights ought to be defended, by force if necessary. Because of European public opinion, and the positions taken by Germany and the United States, only the second option was feasible. Thus, in the aftermath of Srebrenica, there were three crucial changes in the nature of European engagement with the Balkans. First, the United States began to take the diplomatic lead by dispatching a negotiating team headed by Richard Holbrooke to broker a peace settlement. Along the way this involved simply overriding European (especially British) concerns about maintaining Serb consent.[76] Second, the United Kingdom found itself unable to continue to resist the long-standing US preference for "lift and strike" – lifting the arms embargo and launching air strikes against the Bosnian Serbs. The display of American solidarity with BiH remained, however, highly constrained. Although willing to use air power from a safe distance, the Clinton administration remained steadfastly unwilling to place its forces in harm's way by deploying a ground contingent before a comprehensive political settlement was concluded.[77] Third, the United Kingdom and France embraced this shift and placed their ground forces in harm's way. They deployed a joint NATO rapid reaction force on the ground in BiH with robust rules of engagement. It is worth noting that during NATO's subsequent Operation Deliberate Force, more ordnance was delivered by Anglo-French artillery based near Sarajevo than by NATO aircraft.[78] Moreover, the new French President, Jacques Chirac, insisted that if the United Kingdom had failed to act against the Bosnian Serbs, France would have unilaterally launched an attack aimed at reclaiming Srebrenica.[79]

The European security community therefore partially transformed its engagement with the Yugoslav wars of succession during the Bosnian war. Initially, states responded with a similar mindset to that employed in response to the conflicts in Slovenia and Croatia. Key European states such as the United Kingdom and France were unwilling to use force to protect basic human rights in the region because they believed that doing so would place their peacekeepers in harm's way and could potentially undermine regional order. The United States remained unwilling to take the lead, and Germany and Austria were unwilling to act without UN or EC support. Between 1993 and 1995 there were subtle shifts toward a more humanitarian engagement caused in part by the expectation of European publics and in part by the persistent lobbying of a handful of key states. However, with hindsight, the minimally solidarist safe areas strategy was doomed to failure from the outset because there was little interest in making sacrifices to save Bosnians. As a result, the strategy failed disastrously in July 1995. At that point there was a significant shift based on a general acceptance of the view that there was an intimate link between respect for basic human rights and long-term geopolitical stability. In other words, it became clear that "peace through war" would effectively mean endorsing Serbian ethnic cleansing and genocide,[80] something that electorates in most European states were unwilling to do. However, states remained reluctant to make anything other than an arm's length commitment (air power and artillery) to BiH. Nevertheless, combined with Croatian and Bosniak military offensives, the use of NATO air power proved just enough to persuade the Serbian leadership to accept the Dayton peace accords.

After Dayton

There were two significant changes between the European security community's highly constrained display of solidarity toward BiH in 1995 and its humanitarian intervention in Kosovo less than four years later that go some way toward explaining the higher levels of (albeit still constrained) solidarity displayed in the latter case.

First, following Dayton, many of Europe's institutions became intimately involved with governance, security and economic reconstruction in BiH. Through IFOR/SFOR, NATO took the lead in providing military security, disarming and demobilizing the belligerents, apprehending war criminals, promoting military cooperation and assisting the development of a new national army.[81] The European Union (formerly the European Community) developed strategies for economic reconstruction, the centrepiece of which was the so-called "stability pact" that aims to encourage economic growth and cooperation through trade liberalization and inward investment.[82] The OSCE deployed its largest mission (surpassed by the Kosovo Verification Mission in 1998) to facilitate democratization, human rights monitoring, media development and a series of elections. In sharp contrast to critiques of European involvement in BiH prior to Dayton, critics of the post-Dayton order have complained that international institutions have assumed too much responsibility for governance, security and economics in BiH to the detriment of self-determination.[83] For NATO, the European Union and OSCE, this level of engagement was unprecedented. Despite its many flaws, the growth of engagement both produced, and was produced by, a degree of solidarity with the people of BiH. Through these three agencies, European states and societies have invested considerable capital in BiH and have engaged in a wide range of activities. This engagement itself in the implementation of the Dayton peace accords significantly increased the influence of solidarity vis-à-vis narrow national interests. Moreover, through the socializing effect of these institutional engagements states such as the United Kingdom that had traditionally conceived order and justice as contradictory forces in the Balkans shifted toward a position that viewed the two as interdependent.[84] The shift in UK policy was certainly more dramatic than the shift in any other European state, the key factor in the scale of that transformation undoubtedly being the election of a Labour government in 1997.[85] Srebrenica demonstrated that Balkan peace could not be cheaply bought at the price of justice. In the two or so years that followed, a new European orthodoxy emerged, based on the position expressed by Germany in 1991/92 that regional stability depended on the creation of a democratic multicultural state that respected human rights.

The second key transformation between 1995 and 1998 was the transformation of the European security community itself into a solidarist community.[86] As we noted earlier, there was little consensus in the early 1990s about the relative importance of solidarity and national interests. For some, solidarity with the Balkan victims could be traded to maintain order. For others, order itself depended on the preservation of solidarist human rights values in the Balkans. By 1998, however, not only had a broad consensus around the latter view emerged but also the European security community had itself transformed in two important respects. On the one hand, in many ways thanks to post-Dayton BiH, the different institutions of the security community had developed higher degrees of institutional capacity. In other words, by 1998 the European security community had a higher degree of *agency*. On the other hand, a broader consensus had emerged on what the "European idea" meant. Hugh Seton-Watson's comment that "there are many Europes" seems an apposite description of the situation before 1995. The European security community was itself stratified and for all but a minority of European states the Balkans remained an "external" issue to be comprehended through the traditional lenses of geopolitics and national interests.[87] By 1998, a web of institutions and networks underpinned by a common set of liberal, democratic values had joined Europe together into what Mikhail Gorbachev had earlier described as the "common European home".[88]

Moreover, although the former Yugoslavia was certainly not fully "inside" that home, the extensive network of ties between the ex-Yugoslav republics and Europe meant that it was no longer fully on the "outside" either.

The effect of these two transformations, coupled with Europe's social learning from BiH, meant that the outbreak of (by Bosnian standards) relatively low level violence in Kosovo in 1998 was met with a rapid multi-national and multi-institutional response. Although there was significant disagreement within the European security community about the best way to proceed, and especially over the efficacy and legitimacy of intervention, nobody argued against engagement and no European state insisted that geopolitical stability be bought at the expense of human rights. Thus, regardless of the pros and cons of particular arguments related to the question of intervention, there was a discernible shift toward a solidarist discursive framework. In this framework, geopolitical arguments were marginal.

Kosovo

On 5 March 1998, Serb paramilitary police forces raided the home of the Jashari family in Donji Prekaz, Kosovo. Adem Jashari was a leading member of the Kosovo Liberation Army (KLA), which had burst onto the political scene with a number of violent attacks on Serb police stations in late 1997. Fifty-eight people were killed in the assault, including ten children and eighteen women.[89] The European response, if somewhat indecisive, was rapid and based on the presumption that such human rights abuses were wholly illegitimate. Whilst US Secretary of State Madeleine Albright immediately intimated the possibility of a military intervention, German Foreign Minister Klaus Kinkel advocated a multi-pronged approach that involved enhancing NATO's role in Macedonia, strengthening the WEU force in Albania and launching a joint EU–OSCE political process.[90]

As these diplomatic efforts floundered and a pattern of ethnic cleansing began to emerge, the United States and United Kingdom in particular placed the issue of intervention as a last resort firmly on the agenda. Tellingly referring to the "lessons of Bosnia", Clinton insisted that the United States would use force if Milošević continued in his policy.[91] In the United Kingdom, Blair took a very similar line, telling the cabinet that "the only question that matters is whether you are prepared to use force. And we have to be. Reports indicate a level of butchery that risks escalating into another Bosnia".[92] Along similar lines, in early June

Foreign Secretary Robin Cook insisted that Milošević had "crossed the threshold".[93] Although at this point there was little support for intervention, reluctant states such as Greece, Italy and Germany focused on the twin questions of legality (will intervention be legal?) and efficacy (will intervention remedy the human rights problem?) rather than the types of geopolitical arguments used to reject calls for intervention between 1991 and 1995. Furthermore, a broad solidarist consensus had emerged relatively quickly. That consensus held that ethnic cleansing in Kosovo was an intolerable infringement of European solidarity and that the European security community should act to halt those abuses. As demonstrated by the above quotes from Clinton and Blair, the "lessons of Bosnia" loomed large in Western thinking.

Through the summer of 1998, a variety of peace initiatives were launched by the OSCE/European Union and the United States. The main process, headed by Christopher Hill, was based on persuading Milošević to accept a political settlement that accorded autonomy to Kosovo in return for the demobilization of the KLA.[94] Concurrently, Serb forces persisted in their policy of ethnic cleansing and a Western consensus began to emerge in favour of using air power to coerce Serbian acquiescence if necessary. That consensus was briefly interrupted in June when Boris Yeltsin led an ill-fated peace mission that failed to persuade Milošević to change his course of action.[95] The failure of the Russian initiative created a consensus around a stronger course of action, which emerged in earnest in September/October 1998.

On 23 September, the UN Security Council passed Resolution 1199. The resolution condemned "the indiscriminate use of force by Serbian security forces and the Yugoslav army" and demanded the immediate cessation and withdrawal of Serbian forces and rapid progress toward a political settlement.[96] Madeleine Albright immediately insisted that Resolution 1199 contained enough authority to justify the use of force against Milošević, a view vociferously rejected by Russia.[97] To resolve the first problem, the United Kingdom, Canada and Japan tabled a draft resolution authorizing the use of "all necessary means" to resolve the Kosovo crisis. In informal consultations, Russia indicated that it would veto any resolution authorizing force against Yugoslavia, regardless of progress toward a political settlement, and it was widely thought that China would do likewise.[98] For many Western states this amounted to what Tony Blair was later to describe as an "unreasonable veto".[99] It also gave rise to the view, articulated most forthrightly by Albright, that the regional solidarist community in Europe did not require the endorsement of global bodies partly governed by states (such as Russia and China) that did not subscribe to that community's liberal solidarist values.[100] A similar view was expressed at this time by Jacques Chirac, who noted that whilst the use of force "must be requested and decided by the Security Council", "the humanitarian situation [in Kosovo] constitutes a ground that can justify an exception to the rule".[101]

The second primary concern within Europe was the question of efficacy. That is, although there was broad agreement amongst European states and societies (with the exception of Greece) that defence of human rights and conflict resolution should be the primary concern, there remained disagreement about the most appropriate way to achieve those ends. Many states believed that the point of "last resort" had not yet been reached and were therefore unwilling to support the use of force. In late 1998, therefore, US Special Envoy Richard Holbrooke returned to the diplomatic fray and used coercive diplomacy (the threat of air strikes) to persuade Milošević to accept a peace plan that included an immediate ceasefire, a pledge to return Serb and Yugoslav forces to barracks, and a commitment to move toward a political settlement. All of this was to be monitored by a large OSCE verification mission.[102] Although some progress was made in November/December and OSCE inspectors were rapidly deployed into Kosovo and played an effective monitoring role, the process dramatically unravelled in mid-January when evidence emerged that Serb forces had massacred 45 civilians in the village of Racak.[103] The contact group (the United States, the United Kingdom, France, Germany and Italy) still believed that the "last resort" had not been reached and summoned all the parties to last-ditch negotiations at Rambouillet. Only when those negotiations failed, because Milošević refused to accept NATO's terms or even seriously negotiate, and Serb forces recommenced ethnic cleansing in Kosovo did NATO finally decide to launch air strikes.

The European security community's response to the Kosovo crisis, overly simplified in this discussion, demonstrates the changed relationship between geopolitical and parochial interests-based concerns and liberal solidarity for a political group on the community's borders. With the notable exception of Greece, the primary critics of NATO's actions and intentions were states outside the security community. From the outset of the crisis, the debate about how to proceed was guided by a solidarist discursive framework. Although they predominantly converged, where national interests and solidarity collided in this debate, a form of solidarity (albeit constrained) won out: nobody seriously suggested that peace be bought at the price of solidarity. Hence the debate was primarily concerned with the legality and efficacy of different strategies, rather than with the final goal or the overall nature of engagement. However, there was a marked disparity between the tenor of the debate within Europe and the nature of the global debate. The basic claims of key states such as the United Kingdom, Germany, France and the United States – that egregious human rights abuse in Kosovo was simply intolerable – was widely rejected by the broader, pluralist minded, international society.[104]

The regional limit of solidarity is not the only caveat to erode the sense of solidarist triumphalism that the evolution of Europe's engagement with the Balkans might incite. Even after deciding to use force, NATO's display of solidarity remained highly constrained. As early as mid-1998, member states ruled out the use of ground forces in any campaign against Yugoslavia and the primary concern for NATO's military planners was minimizing the danger faced by its soldiers. As a result, in March 1999, NATO embarked on a military strategy that simply could not achieve its stated goal. It became clear in the weeks that followed, as more than a million people were forced from their homes and more than 5,000 killed, that the use of airpower alone cannot prevent small groups of well-armed militia from wreaking havoc. To be sure, NATO did not "provoke" the Serb action. In the aftermath of Rambouillet and the follow-up talks in Paris, NATO still required a "trigger" for the use of force, because some member states believed that the Serb refusal to sign the peace deal did not, by itself, constitute grounds for war. The trigger was provided by a new round of ethnic cleansing. According to UNHCR, between the end of the Rambouillet/Paris peace talks and 20 March (three days before NATO launched its first strikes) more than 20,000 Kosovar Albanians had been "ethnically cleansed".[105] Although NATO neither precipitated nor provoked the ethnic cleansing, it did select a strategy that appeared to prioritize the safety of its own personnel over that of the people it was supposedly defending.[106] This clearly suggests a significant limit on the extent to which solidarity was privileged over national interests. In this case, although solidarity trumped geopolitics, it remained constrained by the domestic political interests of European elites in that it was widely believed that allied casualties would be politically damaging at home.

However, our criticism of NATO and doubt about the depth of its solidarity toward Kosovar Albanians should be tempered by at least four considerations. First, the decision to limit the use of force to air power was driven as much by the need for allied unity as it was by the need to minimize losses. Whilst loss minimization was pivotal in the United States, it was much less central in Europe, and it was European members of NATO that, in early 1999, were most hesitant about using force. Key states such as Germany, France and Italy remained concerned about the legality and efficacy of force and consented to the intervention on the grounds that it would be limited to a carefully calibrated and highly discriminate air assault.[107] Second, the oft-repeated criticism that NATO placed Kosovar Albanians in harm's way by limiting their flying altitude to 15,000 feet in order to avoid Serbian air defences, thereby reducing their accuracy and increasing the likelihood of civilian casualties is misplaced. The optimal altitude for the delivery of precision-guided munitions (PGMs) is 15,000 to 20,000 feet to establish a lock on their target.[108] Greater distance, within these limits, does not reduce the accuracy of PGMs. Furthermore, flying lower would have made pilots less able to spot and attack Serb military movements. Finally, flying low actually reduces the danger to aircraft from surface-to-air missiles.[109] Third, some states, most notably the United Kingdom, were prepared to commit large numbers of ground forces to a land invasion if necessary. In bilateral discussions with William Cohen during the campaign, George Robertson, the British Defence Minister, insisted that the United Kingdom would commit 50,000 troops for "as long as it takes" to guarantee victory.[110] Finally, liberal advocates of a ground war have failed to demonstrate that a contested land invasion over difficult terrain would have saved lives. In the event, approximately 500 non-combatants were killed by the air strikes. Contrast that with the conservative estimate of 13,000 non-combatant deaths during the land invasion of Iraq.[111] It is likely that an invasion of Yugoslavia would have been much bloodier, and would have put many more Kosovar Albanians, as well as non-combatant Serbs, in harm's way.

The Kosovo case demonstrates that within the broad sphere of "interests" we need to distinguish between geopolitics and domestic political interests. Despite strong objections by Russia and other key actors in international society, the European security community did not seek to balance political solidarity with geopolitical interests as they had done prior to 1995. There were two reasons for this. First, there was a broad consensus within the community that order and justice were interdependent, a proposition first aired by Germany in 1991 but evidently not shared by wider international society. The purported "lesson" of Srebrenica was that stability rested on the robust defence of human rights. Second, the transformation of the European security community resulted in key states finding large-scale human rights abuse in Kosovo less tolerable than they had in Bosnia. Thus, the development of the security community helped to transform identities amongst European states, enabling a reconceptualization of their interests. For much of the Bosnian war, those same states were prepared to tolerate gross abuses in order to keep diplomatic channels open, negotiate a settlement based on ethnic partition and protect the lives of their own soldiers. Although force protection remained a significant issue in the Kosovo case, the relative balance between solidarity, force protection and regional order had shifted in favour of the former. However, solidarity was constrained by domestic political interests. Most states were reluctant to place their own citizens in harm's way or jeopardize the wider European integration process by pressuring reluctant allies to expand the use of force.

Conclusion

Whilst there was a clear shift in the nature of European engagement with the Balkans by 1999, the former Yugoslav states remained on the borders of the European security community (in 1991 it was distinctly "outside"). As a result, although the discursive framework that shaped regional responses to the crisis was solidarist, that engagement remained constrained in important respects. Post-Kosovo, there are signs that the former Yugoslavia (with the exception of Serbia and Montenegro) is being socialized into the European security community. Slovenia has become a member of NATO and the European Union, and Croatia and BiH are well on their way to membership in both. In 2001, NATO, the European Union and OSCE all responded swiftly to the outbreak of low-level violence in Macedonia. On the one hand they used diplomatic, economic and military coercion to persuade the Macedonian government to adopt a conciliatory line towards the rebels, and on the other they helped to coerce the Albanian separatists into accepting an EU-brokered peace plan overseen by a NATO peacekeeping deployment followed by an EU operation.[112] The outcome of the 2004 election in Croatia provides further evidence of former Yugoslav states being socialized into the European security community. The former nationalist Croation Democratic Union (HDZ) was returned to power, but the "new" HDZ has reformed itself into a mainstream centre-right European party. It has cooperated with the International Criminal Tribunal for the former Yugoslavia more fully than its left-wing predecessor and has placed NATO and EU membership as the cornerstones of its political programme.[113]

The Balkans case is therefore a study in the development of a regional solidarist community. In the early 1990s, national interests and geopolitical considerations tended to take precedence over solidarity in shaping the policy of most states. Yugoslavia was predominantly seen as outside the European community, though some states argued strongly in favour of viewing Yugoslavia as a member of the community and treating its peoples accordingly. As the level of violence grew, European societies began to demonstrate high levels of solidarity toward the Croat and Bosnian victims. Amongst many governments, however, perceived geopolitical interests continued to dictate an arm's-length engagement but domestic pressure compelled them to "do something" to ease the unfolding humanitarian catastrophe. The result was a series of half-hearted measures. This strategy rapidly unravelled in the summer of 1995, with the collapse of the safe areas policy. The nature of European engagement began to change significantly after Srebrenica. A consensus emerged after Srebrenica that geopolitical interests and solidarist concerns were interdependent, a view that was strongly reinforced by the high levels of institutional involvement in BiH after Dayton. This shift was evidenced in 1998/99 in the swift and relatively decisive response of the European security community to Serbian ethnic cleansing, which succeeded a decade of neglect of the Kosovo problem.[114] From early 1998, that response was framed by a regional solidarist discursive framework that viewed solidarity, national interests and order as interdependent. Thus, unlike in 1991 to 1995, the debate about how to proceed in relation to Kosovo revolved around two core questions: the legality of intervention and the ability of different strategies to accomplish the twin goals of halting the violence and securing a political settlement that guaranteed the rights of Kosovar Albanians. Nevertheless, the extent of solidarity remained constrained by domestic political interests. Thus, although states and societies exhibited a high degree of solidarity toward the people of Kosovo, the level of solidarity remained much lower than levels of communitarian solidarity expressed within European polities.

The Balkans case teaches us at least three things about the relationship between solidarity and interests. First, the relationship can change over time. Such changes may be brought about by the emergence of transversal society-to-society solidarity, social learning from past bad experiences, changes in political leadership, and the internal transformation of security communities into tightly coupled communities. Such communities are predicated on a strong sense of shared identities and solidarity, which are then projected outwards onto those on the community's periphery. Second, expecting the emergence of a global solidarism and overlooking the regional dimension sets the bar too high and causes us to overlook significant change at the sub-global level.[115] An alternative way of conceptualizing the emergence of solidarism is in terms of regional solidarist communities – groups of states that exhibit high degrees of solidarism. It is clear from what has gone above that such a community developed in Europe in the 1990s. This was evidenced by the subtle contrast between the debate that took place within Europe about how best to respond to the Kosovo crisis and the wider debate in international society. Third, regional solidarist communities provide common discursive frameworks that privilege some arguments over others but do not determine action. Within these frameworks there still remains significant room for dissent about the legitimacy and efficacy of particular courses of action and domestic political concerns may still override transnational solidarity.

Notes

1. I would to thank Paul Williams, Luke Glanville, Nick J. Wheeler, Jean-Marc Coicaud and especially Sara Davies for their help and useful comments in putting this chapter together.
2. Laura Silber and Allan Little (1995) *The Death of Yugoslavia*, London: Penguin, p. 174.
3. Silber and Little, *The Death of Yugoslavia*, p. 176.
4. See, for instance, James Gow (1997) *Triumph of the Lack of Will: International Diplomacy and the Yugoslav War*, London: Hurst and Co., p. 48; Christopher Bennett (1995) *Yugoslavia's Bloody Collapse: Causes, Course and Consequences*, London: Hurst and Co.; and Catherine Guicherd (1993) "The Hour of Europe: Lessons from the Yugoslav Conflict", *Fletcher Forum of World Affairs* 17(2).
5. The John Major government maintained this line until after the Srebrenica massacre in 1995. Throughout, Major and Foreign Minister Douglas Hurd were adamant that Britain's primary interest in the conflict was containment. For a thorough discussion of this, see Brendan Simms (2001) *Unfinest Hour: Britain and the Destruction of Bosnia*, London: Penguin.
6. The terms "Europe" and "European security community" are used interchangeably in this chapter. Although I refer to Europe, I include the United States and Canada as members of this community. See Barry Buzan and Ole Waever (2004) *Regions and Powers: The Structure of International Security*, Cambridge: Cambridge University Press, pp. 30–37.
7. Gow, *Triumph of the Lack of Will*, p. 48.
8. Susan L. Woodward (1995) *Balkan Tragedy: Chaos and Dissolution after the Cold War*, Washington, D.C.: Brookings Institution, p. 174. Indeed, the German Constitution still forbade Germany from deploying its forces overseas, undermining the possibility of German leadership. I am grateful to Paul Williams for bringing this point to my attention.
9. This is Nicholas Wheeler's term. See Nicholas J. Wheeler (2001) *Saving Strangers: Humanitarian Intervention in International Society*, Oxford: Oxford University Press. "A supreme humanitarian emergency exists where the only hope of saving lives depends on outsiders coming to the rescue", p. 34.
10. Satish Nambiar (2000) "India: An Uneasy Precedent", in Albrecht Schnabel and Ramesh Thakur, eds, *Kosovo and the Challenge of Humanitarian Intervention: Selective Indignation, Collective Action and International Citizenship*, Tokyo: United Nations University Press, p. 264.
11. See Simon Duke, Hans-Georg Ehrhart and Matthias Karadi (2000) "The Major European Allies: France, Germany and the United Kingdom", in Schnabel and Thakur, *Kosovo and the Challenge of Humanitarian Intervention*, pp. 132–136.
12. Such arguments were articulated within the European security community, especially in Greece and Cyprus, but inhabited the margins. Beyond the security community they were much more prevalent.
13. Alex J. Bellamy (2002) *Kosovo and International Society*, Basingstoke, UK: Palgrave Macmillan.
14. Tony Blair (1999) "Our Responsibilities Do Not End at the English Channel", *Independent on Sunday*, 14 February, p. 24.
15. Jacques Chirac (1999) radio and television broadcast to the people of France, 6 April; Lamberto Dini (1999) "Loyal to NATO, Faithful to Negotiations", *La Stampa*, 30 May; Gerhard Schroeder (1999) "Statement Regarding the Situation in Kosovo", press release (Berlin), 30 May.

16. Jim Whitman (2001) "The Kosovo Refugee Crisis: NATO's Humanitarianism Versus Human Rights", in Ken Booth, ed., *The Kosovo Tragedy: The Human Rights Dimensions*, London: Frank Cass, pp. 164–183.

17. Misha Glenny (1995) "Heading Off War in the Southern Balkans", *Foreign Affairs*, May/June, p. 99.

18. Lord David Owen, interviewed by the author, London, 5 October 2001. Similar views were expressed at length by Dean Katsiyiannis (1996) "Hyper-Nationalism and Irredentism in the Macedonian Region: Implications for US Policy, Part I", *European Security* 5(2): 326–341. I deal at greater length with what I describe as the "Balkan wars" syndrome and "four wolves" thesis in Alex J. Bellamy (2002) "The New Wolves at the Door: The Conflict in Macedonia", *Civil Wars* 5(1), pp. 117–144.

19. I am speaking in general terms. Within NATO, Greeks and Italians in particular expressed deep scepticism about the intervention and, although on NATO's borders states tended to strongly back the alliance, some such as Belarus and Russia staunchly opposed the alliance.

20. The emergence of a regional solidarist community, whereby an ethic of solidarity is interdependent with ideas about self-interest, prevails within, but an ethic of national interests prevails between community members and outsiders. To use the Wendtian triarchy of coercion, calculation and belief, whereas the European security community prior to the 1990s was predicated on a solidarism informed primarily by calculation (a poor human rights record did not necessarily debar entry), post-1990 calculation has been replaced by belief. Alexander Wendt (1999) *Social Theory of International Politics*, Cambridge: Cambridge University Press, pp. 247–250.

21. Michael Ignatieff (2000) *Virtual War: Kosovo and Beyond*, London: Chatto and Windus, p. 4.

22. Emanuel Adler and Michael Barnett (1998) "Security Communities in Theoretical Perspective", in Emanuel Adler and Michael Barnett, eds, *Security Communities*, Cambridge: Cambridge University Press, p. 17.

23. ASEAN is probably the best example of this type of community. See Geoffrey Gunn's contribution to this volume; Alex J. Bellamy (2004) *Security Communities and their Neighbours: Regional Fortresses or Global Integrators?* London: Palgrave Macmillan, pp. 88–117; Jurgen Haacke (2003) *ASEAN's Diplomatic and Security Culture: Origins, Development and Prospects*, London: RoutledgeCurzon; and Amitav Acharya (2001) *Constructing a Security Community in Southeast Asia: ASEAN and the Problem of Regional Order*, London: Routledge.

24. Emanuel Adler and Michael Barnett (1998) "A Framework for the Study of Security Communities", in Adler and Barnett, *Security Communities*, p. 51. This solidarist component of a security community distinguishes it from security regimes, which, according to Robert Jervis, are predicated entirely on self-interested calculations. Robert Jervis (1983) "Security Regimes", in Stephen D. Krasner, ed., *International Regimes*, Ithaca, N.Y.: Cornell University Press, esp. pp. 176–178.

25. Adler and Barnett, "A Framework for the Study of Security Communities", p. 53.

26. Michael Barnett and Martha Finnemore (1999) "The Politics, Power and Pathologies of International Organizations", *International Organization* 53(4).

27. It is important to note that the term "solidarist" typically refers to the depth of common values across states, not, as is commonly argued, to the nature of those values. In other words, there is no necessary general correlation between solidarism and particular values such as human rights. However, because this chapter is primarily interested in European solidarism, I do equate solidarism in this case with a commitment to basic human rights. I am not, however, implying that all solidarisms have that commitment and this is not the arena to discuss that in more detail. For more, see Barry

Buzan (2005) "International Political Economy and Globalization" and Alex J. Bell-amy (2005) "Conclusion: Whither International Society", Alex J. Bellamy, ed., *International Society and Its Critics*, Oxford: Oxford University Press, pp. 115–134 and 283–295 respectively.

28. Hedley Bull, who was first to use to label "solidarism", used it to describe a particular mode of relating between states. Since Bull, however, many writers have associated solidarism with Wight's Kantian tradition and have located it within global civil society, or world society. Although there are good analytical reasons for separating out examples of solidarism in international and world society, such a separation does not accurately describe the role of solidarist values and identities in world politics, which mesh the state and non-state sectors. For me, solidarism operates in both the state and non-state domain. I am avoiding the term "world society" because the phenomena I am describing in this chapter are regional, not global.

29. Barry Buzan (2004) *From International to World Society? English School Theory and the Social Structure of Globalisation*, Cambridge: Cambridge University Press, pp. 143–152.

30. Adler and Barnett, "A Framework for the Study of Security Communities", p. 55.

31. I discuss this relationship in detail in Bellamy, *Security Communities and their Neighbours*.

32. The core of this solidarist community comprises the European Union, United States and Canada. On the periphery of the community are NATO members and states in advanced stages of negotiations for EU membership.

33. Throughout the chapter I refer to transversal and society-to-society relations. These are both transnational relationships that are not mediated by states. Society-to-society relations are straightforward relationships that do not necessarily challenge the "spatial logic of international society". According to Roland Bleiker, transversal phenomena are political practices that not only transgress national boundaries "but also question the spatial logic through which these boundaries have come to constitute and frame the conduct of international relations". Roland Bleiker (2000) *Popular Dissent, Human Agency and Global Politics*, Cambridge: Cambridge University Press, p. 2.

34. Marc Weller (1992) "Current Developments in Yugoslavia", *American Journal of International Law* 86(3): 572.

35. Amongst the best accounts are Woodward, *Balkan Tragedy*; Silber and Little, *The Death of Yugoslavia*; Sabrina Petra Ramet (1996) *Balkan Babel: The Disintegration of Yugoslavia from the Death of Tito to Ethnic War*, Boulder, Colo.: Westview Press; and John B. Allcock (2000) *Explaining Yugoslavia*, London: Hurst and Co.

36. Cited in "Caution Urged in Yugoslavia", *International Herald Tribune*, 26 June 1991.

37. Martin Spegelj (2001) "The First Phase, 1990–1992: The JNA Prepares for Aggression and Croatia for Defence", in Branka Magas and Ivo Zanic, eds, *The War in Croatia and Bosnia-Herzegovina 1991–1995*, London: Frank Cass, p. 31.

38. Woodward, *Balkan Tragedy*, p. 174.

39. Ibid., p. 174; John Zametica (1992) "The Dissolution of Yugoslavia", *Adelphi Papers* No. 270.

40. This issue is superbly documented and analysed in Daniele Conversi (1998) "German-Bashing and the Break-up of Yugoslavia", *Donald W. Treadgold Papers in Russian, East European and Central Asian Studies* No. 16.

41. Cited in Lenard J. Cohen (1995) *Broken Bonds: Yugoslavia's Disintegration and Balkan Politics in Transition*, Boulder, Colo.: Westview Press, p. 218.

42. Ibid., p. 218.

43. Simms, *Unfinest Hour*, p. 16.

44. Cohen, *Broken Bonds*, p. 221.

45. For a discussion of the 10-day war, see James Gow and Cathie Carmichael (2000) *Slovenia and the Slovenes: A Small State and the New Europe*, London: Hurst and Co., pp. 174–184.

46. Although at this point Russia remained part of the Soviet Union, "Russia" is listed here because the poll was conducted only within the Russian Soviet Republic.

47. Eurobarometer Poll, September 1991, presented in full in Cohen, *Broken Bonds*, p. 234.

48. For more on the initial make-up and operating assumptions of UNPROFOR, see Alex J. Bellamy, Paul Williams and Stuart Griffin (2004) *Understanding Peacekeeping*, Cambridge: Polity, pp. 133–137.

49. I am grateful to Nicholas Wheeler for suggesting this to me.

50. James Gow, Richard Paterson and Alison Preston, eds (1996) *Bosnia by Television*, London: British Film Institute Publishing.

51. Tim Riley (1999) *Operation Deliberate Force: The UN and NATO Campaign in Bosnia, 1995*, Lancaster, UK: Centre for Defence and International Security Studies.

52. Noel Malcolm (1994) *Bosnia: A Short History*, London: Macmillan, p. 231.

53. Wheeler, *Saving Strangers*, p. 249.

54. Malcolm, *Bosnia*, pp. 238–239.

55. Gow, *Triumph of the Lack of Will*, pp. 91–92.

56. James Gow (1996) "British Perspectives", in Alex Danchev and Thomas Halverson, eds, *International Perspectives on the Yugoslav Conflict*, London: Macmillan, p. 90.

57. Ed Vulliamy (1996) "How the CIA Intercepted SAS Signals", *Guardian*, 29 January, p. 9.

58. Foreign Office Minister of State Douglas Hogg described the war as "largely ethnic and historic". Cited by Gow, "British Perspectives", p. 89. Britain's senior negotiator at the outset of the war, Lord Carrington, described the region's people as "all impossible people ... all as bad as each other". Cited by Simms, *Unfinest Hour*, p. 17. The prevalence of the "ancient hatreds" thesis in British foreign policy circles is exhaustively demonstrated throughout Simms' book.

59. Woodward, *Balkan Tragedy*, p. 306. Also see Branka Magas (1993) "Bosnia: A Very British Betrayal", *New Statesman and Society*, 10 September, pp. 14–15.

60. Cited in Elizabeth Drew (1994) *On the Edge: The Clinton Presidency*, New York: Simon and Schuster, p. 139.

61. Wayne Bert (1997) *The Reluctant Superpower: United States' Policy in Bosnia, 1991–1995*, Basingstoke, UK: Macmillan, p. 189. Clinton called for "collective action, including the use of force if necessary" to liberate the Serb concentration camps and insisted that the United States should play a major role in such activities. Paul Horvitz (1992) "On Bosnia, Clinton Agressive, Bush Wary", *International Herald Tribune*, 6 August.

62. John Shattuck (2003) *Freedom on Fire: Human Rights and America's Response*, Cambridge, Mass.: Harvard University Press, pp. 154–156.

63. For an excellent first hand account of the problems with implementing this mandate, see Bob Stewart (1993) *Broken Lives: A Personal View of the Bosnian Conflict*, London: Harper Collins.

64. See Mark Duffield (1999) "Lunching with Killers: Aid, Security and the Balkan Crisis", in Carl-Ulrik Schierup, ed., *Scramble for the Balkans: Nationalism, Globalism and the Political Economy of Reconstruction*, London: Macmillan, pp. 118–146.

65. It is worth noting that although the final Dayton accords rejected cantonization, it did by and large accept the proposition of ethnic partition within a multicultural state. For a study focusing on the partition debate, see Radha Kumar (1997) *Divide and Fall? Bosnia in the Annals of Partition*, London: Verso.

66. John J. Mearsheimer (1993) "Shrink Bosnia to Save It", *New York Times*, 31 March; and John J. Mearsheimer and Robert A. Pape (1993) "The Answer: A Partition Plan for Bosnia", *New Republic*, 14 June.

67. David Owen (1995) *Balkan Odyssey*, London: Indigo, p. 392.

68. Austria was a non-permanent member of the Security Council at this point.

69. Jan Willem Honig and Norbert Both (1996) *Srebrenica: Record of a War Crime*, London: Penguin, p. 100.

70. Ibid., pp. 104–105. It is important to note that these debates were running almost concurrently with the unfolding tragedy in Somalia. For a discussion of the practical concerns related to the Mogadishu line, see Michael Rose (1998) *Fighting for Peace: Lessons from Bosnia*, London: Warner Books, p. 186.

71. A strategy endorsed by Mark Kaldor (1999) *New and Old Wars: Organised Violence in a Global Era*, Stanford, Calif.: Stanford University Press.

72. Honig and Both, *Srebrenica*, pp. 113–117.

73. Brendan O'Shea (1998) *Crisis at Bihac: Bosnia's Bloody Battlefield*, London: Sutton; and Joe Sacco (2002) *Safe Area Gorazde: The War in Eastern Bosnia 1992–95*, London: Fantagraphics.

74. The force consisted of approximately 1,700 troops (1,200 from the United Kingdom and 500 from France), equipped with 50 armoured personnel carriers, supported by two divisions of Royal Artillery, with helicopter air cover provided by the United Kingdom's Army air corps.

75. Alex J. Bellamy et al., *Understanding Peacekeeping*, pp. 136–137.

76. Richard Holbrooke (1998) *To End a War*, New York: The Modern Library.

77. Colin McInnes has persuasively argued that this reluctance to place armed forces in harms way is one of the central features of modern Western warfare, particularly humanitarian interventions. Although this is an accurate depiction of the US position, I believe that it overlooks the extent to which the United Kingdom and France did place their forces in harms way in Bosnia and the fact that the UK government was prepared to do the same in Kosovo. Colin McInnes (2003) "A Different Kind of War? September 11 and the United States' Afghan War", *Review of International Studies* 29(2): 165–184.

78. Riley, *Deliberate Force*, p. 174.

79. Bert, *The Reluctant Superpower*, p. 221. Chirac likened the Major government's policy to Chamberlain's policy of appeasing Hitler. According to John Shattuck, a policy insider, in the immediate aftermath of Srebrenica, Chirac called Clinton and proposed using American helicopters and French troops to relieve the town and rescue the survivors. Shattuck, *Freedom on Fire*, p. 153.

80. The legal debate about whether the Serbian onslaught in Bosnia constituted genocide has been largely resolved by the International Criminal Tribunal for the former Yugoslavia. In its judgement on 2 August 2001 in the case of *Prosecutor vs. Krstic*, the judges closely evaluated the question of whether the Bosnian Serbs had committed genocide in detail. Its findings and reasoning (paras. 539–599) marks a significant and authoritative advance in the debate about the legal applicability of the concept of genocide. It found that "the intent to kill all the Bosnian Muslim men of military age in Srebrenica ... must be qualified as genocide" (para. 599), a view that was upheld on appeal. ICTY Judgment, *Prosecutor vs. Krstic*, case no. IT-98-33-T, 2 August 2001.

81. Dana H. Allin (2002) "NATO's Balkan Interventions", *Adelphi Papers* No. 347, pp. 35–46.

82. Vladimir Gligorov (2001) "Notes on the Stability Pact", in Thanos Veremis and Daniel Daianu, eds, *Balkan Reconstruction*, London: Frank Cass, pp. 12–19.

83. Most notably, see David Chandler (1999) *Bosnia: Faking Democracy After Dayton*, London: Pluto.
84. This transition is detailed by Dana Allin, who concluded that "NATO employed military force in the Balkans only when moral imperatives were reinforced by a compelling interest in European stability". Allin, "NATO's Balkan Interventions", p. 99.
85. The United Kingdom's transition in position is in many ways an exceptional case. Between 1991 and 1999 the United Kingdom moved further than any other state. In the early 1990s, it was the most conservative in its privileging of national interests over solidarity. In 1999, it was the most hawkish in insisting that solidarity and national interests were interdependent and in calling for the early use of force. The fact that the United Kingdom travelled so far in these eight years suggests that the effect of the factors outlined in this paragraph was enhanced by the change of government in 1997, which brought to power a party that, since 1991, had endorsed the German position more than the British position on the Balkans.
86. I am not suggesting here that the European security community did not have shared values prior to this. I am suggesting that the content of those values shifted from order-oriented values to an ethic of solidarity.
87. The prevalence of the idea of the Balkans as the "other" of Europe, an image that certainly guided orthodoxy until around 1997, is demonstrated by Maria Todorova (1997) *Imagining the Balkans*, New York: Oxford University Press.
88. These processes started during the Cold War and increased in intensity in the 1990s. As I argued earlier, the Balkan experience was one of the key drivers of that intensification. In terms of the expression of solidarity toward the victims of regional crises, this web became particularly apparent in 1998 in relation to Kosovo but I am not suggesting that it was "created" in 1998.
89. For a detailed account, see Alex J. Bellamy (2001) "Human Wrongs in Kosovo, 1974–99", in Ken Booth, ed., *The Kosovo Tragedy: The Human Rights Dimensions*, London: Frank Cass, pp. 120–121.
90. Klaus Kinkel, press briefing with the Secretary of State, Madeleine K. Albright, Bonn, 8 March 1998.
91. Comments taken from the Joint Press Conference by President Clinton and Italian Prime Minister Prodi, Washington, D.C., 6 May 1998.
92. Private e-mail to the author from a source in Whitehall.
93. "Britain Calls for Action over Kosovo", *New York Times*, 8 June 1998.
94. Richard Caplan (1999) "Christopher Hill's Roadshow", *World Today*, January; Janusz Bugajski (1998) "Close to the Edge in Kosovo", *Washington Quarterly* 21(3); and Michael Ignatieff (2000) *Virtual War: Kosovo and Beyond*, London: Chatto and Windus.
95. For a lengthier discussion of Yeltsin's peace initiative and the pivotal role it played in ultimately securing Russian acquiescence with NATO's intervention see Bellamy, *Kosovo and International Society*, pp. 87–93.
96. UN Security Council Resolution 1199, 23 September 1998.
97. The Russian position was expressed by their ambassador to the Security Council. See S/PV. 3930, 23 September 1998.
98. See UN Press Release, SG/SM/6583, 5 June 1998. Information about the Russian and Chinese position on the draft was given to the author by Russian sources in the United Kingdom.
99. I am grateful to Nick Wheeler for bringing this to my attention.
100. For instance, according to William Cohen, "NATO should not be required in each and every case to go to the United Nations for its authority. It should be in a position to make its own decisions.... NATO works by consensus. That means that all the coun-

tries ultimately agree or there is no action. But to subordinate NATO's concern for security ... to the United Nations is inadvisable and not necessary". "Kosovo at Heart of Debate over NATO Future", CNN, 14 June 1998, available from http://www.cnn.com/WORLD/europe/9806/14/kosovo.analysis/.

101. Cited in Tim Judah (2000) *Kosovo: War and Revenge*, London: Yale University Press, p. 182.
102. For a more detailed discussion of the mission, see Alex J. Bellamy and Stuart Griffin (2002) "OSCE Peacekeeping: Lessons from the Kosovo Verification Mission", *European Security* 11(1): pp. 1–26.
103. The Racak massacre is one of the cornerstones of the ICTY prosecutor's case against Milošević and the details of the massacre have been exhaustively outlined by the prosecutor. An exhaustive study was also carried out by independent pathologists led by Helena Ranta. An executive summary was e-mailed to the author by Helena Ranta on 17 August 2004. Helena Ranta, "Executive Summary on the Work of the Forensic in Kosovo in the Federal Republic of Yugoslavia, 1998–2000", declassified document in the possession of the author.
104. In its 2000 Cartagena declaration, the Non-Aligned Movement reaffirmed: "The distinction between humanitarian assistance and UN peace-keeping and peace enforcement operations ... In order to pursue the independence, neutrality and the impartiality of humanitarian action, such action must be kept distinct from, and independent of political and military action, in accordance with respective mandates and in accordance with international laws. We reject the so-called 'right' of humanitarian intervention, which has no legal basis in the UN Charter or in the general principles of international law". Final document of the XIII Ministerial Conference of the Non-Aligned Movement, Cartagena, 8–9 April 2000, pp. 41–42.

The fact that similar arguments were not made during Russia's bloody assault on Grozy, Chechnya, in 1999/2000, amplifies my point that the European solidarist community is a bounded community not a global one. The evidence from the Chechnya case suggests that the community does not extend to the Russian region.
105. "New Violence Hits Kosovo", *The Times*, 21 March 1999.
106. This argument has been expressed most persuasively by Nicholas J. Wheeler (2004) "The Kosovo Bombing Campaign", in Christian Reus-Smit, ed., *The Politics of International Law*, Cambridge: Cambridge University Press, esp. pp. 199–207 and 213–216; and Ignatieff, *Virtual War*, esp. pp. 162–164.
107. As we now know, this view later led to stark differences of opinion on targeting policy, with the United States and France as the main protagonists. As NATO Commander Wesley Clark put it, "What was becoming increasingly clear to me ... was just how difficult the process of target approval was going to become. Once we moved past the obvious air defence target set, every target ... was, in one way or another, likely to become controversial". Wesley K. Clark (2001) *Waging Modern War*, New York: Public Affairs, p. 201.
108. The purported "cloud cover" problem – the fact that NATO aircraft did not launch strikes on cloudy days – was more about Rules of Engagement than technical limitations. The accuracy of a PGM against a fixed target through cloud is not significantly diminished and on days where there is low cloud it is important to remember that a PGM dropped from less than 10,000 feet takes on all the characteristics of a "dumb" bomb. NATO's Rules of Engagement privileged visual contact with all but well-known fixed targets. This reduced the level of bombardment on cloudy days but did not halt it.
109. These points all from Benjamin S. Lambeth (2001) *NATO's Air War for Kosovo: A Strategic and Operational Assessment*, Santa Monica, Calif.: RAND, p. 140.

110. Louise Richardson (2001) "Britain's Role in the Kosovo Crisis", in Pierre Martin and Mark R. Brawley, eds, *Alliance Politics, Kosovo, and NATO's War: Allied Force or Forced Allies?* London: Palgrave, p. 151.
111. See http://www.iraqbodycount.com/.
112. For a more detailed discussion of conflict prevention efforts in Macedonia, see Bellamy, "The New Wolves at the Door".
113. For more detail on the security policy of the new Croatian government, see Alex J. Bellamy and Tim Edmunds (2005) "Civil-Military Relations in Croatia: Politicization and the Politics of Reform", *European Security* 14(1): 71–93.
114. Bellamy, *Kosovo and International Society*, pp. 16–65.
115. Buzan, *From International to World Society?*, esp. pp. 205–227; and Buzan, "International Political Economy and Globalization", esp. pp. 129–131.

9

Is East Timor an exception in the Southeast Asian landscape?

Geoffrey C. Gunn

After some two and a half years' stewardship under UN auspices, East Timor was admitted to the UN General Assembly as its 191st member on 20 May 2002. The international humanitarian rescue and rebuilding of East Timor is seen by some as a model for future interventions, just as the East Timor case also starkly illustrates the tension between geostrategic perspectives and the possibilities of an ethic of global solidarity.

In line with our sense of the emergence of solidarist communities conjoining states and citizens in developing a new politics of humanitarian intervention, we might recall the words of Secretary-General Kofi Annan in Dili on 19 March 2002. As he stated, "Without the support of the international solidarity movement East Timor would not have won its freedom". The tenor of these remarks was repeated the same evening by incoming President of the Democratic Republic of Timor-Leste, José "Xanana" Gusmão, and foreign minister José Ramos Horta, at the ceremony to transfer power from the UN to the independent state. Annan was undoubtedly reflecting upon the role of pro-democracy forces in Indonesia; the years of activity by East Timorese and their international supporters in pressing the legality of East Timor's claims; the media people who videotaped the 1991 Dili cemetery massacre; the heroic role of the East Timor student groups in calling for a referendum; the international observers and media who also became victims of violence surrounding the historic ballot of 30 August 1999; the United Nations Volunteers (UNVs) whom Annan also credited with the task of helping to

National interest and international solidarity: Particular and universal ethics in international life, Coicaud and Wheeler (eds),
United Nations University Press, 2008, ISBN 978-92-808-1147-6

rebuild the social fabric of the country; and modestly perhaps, his own role.[1]

Invaded and occupied by Indonesia in 1975/76, the former Portuguese colony was subject to three closely linked but sequential UN interventions, after 24 long years of virtual non-engagement. This chapter will subject each of these interventions to some scrutiny, as each sprung from different levels of international solidarity, in quite different geosecurity contexts. But it is also important to remember that the East Timor problem is a regrettable legacy of failure on the part of the international community to live up to obligations at a number of key moments over a number of decades. In setting the scene, I demonstrate how a culture of geostrategy derailed East Timor's quest for decolonization, making the point that not even the end of the Cold War brought redress to the suffering people of East Timor. I then turn to an examination of the first international intervention flowing from the 5 May 1999 Agreements in New York, which saw the arrival in East Timor of UNAMET (United Nations Assistance Mission for East Timor) leading up to the 30 August 1999 "consultation" on whether or not East Timorese would accept "special autonomy" status within the Republic of Indonesia. The second intervention followed quickly on a serious and deadly betrayal on the part of Indonesian forces charged with guaranteeing the security of the ballot. This took the form of a Security Council-mandated military/humanitarian operation (the International Force for East Timor, hereafter INTERFET). Unlike the case of Rwanda, East Timor demonstrated that in a clear-cut case of state-orchestrated crimes against humanity, opposition to an ethic of solidarity could be overcome even among concerned regional states. And unlike the case of Kosovo where the threat of a Russian and Chinese veto had frustrated effective UN action, East Timor demonstrated that once Indonesia had offered the "invitation" to intervene, albeit extracted through a mixture of financial and moral pressure, it was possible to forge unity among the five permanent members of the Council on the need for humanitarian action.

The chapter concludes with an analysis of the third intervention under the banner of UNTAET (United Nations Transitional Mission in East Timor), which saw a virtual UN/World Bank takeover of government in East Timor assisted by a UN blue beret force. Obviously, international interventions cost money and the mechanisms of international donor coordination come to the heart of such actions. Here I show that raising the funds and following through with commitments also conforms to our sense of solidarity at the intra-state level, in terms of responsibilities that states and peoples have in disaster situations (even if, as in Afghanistan, the scale of operations and local complexities sometimes proves too daunting to many potential donors).

In stressing the international modalities surrounding the three-stage UN intervention in East Timor; the 5 May Agreements in New York leading to the 30 August consultation; the INTERFET intervention; and the UNTAET takeover, I seek to examine how far East Timor suggests itself as a model for collective enforcement of global humanitarian norms in other parts of the world. As Nicholas Wheeler and Tim Dunne have argued, with specific reference to the responses of the international community to the violence in the wake of the UN-conducted ballot in East Timor in September 1999, "East Timor is a barometer for how far the normative structure of international society has been transformed".[2] Consonant with the overarching thesis of this book, I aim to show from the East Timor example that – provided certain other procedural steps have been met – a full-blown ethic of solidarity in the interest of humanitarian intervention can emerge, notwithstanding the most severe geopolitical constraints.

Dilemmas of international action: The East Timor problem

A major feature of the post-war history of East Timor was the Portuguese failure to decolonize its Asian colony and Western inaction in support of a NATO ally.[3] And when, in 1974, Portugal belatedly offered a timetable for decolonization, the sorry result was civil war and the annexation and occupation in 1975/76 of the territory by Indonesia as its 27th province. Condemned in successive Security Council and General Assembly resolutions,[4] regional states along with Australia, the United States and Japan nevertheless placed pragmatism over principle in dealing with Indonesia over East Timor. Alone among Western countries, Australia went as far as offering *de jure* recognition of Indonesia's occupation,[5] although, as now well documented, the United States played an active role in facilitating the Indonesian invasion.[6] As American foreign policy critic Noam Chomsky has written with some force, "East Timor was 'Indonesian territory' only in that leaders of the liberal democracies effectively authorized the conquest in violation of Security Council directives and a World Court ruling".[7]

In 1982, the UN Secretary-General Perez de Cuellar began informal consultations with the governments of Indonesia and Portugal aimed at improving the humanitarian situation and achieving a comprehensive solution to the problem. But East Timor remained a "closed province" and most humanitarian organizations were simply denied access. A geostrategic culture poisoned East Timor's chances of early independence. Not only were East Timor's political rights betrayed by the international community but the territory suffered a devastating 24-year occupation, which led the 1996 Nobel Peace Prize Committee to deplore the loss of up to one third of the population to death through violence, famine and sickness. But why the eventual exposure of military abuses and crimes against humanity in East Timor did not translate into Western support for East Timor's self-determination is a long story.[8]

During the Cold War years, East Timor actually became a paradigm of the conflict between human rights discourse and practice and traditional concepts of nationalism and sovereignty.[9] The Indonesian New Order government of President Suharto, along with the ASEAN countries, frequently invoked their shared principle of mutual non-interference in the internal affairs of member states to deflect charges of military excesses and violations of human rights. Specific to East Timor, the Philippines, Malaysia and Thailand periodically harassed, deported and imprisoned even academic supporters of East Timor self-determination, both testing (the Philippines) and exposing (Malaysia) the weakness of these countries' judicial systems.[10] But even when "corruption, collusion and nepotism" came under challenge in the wake of the Asian economic crisis of 1997, not the least by the IMF, the "Asian values" defence actually bought time for the Indonesian dictator. The bankruptcy of the ASEAN approach was actually unmasked by the East Timor debacle. At the time of the Indonesian military (TNI) rampage in September 1999, arguably, ASEAN reached its nadir. Then meeting in Bangkok, ASEAN produced no statement on the problem much less action.

Given this history of neglect or inaction, we may well ask, how and why did the international community re-engage in the East Timor question? While the rise of the pro-democracy movement inside Indonesia in tandem with economic crisis and financial collapse was undoubtedly critical, as discussed below, so was the re-engagement in the issue by the incoming UN Secretary-General Kofi Annan, who in February 1997 appointed a special representative, Pakistani diplomat Jamsheed Marker, to solicit opinion in the territory as to the prospects of a referendum, while placing Portugal and Indonesia on notice as to a negotiation of the problem under UN auspices.

Culture of international solidarity: The East Timor struggle for self-determination

The foregoing also raises the question as to how the East Timorese themselves responded to international norms surrounding the self-determination question, along with claims to international human rights law, and how their appeals resonated with a culture of international solidarity. In reality, the East Timor struggle was two-pronged. The first was the legal–diplomatic struggle that, after a two-decade hiatus, eventually prevailed. Portugal's failure to win a case against Australia in the July 1995 World Court ruling over the Timor Gap dispute actually brought down a ruling confirming East Timor's status as a non-self-governing territory: "East Timor remains a Non-Self-Governing Territory and its people has [sic] the right to self-determination."[11] The award of the 1996 Nobel Peace Prize to two sons of East Timor, José Ramos Horta and Bishop Carlos Ximenes Belo, was an important moral albeit not diplomatic victory for East Timor's independence struggle.

The second struggle, albeit taking various forms, is glossed by East Timorese as the "clandestine". Foremost was the pride of many East Timorese in their invincible guerrilla movement, Fretilin/Falintil, which survived in the mountains of East Timor from the moment of the Indonesian invasion down until the exodus of the last remaining occupation forces in September 1999. Long under the leadership of the charismatic José "Xanana" Gusmão, until he was captured in 1992, Falintil was the rump of the armed forces of the stillborn Democratic Republic of East Timor that effectively controlled the territory from October to December 1975.

As became known to the world following the massacre of student-mourners in November 1991 (the "Dili massacre"), the guerrillas were backed, or at least complemented, by the clandestine movement of young Indonesian-educated East Timorese activists not only in Dili but on the campuses of universities in Java and Bali, and, with the advent of the pro-democracy movement in Indonesia, on the streets in Jakarta. While victims of horrific violence and loss of life at the hands of the TNI, East Timorese were not passive actors in their struggle, although, singularly, they did not go down the route of bombs or terror.

International or global human solidarity constituted an additional tier of support, albeit closely networked in some instances with the clandestine movement. In part stemming from activities of East Timorese in the diaspora in Portugal, Macau, Australia and North America, in part drawing upon East Timor support groups around the world, the movement also took various forms and adopted various strategies. There is reason to believe, for example, that international lobbying was responsible for influencing the award of the 1996 Nobel Peace Prize. Similarly, the East Timor Action Network (ETAN) mounted a major and successful campaign to influence opinion makers within the US Congress. Just as the pro-democracy movement in Indonesia wielded the new electronic media to advantage, so the Internet emerged as a key tool in the hands of East Timor support groups around the world in coordinating strategy.[12]

Not surprisingly, the political conjuncture stemming from Indonesia's economic collapse, the resignation of President Suharto, the advent of the "reformist" government of B. J. Habibie and widespread public disdain across the archipelago for the military made its impact felt in distant Dili.[13] Adding fuel to the fire, as it were, was Habibie's June 1998 announcement that he was willing to grant East Timor "wide ranging autonomy" within the Republic of Indonesia.

In early July 1998 Dili began to replay the events in Jakarta during Suharto's last days, namely in the form of demonstrations between pro-independence groups and pro-integrationists. The pro-independence movement quickly moved from the streets to the main campus of East Timor University. According to *Time* magazine, it was in these circumstances that on 8 June Antero Benedito da Silva launched the Student Solidarity Council "with the goal of building a bridge between the two groups by limiting the debate to seeking a referendum on Timor's future".[14] According to da Silva, it was Jamsheed Marker who granted the Timorese students the mandate to set up regional dialogues to ascertain the aspirations of the people. This apparently occurred in a meeting between Marker and student representatives on the occasion of his visit to the town of Baucau on 6 June.[15]

It then seemed imperative that Indonesia, Portugal and the UN would somehow get the students' message before the window of opportunity in Jakarta arising from the political and economic crisis slammed shut. Importantly, the actions of the Student Solidarity Council demonstrated to those who were listening that, notwithstanding overwhelming pressures and constraints, sentiment inside East Timor was to reject talk of autonomy and to seek independence through a referendum.

In proposing autonomy for East Timor but linked to international recognition of the territory's incorporation into the Republic of Indonesia, Habibie offered what even Suharto had rejected. But what was the role of the UN in answering Jakarta in these circumstances? Even prior to the Indonesian economic crisis and the fall of Suharto, Annan had moved further and faster than his predecessor by stepping up the pace on tripartite talks between the Indonesian and Portuguese Foreign Ministers and his own office. Marker had likewise moved ahead to consult all interested parties to the question in Lisbon, in Jakarta, inside East Timor and with Gusmão, then incarcerated in prison in Jakarta.

Nevertheless, the logjam in negotiations only really broke with Marker taking up the Habibie autonomy proposal as one that could be parlayed without prejudice to the positions of Indonesia and Portugal. In fact, the central role of Gusmão, as the acknowledged leader of the umbrella resistance organization, the National Council of the Timorese Resistance (CNRT), and the key Timorese interlocutor with the UN, became apparent from May 1998 onwards. The future President of Timor-Leste was also sought out in prison by a string of international ambassadors and concerned officials.

Talks proceeded in New York in August 1998 between the Secretary-General and the foreign ministers of Portugal and Indonesia concerning Indonesia's proposals for special status based on wide ranging autonomy for East Timor. Both sides agreed to set aside the issue of the territory's final status, while the UN proposals called for the organization of free elections to form an autonomous government in Dili. Indonesia also pledged to decrease its military presence in Indonesia (never honoured) while expediting the release of East Timorese political prisoners, honoured in the main with the notable exception of Gusmão transferred to house arrest on 11 February 1999, making him more accessible to the UN process.

In October 1998, the UN submitted a proposal for self-administration of East Timor in discussion with East Timorese leaders. In November, Marker revealed that this plan was based on the Indonesian autonomy proposals with the caveat, "But we have decided to go further and prepare a more substantial document which could be accepted by both countries, whatever the final decision on the territory's status".[16] The sovereignty question remained fuzzy, just as Lisbon and CNRT leaders continued to view the UN plan as a transitional arrangement pending an internationally monitored popular vote or referendum. Indonesia, on its part, held to the view that the autonomy "concession" would be offered only if the international community accepted Indonesia's sovereignty over East Timor. Marker later stated in an interview published in the Portuguese daily *Diário de Notícias*,[17] ahead of the 19 December meeting in New York between the UN Secretary-General and the foreign ministers, that, while the Timorese leaders were not directly involved in these negotiations, he had sought to canvass the views of leaders by means of questionnaire.

Guided by Portugal, the EU countries pressured Indonesia to abide by its pledges and, on 12 December 1998, backed calls for a referendum and a permanent UN presence in East Timor. For some of the EU states this position meant drawing a line between arms sales to Jakarta and a moral position on East Timor. While official US policy on East Timor had always been guarded in the interests of preserving business and military ties with a "moderate" Muslim country, in a landmark decision on 28 October 1998, the US Congress voted to ban the use of US-supplied weapons in East Timor and, for the first time, to support self-determination for East Timor.

But, by late 1998, despite an apparent deadlock at the foreign ministers' meeting in December, there was a sense that Portugal and Indonesia had reached a rapprochement. In January 1999, following symbolic exchanges of officials, each country opened interest sections in each other's capitals, a decision made the previous August, although it would not be until March 1999 that a Portuguese envoy visited Dili, the first since the invasion of 1975.

Swinging its support in favour of a referendum in East Timor, the opposition Labor Party in Australia breached a long-standing consensus in Canberra on sensitivity to Jakarta. Rising to this challenge in late 1998, Australian Prime Minister John Howard wrote to Habibie that while he favoured the status quo he also wished a New Caledonia-style solution, namely a distant timetable for a popular consultation. Dramatically, on 27 January 1999, virtually answering back to Howard, the Indonesian president made it known that his government might be prepared to consider independence for East Timor, the so-called "second option". As it happened, this remark spooked the Australian defence establishment, prompting Canberra to anticipate chaos and general worst-case defence scenarios. Canberra began its military build-up in the Northern Territory.[18]

Further progress was made in New York on 8 February 1999 where Marker and the Directors-General of the Foreign Ministries of Indonesia and Portugal reached understanding on a number of issues on the autonomy proposal. Finally, on 11 March, agreement was reached on a direct ballot to consult the East Timor people as to whether they accepted or rejected the autonomy proposal. This initiative was strengthened in negotiations in New York on a popular consultation. At this venue Indonesian Foreign Minister Ali Alatas offered the now hollow assurances that the Indonesian military and police would be responsible for security during the consultation process.

But Alatas would also have been emboldened by arguments made by the Secretary of the Australian Department of Foreign Affairs, Dr. Ashton Calvert, in Washington in February in conversations with US State Department official Stanley Roth that deployment of an international peacekeeping force prior to the ballot would not be necessary.[19] Clearly, the Canberra government could have gone further in mobilizing international opinion at this juncture, especially when US officials such as Roth were apparently in favour of stronger security guarantees.[20] At that point there was already a crying need to rally humanitarian assistance for growing numbers of internally displaced persons (IDPs) inside East Timor. As the negotiations played out in New York, the TNI commenced with deadly efficiency to unfold its plan of subversion of the very agreement that Indonesian diplomats were then cementing. Notably, on 8 April, military-linked militias committed a deadly atrocity in the town of Liquica, a prelude to major crimes against humanity, gravely calling into question Indonesian assurances of fair play.[21] Official Australian descriptions of these militia actions as the work of "rogue" elements within the TNI were not only deceptive but also dishonest.

In a shift announced on 25 April 1999, the Australian government also offered to send troops to East Timor for peacekeeping duties but only after the vote on self-determination and as part of a wider UN involvement. Ireland, Canada, Brazil and New Zealand, with various conditions, all offered to supply peacekeepers to a UN mission in East Timor. Even so, the Canberra government did not depart from its fine-tuned position of recognition of Indonesian sovereignty over East Timor.[22]

This announcement was ahead of a "historic summit" between Prime Minister Howard and Australian military brass and their Indonesian counterparts, held on the Indonesian island of Bali on 27 April. Although this meeting was portrayed in Australian media as bravely standing up to Jakarta, in fact it was the occasion in which the regime let it be known to the world ahead of the 5 May agreement in New York that it would countenance only unarmed UN "police advisors" in East Timor. The world could not but notice that Howard fell short of obtaining crucial guarantees from Indonesian Defense Forces chief General Wiranto or Habibie as to a disarmament of the militia groups. While the Bali meeting was clearly a high-wire act of diplomacy, this writer believes that Australia could have done more without jeopardy to the ballot. There was also a moral dimension, especially as Australian intelligence was well apprised of the militia, their TNI links, their chain of command and likely post-ballot scenarios. As William Maley has persuasively argued, Australian negotiators "consciously decided" not to vigorously press Indonesia on a neutral force.[23]

Geopolitical culture triumphs over solidarity: The 5 May agreement and its derailing

Meeting on 5 May 1999 in New York at UN headquarters, the foreign ministers of Portugal (Jaime Gama) and Indonesia (Ali Alatas) signed a "historic" agreement on the question of East Timor, along with two protocols pertaining to the modalities of a popular ballot slated for August 1999 as to whether or not the East Timorese would accept or reject autonomy within the Republic of Indonesia and another pertaining to security arrangements during and after the vote. Annexed to the agreement was Indonesia's "Constitutional Framework for a Special Autonomy for East Timor", otherwise known as the autonomy package. This agreement, endorsed by the Security Council on 7 May [Resolution 1236 (1999)], was widely portrayed as the triumph of 16 years of

UN diplomacy on the question. But in a highly creative act of diplomacy, to say the least, Portugal was obliged to step back as power responsible for the decolonization of its former ward, with the UN tacitly recognizing Indonesia's 1976 sham incorporation of East Timor as its 27th province. In recognition of this move, Jakarta "invited" the UN to conduct a ballot on a "Constitutional Framework for a Special Autonomy for East Timor" within the Republic of Indonesia.

The 5 May document also offered that should the proposed constitutional framework for special autonomy be acceptable to the East Timorese people, then Portugal would initiate the procedures necessary to remove East Timor from the list of Non-Self-Governing Territories and Indonesia would make its constitutional adjustments in line with the autonomy package. On the contrary, should the autonomy proposals be rejected, then Indonesia would terminate its links with East Timor and the territory would revert to its pre–17 July 1976 status (a reference to the Indonesian parliament's incorporation of East Timor) and authority in East Timor would be transferred to the UN pending a transfer of power to an independent East Timor state. Such language masked the pact with Jakarta that required the new Indonesian parliament elected in June 1999 to actually vote to release East Timor from the illegal 1976 annexation.

The document was also historic in the sense of heralding the almost immediate arrival in East Timor of an advanced UN mission, prelude to the full-blown United Nations Assistance Mission in East Timor (UNAMET) budgeted at some US$53 million. This was formalized by the Security Council on 11 June. UNAMET would include up to 280 civilian police officers to "advise" the Indonesian police, as well as 50 military liaison officers to maintain contact with the Indonesian armed forces. Budgeted at US$52.5 million, UNAMET was strengthened with 4,000 international and local staff as well as 400 UNVs.

Obviously, as discussed below, the major flaw in the 5 May agreements was UN sanction of Indonesian military control over ballot security, especially as Western intelligence, along with critical media and the global solidarity movement, foresaw that the side widely predicted to lose the ballot was in advanced preparation to unleash a bloodbath upon the victors, namely a basically defenceless East Timorese population. To astute observers it was clear that Jakarta was playing a wily dual diplomatic and military strategy over East Timor, on the one hand snaring the UN into mounting a flawed ballot with Portugal's acquiescence, and, on the other hand, setting the trap masterminded by the TNI. The Foreign Ministry role was clearly to drag out the discussions to win time for a strategy aimed at routing out the pro-independence supporters, while the TNI through its agents provoked terror and coercion to prepare a favourable outcome. The strategy on the ground was to create the myth of equivalence between the militias and Falintil as the so-called "warring parties". Ipso facto, in this logic, disarmament of the factions would involve not only the militias but also Falintil. TNI, the invader and tormentor of the Timorese people were, accordingly, elevated to the status of keeper of security, while Falintil, the protector of the Timorese people over 24 years, became the equivalent of the murderous TNI-sponsored militias of three months. All these paramilitary death squads came into being or were reactivated after the announcement of a "second option". All were led by pro-integration figures, all gained support from the TNI. All advocated or used violence in recruitment and in waging war on the Timorese people. TNI, along with pro-integrationist forces, were widely observed at inauguration ceremonies.

As the security protocol of the May 5 agreement (Annex III) outlined, a prerequisite for the vote was a "secure environment devoid of violence or other forms of intimidation". Even so, the major contradiction in the agreement was, as feared by independence supporters, that "the maintenance of law and order rested with the appropriate Indonesian security authorities". Still, the "absolute neutrality" of the TNI was demanded. But this was a matter of faith, as Kofi Annan explained in a press conference.

But just who was in charge of decision-making in New York and why the evident failure of contingency planning? Geoffrey Robertson, a historian serving with UNAMET, explains that while the Department of Political Affairs (DPA) was the lead agency concerned with formulating policy on East Timor, the Department of Peacekeeping Operations (DPKO) was also closely involved. But at the political level, East Timor policy at the UN was also informed and guided by a group of five countries, the United States, United Kingdom, Australia, New Zealand and Japan, together known as the "core group".[24]

In any case, the security question was to be subject to a number of tests, the first accounting of which was registered by the advance mission in its report to the Secretary-General submitted to the Security Council on 22 May. In this, Kofi Annan declared, "I regret to inform the Security Council that credible reports continue to be received of political violence, including intimidations and killings, by armed militias against unarmed pro-independence civilians. There are indications that the militias, believed by many observers to be operating with the acquiescence of elements of the army, have not only in recent weeks begun to attack pro-independence groups, but are beginning to threaten moderate pro-integration supporters as well."[25] He also raised for the first time the possibility of assigning military liaison officers to assist UNAMET. More the pity, as this author witnessed of the mayhem in Dili in the days leading up to the consultation.

Robertson claims that it was immediately apparent to his colleagues in UNAMET's Political Affairs Office that the presence of Indonesian armed militia precluded the conditions for a free and fair ballot. Such advice no doubt translated into two minor postponements of the ballot but the order to proceed, he argues, also had merit, because the core group "feared that delay might lead to a decline in international support for the mission", especially within the Security Council.[26] While this view has merit, it should also not be forgotten that, by this stage, Indonesian actions in East Timor were under intense scrutiny by the international media along with a significant observer presence, meaning that more pressure could have been applied to achieve compliance.

As closely monitored by international media and other observers, this process culminated in the historic "popular consultation" of 30 August 1999, whereupon a majority of East Timorese rejected the autonomy option. Having invited the UNAMET presence, the Indonesian parliament was also required to concede the result of the 30 August ballot and thus "invite" the Security Council-mandated INTERFET. According to the UN formula, the Indonesian government was then obliged to "terminate its links with East Timor". This was subsequently achieved on 19 October 1999 through an act of the Indonesian parliament, allowing a "peaceful and orderly transfer of authority" to the UN.[27]

The Security Council, INTERFET and an ethics of solidarity

With the post-ballot violence leaving a majority of the population displaced, over a thousand dead, and 70 to 80 per cent of infrastructure destroyed, the stakes for international action on East Timor were critically raised by procedural issues surrounding the need to extract an "invitation" for intervention from Indonesia. Dilemmas over timing, mandate and regional leadership were also at issue, especially as a veto in the Security Council by states sensitive to interference in their own territorial or domestic issues was always a concern. The subject of a number of scholarly papers and books, Security Council decision-making on East Timor is especially instructive as a test case for international solidarity in circumstances where a government is not complying with international human rights standards and where the unilateral use of armed force to attain those ends is simply not in the cards.[28] Just as some have observed a normative shift in the Security Council toward overcoming resistance to interventions in cases of genocide or mass murder, I will argue here that consensus achieved in the Security Council on humanitarian intervention in East Timor has actually worked to strengthen the definition of international solidarism and perhaps even to enhance the status and efficacy of the Council itself.[29]

A basic chronicle and interpretation of the close-packed events of September 1999 relating to East Timor would be illustrative. On 3 September, the Secretary-General announced the result of the ballot (94,388, or 21.5 per cent, of registered voters voted in favour of the special autonomy proposal and 344,580, or 78.5 per cent, voted against). Responding to the killings of local UNAMET staff, UNHCR's Mary Robinson urged the Security Council to consider deployment of international or regional forces should the Indonesian authorities fail to fulfil security obligations. In fact they had failed.

The President of the Security Council, Peter van Walsum of the Netherlands, in communication with DPA and the "core group", informed the Secretary-General that the members of the Security Council had agreed to dispatch a mission to Jakarta to discuss with the Indonesian government "concrete steps to allow the peaceful implementation of the ballot result".[30] Headed by Namibian Ambassador Martin Andjaba, the mission was accompanied by ambassadors or ministers from Malaysia, the Netherlands, Slovenia and the United Kingdom. The terms of reference stated that Indonesia had "not been able to prevent an intensification of violence in the territory", including the "campaign of violence" against the UN mission in East Timor "under virtual state of siege". In this missive, the Security Council "urged" Indonesia's cooperation in "ensuring security", and in allowing UNAMET to implement its mandate (phase III of the transition process in bringing East Timor to independence).[31]

On 4 September, with the announcement of the results of the vote in Dili, the systematic campaign of arson, killings, mass deportations and looting accelerated. Most foreign nationals, including remaining UN staff, were confined to a beleaguered UNAMET compound, pending almost complete evacuation on 14 September. Through 5 and 6 September, the Secretary-General kept up the rhetoric of concern, revealing he had been in contact with the President of the United States, the Prime Ministers of Australia and New Zealand, and the President and Prime Minister of Portugal, among other leaders, as well as President Habibie of Indonesia.

Beginning its meetings in Jakarta on 8 September, the mission found President Habibie and Foreign Minister Ali Alatas reluctant to agree to any foreign military presence before the Indonesian Parliament had acted on the consultation result. Habibie also wished to declare martial law, possibly, as Ian Martin interprets, as a demonstration to Wiranto that, if things didn't improve on the ground, then international assistance could be agreed to.[32]

On 8 September the Security Council weighed in as did the Secretary-General, who revealed that in overnight talks he had made it clear to the Indonesian president that if the government of Indonesia were unable to maintain law and order, it would have to "invite and accept" international assistance to bring order to the territory. Indonesian "consent" was the operative word. As he revealed, "The governments that I have been in touch with, who are prepared to make troops available, would all want to see Indonesian consent". Clearly, as Wheeler and Dunne underline, unilateral action on the model of NATO's intervention in Kosovo was not acceptable and simply not part of the discourse.[33]

On 10 September, with a large-scale UNAMET evacuation, all but 100 UN staff remained in Dili. Genuine fears were expressed in solidarity circles that the UN was abandoning the people of East Timor to their fate. Again the Secretary-General reiterated his request for action on the part of the government of Indonesia "for what could amount, according to reports reaching us, to crimes against humanity".

On 11 September, the UN delegation (in the company of General Wiranto, the Indonesian Defence Minister) visited Dili via Jakarta for an inspection, and duly registered their concerns at the destruction and human misery as well as the urgent necessity for humanitarian intervention.[34] On that day the Security Council met in formal session to consider the situation in East Timor. Martin describes in detail the atmosphere of the Security Council session with orations by more than 50 delegations. Again, China and Russia stressed the need for Indonesian consent to intervention, but it was evident from the Council's deliberations that Indonesia's support among Asian nations was clearly waning.[35]

It is instructive to examine the role of other concerned actors. As Don Greenless and Robert Garran confirm, with Kosovo in mind the United States was reluctant to splash out in a zone of no strategic interest at least alongside the weight of a democratic ally in Indonesia.[36] Washington dithered at least until 6 September, the day that the Bishop's Dili residence was burnt amidst a small orgy of killing. Australian Prime Minister Howard was disappointed that US President Clinton declined an invitation to insert US combat troops. But Washington also intervened in the form of a strong demarche delivered on 8 September by the commander-in-chief of the US forces in the Pacific, Admiral Dennis Blair, directly to Wiranto. Portugal, where sentiments ran even higher than in Australia, rescinded landing rights for US military aircraft in the Azores and threatened to pull its troops out of Kosovo.[37]

On 7 September the IMF also added its voice of concern, later postponing a mission scheduled for mid-September. World Bank President

James Wolfensohn was more explicit, warning Habibie in a letter that "for the international financial community to be able to continue its full support, it is critical that you act swiftly to restore order and that your government carry through on its public commitment to honor the referendum outcome". Martin declares the Bank's intervention as "perhaps its strongest-ever public statement regarding a political situation".[38] On 9 September, Clinton also threatened to stop crucial IMF and World Bank loans to Indonesia, a linkage I take up below.[39] It is undoubtedly true, as Huntley and Hayes point out, that Indonesia's eventual acceptance of an international force reflected its "continuing sensitivity to US pressure".[40]

It was all the more fortuitous that, concurrent with the events being played out in East Timor on 9 September, the annual summit of Asia Pacific Economic Cooperation (APEC) was being hosted in Auckland, New Zealand, a rare assembly of leaders of the Pacific rim countries. It is understood that the President of South Korea, Kim Dae-jung, an early convert, along with Japanese Premier Kazuo Obuchi and President Clinton, were brought alongside on the question of some form of international humanitarian rescue of East Timor involving a peacekeeping force.[41] But just prior to departing Washington for Auckland, Clinton told a press conference that Indonesia "must invite" the international community to assist in restoring security. Prime Minister Howard had also worked the phone with Habibie, raising the prospect of an Australian contribution to an international force. But Australia well knew that that force would require substantial US backing, as well as an "invitation" from Jakarta.[42] In any case, Australian forces were on high alert.

The role of China in joining the Security Council consensus bears some discussion. It is instructive here to recall an expressed Australian view in the run-up to the UNAMET mission, that China would undoubtedly veto moves to insert armed civilian police in East Timor.[43] In the event, China joined the consensus on INTERFET and went on to become a first-time participant in a UN civilian police mission, and even emerged as a credible donor in supporting post-conflict reconstruction. For China, East Timor was not another Kosovo; the US was not in the driving seat; Russia did not veto; and crucially, it did not involve such an infraction of the sovereignty principle because Indonesia had – albeit reluctantly – consented to an international presence. For China, at least, joining the UN mission in East Timor represented a new level of international solidarity on humanitarian interventions.

Just as the diplomats and military planners drove decision-making on East Timor in the crucial days of the crisis, so as Martin (ex-Amnesty) argues, the global human solidarity movement, including church and media circles, also went into overdrive.[44] While major international news media had long neglected East Timor[45] or had been fobbed off by editors,[46] East Timor became *the* major international media story at this juncture.[47] Flowing on from the militia attacks on media people and observers in Dili during the ballot, media coverage of the destruction in Dili, refugee arrivals in Darwin and even satellite images of a burning country sent a vivid image to a world which pledged no more Rwandas. As a media-driven issue especially in Australia, but also in the United States, Japan and Europe, it would have been unconscionable for the world community to back away at this stage. In any case, East Timor had become mainstreamed, although hardly in the way that East Timorese victims and pro-referendum supporters had wished. The major exception to the "mainstreaming" of the East Timor humanitarian cause of course arose from diehard nationalist elements inside Indonesia and their allies in certain ASEAN capitals who, as discussed below, literally refused to blink.

Given this combination of pressures operating at both state and non-state levels, President Habibie issued a statement on 12 September that his government would unconditionally accept international assistance to restore peace and security in East Timor. In Geneva, Sadako Ogata, UN High Commissioner for Refugees, allowed that Indonesia's statement would pave the way for a "feasible humanitarian operation". Similarly, back in New York, the UN delegation that had earlier visited Dili argued that the humanitarian crisis be given the topmost priority. On 15 September 1999, acting under Chapter VII of the UN Charter, the Council adopted resolution 1264 (1999) "to take all necessary measures" to restore peace and security in East Timor. Expressing deep concern over continuing violence and large-scale displacements and relocation of East Timorese civilians, attacks on UNAMET staff, a worsening humanitarian situation deeply affecting vulnerable groups and widespread and flagrant abuse of human rights, the resolution also determined that the present situation in East Timor was a threat to "peace and security". Importantly, Resolution 1264 authorized the establishment of a multinational force under a unified command structure, not only to restore peace and security, but also to facilitate humanitarian assistance. This would be dubbed INTERFET. Habibie's invitation or statement of readiness to accept an international peacekeeping force was reiterated but certain obligations were also imposed upon Indonesia, namely to ensure the safe guarantee of refugees to East Timor and to guarantee security in an interim phase. The modalities of Indonesian withdrawal were not spelled out.[48]

Approved by the Security Council to restore peace and security and support the beleaguered UNAMET mission, INTERFET was not ostensibly a UN blue beret force. Rather, INTERFET constituted a "coalition of the willing" with UN approval. Unlike UN peacekeepers, INTERFET did not have to wait to be fired upon to return fire but were granted robust terms of engagement, necessary in the circumstances.[49] Reflecting the importance and readiness of Australian forces positioned in nearby Darwin, an Australian was appointed commander of INTERFET. Notably, as mentioned below, a Thai national was appointed deputy force commander. The first INTERFET deployment commenced on 20 September. By 29 September, as revealed by the first INTERFET report to the Security Council, the mission had deployed 3,700 personnel in East Timor drawn from Australia, Brazil, Canada, France, Italy, Malaysia, New Zealand, Norway, the Philippines, the Republic of Korea, Singapore, Thailand, the United States and the United Kingdom. As noted in this report, Australia was keen to expand regional participation.[50] At full strength, INTERFET forces totalled 8,000, of which Australia committed over half.

Commencing on 17 September, even prior to deployment, INTERFET working with the World Food Programme (WFP) initiated airdrops of food and other relief goods in strategic locations while the International Committee of the Red Cross (ICRC) landed emergency supplies in Dili harbour. The limits of INTERFET in policing and detention were also highlighted in the report, foreshadowing future needs in civil administration in East Timor such as would subsequently be addressed with the formation of the United Nations Transitional Administration of East Timor (UNTAET).[51]

Early Thai and Philippine participation in INTERFET was seen by Australia as politically important if it was going to allay hard-line ASEAN concerns of Western interference. Although not a member of the core group, South Korea was an early supporter of intervention and a significant contributor to the military mission. INTERFET was funded by a trust fund agreed upon on 29 September with contributions from Portugal, Switzerland and, significantly, US$100 million contribution from Japan. Domestic political pressure had confined Japanese "Self Defense Force" aircraft to flying relief missions to the non-combat zone of west Timor.

As the first INTERFET report to the Security Council makes clear, even prior to INTERFET deployment, the Commander and Deputy Commander visited Dili to discuss the modus operandi of deployment with the Indonesian military. Undoubtedly, this basis of cooperation was essential to the absence of major clashes and the eventual success of the mission. But such consultations were also coordinated with Indonesian officials in New York and Jakarta. This was termed Phase I, or establishing the preconditions of deployment. Phase II, or insertion, began, as mentioned, on 20 September. Phase III was restoration of peace and security, and phase IV was eventual transfer to a UN peacekeeping mission.[52]

Financing UNTAET: The UN/World Bank-coordinated donor approach to intervention and reconstruction

The UN intervention in East Timor was not only a military exercise but, building upon the Cambodia[53] and Kosovo[54] experiences, also combined humanitarian and state-building components. In the case of East Timor, the UN was called upon to substitute itself for the government, with a view to preparing East Timor for independence. Unlike in Cambodia, where a functioning government was in place, in East Timor the first-arriving international forces and civilians witnessed a smoking ruin. Just as basic services had to be restored often from scratch, so former civil servants had to be identified and screened prior to their induction in the parallel administration that UNTAET established. Obviously, numerous elements and agencies were involved in this exercise, whether delivering basic humanitarian assistance, restoring peace and order, rebuilding infrastructure, or rebuilding capacity. More than is often conceded, the key decisions made in the early planning period set the parameters under which the civil side of UNTAET would operate, although there was much innovation and even experimentation in the way that many World Bank-funded projects were implemented.

Originally established by Resolution 1272 (1999) of 25 October, the Security Council endowed UNTAET "with overall responsibility for the administration of East Timor empowered to exercise all legislative and executive authority including the administration of justice". UNTAET operated according to a strict mandate, but with no specific timetable:

2 (a) To provide security and maintain law and order throughout the territory of East Timor;
  (b) To establish an effective administration;
  (c) To assist in the development of civil and social services;
  (d) To ensure the coordination and delivery of humanitarian assistance; rehabilitation and development assistance;
  (e) To support capacity-building for self-government;
  (f) To assist in the conditions for sustainable development.

Overlapping with INTERFET, UNTAET commenced to become fully operational in East Timor only in January/February 2000. Military command was officially transferred from INTERFET to UNTAET on 23

February. Operationally, the staff of the former UNAMET mission were incorporated into UNTAET.

Clearly the mechanisms of international donor coordination come to the heart of such financial interventions as those required to support UNTAET. Raising the funds, sustaining donor interest, and following through also conforms to our sense of solidarity at the intra-state level, in terms of responsibilities that states and peoples have in disaster situations. In fact it might be said (and Japan's famous check book diplomacy offers a prime example here), that, next to sending peacekeepers, putting up the money is the highest level of solidarism.

Just as financing of post-conflict peacekeeping situations has gained some attention within UN circles,[55] this section looks at the "coordinated" donor approach to early intervention in East Timor. As explained, drawing upon broad institutional experience, the Security Council, DPKO, World Bank, IMF, Asian Development Bank (ADB), UNDP, the Office for the Coordination of Humanitarian Affairs (OCHA) and UNOPS, along with the key donors, all became engaged in the East Timor question at an early date once the "coalition of the willing" had kicked into action.

As with the earlier Cambodia intervention and the subsequent Afghanistan intervention, a series of high-profile donor's conferences were organized to coordinate international approaches to East Timor. All the key "players" were involved in these conferences, including members of CNRT and concerned non-governmental organizations (NGOs). On 17 December at an international donor conference hosted by the government of Japan in Tokyo, over US$500 million was pledged to rebuild East Timor, with US$156 million allocated to a Consolidated Inter-Agency Appeal (CAP) programme. Japan alone extended around US$100 million for a three-year period, earmarked for rehabilitation and development. Japan would emerge as East Timor's primary donor, ahead of Australia and Portugal, although with significant contributions from the European Union, the United States and other bilateral donors. Other donor conferences followed. Earlier at the December 1999 Tokyo Donor's meeting, the World Bank's Board of Governors established a Trust Fund for East Timor.

During the transitional period, funding for UNTAET and the embryonic national government was drawn from a Consolidated Fund using donor contributions and government revenue. Just as UNTAET made humanitarian recovery, security and the rebuilding of institutions its priority, so macroeconomic planning and management was left in the hands of the World Bank. Notably, it was an IMF initiative that led to the choice of the US dollar as East Timor's official currency.

The first major initiative by the World Bank to bring the East Timorese leaders alongside was on 29 September 1999, when Gusmão, recently released from prison, and José Ramos Horta met in Washington
with the World Bank President, along with a group of potential institutional and international donors.[56] At this meeting, a Joint Assessment
Mission was established to assess current needs in East Timor and to
evaluate and propose priorities for meeting reconstruction needs. As proposed, the International Development Association-led mission identified
recurrent budget needs and priority activities in each key sector. Coordinated by the World Bank and working in liaison with DPKO, UNAMET
and other UN agencies, the Bank argued in favour of a rapid deployment
in the light of "lessons of other post-conflict countries where lack of coordination between relief and development planning has delayed the
transition from emergency relief to more sustainable development".[57]
Arriving in October/November 1999, the Mission of 40, half of whom
were Timorese, targeted two broad areas, agricultural recovery and state
capacity.[58] The ADB were delegated responsibility as lead agency for infrastructure development.

A hallmark of the East Timor model was undoubtedly the success with
which the mission responded efficiently to the humanitarian crisis. Targeting some 100,000 IDPs, the relief effort was coordinated by OCHA,
the lead UN agency responsible for handling humanitarian emergencies.
Financing for refugees was raised by the CAP, while administering
agencies included UNICEF, UNDP, UNHCR, WFP, WHO, the International Organization for Migration, and the ICRC.[59]

Refugee repatriation from West Timor was not only a major humanitarian and logistical problem for UNHCR and other agencies, but came
to the heart of political relations between UNTAET and Indonesia, especially as highlighted by the September 2001 slaying of three UN workers
in West Timor. In a second rebuke to the Indonesian authorities, the
World Bank president joined a chorus of international voices (the Security Council included), calling for concerted action to neutralize militia
activities.[60] Otherwise much controversy surrounded UNTAET's efforts
to rebuild the justice system and to bring those guilty to justice. While in-
dictments have been made against militia suspects, to date no convictions
have been brought against the TNI. Regrettably, Indonesia has disal-
lowed extradition of suspects. It is also regrettable that, in giving Indonesia's own judicial processes the benefit of the doubt, the UN has held
back from convening an international tribunal along, say, the Rwanda
model.[61]

In a second phase, more or less coinciding with the arrival in the
territory on 17 November 1999 of the Special Representative of the
Secretary-General and Transitional Administrator, Brazilian diplomat

Sergio Vieira de Mello, and his team, the focus switched to "capacity building" of what would eventually become the parallel East Timor Transitional Administration looking ahead to the day when UNTAET would be truly redundant. From an early date de Mello entered into consultations with East Timorese leaders and CNRT who had quickly moved in to fill an administrative vacuum especially at the district level. On 2 December the SRGC created a National Consultative Council, a 15-member joint UNTAET–East Timorese body in the endeavour to better facilitate coordination of decision-making and to allay East Timorese concerns of UN "colonization".

In part responding to local political pressure, but also with the end of mission in mind, Timorization of administrative functions became accelerated by mid-2001. Especially following the Consultative Assembly elections of 30 August, East Timorese progressively occupied senior administrative positions. By the end of 2001, the civilian component of UNTAET had been rapidly downsized. On 20 May 2002, a successor mission, UN Mission of Support in East Timor (UNMISET), was installed with a vastly reduced civilian and military component in support of the newly independent state.

Conclusion

Looking back on the "culture of solidarity" among nations that gelled in the critical weeks of early September 1999, the then-President of the Security Council, Peter van Walsum, described the INTERFET intervention in East Timor as a "miracle" in the sense that Indonesia capitulated to international opinion. He was also referring to the fact that two permanent members of the Security Council, Russia and China, made it very clear that "they would not consider giving the green light for any intervention unless it was in agreement with the Indonesian government". In other words, with the recent Kosovo experience in mind, Russia and China backed international intervention in East Timor but not without Security Council backing (thus demonstrating the limits of the norm of solidarist intervention developed in the 1990s). But van Walsum also suggested that in the light of what actually happened in Kosovo, "Humanitarian intervention without a Security Council mandate was not unthinkable". He believes that Indonesia must also have weighed that possibility. In other words, Indonesia relented for fear that the international community might intervene regardless of Security Council approval.[62]

As examined above and as corroborated by Mark Quarterman in a careful study on UN leverage in East Timor, while other actors in the system played crucial roles, the presence of the UN mission in East Timor, along with the Secretary-General, the Security Council and the Secretariat were central as the focal points of activity in seeking compliance on the part of Indonesia.[63] But in tracing the emergence of a new ethic of solidarity around some form of humanitarian intervention, we have not ignored the geopolitical interest of states, notably Australia with its special regional interests, but also the US along with China and the ASEAN countries. But we have also been at pains to emphasize the role of the international media and a range of focus and solidarity groups unrelenting in their exposure of Indonesian complicity in breaches of global humanitarian norms. Exceptionally, East Timorese leaders, including the consummate diplomat José Ramos Horta were also in the forefront of international advocacy actions.

The response to East Timor by the international donor community, the response by civil society groups (NGOs and UNVs) and even the response by nations dispatching civilian police and peacekeepers, is further evidence of an ethic of solidarity at the intra-state level. Returning to the theme of "normative shift", as outlined by Wheeler and Dunne,[64] significant participation in UNTAET and policing roles by Asia, including ASEAN nations, reveals how ASEAN (and China) could begin to overcome a prevailing logic/culture of non-intervention by accepting the humanitarian imperative to act, even if considerable reservations remained.[65]

The tragedy of the East Timor case is that after human rights concerns had finally propelled it onto the world's agenda in the late 1990s, more was not done to protect humanitarian values during the ballot process. I have also been critical that the Canberra government did not dissent from the mistaken view that security for the ballot should be in the hands of the perpetrators of the violence, the TNI, or that a more robust UN security detail be involved in line with worst case scenarios such as those being painted by media and NGO groups. After all, it was Australia that possessed key intelligence on the activities of the TNI and militias, intelligence that should have been shared with the UN Secretariat and other key actors. But in making the decision to dispatch only unarmed civilian police monitors into a situation of rapidly deteriorating law and order, the UN also erred by not building a strong humanitarian component into the electoral mission. Such delay inevitably cost lives in the crucial weeks of September 1999. However, the UN also redeemed itself in the following weeks with the expeditious arrival of INTERFET along with concerned UN relief agencies. A major humanitarian disaster was averted while military and militia threats were quickly neutralized.

Notwithstanding operational questions and problems in implementation, the World Bank "coordinated donor approach" merits attention in situations of transition from conflict to stability and where rapid assessments are both necessitated and justified. Otherwise, I would argue, the role of multilateral funding in the coordination and supervision of post-conflict situations has been underwritten in the literature, just as the approach appears to be gaining new ground as the tested operational model for complex interventions requiring the broadest possible international donor support.

The outcome in East Timor has not been lost upon the peoples of the Indonesian provinces of Aceh, Papua and the Malukus, nevertheless, no other regional Southeast Asian movement for ethnic autonomy or secession ever gained the degree of support or international solidarity as East Timor. Neither is the UN re-engaging or endorsing intervention in these "internal" disputes, although humanitarian intervention has been raised in the case of the Malukus. Even so, we cannot preclude deeper international mediation of the Aceh dispute and the US "war against terror" has already seen direct US military intervention in the Mindanao area of the Philippines.

We might conclude that the UN-sanctioned INTERFET intervention in East Timor and post-conflict rehabilitation under World Bank/UNTAET has been an exception within the region, just as UNTAET represented a new stage in UN state-building.[66] But, in stressing the international modalities surrounding the three-stage UN intervention in East Timor; the 5 May agreements in New York leading to the 30 August consultation; the INTERFET intervention; and the UNTAET takeover, the East Timor experience raises itself as a model for collective enforcement in other parts of the world. In the language of solidarism, we could argue that the East Timor experience has gone far in reinforcing acceptance of the ethic of solidarity in the interests of humanitarian intervention, notwithstanding the most severe geopolitical constraints.

Notes

1. The occasion was the opening of a "peace park" in Dili dedicated to the volunteer spirit of UNVs. Annan's speech (not circulated) was heard by the author.
2. Nicholas J. Wheeler and Tim Dunne (2001) "East Timor and the New Humanitarian Interventionism", *International Affairs* 77(4): 806.
3. See Geoffrey C. Gunn (2000) *New World Hegemony in the Malay World*, Trenton, N.J.: Red Sea Press, pp. 165–213 on the "Azores connection".
4. See Geoffrey C. Gunn (1997) *East Timor and the United Nations: The Case for Intervention*, Trenton, N.J.: Red Sea Press, for a compilation of the relevant UN resolutions.
5. Major political recriminations emerged in the wake of Australia's intervention in East Timor, recalling the past 24 years of policies of appeasement of Jakarta. The Australian government answered back in part with the following two useful, but selective, sets of documents.

a. Commonwealth of Australia, Department of Foreign Affairs and Trade: Wendy Way, ed. (2000) *Documents on Australian Foreign Policy: Australia and the Indonesian Incorporation of Portuguese Timor, 1974–1976*, Melbourne: Melbourne University Press.

b. Commonwealth of Australia: Department of Foreign Affairs and Trade (2001) *East Timor in Transition 1998–2000: An Australian Policy Challenge*, Canberra: Department of Foreign Affairs and Trade.

6. The specific role of US President Ford and Secretary of State Henry Kissinger in offering the green light for invasion of East Timor was long surmised and progressively revealed by declassified or leaked US documents, eventually reaching an Indonesian audience. For example, see Jim Wolf (2001) "U.S. Okayed E. Timor Invasion in '75: Document", Reuters, *Jakarta Post*, 8 December, p. 3.

7. Noam Chomsky (2000) *A New Generation Draws the Line: Kosovo, East Timor and the Standards of the West*, London: Verso.

8. Noam Chomsky (2979) *The Washington Connection and Third World Fascism: The Political Economy of Human Rights*, vol. 1, Boston: South End Press; Geoffrey C. Gunn with Jefferson Lee (1994) *A Critical View of Western Journalism and Scholarship on East Timor*, Manila: Journal of Contemporary Asia Press; and Sonny Ibaraj (1995) *East Timor: Blood and Tears in ASEAN*, Chiang Mai, Thailand: Silkworm Books.

9. Paula Escarameia (1995) *Formation of Concepts in International Law: Subsumption under Self-Determination in the Case of East Timor*, Lisbon: Fundação Oriente.

10. Ibaraj, *East Timor*. Unlike, say, the European Union, ASEAN hosts no Strasbourg or European Court of Human Rights.

11. Gunn, *East Timor and the United Nations*, p. 217.

12. See Charles Scheiner (2001) "Grassroots in the Field: Observing the East Timor Consultation", in Richard Tanter, Mark Selden and Stephen R. Shalom, eds, *Bitter Flowers, Sweet Flowers: East Timor, Indonesia, and the World Community*, Lanham, Md.: Rowman & Littlefield, pp. 109–124.

13. Gunn, *New World Hegemony*. Analysis of student solidarity movement is adapted from pp. 253–265 (chapter 11).

14. Although Jakarta-based Western embassies were well apprised of these events, news media were shy. One exception was *Time* magazine (13 July 1998). Another was freelancer Stephanie Coop (1998) "Hopes for Referendum: Defying Guns and Goons, East Timorese Speak Out", *Japan Times*, 23 October. *Far Eastern Economic Review* declined to publish the author's own eyewitness account. For a retrospective view, see John Martinkus (2001) *A Dirty Little War*, Sydney: Random House. Also see Dan Nicholson (2001) "Lorikeet Warriors: East Timorese New Generation Nationalist Resistance, 1989–1999", BA (honours) dissertation, Department of History, University of Melbourne, October, for a wide-ranging study of East Timorese student and youth movements.

15. *Suara Timor Timur* (Dili), 15 August 1998, cited in Gunn, *New World Hegemony*, p. 289.

16. *Agence France Press*, 12 November 1999, cited in Gunn, *New World Hegemony*, p. 255.

17. C. Albino and L. Ferreira (1998) "Just a Step Forward: East Timor Jamsheed Marker", *Diário de Notícias*, 4 December, cited in Gunn, *New World Hegemony*, p. 257.

18. James Cotton (1999) "'Peacekeeping' in East Timor: An Australian Policy Departure", *Australian Journal of International Affairs* 53(3): 237–246.

19. See Wheeler and Dunne, "East Timor and the New Humanitarian Interventionism", p. 813. They cite Desmond Ball (2001) "Silent Witness: Australian Intelligence and East Timor", *Pacific Review* 14(1): 47.

Mine is not a retrospective view. Disturbed at the time by the naivety of the trust-in-diplomacy position I was moved to write the following lines to Calvert on 26 February.

There was no response. "I am heartened to learn of your recent conversations with UN Secretary-General Kofi Annan reflecting the seriousness of the situation, just as I am gratified that the Secretary-General has called for restraint on all sides. Nevertheless East Timor is not a level playing field and I sincerely believe that before the situation spirals out of hand, Jakarta's timetable must be interrupted in the sense of placing international monitors in situ. This is not exactly a Rwanda situation, but a failure on the part of the international community to act now could have irreversible consequences."

20. William Maley (2000) "The UN and East Timor", *Pacifica Review* 12(1): 70.

21. Lansell Taudevin (1999) *East Timor: Too Little Too Late*, Sydney: Duffy & Snellgrove. Taudevin, an Australian aid worker in East Timor, reveals that he witnessed the clandestine militia build-up from early 1998 and, until "pulled out" in mid-1998, kept up a stream of reports to his Australian employers in the Jakarta Embassy. Failure on the part of the government of Australia to share its intelligence assets obviously created severe and controversial distortions, not only to public perceptions of events unfolding in East Timor but to the key international actors (Washington) and those planning contingency scenarios (no doubt including the UN Department of Peacekeeping Operations).

22. Australia had long distinguished itself in its *de jure* recognition of East Timor as part of the Republic of Indonesia. Gunn with Lee, *A Critical View*; James Cotton (2001) " 'Part of the Indonesian World': Lessons in East Timor Policy-Making, 1974–76", *Australian Journal of International Affairs* 55(1): 119.

23. William Maley, "The UN and East Timor", p. 70.

24. Geoffrey Robertson (2001) "With UNAMET in East Timor: An Historian's Personal View", in Richard Tanter, Mark Seldon and Stephen R. Shalom, eds, *Bitter Flowers, Sweet Flowers: East Timor, Indonesia and the World Community*, Lanham, Md.: Rowman & Littlefield, pp. 5–72.

25. S/1999/599, 22 May 1999; and see Gunn, *New World Hegemony*, pp. 276–277.

26. Robertson, "With UNAMET in East Timor".

27. See Ian Martin (2001) *Self-Determination in East Timor: The United Nations, the Ballot, and International Intervention*, International Peace Academy Occasional Paper Series, London: Lynne Rienner, for the best retrospective analysis of UNAMET by its former head.

28. For example, see James Cotton, " 'Peacekeeping' in East Timor"; Leonard C. Sebastian and Anthony L. Smith (2000) "The East Timor Crisis: A Test Case for Humanitarian Intervention", in *Southeast Asian Affairs 2000*, Singapore: Institute of Southeast Asian Studies, pp. 64–85; Wheeler & Dunne, "East Timor and the New Humanitarian Interventionism"; Alvaro Vasconcelos (2000) "L'intervention au Timor et le multilatéralisme impossible", *Politique Etrangère* No. 65, Paris, April; and books: William Shawcross (2000) *Deliver Us from Evil: Warlords and Peacekeepers in a World of Endless Conflict*, London: Bloomsbury; Don Greenless and Robert Garran (2002) *Deliverance: The Inside Story of East Timor's Fight for Freedom*, Sydney: Allen & Unwin.

29. Cf. Sebastian and Smith, "The East Timor Crisis", pp. 65–66.

30. "Letter dated 5 September 1999 from the President of the Security Council Addressed to the Secretary-General", S/1999/946, 6 September 1999.

31. UN Security Council documents S/1999/944, 3 September 1999; S/1999/946, 6 September 1999; and S/1999/972, 14 September 1999.

32. Martin, *Self-Determination in East Timor*, p. 106.

33. Wheeler and Dunne, "East Timor and the New Humanitarian Interventionism", p. 822. And see Greenless and Garran, *Deliverance*, pp. 234–235, on van Walsum's difficulty in getting the Indonesian government to accede in what was clearly a step toward inserting foreign troops into East Timor. Tracing Annan's telephone log for 5 September, these

authors reveal the Secretary-General's behind-the-scenes activism (and concern to rescue the UN's stillborn child).

34. This was UN Security Council document S/1999/976, 14 September 1999.
35. Martin, *Self-Determination in East Timor*, p. 112.
36. Greenless and Garran, *Deliverance*, pp. 240–243. While a key source on the diplomacy between the key nations in the run-up to the INTERFET intervention, Greenless and Garran allow no special agency to the East Timorese and, contra Martin, *Self-Determination in East Timor*, are dismissive of the global human solidarity movement.
37. Greenless and Garran, *Deliverance*, pp. 243–246.
38. Martin, *Self-Determination in East Timor*, p. 107; Greenless and Garran, *Deliverance*, pp. 244–245.
39. Cf. Wheeler and Dunne, "East Timor and the New Humanitarian Interventionism", p. 819.
40. Wade Huntley and Peter Hayes (2001) "East Timor and Asian Security", in Richard Tanter, Mark Selden and Stephen R. Shalom, eds, *Bitter Flowers, Sweet Flowers: East Timor, Indonesia, and the World Community*, Lanham, Md.: Rowman & Littlefield, pp. 173–185.
41. Cf. Martin, *Self-Determination in East Timor*, pp. 106–107.
42. Greenless and Garran, *Deliverance*, pp. 235–239.
43. Interview with Australian military attaché in Dili, 23 August 1999. See James Cotton (2004) *East Timor, Australia and Regional Order: Intervention and Its Aftermath in Southeast Asia*, London and New York: RoutledgeCurzon, p. 57.
44. Martin, *Self-Determination in East Timor*, pp. 106–107.
45. Gunn with Lee, *A Critical View*.
46. Martinkus, *A Dirty Little War*, p. xv.
47. The author's UNAMET press card from this era is numbered 337, suggesting a very large press contingent. Also see Rodney Tiffen (2001) *Diplomatic Deceits: Government, Media and East Timor*, Sydney: University of New South Wales Press, for the best analysis of media coverage of the crisis; although it is regrettable that Tiffen did not interview news gatherers in situ.
48. Security Council, S/RES/264 (1999), 15 September 1999.
49. Cf. Sebastian and Smith, "The East Timor Crisis", p. 74; and see Bob Breen (2000) *Mission Accomplished, East Timor: The Australian Defense Force Participation in the International Forces East Timor (INTERFET)*, Sydney: Allen & Unwin.
50. UN Security Council document S/1999/1025, 4 October 1999.
51. Ibid.
52. Ibid.
53. Janet E. Heininger (1994) *Peacekeeping in Transition: The United Nations in Cambodia*, New York: The Twentieth Century Fund Press.
54. Valerie Epps (2000) "Self-Determination after Kosovo and East Timor", *ILSA Journal of International and Comparative Law* 6, available from http://www.nsulaw.nova.edu/student/organizations/ILSAJournal/6-2/Epps%206-2.htm. On Kosovo, see Nicholas J. Wheeler (2000) *Saving Strangers: Humanitarian Intervention in International Security*, Oxford: Oxford University Press.
55. See for example Mukesh Kapila (2002) "Setting-up of UNTAET: Post-UNAMET, Planning, Drafting Resolution and Finance", paper presented to UNTAR-IPS-JIIA Conference on "UNTAET: Debriefing and Lessons", September 2002, UNU, Tokyo, pp. 16–18.
56. Lynn Fredriksson (1999) *Estafetta* 5(3), Autumn.
57. Report of the Joint Assessment Mission to East Timor, 08/12/99.

58. In August/September 2000, the author was engaged by UNTAET as "consultant sociologist" and head of a "social team" to visit all districts to explain and solicit opinions on World Bank/UNTAET agricultural policies. See Geoffrey C. Gunn (2000) "Showdown in Timor: Notes from the (Battle) Field", *Bulletin of Concerned Asian Scholars* 32(4), October–December: 52–54.

59. Cf. *La'o Hamutuk Bulletin* (Dili), April 2001.

60. Gunn, "Showdown in Timor".

61. There was also a great willingness on the part of the Timorese elite for reconciliation over justice although the risk remains that the principle of impunity will be sidestepped, sending all the wrong lessons. Also see Suzannah Linton (2001) "Cambodia, East Timor and Sierra Leone: Engagements in International Justice", *Criminal Law Forum*, 12: 185–246; and Anon (2002) "Indonesia: Implications of the Timor Trials", *Indonesia Briefing* (International Crisis Group), 8 May. For an Indonesian perspective on the "UN conspiracy", incorporating possibly incriminating remarks attributed to General Wiranto, see Suhardi Somomoedjono (2001) *Menguak Konspirasi Internasional di Timor Timur: Sebuah Analisis Yuridis*, Jakarta: Lembaga Studi Advokasi Peradilan Indonesia.

62. Peter Mares interview with Peter van Walsum (2002) "Timor: UN Peace-Keeping 'A Miracle'", 5 February, Australian Broadcasting Commission (ABC), Asia Pacific programme.

63. Mark Quarterman (2003) "UN Leverage in East Timor: Inducing Indonesian Compliance through International Law", in Jean Krazno, Brad C. Hayes and Donald C. F. Daniel, eds, *Leveraging for Success in United Nations Peace Operations*, Westport, Conn. and London: Praegar, p. 164.

64. Wheeler and Dunne, "East Timor and the New Humanitarian Interventionism", p. 806.

65. By attending the 20 May 2002 independence ceremonies, Indonesian President Megawati could also reveal to her political constituency that she could make a choice between geostrategy (UN/Australian plots) and solidarity. As demonstrated by the illegal deployment of six Indonesia warships to East Timor waters on the eve of independence, the reverse could also apply.

66. This is not the place to pass judgments upon UNTAET. In any case, a secondary literature has already emerged. See Jonathan Steele (2002) "Nation Building in East Timor", *World Policy Journal* 19(2), Summer. Steele argues that the UN operation in East Timor was the "most successful colonization since the Middle Ages" but that UNTAET made mistakes that should not be repeated in future UN missions.

Conclusion: Making sense of national interest and international solidarity

Jean-Marc Coicaud

We end by outlining some of the lessons that this book has brought to the fore. These concern the six following sets of issues: the identity of actors, the projection of power and the rationale for action; the paradoxical relationship between national power and international solidarity; the national/international interest quandary that the democratic global power status of the United States brings upon its foreign policy; the social nature of international life revealed by its hybrid and multilayered character; the need to further dovetail solidarity and global public policy; and international legitimacy as the quest to balance the demands of particularism with those of universality.[1]

Identity of actors, projection of power and rationale for action

This book has examined case studies that are of particular relevance to the discussion of national interest and solidarity in the international arena. In doing so, it has analysed the role of external actors in the management of crises, including the rationale behind their involvement. We have seen that the elements that enter into the fabric of the identity of actors, especially interests and values, matter. Differences and similarities in identities have also proved to be a significant variable.

Differences in the key interests and values that are part of the identity of actors shape how they relate to the international realm and get in-

National interest and international solidarity: Particular and universal ethics in international life, Coicaud and Wheeler (eds),
United Nations University Press, 2008, ISBN 978-92-808-1147-6

volved in unfolding crises. For example, as we have seen in Mira Sucharov's chapter, the rationale behind why and how the European Union and the United States address the Israeli–Palestinian conflict are somewhat different. The differences go back to the specific interests and values of their respective identities and how they are projected in terms of conflict management. Similarly, in her chapter, Ekaterina Stepanova mentions that Russia's conflict management policies, to the extent that they differ from those of Western powers, owe much to its idiosyncratic interests and values, significantly at odds with those of the West.

This being said, differences of identity and, subsequently, of rationale for actions and ways of implementing them, are not the only discernible element. The similarities that bring actors closer together are just as noticeable. As we have seen, actors are more and more shaped by, and concerned with, not only national interest, but also international solidarity.

This state of affairs echoes the normative and political duality of contemporary international life, in a context where national interest and international solidarity are increasingly intertwined. This makes it difficult for actors to pursue their national interest without considering international solidarity and vice versa. While states continue to focus on their national interest, legitimacy requirements for their foreign policy and international legitimacy in general call for them to take other states' interests and points of views into account. They also call for the states to act to some extent as the custodians of the interests of other states, or as the custodians of the interests of these states' populations (defence of human rights and humanitarian interventions). Hence, how the entanglement of national interest and international solidarity logics should best be balanced in the normative and political duality of international life and in the behaviour of actors is now a highly debated matter of international politics and of the quest for justice and security at the international level.[2]

The paradox of national power and international solidarity

Another lesson that emerges from this book is the paradoxical relationship between national power and international solidarity. It boils down to the fact that in order to project and implement a sense of international solidarity, power, more specifically, national power (as the national realm continues to be a, if not *the*, major source of power)[3] is needed.

Unless a country is doing well, it is unlikely to be willing and able to do good, and international solidarity becomes the last item on its agenda. Indeed, countries in a weak position tend to be too busy trying to keep themselves afloat to think about the fate of others. Moreover, weakness, and the sense of insecurity that comes with it, can become a psychological obstacle to connecting with other countries. Weakness is not conducive to empathy. It can even contribute to generating a victim mentality that risks deepening the gap vis-à-vis others. This often comes hand in hand with blaming others for one's own misfortune, a fertile ground for the development of resentment that is likely to trigger a disregard for the other, particularly in the absence of shared values. In contrast, powerful countries shaped by democratic values are the ones that have historically been the advocates and underwriters of international solidarity. The combination of their material empowerment (through their wealth and power) and normative disposition to empower others (through the universality of democratic values) has served as a basis for extending a sense of solidarity and responsibility beyond borders.

At the same time, however, if being strong nationally helps being a strong power internationally, this can also be an obstacle. Being strong nationally, rather than bridging the "we versus they" divide and the hierarchy of priorities that comes with it, can serve to further that divide. When a country is benefiting from a position of power, it is likely to be tempted to use this in a self-serving manner and abuse its position, especially since the national tendencies of international life make it highly competitive and put a premium on self-interest.

Democratic national power is not immune from this trend. It unfolds within the context of the five-centuries' old problem of modernity: the oscillation of the West vis-à-vis the rest of the world between humanism (with the universality of human rights and the extension of international solidarity) and domination (with a drive to power expansion and a tendency to predation), between discriminatory and embracing approaches – without ever decisively opting for one over the other. Against this background, the reluctance of non-Western countries to see the Western-led humanitarian interventions of the 1990s as simply driven by solidarity considerations is not surprising.[4] For, ultimately, democratic values of international solidarity are hardly able to restrain or control the projection of power for self-centred reasons. In a sense, the United States' foreign policy serves as a case in point.

US foreign policy; the challenge of national interest and international solidarity; and the question of world order

In this book a number of chapters deal directly or indirectly with US foreign policy. This is only natural considering that the United States is a global power, involved, in one way or another, in the management of most crises around the world, large and small. As such, these chapters touch upon the challenge that the democratic global power status of the

United States brings upon its foreign policy: the difficulty in balancing national interest and international solidarity imperatives. In the process, the chapters allude to one of the key contradictions of the current world order: the principles of international solidarity (especially those of human rights) have increasingly become a factor of legitimacy at the international level;[5] but the sole superpower, while normatively committed to democratic and solidarist values, is increasingly prone to see its national interest as the principal benchmark of its foreign policy as well as of international politics.[6]

The difficulty in balancing national interest and international solidarity is not limited to the United States. Reconciling the empowerment process that democratic values and their propagation favour and call for, and the power boost that this process earns to the countries championing them, has been a challenge for all democratic powers eager to project their influence internationally since the end of the eighteenth century (beginning with the foreign policy of the French revolution). Nevertheless, in light of its current sole superpower status and unique role in the diffusion of Western values and interests, also in light of the increasing role that democratic/solidarity ideals and values play in shaping international political discourse and practices, the challenge is now greater for the United States than perhaps it has ever been for any other major democratic power.

This is all the more the case considering that, as the United States becomes more powerful its sphere of national interest extends, and as its sphere of national interest extends its exposure increases and, along with it, its vulnerability. The sense of American insecurity that grows exponentially with its reach, rather than being conducive to a policy of international reciprocity, international solidarity and inclusiveness, encourages US foreign policy to further emphasize its national interest and the need to defend it at all costs, wherever and whenever possible. The 11 September attack and the way it has been interpreted and acted upon by the Bush administration has deepened this orientation.[7] Consequently, American foreign policy as a whole is driven by a self-centred conception of national interest (and national security), and the US political establishment becomes increasingly accustomed to considering other countries' national interest hardly legitimate compared to that of the United States. This is exemplified in the belief, especially in the post–Cold War era, among American decision-makers that their country is one of the best things that has ever happened to modern history.

In this context, the dual nature and use of democratic power (with power helping the spread of democratic/solidarist values, and democratic/solidarist values helping the spread of power) entails the risk that the pursuit of power will become an end in itself, taking over and invalidating

the quest for democratic/solidarist values. This makes the tension between democratic/solidarist empowerment on the one hand, and power
enhancement in American foreign policy on the other, a tension that de-
fies easy resolution.

Solidarity and the social nature of international life

Questioning the legitimacy of the foreign policy of major (democratic)
powers and of the international order that they contribute to underwriting (and undermining) because of their inability to find a credible balance
between national interest and international solidarity should not lead to
pessimism. After all, it also points to the right direction regarding what
international life currently is, and what it ought to be.

From a general point of view, an assessment of legitimacy is based
upon values (core values) that are used as criteria for evaluation and
judgment. Values serve both as a foundation and horizon in relation to
which the legitimacy of social reality (including political and economic arrangements) is measured. They serve as a foundation in the sense that
they constitute the normative (or axiological) source from which the legitimacy of reality springs, and which reality, if it is going to be legitimate, has to express or represent; and they serve as a horizon in the
sense that the legitimacy of reality rests upon the aspiration to as much
as possible implement these values – nevertheless without reaching a
state of perfection where values and reality are in complete harmony
(after all, values are also ideals). In this perspective, the legitimacy of reality depends upon the characteristics of the values, the prescriptions that
these entail and what the expectations on the extent and limits of the
harmony between values and reality are (based on the characteristics of
values).[8]

But there is more to the relationship between values and reality. Although values are destined to somehow remain out of reach for reality,
they are essential components of the reality that is under evaluation. If
values are an ideal extension of reality, they are not external to the reality that they help to evaluate. They are part of it. The distance that they
stress between what reality is (in its imperfect embodiment of value-
ideals) and what reality should be, does not eliminate the fact that these
values are part and parcel of the reality that is assessed. Otherwise values
would neither be considered nor would they mean anything to people,
and therefore they would not be used as benchmarks. The fact that a
(revolutionary) change of identification with core values comes with a

(revolutionary) change of reality illustrates this internal, or symbiotic, relationship between values and reality.[9]

In the context of current relations between national interest and international solidarity, this translates into the following: the criticism of the
self-centred character of the foreign policies of major democratic
powers, of their failure to take international solidarist values seriously in
the various fields of international justice,[10] indicates the growing importance that the imperative of international solidarity occupies in international reality.

This criticism indicates that the harmonization process between values
of international solidarity and international reality as a whole is still very
unsatisfactory. But it also tells us that values of international solidarity
are already a large enough part of reality to not be ignored. It shows
that they are important enough to reality to serve as a criterion of evaluation and judgment, and a major source of legitimization for power projection beyond state borders. It shows that the logic of power projection
at the international level is more and more a social one, that is, one based
on the recognition of the legitimacy of the interest of others (states and
individuals); one in which, consequently, the interests of the other are
made into rights, leading to the need to have the dynamics of rights and
duties factored in. Ultimately, this tells us that the logic of power projection now has to be strongly geared toward global public goods. International reality, including the values springing from it and shaping it, makes
this so while also calling for it.

Questioning the legitimacy of the foreign policy of major democratic
powers, and of the international system because of their inability to deliver more in terms of international solidarity, shows the way for future
generations. The power of international solidarity to criticize the present
international order and its main supporters constrains and guides foreign
policies and the organization of international architecture. In particular,
it invalidates the idea that national interest, narrowly understood, can be
the sole benchmark of foreign policy. National interest can be a benchmark only within the limits of rights and duties assigned to international
actors, that is, within the conditions of co-existence among states and of
the quality of existence for individuals within borders.

The role of international law and of its various regimes is to outline these conditions of co-existence and quality of existence and the
need to follow them. In the field of the international law of collective
security, of the law of war and peace, this role springs from key international principles. The principles are: sovereign equality of states; non-
intervention in the internal or external affairs of other states; good faith;
self-determination of peoples; prohibition of the threat or use of force;

peaceful settlement of disputes; respect for human rights; and international cooperation.[11] Following and adhering to these principles is not automatic. It requires interpreting these principles and their relations, and coming up with priorities and choices.

Although it has been the historical trend to interpret and act upon these principles mainly in accordance with the servicing of a particularist vision of the international order (with enclosed national sovereignty being politically and normatively favoured time and time again), this is not set in stone. The growing influence of the democratic vision of sovereignty and the international spread of the imperative of solidarity introduce a form of responsibility and accountability that is not contained within state borders.[12] Failing to recognize that this is increasingly the world in which we live is destined to weaken any claim of legitimacy, domestically and internationally. In this regard, the leftover from the past focus on a self-centric (asocial) understanding and pursuit of national interest and national security, which, rather than enhancing the security of each, is prone to bring insecurity to all.

From moral and public policy solidarity to the rule of law

At the heart of the idea and dynamic of solidarity, be it at the individual, national or international level, is the idea that the disparity between those who have and those who have not has to be addressed and minimized. Among the justifications called upon over time to minimize these disparities, two types of arguments have been particularly significant – one moral and the other prudential.

The moral argument amounts to saying that the gaps have to be addressed for the sake of doing the right thing for human beings – human beings who are fellow human beings regardless of their unfortunate circumstances and, more fundamentally, human beings who are all the more fellow human beings because of their unfortunate circumstances.

The prudential argument refers to the interdependent condition of human existence. As human existence is from the beginning to the end a social affair, one in which each actor lives through and among others and in which actors need each other, overlooking others' needs and rights, even those of the powerless, is done at one's own peril. It contributes to generalized distrust. And general distrust is a dangerous way of life.[13] Hence comes the calculus that, rather than leaving them to run their course unmonitored, it is better to organize and institutionalize interactions among actors in a social structure of cooperation, including a policy of solidarity in favour and in support of those who have less.

Now, the deeper the democratic integration, the more moral solidarity and prudential solidarity work together. And the more we are unlikely to find one without the other. It is one and the same thing to recognize the self in the other and, therefore, show solidarity based on moral principles, and to ensure, directly or indirectly, the cooperation of others by factoring in their needs and rights based on prudential considerations. With democratic integration, connecting with the other on a moral basis and connecting on a self-interested basis are mutually reinforcing. The sense of self (including the image of oneself) of the actor becomes dependent on identifying with the other both on moral and prudential grounds. Such convergence is instrumental for the possibility of a public policy of solidarity. A lack of this endangers the fabric of social integration, its moral and cooperative dimensions, and puts at risk not only the weakest members of society but also its most powerful ones. For the latter in particular, it is the legitimacy of their claims in terms of rights and being in the right that is threatened and, as such, the very comfort of their material existence.[14]

In the modern era, democratic integration has essentially taken place at the national level. This echoes the national tendencies of international life and the "we versus they" divide that shapes international relations. That democratic integration has essentially taken place at the national level does not mean that in this context moral solidarity and prudential solidarity have smoothly and fully come together. It does not mean that they have come together in democratic national politics to a point where moral solidarity systematically becomes a key aspect of public policy solidarity, an organizing principle of the functioning of society as a whole. After all, the history of modern democratic national politics is very much about the struggles (normative, economic, legal and political) surrounding the extent to which, and the concrete ways in which, moral solidarity should structure relations between members of society.[15] For instance, the liberal version of modern democratic politics, emphasizing the self-reliance and personal responsibility of the individual, has been reluctant to make moral solidarity central to the (public) structure of society. Its inclination has been to try to constrain it to a private-individual choice-based initiative (see the culture of philanthropy in the United States).[16] On the other hand, the (continental European) republican and socialist (non-communist) versions of modern democratic politics, banking on the public and private good benefits that this approach is envisioned to generate, have been prone to make it foundational to justice.[17] In this case, moral solidarity toward those in need becomes part of the public policy of the state.[18] Yet, beyond the differences of modern democratic cultures and their specifics of social solidarity, what they have in common is a generic understanding of the rule of law and of its elevation as a central feature of society.[19] In this context, the rule of law is a normative stance about what is right in terms of moral values and a prudential device called upon to secure the cooperative structure of society. The idea is, in principle, to look after the interest of all by equal defence of everybody's rights.[20]

International legitimacy as a bridge between national and international solidarity

At the international level, social integration has never reached the degree that it has in the democratic national realm. Consequently, in the exercise of international solidarity, moral solidarity overshadows public policy solidarity. Multilateralism is the best that international life has to offer in terms of solidarity, in particular in the context of the various international instruments of human rights protection. But this "best" limits solidarity to being marginal, as can be seen in the fact that the international community's commitment to the defence of human rights, despite the progress made, remains more often than not declaratory. Human rights are rarely acted upon in decisive ways, and even less so within a global public policy framework that could potentially make the defence of human rights a strategic matter and a key principle of social organization at the global level.[21]

Weak international integration, not to mention weak international democratic integration, leads the exercise of international solidarity in favour of human rights to rely on moral considerations. It becomes mainly a matter of doing the right thing. The fact that morality, while a foundation of law, is weaker than law because it does not benefit from the type of enforcement mechanisms that are at the disposal of a system of national law in an integrated society helps to understand this point. With international law creating no real human rights obligations for states beyond borders, international solidarity ends up being a moral conception of international obligation, at the mercy of the good will and diplomacy efforts of actors. As such, international solidarity stands short of being part of a public policy of a global anticipatory and preventive (early conflict management), reparatory and punitive (post-conflict) and distributive (including mechanisms to ensure fair access to goods) system of justice.

The furthest international solidarity has gone in terms of being part of a public policy system of justice has been in the context of the European project. This project has many faces. Among these, the one associated with the pursuit of the national interest is not the least important.[22] Still, the expansion of the European Union beyond its initial founders to less developed countries in the region (in particular, with the latest enlargement toward Central and Eastern Europe) is also about moral solidarity embedded into public policy solidarity. The European project goes much beyond loosely coupled security communities.[23] In its most integrative version, it aims at defending and upgrading (economically in particular) the standing of all, nations and individuals.[24] More than being simply an aggregation of multilateral regional arrangements, it is an attempt to dovetail the quest for security (internal and external) with (re-)distributive justice considerations at the supra-national level – in a sense, a regional rule of law.[25]

The international realm is far from envisioning, let alone implementing, such a scenario. The European project is a revolutionary one that it will be difficult to duplicate and extend at the global level for a number of reasons. One of them is the fact that it itself is not foreign to the ambiguities and tensions of modern international politics. The European Union lends its universalist values and resources inwards, as well as outwards, in support of multilateralism and international solidarity. But it continues to put a premium on regional solidarity and, within the regional realm, on national solidarity. European foreign policies are a case in point, be it for instance in the context of security and human rights, as we have seen in the chapter dealing with the Balkans, or in the context of trade policies beyond Europe and subsidies within Europe (the two overlap to a certain extent).[26]

Concluding thoughts

We are left with the following question: is there any hope for going beyond moral solidarity at the international level? Is international life, for all its reality and progress, still so un-socialized that it forbids solidarity to go beyond the moral dimension and become more a matter of international public policy?

It is very difficult to believe that the international realm will ever (or, at least, for many years to come) generate a thickness of solidarity similar to the one existing in the best functioning democratic polities, or at the regional level as in the case of Europe. This is especially true in light of the fact that the (Western) developed countries that have been historically committed to intertwining social solidarity and security policies, and which tend to be among the most active internationalist actors, are increasingly moving away from a "social state" approach nationally.[27] Giving in to the pressures of economic liberalism and global competition, embedding the political and legal dimensions of the rule of law in welfare policies meant to tame the individual mischance, is less and less a policy of choice.[28] How, then, could a philosophy of order and justice that is in the process of being dismantled at the domestic level be endorsed in the international realm? And, indeed, considering how selective and self-centred powerful states are in their handling of international crises,[29] one is inclined to be rather pessimistic. One is inclined to think that the politics of traditional national interest, at times itself hijacked by the interests of a powerful few within countries, is destined to continue to flourish and represent the lion's share of rationale for action in international affairs.

Yet, as the legitimacy constraints weighing on foreign policies become heavier, as it becomes less and less manageable for the unilateral or exclusively self-interested international projection of power to make might right, the possibility of an international rule of law, of a sense of international legitimacy, could expand.

Much of the realization of this possibility will depend upon the ability of states and other institutional international actors (international organizations, regional organizations) to come to terms with the responsibility that they hold toward people in general, whoever and wherever they are. It has been said that with great power comes great responsibility. This is all the more the case in the democratic context. With great democratic power comes great democratic responsibility. And one of these democratic responsibilities is trying to achieve the right balance between particularist and universalist solidarity. While it is of course too much to ask them to dedicate the majority of their national resources to universalist demands, democratic powers can less and less see particularist demands as their only primary source of responsibility, and legitimacy. For them, accountability and the legitimacy of their foreign policy as well as of the international system that they endorse, come with helping to empower others. It comes with using their power and resources so that states and individuals in need can stand on their own.

*   *   *   *   *

Judging from the various cases studied in this book, the overall picture given by the current state of international affairs, and of the rationale for power projection beyond borders, is a mixed one. Clearly, outright predatory behaviours are less and less tolerated. In particular, to benefit from an international recognition of legitimacy, state-actors have to give the impression of being, if not actually being, good international citizens. This helps to explain the resources that key international powers dedicate to help solve crises abroad. Surely, depending on whether or not the crises entail traditional matters of national interest, the resources spent tend to vary. But sheer indifference toward the international realm is not an option, as questions of national interest and international solidarity are becoming difficult to disassociate.

When it comes to the extent to which this hybrid attitude is contributing to a safer and more just world, the management of the various crises or states of crisis examined in this book presents a mixed picture. Only two are now more or less resolved or under control: East Timor and the Balkans (although much remains to be done in both). The others still make up for part of the troubles of the international realm. Three present some sort of status quo, with a situation that is hardly resolved but not unraveling either: India/Pakistan, US/China relations with the status of Taiwan in the middle and, at a more local level, Colombia. Two other theaters seem to now receive relatively little attention: Russia and Central Asia. As for the Israeli–Palestinian conflict and Africa, they represent, each in their own way, two major unresolved questions that are likely to remain so in the coming years.

This shows that the need for addressing tensions and crises in the international realm, far from being a thing of the past, has a "bright" future. As relations between values and interest will continue to be tense within and across borders, there will be a need for an international projection of power. Whether or not this international projection of power takes place mainly in the name of traditional national interest or in that of international solidarity will depend upon the nature and the extent and limits of the pressure of democratic demands exercised on actors, inwards and outwards.[30]

Notes

1. This chapter has benefited from the comments and suggestions of Nicholas J. Wheeler, Louise Bergström, Jibecke Jönsson and Lamis Abdel-Aty.
2. See for instance Michael Walzer (2004) "Governing the Globe", in Walzer, *Arguing about War*, New Haven, Conn.: Yale University Press, pp. 171–191.
3. The relationship between international organizations and member states illustrates this situation. The strength of international organizations is closely linked with the strength of support that they receive from powerful member states. On the other hand, the strength of support from powerful member states can also turn into a source of weakness for international organizations, as it creates a relation of dependency.
4. To be suspicious of the intentions and goals of a country's international projection of power is not the monopoly of non-Western countries vis-à-vis Western powers. It is also at work in the West, among competitive powers. The unease with which France sees the United States trying to increase its presence in central Africa, as alluded to in Tim Docking's chapter, is a case in point.
5. Ruth W. Grant and Robert O. Keohane (2005) "Accountability and Abuses of Power in World Politics", in *American Political Science Review* 99(1), February: 29–43, esp. p. 35.

6. This tendency transcends the Democratic/Republican political divide.

7. Beyond its mere factuality, the way an event is interpreted and how an actor reacts to it enter into its fabric and identity. It would have been interesting to see what a Democratic administration would have made of 11 September.

8. The expectations on the extent and limits of such harmony vary with the characteristics of values and the prescriptions that they entail. Not surprisingly, political struggles revolve around the definition, interpretation and implementation of (core) values, and how they impact the evaluation of the legitimacy of reality.

9. On this issue, refer for example to Mlada Bukovansky (2002) *Legitimacy and Power Politics: The American and French Revolutions in International Political Culture*, Princeton, N.J.: Princeton University Press.

10. See for instance Thomas W. Pogge (2002) *World Poverty and Human Rights: Cosmopolitan Responsibilities and Reforms*, Cambridge: Polity Press.

11. For a detailed analysis of each of these international principles, see Antonio Cassese (1994) *International Law in a Divided World*, Oxford: Clarendon Press, pp. 129–157. On the non-exhaustive character of this list and the status of international principles, see Michel Virally (1990) *Le droit international en devenir: Essais écrits au fil des ans*, Geneva: Presses Universitaires de France, pp. 206–212. On the interpretation and implementation of these principles and their relations in the post–Cold War context, see Jean-Marc Coicaud (2007) *Beyond the National Interest: The Future of UN Peacekeeping and Multilateralism in an Era of U.S. Primacy*, Washington, D.C.: United States Institute of Peace Press.

12. On the evolution of socialization and the historicity of principles of justice, national and international, refer for instance to Philip Allott (1990) *Eunomia: New Order for a New World*, Oxford: Oxford University Press. See also Philip Allott (2002) "International Law and the Idea of History", in Allott, *The Health of Nations: Society and Law Beyond the State*, Cambridge: Cambridge University Press, pp. 316–341.

13. As Jean-Jacques Rousseau states, "The strongest is never strong enough to be always the master, unless he transforms strength into right". Rousseau (1968) *The Social Contract, or Principles of Political Right*, translated from the French by Maurice Cranston, London: Penguin Books, p. 53.

14. Hence, among other things, John Rawls's second principle: "Social and economic inequalities ... are to be to the greatest benefit of the least-advantaged members of society (the difference principle)". Rawls (2001) *Justice as Fairness: A Restatement*, Erin Kelly, ed., Cambridge, Mass.: The Belknap Press of Harvard University Press, pp. 42–43.

15. Andrew Linklater (1998) *The Transformation of Political Community: Ethical Foundations of the Post-Westphalian Era*, Columbia, S.C.: University of South Carolina Press.

16. The fact that the practice of philanthropy is encouraged by tax laws mitigates its private dimension.

17. Communism is a version of modern democratic culture. But its conception and implementation of moral solidarity and of the public structure of solidarity, together with their relations, put it in a category which is very different from the liberal, republican and socialist versions of democratic politics.

18. These differences among the political theories of modern democracy are echoed in international relations debates.

19. On the rule of law in general, see Brian Z. Tamanaha (2004) *On the Rule of Law: History, Politics, Theory*, Cambridge: Cambridge University Press.

20. In John Rawls's theory of justice, the ideas of the original position and of the veil of ignorance reflect both moral and self-interested considerations. Refer to Rawls, *Justice as Fairness*, pp. 14–18.

21. Regarding global public policy, see also Jürgen Habermas's notion of "world domestic policy", for example in Hubermas (2001) *The Postnational Constellation: Political Essays*, trans. Max Pensky, Cambridge, Mass.: MIT Press.

22. These faces are neither altogether convergent nor compatible. Note also that the European project has even been called "an empire by self-determination". See Michael Johnson, workshop on *The Rule of Law and Transitional Justice: The Way Forward?*, organized by the United Nations University, New York, 27 January 2005.

23. On security communities, see Emmanuel Adler and Michael N. Barnett, eds (1998) *Security Communities*, Cambridge: Cambridge University Press.

24. Needless to say this picture of the European project is not comprehensive. It only brings to the fore the elements required by our line of argument. There are obviously various visions of the European project in competition, in the normative, political, economic and social spheres. Moreover, whether or not greater regional prosperity will be achieved remains an open question.

25. On dovetailing security and justice in the rule of law, refer to Jean-Marc Coicaud (2007) "Quest for International Justice: Benefits of Justice *versus* the Trappings of Paranoia", in Hans Günter Brauch, John Grin, Czeslaw Mesjasz, Pal Dunay, Navnita Chadha Behera, Béchir Chourou, Ursula Oswald Spring, P. H. Liotta and Patricia Kameri-Mbote, eds, *Globalisation and Environmental Challenges: Reconceptualising Security in the 21st Century*, Berlin: Springer-Verlag.

26. M. Ataman Aksoy and John C. Beghin, eds (2005) *Global Agricultural Trade and Developing Countries*, Washington, D.C.: The World Bank for Reconstruction and Development.

27. Robert Castel (2002) *From Manual Workers to Wage Laborers: Transformation of the Social Question*, trans. Richard Boyd, Somerset, N.J.: Transaction Publishers.

28. Zygmunt Bauman (2005) *Wasted Lives: Modernity and Its Outcasts*, Cambridge: Polity Press, pp. 51–53.

29. As Samina Yasmeen alludes to in her chapter regarding the US handling of India/Pakistan tensions, or as Parviz Mullojanov indicates in his analysis of Russian and American interests in Central Asia.

30. Such democratic demands are neither necessarily positive nor convergent. As for not necessarily positive, democratic demands can lead, especially when the domestic economy of a democracy is under stress, to a reluctance to divert resources internationally. Also, there is the complex relationship between democracy and capitalism, namely with the spread of democracy going hand in hand with the spread of capitalism, and the former running the risk of being undermined by the latter. The tensions that can exist between democracy and capitalism are one example among many that democratic demands are not necessarily convergent.

Index